Percy B. Shelley

THE LIFE

OF

PERCY BYSSHE SHELLEY

BY

EDWARD DOWDEN

LITT. D., DUBLIN; LL.D., EDINBURGH; D.C.L., OXFORD;
PROFESSOR OF ENGLISH LITERATURE IN THE UNIVERSITY OF DUBLIN;
CLARK LECTURER IN ENGLISH LITERATURE, TRINITY COLLEGE, CAMBRIDGE

NEW EDITION

LONDON
KEGAN PAUL, TRENCH, TRUBNER & CO., Ltᵈ
BROADWAY HOUSE, 68/74, CARTER LANE, E.C.
1920

PREFACE.

---◦◦◦---

In shaping this shorter "Life of Shelley" from my larger biography, I have had much help from my friend Mr. Kegan Paul, which I gratefully acknowledge.

From the reviews of the larger "Life" I have not gained much in the way of correction, nor much from the discoveries and alleged disclosures of the years since that "Life" appeared. I have disregarded what I believe to be without value. But I have to thank many correspondents for communications which have helped me to correct errors in detail. I have seen no reason for altering anything of importance.

If any perplexities should arise in the mind of a reader, I can only ask him to consult my larger work.

E. D.

PREFACE.

In shaping this shorter "Life of Shelley" from my larger biography I have had much help from my friend Mr. .... but which I gratefully acknowledge.

From the reviews of the larger "Life," I have not gained much in the way of correction, nor much from the discoveries and alleged disclosures of the years since that "Life" appeared. I have disregarded what I believe to be without value. But I have to thank many correspondents for communications which have helped me to correct errors in detail. I have seen no reason for altering anything of importance.

If any perplexities should arise in the mind of a reader, I can only ask him to consult my larger work.

E. D.

CONTENTS.

—◦◦◦◦—

LIFE OF SHELLEY.

CHAPTER I.

BOYHOOD.

THE Shelleys are an ancient family of Sussex. To Sir William Shelley, brother of Sir Thomas—"that was attainted for endeavouring to set up King Richard II.," and perished on the scaffold—the ancestry of Percy Bysshe Shelley has been traced. From an Edward Shelley, of Worminghurst, who died in the year of the Spanish Armada, son of Sir John Shelley, of Michelgrove, that branch of the family, in no respect illustrious before the present century, is said to have descended which, on the other side of the Atlantic, a hundred and fifty years ago, was represented by Timothy Shelley and by his son Bysshe (so named after his grandmother's maiden name), who returned to England, married two heiresses, obtained a baronetcy in gratitude for favours expected by the Whigs, and lived long enough to hear of the poem "Queen Mab," written by his grandson and namesake, Percy Bysshe.

Bysshe Shelley was a gentleman of the old school, with a dash of New World cleverness, push, and mammon-worship. Six feet high, handsome, stately in bearing, clear-witted, yet wilful, he achieved greatness by bold and dexterous strokes. He was not more than one and twenty

B

years of age when a Sussex heiress, Miss Mary Catherine
Michell, only child of the Rev. Theobald Michell, of
Horsham, became Mrs. Bysshe Shelley. We are told that
Miss Michell's guardian would not consent to his ward's
marriage, that it was a runaway match, and that the
wedding was celebrated in London at May Fair Chapel.
This Mary Michell was the grandmother of Percy Bysshe
Shelley. Beside the poet's father, she bore to her husband
two daughters, and died almost immediately after the birth
of the second. Mr. Bysshe Shelley was thus, before thirty,
a widower with three young children. Nine years later
he won the hand of another great heiress, Elizabeth Jane
Sidney, daughter of William Perry, of Penshurst, Kent.

In 1806, Bysshe himself became Sir Bysshe Shelley,
Baronet; he had been a staunch Whig, attached to the
Duke of Norfolk's party in the county, and this was the
reward of his loyalty and the incentive to its continuance.
But though Bysshe was now a baronet, and had spent
some £80,000, it is said, in building himself Castle Goring,
the old man cared little to enjoy his honours or his wealth.
He lived at Horsham, in a cottage house hard by the
church, vexed with gout and infirmities of age, and waited
on by a solitary servant.

Bysshe's son, Timothy Shelley, was nearly forty years
old when his first child was born. He went as a youth to
University College, Oxford, and afterwards travelled on the
Continent. He was slight of figure, tall, very fair, with
the blue Shelley eyes. He had a better heart than his
father, and not so clear a head. Timothy Shelley had a
wrong-headed way of meaning well and doing ill; he had
a semi-illiterate regard for letters, a mundane respect for
religion; he dealt in public affairs without possessing
public spirit, and gave his party an unwavering vote when
a member of the House of Commons; in private life he

was kindly, irritable, and despotic ; in manners an aspirant Chesterfield, yet one who could on occasions bustle and fret and scold ; when least venerable he insisted most on his paternal prerogative. Mingling with his self-importance there was a certain sensibility, genuine though not deep, and tears of tenderness or vexation came readily to his eyes : a kindly, pompous, capricious, well-meaning, ill-doing, wrong-headed man. Mr. Timothy Shelley was married, in October, 1791, to Elizabeth, daughter of Charles Pilfold, of Effingham, county Surrey, whose rare beauty descended to her children. We are told that she was a woman of strong good sense, and, though not a lover of literature, an excellent letter-writer. There is testimony to show that her temper was violent and domineering. " Mild and tolerant," her son once called her, " yet narrow-minded ; " but there were times when her mildness disappeared. She had a special grievance against the boy because he was little of what every country gentleman ought to be—a follower of field sports.

Mr. and Mrs. Timothy Shelley had their abode at Field Place, in the parish of Warnham, Sussex, a property which came into the family through the marriage of Bysshe Shelley with Miss Michell. Field Place lies a mile south of the village of Warnham—a comfortable eighteenth-century mansion, with the many windows of one story showing above an open portico along its front which faces the west. From the garden looking westward is seen the mountainous outline of Hind Head ; to the south, the downs are faintly visible, with their suggestions of peace and endless pasture. Here Percy Bysshe Shelley, the first child of his parents, was born on Saturday, August 4, 1792 —a pretty fledgling, distinguished by his delicate hands and feet, his bright down of baby hair (afterwards curling in ringlets), and his great blue, luminous eyes. They

called him Bysshe after his grandfather; Percy had been
a name in the family for two or three preceding generations.

It was happy for Shelley that his childhood was not
solitary. Companionship became the counterpoise to
reverie. At nine years old he was the brother of four
living sisters; another, the earlier Hellen of two who bore
that name, had died after a handbreadth of existence, before
Bysshe was yet four years old. In 1806 Shelley's only
brother was born. John Shelley lived to be sixty, but he
can have been little of a companion to Bysshe, who was
so much his elder, who spent only brief snatches of time at
Field Place after John had passed out of babyhood, and
who left England for ever when John Shelley was a boy
of twelve.

What we know of Shelley's home life during his early
years is told by the second Hellen, who was born in 1799,
and saw a good deal of her brother up to his entrance at
Oxford, and saw little or nothing of him after that date.
He was the companion of the little girls on walks; at
other times he would sing for them; or, when his sisters
came to the dining-room for dessert, would take one upon
his knee, and delight her with endless tales of mystery
and wonder. Sometimes Bysshe and his sisters became
a crew of supernatural monsters: the little girls, in strange
garbs, were fiends; Bysshe the great devil bearing along
the passage to the back door a fire-stove flaming with his
infernal liquids. When Bysshe one day set a fagot-stack
on fire, the excuse was a novel one—he did so that he
might have "a little hell of his own." The fairy-land of
science lay bordering the land of fantasy and romance;
to pass from one to the other was easy. Now it was
chemistry whose marvels and metamorphoses Bysshe displayed; now electricity, when the sisters would hold hands

and form a chain, Hellen hiding in her heart certain
tremors, until they could be no longer concealed, when her
brother, with a magnanimity rare among men and boys of
science, released her from all future part in such demon-
strations.   In Bysshe's pranks we hear of no unkindness
to any living creature ; but there was in them much cheerful
fun, sometimes taking wild or fantastic form, and a delight
in merry mystifications.   But the serious mood was present
in boyhood too.   He loved to walk out alone under the
stars, contemplating and musing.   What could these
lonely night-wanderings mean ?   " The old servant of the
family would follow him, and bring in his report that
' Master Bysshe only took a walk, and came back again.' "

Such an elder brother as this—so kind, so fertile in
wondrous devices, so playful, so serious, so beautiful whatever was his mood—how could he fail to be the hero of
his sisters ?

At six years old, Shelley was placed under the instruction
of a Welsh parson, the Rev. Mr. Edwards, who ministered
at Warnham—a good old man, but, says Medwin, " of very
limited intellects."   Four years later, a new pupil appeared
at Syon House Academy, Isleworth, near Brentford, where
Dr. Greenlaw and his assistants instructed fifty or sixty
lads, chiefly of the middle class, in Latin, Greek, French,
writing, arithmetic, geography, and the elements of astronomy.   Bysshe Shelley, the new boy, was tall for ten years
old, slight of figure, with a well-set head, on which abundant
locks, now of a rich brown hue, curled naturally ; his complexion was fair and ruddy, like a girl's.   The luminous,
large blue eyes had at one time a dreamy softness, at
another a fixed wild beauty, or under the influence of
excitement became restlessly brilliant ; and then his voice,
usually soft and low, grew tuneless and strident ; the
expression of his countenance " was one of exceeding

sweetness and innocence," full of animation when his interest
had been aroused. ⎷ Syon House Academy was a large,
somewhat gloomy brick building, formerly belonging to
the Bishop of London ; its situation was open and healthy ;
a garden and playground were attached. There was certainly no luxury or refinement at Syon House ; but a boy
who was not dainty had not much to complain of in the
matters of bed and board. The doctor's eldest daughter
taught novices their letters. Dr. Greenlaw himself, a vigorous old Scotch divine, choleric and hard-headed, but not
unkindly—"a man of rather liberal opinions," said Shelley—
led the more stalwart scholars in the attack on Virgil,
Homer, and the choruses of Sophocles. With spectacles
pushed high above his dark and bushy eyebrows, the
dominie would stimulate the laggard construers. Frequent
dips into his mull of Scotch snuff helped him to sustain
the wear and tear of the class-room.

The change was great for Shelley from the freedom of
the Sussex fields and lanes, and the loving companionship
of younger sisters, to enclosure within the walls of Syon
House Academy, and the battling of an obstreperous
crowd. To their impertinence "he made no reply," says
Medwin, "but with a look of disdain written in his
countenance turned his back on his new associates, and
when he was alone found relief in tears."

The writer of these words, Shelley's cousin, Thomas
Medwin, some years his senior, was a pupil under Dr
Greenlaw when the new boy arrived. As a relation and
an elder, Medwin assumed the part of a patronizing superior,
but we do not find that he undertook the more troublesome
office of protector. His companions were quick to discover
that Shelley was highly sensitive to pain, easily excited,
and subject to paroxysms of passion when thwarted or
provoked. When driven desperate, he would seize the

first thing that came to hand—even any little boy, says his schoolfellow Rennie—to fling at his persecutors. When it was possible he kept aloof from the swarm, and took no part in their sports or strife. " He passed among his schoolfellows," says Medwin, "as a strange and unsocial being ; for when a holiday relieved us from our tasks, and the other boys were engaged in such sports as the narrow limits of our prison court allowed, Shelley, who entered into none of them, would pace backwards and forwards—I think I see him now—along the southern wall," secluded by his vivid imaginings from the riot and the din. Strange and unsocial in the eyes of some, yet "if treated with kindness," says a schoolfellow, " he was very amiable, noble, high-spirited, and generous."

Shelley grew in scholarship almost unawares, and stood high in the school before he left for Eton. He can hardly have been a favourite with the doctor, for he was guilty of the grievous offence of refusing to laugh at the doctor's unsavoury jests (all through his life Shelley was intolerant of gross or immodest mirth) ; and to blow up the boundary palings with gunpowder, or his desk-lid in mid school-hours, to the amazement of masters and boys, was not precisely the way to soothe the temper of a choleric old gentleman. Then, too, in some things he was a hopeless dunce. Shelley fled from the dancing-lesson, if possible ; if not, he went through his paces, a recalcitrant martyr.

And yet he was learning many things. For tales of marvel and mystery his appetite was unappeasable; six-penny volumes, bound in blue wrappers, telling of haunted castles, necromancers, bandits, murderers, were eagerly purchased and devoured. What occupied Shelley's imagination became for him a reality ; his waking dreams were of frequent recurrence, and were followed by much nervous excitement. One summer night he came gliding by moon-light into Medwin's dormitory, open-eyed, but wrapt in slumber. He advanced to the window, which was open ; his cousin sprang out of bed, seized his arm and waked him. " He was excessively agitated, and after leading him back with some difficulty to his couch, I sat by him for some time, a witness to the severe erethism of his nerves which the sudden shock produced." To check any future tendency to forbidden roamings by night, he was punished with all proper severity.

At this time, fathers who had heard of Herschel and Priestley and Davy, and their great doings, were beginning to think it a fine thing that their boys at school should become youthful natural philosophers. Adam Walker, a self-taught genius, the inventor of a score of scientific toys, had been engaged to deliver scientific lectures at Eton, and Dr. Greenlaw would have him also for the benefit and credit of his academy. For Shelley, as a boy, science transformed the world into a place of enchantment ; it was the true nineteenth-century magic ; the bounds of existence receded before its touch, and the possibilities of human achievement became incalculable.

/ Thus his intellect was startled, and grew wide-eyed and full of wonder. Nor was his heart asleep. His love for his kindred, especially for his mother and sisters, was quick and tender ; it was not without manifest joy, says one who knew Shelley well at a later period, that he received a letter from them. Shelley had also found a spring of exquisite happiness in comradeship with one chosen friend. In delicate natures such friendship is sometimes the harbinger of yet unimagined love—the opening of the curtains of the dawn ; the illumination which precedes the uprising of the sun. " The object of these sentiments," wrote Shelley, " was a boy about my own age, of a character eminently

generous, brave, and gentle ; and the elements of human
feeling seemed to have been, from his birth, genially com-
pounded within him.　There was a delicacy and a simplicity
in his manners inexpressibly attractive. . . . . The tones of
his voice were so soft and winning, that every word pierced
into my heart ; and their pathos was so deep, that in
listening to him the tears have involuntarily gushed from
my eyes.　Such was the being for whom I first experienced
the sacred sentiments of friendship."

In 1804, Shelley's schooling under Dr. Greenlaw ended.
He had left Syon House by midsummer of that year, for
his boyish handwriting may still be seen in the entrance-
book of the head master of Eton under the date July 29,
1804.　The tall, handsome, courteous, dignified gentleman,
wearing eighteenth-century costume, with wig newly dressed
each morning, conservative in all his thoughts and ways, in
whose presence Shelley, not yet quite twelve years old, stood
while he signed his name, was Dr. Goodall, who held the
head mastership from 1802 until he was elected provost in
1809.　An excellent scholar, a gracious gentleman, of
joyous temper and genial wit, there was lacking in Goodall
some of that sterner stuff which goes to make up a vigorous
ruler.　The sterner stuff was to be found superabundantly
in Dr. Keate, lower master when Shelley entered, who
succeeded Goodall in the place of supreme authority a year
before Shelley went to Oxford.　The moral contrast was
not greater than the visible and material one between the
two masters.　Little more than five feet high, and not very
great in girth, was Keate ; but there was concentrated
within this space, says the author of " Eöthen," " the pluck
of ten battalions."　His manner was harsh and dictatorial,
as, in his belief, a schoolmaster's ought to be.　The flogging-
block was an altar at which Keate devoutly officiated as
high priest.　Yet he is said to have had a kindly side.

most often shown when out of office ; he could be courteous to his equals ; he was certainly an excellent scholar, and an admirable teacher ; an upright and honourable man.

Shelley's tutor, an assistant-master, was a very magnificent person, but, though kind and good-humoured, unluckily the dullest man in Eton—George Bethell. He is remembered by his famous comment on a classical text, " Postes æracos," read a boy at construing—" brazen gates." "Yes," interrupted Bethell, "that is right ; probably so called because they were made of brass." The old house in which Shelley boarded as a pupil of Bethell was pulled down in 1863 ; it stood just behind the lime-trees which face the railing now to be seen in front of the new schools. But, at his entrance, Shelley resided with Mr. Hexter, the professor of pothooks and hangers. Hexter had the honour of being, not only an Eton writing-master and a " dame," but also a magistrate of the county and a major in the militia. " Hector" the boys nicknamed this learned Trojan. " Major, will you mend my pen ? " was an often-repeated request which charmed them by its pacific-martial incongruity.

In some respects Shelley's life at Eton was but a continuation of his life at Syon House Academy, only that five hundred boys surrounded him instead of sixty. " He stood apart from the whole school," wrote a contemporary at Eton ; " a being never to be forgotten." Refusing obedience to the orders of his fag-master, and proclaiming war against the fagging system, which seemed to him an organized tyranny, he could hardly expect protection from the elder lads. He stood convicted as a rebel against authority ; while to boys of his own standing, except a few chosen friends, his refusing to join in the common sports, his shyness, his singularity, his careless attire, his interest in strange studies, his gentleness united with an unusual

excitability of temper, pointed him out as a proper victim
on whom to wreak all the exuberance of their animal spirits.

Yet it would be an error to suppose that Shelley lived
in isolation, or had no happy hours and days at Eton. In
public events of the little world he bore his part. The
years 1805 and 1808 were made glorious by the Montem
processions. On the first of these occasions, Shelley, dressed
in blue jacket, white trousers, silk stockings and pumps,
the uniform of a midshipman, and bearing the wand of his
office, assisted in the ceremony at Salt Hill as pole-bearer ;
at the second Montem, being a fifth-form boy, he walked
as full corporal, Lord Sondes by his side, and his own pole-
bearers attending. Two years later, just before he left
Eton, he pronounced a speech of Cicero against Catiline
on Election Monday, July 30, among the rest of the sixth
form. He boated, and was " in the boats." That Shelley
earned the good-will of several among his schoolfellows
cannot be doubted ; but his intimate friends were few.
For a time Amos (afterwards a distinguished barrister) was
one of these. In Hexter's house there were only three
lower boys, Shelley, Amos, and another. The three messed
together. "Shelley and I," wrote Mr. Amos, "used to
amuse ourselves in composing plays and acting them
before the lower boy, who constituted our sole audience.
Shelley entered with great vivacity into this amusement.'
Packe, an excellent but matter-of-fact young gentleman
possessing little in common with Shelley, was, like him, a
pupil of Bethell's, and sat near him in school. "I always
liked him," says Mr. Packe ; "he was such a good,
generous, open-hearted fellow." But no one seems to have
been nearer to Shelley's heart than the younger of two
brothers Halliday, whose gentleness, delicacy of feeling,
and romantic fancy were the grounds of a tender attachment. "Many a long and happy walk have I had with

nim," wrote Mr. Halliday, "in the beautiful neighbourhood of dear old Eton. I was a delighted and willing listener to his marvellous stories of fairy-land, and apparitions, and spirits, and haunted ground ; and his speculations were then (for his mind was far more developed than mine) of the world beyond the grave. Another of his favourite rambles was Stoke Park, and the picturesque churchyard where Gray is said to have written his ' Elegy,' of which he was very fond. I was myself far too young to form any estimate of character, but I loved Shelley for his kindliness and affectionate way. . . . He had great moral courage, and feared nothing but what was base and false and low."

Shelley at Eton became an eager and wide-ranging, if not an exact classical, scholar. He rose steadily from form to form ; his lessons, declares Halliday, "were child's play to him." He grasped the contents of a page with a few swift and searching glances, and what interested him became a portion of himself, never to be lost or forgotten. Possibly it was his devotion to such writers as Pliny and Lucretius that earned for Shelley the title of "Atheist" from his schoolfellows ; a term, says Hogg, applied in Eton to the most daring revolter against the higher powers of the school, and having no theological reference, but of which no trace as used in such a sense can now be discovered in the shifting Etonian dialect.

Shelley's awakened interest in science—more, perhaps, a thing of the imagination than the reason—continued vivid and grew perilously energetic during the Eton years? Here again old Walker exhibited his wonders before the eager-eyed spectator. "Night," says a schoolfellow, "was his jubilee." He launched his fire-balloons on errands to the sky. He borrowed forbidden books on chemistry. When he returned in the holidays to Field Place, it was with face and hands smudged and stained by explosive powders and virulent acids; evidence of the young physicist's industry might also be seen in many a spot and streak on those pretty white frocks in which his assistants and admirers had stood around his table, gladly beguiled into the Hall Chamber, Bysshe's room, to witness their brother's mysterious experiments. In Hexter's house he brewed strange and fiery liquids; and as he ran nimbly upstairs, might be heard singing cheerily the chorus of Shakespeare's concocters of hell-broth—

"Double, double, toil and trouble;
Fire burn, and cauldron bubble."

Once, it is said, he nearly blew up himself and his quill-driving "dame;" once he half-poisoned himself with some arsenical mixture, or believed that such was the case; and once he set ablaze a willow stump with burning-glass and gunpowder. Walker's attendant had picked up some of his master's skill, and gained an honest penny by selling small electrical machines to the schoolboys. Shelley was a delighted purchaser, and a little later became possessed of a galvanic battery. One day Mr. Bethell, suspecting from strange noises overhead that his pupil was engaged in nefarious scientific pursuits, suddenly appeared in Shelley's room; to his consternation he found the culprit apparently half enveloped in a blue flame. "What on earth are you doing, Shelley?" "Please, sir," came the answer in the quietest tone, "I am raising the devil." "And what in the world is this?" resumed the pedagogue, seizing hold of some mysterious-looking apparatus on the table. In an instant the intruder was thrown back—Bethell the magnificent—against the wall, having undesignedly exhibited a very pretty electrical experiment, and received an unstinted discharge.

What may be termed the romantic side of science had a peculiar fascination for Shelley. Of the best training which science affords the intellect he had little or none ; he was impatient or incapable of mathematical studies ; careful and well-directed experiment, the prudent interrogation of nature, the slow and cautious processes of induction, were unknown to him ; hence he passed readily and with ease from the wonder-world of fact to the wonder-world of imagination. He pored on books that treated of magic and witchcraft ; he knew the spell by which to summon up a ghost ; he planned, when at his father's dwelling, how to get admission by night to the vault or charnel-house of Warnham Church ; he might indeed have been engaged in raising the devil when Mr. Bethell broke into his solitary chamber.

One living mage Shelley actually found in the immediate neighbourhood of Eton. Dr. Lind, of Windsor, had been in early life surgeon to an East Indiaman ; while a wanderer in strange lands he had brought together a remarkable collection of Eastern curiosities. With these and his handsome wife, as tall as himself and six times as stout, he had settled in Windsor, and was well known to the court and to court ladies. He was a man of remarkable sweetness and gentleness of disposition, yet one who asserted his right to think in ways of his own. It looked as if nature had fashioned him to become in old age the venerable friend of such an inspired boy as Shelley. The relation seems to have been a wholly beautiful one ; on this side, the tall, spare figure of the physician—"lean as a lath," says Dr. Burney—still light of foot, hoary-headed, with eyes undimmed by years, gleaming under aged brows ; on the other, the illuminated face of an eager stripling ; on this side, age and experience, undulled by custom or the enfeebling touch of time ; on the other, all the wonder, desire, and hope of a young and winged spirit. Never did Shelley mention Dr. Lind's name in after years, writes Mary Shelley, without love and veneration. He lives in Shelley's verse as the old hermit who liberates Laon from the dizzy platform on which he stood enchained until his brain reeled and maddened, who bears the youth to that curious chamber strewn with rarest sea-shells and tapestried with moss, where the sage had gathered many a wise tome, and tends him there until Laon's wildered brain is soothed and healed. Nor is the record of this friendship between old and young less beautiful as we find it in the fragment " Prince Athanase," written not long before Shelley set forth on his last voyage to the Continent..

Such were the main influences which went to mould the mind of Shelley in boyhood. While gaining the usual equipment of classical erudition from his teachers, he had himself started forward into untried and perilous ways of speculation and of fantasy. His interest in science connected itself on the one hand with free speculation in the regions of religion and of politics, and on the other hand with a world of imaginative wonder and romance. His chief friends were books, and perhaps among these the most influential was Godwin's " Political Justice." It supplied him with a ready-made creed, apparently based upon morality and reason, and Shelley became forthwith a preacher and propagandist of revolutionary ideas in his little world of Eton. " I was twice expelled," he wrote at a later time to Godwin, " but recalled by the interference of my father ; " and it is likely enough that a boy who raised the devil might get into grave trouble when seniority in the school would seem to render his aberrations less excusable.

With such a spirit and in such a life as Shelley's

habitual influences and periods of development may count
for much, but now and again comes some shining moment,
one and infinite, which does more than the work of years.
The experiences of two such moments coming to Shelley
in boyhood may be found recorded in his verse. It was
almost certainly at Syon House Academy—not at Eton—
that suddenly the revelation came to him of the misery
of the oppressors and the oppressed in the world in which
he lived and moved, of the misery of his own extravagant
and impotent rages ; and with this discovery arose the
resolve henceforth to be wise and gentle, and just and free.

> "I do remember well the hour which burst
>   My spirit's sleep. A fresh May-dawn it was,
>   When I walked forth upon the glittering grass,
> And wept, I knew not why : until there rose
>   From the near schoolroom voices that, alas !
> Were but one echo from a world of woes—
> The harsh and grating strife of tyrants and of foes.
>
> "And then I clasped my hands and looked around ;
>   But none was near to mock my streaming eyes
> Which poured their warm drops on the sunny ground.
>   So, without shame, I spake : 'I will be wise,
>   And just and free, and mild, if in me lies
> Such power ; for I grow weary to behold
>   The selfish and the strong still tyrannize
> Without reproach or check.' I then controlled
> My tears, my heart grew calm, and I was meek and bold."

The inspiration of this memorable moment was to
elevate and purify Shelley's moral being ; but what if his
imagination were still held in bondage by the fascination
of superstitious fancies and nightmares of gross or vulgar
horror ? His imagination also needed to be purified. To
dedicate his moral being to justice, gentleness, and freedom,

it was the first thing needful; but it was hardly less
essential that he should dedicate his imagination to the
spirit of beauty. This also was accomplished—accomplished almost involuntarily on Shelley's part, and in a
moment of time. We read the record of this second
spiritual crisis in the "Hymn to Intellectual Beauty."
Like the former discovery of moral truth, this unveiling
of intellectual loveliness came on a morning of springtime.

> "While yet a boy I sought for ghosts, and sped
>   Through many a listening chamber, cave, and ruin,
>   And starlight wood, with fearful steps pursuing
> Hopes of high talk with the departed dead.
> I called on poisonous names with which our youth is fed.
>   I was not heard, I saw them not;
>   When, musing deeply on the lot
> Of life, at that sweet time when winds are wooing
>   All vital things that wake to bring
>   News of birds and blossoming,
>   Sudden thy shadow fell on me:—
> I shrieked and clasped my hands in ecstasy!
>
> "I vowed that I would dedicate my powers
>   To thee and thine: have I not kept the vow?"

These two moments were the consecration of Shelley's
boyhood. Never after the years of boyhood did his
imagination cloud itself with the gross stimulants of mind-
less wonder, and horror unallied with beauty. Other
poets have more faithfully represented the concrete facts
of the world, the characters of many men, the infinite
variety of human passions. No other poet has pursued
with such breathless speed on such aerial heights the spirit
of ideal beauty.

CHAPTER II.

OXFORD.

EIGHTEEN hundred and ten, the year in which he removed from Eton to Oxford, was one of the most joyous periods of Shelley's life, until the closing days of that year were darkened by the shadow of disappointed love. It was a happiness to pass from the gregarious school-life and such rigorous discipline as that of Keate to the freedom and seclusion of college chambers. During 1810 Shelley's bodily health seems to have been unusually good, and his spirits unusually buoyant. In the Christmas vacation, 1809–10, he walked the Sussex fields and woods with vigorous step, a gun upon his shoulder, his cousin Medwin by his side. "On such days," says Medwin, "Shelley's spirits used to run riot ; his 'sweet and subtle talk' was to me inebriating and electric." Later in the year hope spanned with a double rainbow the interval between Eton and Oxford—first the hope of a youthful poet and romancer, and, above this, the brighter but more uncertain iris of a lover's hope.

It is curious to note how, from very early days, Shelley, with no literary surroundings or traditions, aspired to authorship. Being urged as a boy by his own fervid thoughts or fancies to give them utterance in prose or verse, he must forthwith put them in a book and present that book to the world. He lived intensely in his own imaginings, wise or idle, beautiful or feebly extravagant, and was insensible to those checks of common sense which come from a power of passing in and out of our own imaginings, and seeing many things, even imperfectly, at a single view. It was his misfortune as a boy to fall under the influence of detestable literary models, and to these he abandoned himself with single-hearted zeal. With what is robust and realistic in eighteenth-century fiction Shelley was out of sympathy. He found what suited his boyish passion for romance and mystery and horror in such ballads as those of Matthew Gregory Lewis, whose false gallop of rhyme readily took the ear, and in forgotten tales by forgotten writers for the Minerva Press, or extravagant romances from the German.

We find it impossible to imagine Shelley at work upon any of his characteristic writings with a collaborator by his side. But nearly all his earlier attempts in prose and verse were made in partnership. With his eldest sister as joint-author he secretly wrote a play and sent it to Matthews, the comedian, who returned the manuscript with the courteous reply that it would not do for acting. He encouraged his sister Hellen in verse-making. In the winter of 1809–10 Shelley and his cousin Medwin wrote, in alternate chapters, the opening of a romance with the title " Nightmare," in which a gigantic witch played a principal part. A more important undertaking was a romantic narrative poem, in which also Medwin was his fellow-labourer, on the subject of the Wandering Jew. Shelley or his cousin had picked up in Lincoln's Inn Fields a printed fragment containing the translation of part of Schubart's poem, " Der Ewige Jude." The subject was one which had within it strange springs of pity and awe, and Ahasuerus—a fellow-sufferer of Prometheus, but in

Christian legend—henceforth haunted Shelley's imagination, and was not lost to view in after-years. Now he rises beside those airy battlements that surmount the universe, to reveal forbidden lore to Ianthe's spirit; now he hangs, a mangled ruin of manhood, yet calm and triumphant, in the cedar tree of the Assassins' valley, or gazes over the precipice while the innocent Assassin children fondle or sport with their favourite snake; and now he comes forth by moonlight from his sea-cavern of a foamless isle, with glittering eye and snow-white hair and beard, to show as in a dream to the Turk the mutability of empire and the ever-new renascence of liberty. Some seven or eight cantos of "The Wandering Jew," Medwin tells us, were written, the first three or four being almost entirely his own. These remain to us, but Shelley's portion of the poem is unascertained or undiscovered. The manuscript was sent by Shelley to Thomas Campbell for his opinion, who returned it with the comment that there were only two good lines in the poem—

> "It seemed as if some angel's sigh
> Had breathed the plaintive symphony."

From the Scotch poet, Shelley appealed to a Scotch publishing firm. Messrs. Ballantyne and Co. kept him long in suspense; then gave a prudent reply—they did not doubt the success of the poem, but it was perhaps better suited to the liberal feelings of the English than "the bigoted spirit which yet pervades many cultivated minds in this country."

Before he had ceased to be a schoolboy Shelley was author of a romance for which, though the statement may seem hardly credible, a publisher of Paternoster Row is said to have been venturesome enough to pay the sum of forty pounds. "Zastrozzi," which bears upon its title-page

the initials " P. B. S.," was in great part written by May of
the year 1809, perhaps considerably earlier.   On April 1
of the following year it was published, or was almost ready
for publication.

" Zastrozzi " is a boy's attempt to rival and surpass
the pieces of contemporary fiction which for a time had
caught his fancy—romances of pseudo-passion and the
pseudo-sublime written in staccato sentences of incoherent
prose.   In " Zastrozzi " the boy-author abandons himself,
with characteristic singleness of feeling, to his conceptions,
and lives with enthusiasm prepense in a world of elaborated
absurdity.   It is all a marvel of the grotesque-sublime ;
and yet not without a curious interest for those who would
study the psychology of genius, since it was the brain that
conceived Zastrozzi which created Count Cenci, and the
inventor of Julia and La Contessa di Laurentini who
in after-years made Asia the consoler and sustainer of
Prometheus.

Some chapters of " Zastrozzi," if we may trust Medwin s
statement, were written by Shelley's cousin, Harriet Grove,
whom he had known as a child, and with whom his acquaintance ripened into close intimacy in 1809 or 1810.   It may
be that during all his Eton days he cherished the memory
and vision of her in his imagination.   Certainly in his
eighteenth year Shelley loved her with the single-hearted-
ness and sincerity of youth.   Harriet Grove was of his
own age, and resembled him in her looks.   In the summer
of 1810, when Shelley, no longer a schoolboy, felt within
him the stir and hopes of dawning manhood, there was a
family gathering of the Grove household at Field Place—
father, mother, Charlotte, Harriet, and Charles, a lad of
fifteen just released from service in the navy.   " Bysshe,"
writes Charles Grove, " was at this time more attached
to my sister Harriet than I can express, and I recollect

well the moonlight walks we four had at Strode, and also
at St. Irving's, the name, I think, of the place then the
Duke of Norfolk's at Horsham." The attachment of the
cousins was seen and sanctioned by the elders, and though
no engagement of marriage was given or received, it was
felt that this might be not far off.

Meanwhile another literary project was on foot. Early
in the autumn of 1810, a very young man—not looking
more than eighteen, says the publisher—introduced himself
to Mr. Stockdale, of 41, Pall Mall, explaining that he was
the eldest son of Mr. Timothy Shelley, M.P. ; that he had
printed a volume of poems at Horsham—no fewer than
fourteen hundred and eighty copies had been struck off—
and unhappily he knew not where to find a sum sufficient
to pay the account : would Stockdale take the quires, bind
them, and offer the volume for sale ? Somehow the Horsham printer's account was discharged, the unbound sheets
arrived at Pall Mall, and on September 18 and 19 appeared
an advertisement in the morning papers : "This day is
published, in royal 8vo, price 4*s.* in boards, ' Original Poems,'
by Victor and Cazire." Like other early productions of
Shelley, this octavo of sixty-four pages was the joint
work of himself and some co-labourer under the Muses—
not Medwin now, but one who was assumed at the time to
be a lady. Was "Cazire" Shelley's sister Elizabeth ? or
the colleague who had elaborated with him some of the
nonsense of "Zastrozzi"—his cousin Harriet Grove ? Or
can "Cazire" have been a mask for his friend, Edward
Graham, a youth of musical talent who had been educated
at the expense of Shelley's father ? A few days after its
publication, Stockdale, looking through the little volume
with more care than he had previously had leisure to bestow,
recognized one of the pieces as a transcript from the pages
of Matthew Gregory Lewis, author of "The Monk" and of

many tales of wonder and tales of terror in ballad form.
He made haste to communicate his discovery to Shelley.
" With all the ardour incidental to his character," writes
Stockdale, "which embraced youthful honour in all its
brilliancy, he expressed the warmest resentment at the
imposition practised upon him by his coadjutor, and
entreated me to destroy all the copies." Already, however,
about one hundred copies were in circulation, and the
volume was in the hands of the reviewers. The thin octavo
has wholly disappeared from human ken, but of a hundred
copies put into circulation one may somewhere lurk for
future discovery. Meanwhile we can await its reappearance
with equanimity, and may be willing to accept as not
unjust the decision of a contemporary critic :—" Original
Poetry by Victor and Cazire. There is no original *poetry*
in this volume ; there is nothing in it but downright
scribble."

On April 10, 1810, Percy Bysshe Shelley signed his
name as a student in the books of University College,
Oxford, " Sub tutamine Magistri Rowley et Domini
Davison." Having matriculated, he returned to Eton, and
there remained until he had ended his schooling, on July
30. At the beginning of Michaelmas Term, he was again
in Oxford, now about to enter on residence. On one or
other of these occasions—probably the second—his father
accompanied him. University College had in former days
seen Timothy Shelley as a student within its walls, and
now the son was to follow in his father's steps ; there was,
moreover, an exhibition held in the college, styled the
Leicester Exhibition, to which Bysshe had been nominated
in April by Sir John Shelley-Sidney, of Penshurst, as heir
of the Sidney Earls of Leicester. Surrounded by objects
which recalled his early days, and lodging in his old
quarters, with the son of his former host, Mr. Timothy

Shelley was in a gracious mood. One of the sons of Mr. Slatter, his departed host, was about to embark in business as partner with a bookseller and printer. To the place of business Mr. Timothy repaired with Bysshe, and enjoined the young student to purchase there whatever he might need in books and stationery. "My son here," he went on, "has a literary turn ; he is already an author, and do pray indulge him in his printing freaks." One of these printing freaks, before many months had gone by, was to drive Shelley forth into banishment from Oxford, and to close against him the doors of his father's house.

In first-floor rooms, now known as "The Shelley Lecture-room," in the corner next the hall of the principal quadrangle of University College, the new-comer took up his abode. The venerable traditions of Oxford probably affected little a mind at all times singularly insensible to the wisdom or the sentiment of history. Oxford in 1810 represented the past ; it was Shelley's aspiration to break with the past, and belong, as he conceived it, wholly to the present or the future. The routine of instruction was not attractive to a young and eager mind ; tutors' lectures and compulsory chapels are perhaps fuller of charm and inspiration when remembered after a decade or two than when actually endured. The special charm of Oxford for Shelley lay in the comparative freedom of his student's life. He could pursue his own studies without interruption, and in the citadel of his chambers, be poet, natural philosopher, metaphysician, in turns as it pleased him. If he desired the companionship of some chosen friend, there was all the afternoon free for country rambles, all the endless hours from five till long past midnight for converse and debate.

One such friend, and only one during the months at Oxford, Shelley found. Thomas Jefferson Hogg, son of a gentleman of old family and high Tory politics, residing at Stockton-on-Tees, had entered University College in the early part of the year 1810, a short time before Shelley. Early in Michaelmas Term they met for the first time, and speedily followed a close alliance, which for a season excluded every other friendship, and was momentous in its consequences for each of the inseparable pair. There was little resemblance between the friends. Hogg had intellectual powers of no common order, and all through his life was an ardent lover of literature ; but he cared little or nothing for doctrines and abstract principles such as formed the very food on which the revolutionary intellect of Shelley fed ; and his interest in literature was that of a man of the world who finds in poetry a refuge from the tedium of common life. For the foibles and follies and false enthusiasms of individuals or coteries, Hogg had a keen eye and a mocking tongue ; yet he tolerated all novelties of opinion or of practice as bright oases in the desert of common sense. In Shelley there stood real and living before him "the divine poet"—all that he himself could never be, and could not even choose to be. For "the divine poet" Hogg's admiration was genuine and vivid ; but with his admiration for the poet there mingled a man of the world's sense of superiority to the immortal child. Accordingly Shelley appeared to Hogg at once sublime and ridiculous, a being fashioned to serve as an inexhaustible source of delight and diversion to men of sense and wit. The peculiar piquancy of Hogg's account of his relations with Shelley lies in this—that in Hogg the lover of the ideal was at the same time a man of the world, and the man of the world was a lover of the ideal, so that underlying his admiration we can always discover a kind of amused disdain, and again under his disdain a certain involuntary loyalty and admiration.

For Shelley's six months at Oxford, Hogg is our sufficient and almost our only witness. We should spoil his narrative if we were to interrupt it with cross-questioning or rebuke. The veracity of the historian and the veracity of the artist are not identical. Allowing for Hogg's peculiar point of view, for his egotism, and for the fact that at all hazards he must be witty, we may assert that in his chapters on Shelley at Oxford he has painted an admirable portrait, true in the essential qualities of being characteristic and living.

"At the commencement of Michaelmas Term," writes Hogg, "that is, at the end of October in the year 1810, I happened one day to sit next a freshman at dinner; it was his first appearance in hall. His figure was slight, and his aspect remarkably youthful, even at our table, where all were very young. He seemed thoughtful and absent. He ate little, and had no acquaintance with any one. I know not how it was that we fell into conversation, for such familiarity was unusual, and, strange to say, much reserve prevailed in a society where there could not possibly be occasion for any. We have often endeavoured in vain to recollect in what manner our discourse began, and especially by what transition it passed to a subject sufficiently remote from all the associations we were able to trace. The stranger had expressed an enthusiastic admiration for poetical and imaginative works of the German school. I dissented from his criticisms. He upheld the originality of the German writings. I asserted their want of nature. 'What modern literature,' said he, 'will you compare to theirs?' I named the Italian. This roused all his impetuosity; and few, as I soon discovered, were more impetuous in argumentative conversation. So eager was our dispute, that when the servants came to clear the tables, we were not aware that we had been left alone. I

remarked that it was time to quit the hall, and I invited
the stranger to finish the discussion at my rooms. He
eagerly assented. He lost the thread of his discourse in
the transit, and the whole of his enthusiasm in the cause
of Germany ; for as soon as he arrived at my rooms, and
whilst I was lighting the candles, he said calmly, and to
my great surprise, that he was not qualified to maintain
such a discussion, for he was alike ignorant of Italian
and German, and had only the works of the Germans in
translations, and but little of Italian poetry, even at second-
hand. For my part, I confessed, with an equal ingenuousness, that I knew nothing of German, and but little of
Italian ; that I had spoken only through others, and like
him had hitherto seen by the glimmering light of translations."

Over their dessert and wine the talk went on. It
mattered little, declared Shelley, whether German or Italian
literature were the more excellent, for what was all literature but vain trifling ? What was the study of ancient or
modern tongues but merely a study of words and phrases,
of the names of things? How much wiser it were to
investigate things themselves! Feeling little interest in
the subject of his discourse, Hogg had leisure to examine
the appearance of his extraordinary guest. "It was a sum
of many contradictions. His figure was slight and fragile,
and yet his bones and joints were large and strong. He
was tall, but he stooped so much that he seemed of a low
stature. His clothes were expensive, and made according
to the most approved mode of the day ; but they were
tumbled, rumpled, unbrushed. His gestures were abrupt,
and sometimes violent, occasionally even awkward, yet
more frequently gentle and graceful. His complexion was
delicate, and almost feminine, of the purest red and white ;
yet he was tanned and freckled by exposure to the sun,

having passed the autumn, as he said, in shooting. His features, his whole face, and particularly his head, were, in fact, unusually small ; yet the last *appeared* of a remarkable bulk, for his hair was long and bushy, and in fits of absence, and in the agonies (if I may use the word) of anxious thought, he often rubbed it fiercely with his hands, or passed his fingers quickly through his locks unconsciously, so that it was singularly wild and rough. In times when it was the mode to imitate stage-coachmen as closely as possible in costume, and when the hair was invariably cropped, like that of our soldiers, this eccentricity was very striking. His features were not symmetrical (the mouth, perhaps, excepted), yet was the effect of the whole extremely powerful. . . . But there was one physical blemish that threatened to neutralize all his excellence "—his voice, which was " excruciating "—" it was intolerably shrill, harsh, and discordant ; of the most cruel intension,—it was perpetual, and without any remission,—it excoriated the ears." * As the shrill discourse proceeded, suddenly a clock without chimed the quarter to seven, and Shelley was away on flying foot to attend a lecture on mineralogy. An hour later and he burst into Hogg's room, threw down his cap, and stood chafing his hands over the fire. The lecture was dull and miserably attended ; the man talked " about stones ! about stones ! " and so

---

* Peacock writes of Hogg's statement, " There is a good deal in these volumes about Shelley's discordant voice. This defect he certainly had ; but it was chiefly observable when he spoke under excitement. Then his voice was not only dissonant like a jarring string, but he spoke in sharp fourths, the most unpleasing sequence of sound that can fall on the human ear : but it was scarcely so when he spoke calmly, and not at all so when he read ; on the contrary, he seemed to have his voice under perfect command ; it was good both in tune and in tone ; it was low and soft, but clear, distinct, and expressive. I have heard him read almost all Shakespeare's tragedies, and some of his more poetical comedies, and it was a pleasure to hear him read them."

dryly, said Shelley, with a downcast look and melancholy tone; he would never endure another lecture about stones. Again after supper the theme of chemistry and its wonders was taken up; the service it was destined to render to the race of man; the supply of unstinted stores of artificial food; the watering of arid African wastes by streams and lakes won from the elements by chemistry; the production of artificial heat in arctic climates, and for our poor during the cruel English winters; the mighty energies of the galvanic battery; the art of aerial navigation in balloons. Thus sped by the inspired hours, Shelley pacing the room with slow, prodigious strides, and when the mysteries of matter failed, descanting as eloquently on mysteries of mind—the analysis of the substance of the soul, a future state, pre-existence, personal identity—until the fire sank low and the candles glimmered in their sockets. "I lighted him downstairs," writes Hogg, "with the stump of a candle which had dissolved itself into a lamp, and I soon heard him running through the quiet quadrangle in the still night. That sound became afterwards so familiar to my ear, that I still seem to hear Shelley's hasty steps."

A meeting in Shelley's rooms had been appointed for the afternoon of the ensuing day. An hour behind his time, Hogg arrived at two o'clock; but to the young chemist, absorbed in his experiments, it seemed still early morning. "I perceived," says Hogg, "that he took no note of time; if there was a virtue of which he was utterly incapable, it was that homely, but pleasing and useful one, punctuality.' Shelley cowered over the fire, stricken with a chill, and oppressed, until the officious scout withdrew, by a fear that his rooms were to be put in order, and everything restored to its proper place. The rooms had been just papered and painted; carpet, curtains, and furniture were quite new; but the general air of freshness, observes Hogg, was greatly obscured by the indescribable confusion in which the various objects were mixed. Shelley did not gather, arrange, and possess in the manner of a collector; the objects which made up the chaos that surrounded him were means for bringing close to him the quick and mysterious forces of nature as his guests or playfellows; and he loved to feel that the chaos of his chambers was instinct with fiery life and pregnant with wonder. In a moment he was vehemently turning the handle of the electrical machine, making the sparks crackle and fly; or stood on the insulating stool, charged with the fiery stream, his wild locks extravagantly dispread, while Hogg worked the apparatus. Or he discoursed eagerly of a method by which, with the aid of electrical kites, man might become master of the thunderstorm and lord of the clouds; or passed on, forgetful of his declaration that literature is vain trifling, to speak with fervour of poets and poetry. "I participated in his enthusiasm," says Hogg, "and soon forgot the shrill and unmusical voice that had at first seemed intolerable to my ear. He was indeed a whole university in himself to me, in respect of the stimulus and incitement which his example afforded to my love of study."

This meeting in Shelley's rooms confirmed an alliance between the two freshmen, who henceforth were inseparable. After morning chapel, lectures, and some hours of private study, the friends would meet at one o'clock, and again in the evening after dinner in hall. "I was enabled," writes Hogg, "to continue my studies in the evening in consequence of a very remarkable peculiarity. My young and energetic friend was then overcome by extreme drowsiness, which speedily and completely vanquished him; he would sleep from two to four hours, often so soundly that his slumbers resembled a deep lethargy; he lay occasionally upon the sofa, but more commonly stretched upon the rug before a large fire, like a cat; and his little round head was exposed to such a fierce heat, that I used to wonder how he was able to bear it. Sometimes I have interposed some shelter, but rarely with any permanent effect; for the sleeper usually contrived to turn himself, and to roll again into the spot where the fire glowed the brightest. His torpor was generally profound, but he would sometimes discourse incoherently for a long while in his sleep. At six he would suddenly compose himself, even in the midst of an animated narrative or of earnest discussion; and he would lie buried in entire forgetfulness, in a sweet and mighty oblivion, until ten, when he would suddenly start up, and rubbing his eyes with great violence, and passing his fingers swiftly through his long hair, would enter at once into a vehement argument, or begin to recite verses, either of his own composition or from the works of others, with a rapidity and an energy that were often quite painful. During the period of his occultation I took tea, and read or wrote without interruption. He would sometimes sleep for a shorter time, for about two hours; postponing for the like period the commencement of his retreat to the rug, and rising with tolerable punctuality at ten; and sometimes, although rarely, he was able entirely to forego the accustomed refreshment." At ten, when he awoke, he was always ready for his supper, a meal which he enjoyed. After supper "his mind was clear and penetrating, and his discourse eminently brilliant." The students read each his own book, or more often read together, long discussions interrupting and prolonging their hours of study. When the college clock struck two Hogg would rise, in spite of Shelley's entreaty or remonstrance, and retire for the night.

Each afternoon, at one o'clock, Shelley and his companion were accustomed to sally forth for a walk. " It was
his delight to strike boldly into the fields, to cross the
country daringly on foot, as is usual with sportsmen in
shooting ; to perform, as it were, a pedestrian steeple-chase.
He was strong, light, and active, and in all respects well
suited to such exploits." Shelley's ordinary preparation
for a rural walk, says Hogg, formed a very remarkable
contrast with his mild aspect and pacific habits. " He
furnished himself with a pair of duelling-pistols, and a good
store of powder and ball ; and when he came to a solitary
spot, he pinned a card, or fixed some other mark upon a
tree or a bank, and amused himself by firing at it : he was
a pretty good shot, and was much delighted at his success."
The duelling-pistols were handled with inconceivable care-
lessness, and Hogg, fearing some misadventure, would
secretly abstract, when Shelley equipped himself for the
field, the powder-flask or the flints ; and thus, after a time,
the pistols, often found unserviceable, were left at home.
One day, on discovering the trick that had been played to
render his weapons harmless, Shelley was seriously offended.
He determined instantly to return to college for the flints
and steel. " I tempted him, by the way, to try to define
anger, and to discuss the nature of that affection of the
mind ; to which, as the discussion waxed warm, he grew
exceedingly hostile in theory, and could not be brought to
admit that it could possibly be excusable in any case."
While the disputation *De Ira* proceeded, Shelley forgot his
wrath and his purpose, and suffered himself to be led by
the ingenious Hogg into another path towards another end
and aim. In these country walks Shelley loved to find
himself among the woods, or on the banks of the Thames,
or by the waterside of an old quarry-pond at the foot of
Shotover Hill. On the edge of this pond " he would linger

until dusk, gazing in silence on the water, repeating verses aloud, or earnestly discussing themes that had no connection with surrounding objects."

The inducements to study offered by college or university were few and slight; at least they operated but feebly on the freshman class. Learning was neglected; discipline was decayed. At University College " in the evening unceasing drunkenness and continual uproar prevailed." Shelley, prone beyond all other men to admire, and with a youthful scholar's veneration for men of learning and genius, found little to admire or venerate among those who should have been the masters of his mind. At Oxford as at Eton his closest friends were the books he loved. " The devotion, the reverence, the religion with which he was kindled towards all the masters of intellect," declares Hogg, ' cannot be described. The irreverent many cannot comprehend the awe, the careless apathetic worldling cannot imagine the enthusiasm, nor can the tongue that attempts only to speak of things visible to the bodily eye express the mighty emotion that inwardly agitated him, when he approached for the first time a volume which he believed to be replete with the recondite and mystic philosophy of antiquity; his cheeks glowed, his eyes became bright, his whole frame trembled, and his entire attention was immediately swallowed up in the depths of contemplation." Shelley took the scholastic logic, says Hogg, very kindly, and seized its distinctions with his accustomed quickness. But " he rejected with marvellous impatience every mathematical discipline that was offered; no problem could awaken the slightest curiosity, nor could he be made sensible of the beauty of any theorem." Nor was his an intellect which could spell out patiently the lessons of nature. It was Shelley's dream that man should seize the mysterious forces of nature and wield them for the uses of

D

humanity—a dream which the century is bringing true ; but he lacked the scientific habit of mind. " I was never able," says Hogg, " to impart even a glimpse of the merits of Ray or Linnæus." Method and classification were not Shelley's province ; when he fixed his gaze upon external nature, he desired to penetrate in imagination through and beyond the sensible phenomena to living energies of which they are the manifestation, and to recreate a nobler world of dream from these energies unimpeded by the cold obstruction of earth.

At Oxford, as at Eton, Shelley's mind moved upon lines of its own ; but its susceptibility was extreme to influences that were in any degree kindred to itself. " He was to be found, book in hand, at all hours ; reading in season and out of season ; at table, in bed, and especially during a walk ; not only in the quiet country and in retired paths ; not only at Oxford, in the public walks and High Street, but in the most crowded thoroughfares of London. Nor was he less absorbed by the volume that was open before him in Cheapside, in Cranbourne Alley, or in Bond Street, than in a lonely lane or a secluded library. Sometimes a vulgar fellow would attempt to insult or annoy the eccentric student in passing. Shelley always avoided the malignant interruption by slipping aside with his vast and quiet agility." More often he would glide through the throng, gazed at but unmolested, almost unconscious of his surroundings, " stooping low, with bent knees and out-stretched neck, poring earnestly over the volume, which he extended before him." " I never beheld eyes," says Hogg, " that devoured the pages more voraciously than his ; I am convinced that two-thirds of the period of day and night were often employed in reading. It is no exaggeration to affirm that out of the twenty-four hours he frequently read sixteen. At Oxford his diligence in this respect was exemplary, but it greatly increased afterwards. . . . Few were aware of the extent, and still fewer, I apprehend, of the profundity of his reading ; in his short life, and without ostentation, he had in truth read more Greek than many an aged pedant, who, with pompous parade, prides himself upon this study alone. Although he had not entered critically into the minute niceties of the noblest of languages, he was thoroughly conversant with the valuable matter it contains. A pocket edition of Plato, of Plutarch, of Euripides, without interpretation or notes, or of the Septuagint, was his ordinary companion ; and he read the text straightforward for hours, if not as readily as an English author, at least with as much facility as French, Italian, or Spanish."

"Hume's 'Essays' was a favourite book with Shelley, and he was always ready to put forward in argument the doctrines they uphold." The sceptical philosophy, observes Hogg, though uncongenial with a fervid and imaginative genius, gave Shelley a vantage-ground as a disputant ; and to question and contend was to his intellect like the breath of life. It demanded a clear space wherein to rear ideal fabrics. The French Revolution, sweeping away so many landmarks and crumbling structures of the past, and speeding onward with a dreadful voice of hope, created the very conditions which were most favourable to the free development of Shelley's imagination. But to be a portion of the Revolution meant that one had imbibed the critical philosophy which preceded, and in part inspired, the revolutionary movement.

With great audacity of intellect Shelley united a grave, earnest, and reverential spirit, a "meek seriousness" of heart, a "marvellous gentleness" of disposition. Amid the turbulent animalisms of young Oxford, he remained untouched by grossness; "the purity and sanctity of his life," says his closest friend, "were most conspicuous.'

Although Shelley's seriousness permitted him now and again to indulge in some freak or elvish trick, and although he was "vehemently delighted by exquisite and delicate sallies," in which a fanciful or fantastic wit disported itself, he was offended, declares Hogg, "and indeed more indignant than would appear to be consistent with the singular mildness of his nature at a coarse and awkward jest, especially if it were immodest and uncleanly; in the latter case his anger was unbounded, and his uneasiness pre-eminent." With exceeding gentleness and refinement of feeling he united a generous indignation at the sight of cruelty or injustice ; the indignant ardour, on his witnessing the infliction of pain, being "too vivid to allow him to pause and consider the probable consequences of the abrupt interposition of the knight-errantry which would at once redress all grievances." Hogg relates how one afternoon in Bagley Wood they came upon a boy driving a very young and very weak ass, overladen with a weight of fagots ; the tyrant was belabouring his victim's lean ribs violently with a cudgel. Shelley sprang forward, roused to an unusual degree of excitement, and was about to take action with indignant vehemence, when the judicious Hogg interposed, and by legal methods of pleading and cross-examination gained the cause of his long-eared client.

" The most docile, the most facile, the most pliant, the most confiding creature, that ever was led through any of the various paths on earth "—with such superlatives Hogg, apologizing for a description which looks like an unqualified panegyric, is constrained to place on record his impression of Shelley at Oxford. His charities flowed forth wherever and whenever human suffering or sorrow made its appeal to his human pity and love. " Out of a scanty and somewhat precarious income," writes Hogg, thinking of all the years of Shelley's life, not merely of the months at Oxford

—"an income inadequate to allow the indulgence of the most ordinary superfluities, and diminished by various casual but unavoidable incumbrances—he was able, by restricting himself to a diet more simple than the fare of the most austere anchorite, and by refusing himself horses and the other gratifications that appear properly to belong to his station, and of which he was in truth very fond, to bestow upon men of letters, whose merits were of too high an order to be rightly estimated by their own generation, donations large indeed, if we consider from how narrow a source they flowed." But to speak of these acts of generosity in detail would be a violation, adds Hogg, of the "unequalled delicacy " of the donor.

Shelley's love of children was early developed, and of unusual strength. He would pause in his swift course to admire the bright face of some cottage child ; then sadden to think of what might be its future lot, what hereafter the piteous or sullen expression of that glad countenance. In a whimsical way he would apply the Platonic doctrine that all knowledge is reminiscence, so as to justify an interest in babyhood which is not a usual characteristic of under graduate philosophers.

" One morning," writes Hogg, " we had been reading Plato together so diligently that the usual hour of exercise passed away unperceived. We sallied forth hastily to take the air for half an hour before dinner. In the middle of Magdalen Bridge we met a woman with a child in her arms. Shelley was more attentive at that instant to our conduct in a life that was past, or to come, than to a decorous regulation of the present, according to the established usages of society, in that fleeting moment of eternal duration styled the nineteenth century. With abrupt dexterity he caught hold of the child. The mother, who might well fear that it was about to be thrown over the parapet of the bridge into the sedgy waters below, held it fast by its long train. 'Will your baby tell us anything about pre-existence, madam?' he asked, in a piercing voice and with a wistful look. The mother made no answer, but perceiving that Shelley's object was not murderous, but altogether harmless, she dismissed her apprehension and relaxed her hold. 'Will your baby tell us anything about pre-existence, madam?' he repeated, with unabated earnestness. 'He cannot speak, sir,' said the mother, seriously. 'Worse and worse,' cried Shelley, with an air of deep disappointment, shaking his long hair most pathetically about his young face; 'but surely the babe can speak if he will, for he is only a few weeks old. He may fancy perhaps that he cannot, but it is only a silly whim. He cannot have forgotten entirely the use of speech in so short a time; the thing is absolutely impossible.' 'It is not for me to dispute with you, gentlemen,' the woman meekly replied, her eye glancing at our academical garb; 'but I can safely declare I never heard him speak, nor any child of his age.' . . . Shelley sighed deeply as we walked on. 'How provokingly close are those new-born babes!' he ejaculated; 'but it is not the less certain, notwithstanding the cunning attempts to conceal the truth, that all knowledge is reminiscence.'"

Shelley's kindly or fantastic familiarities with persons of a humbler social position than his own were helped, not hindered, by his high-bred courtesy of feeling and of manner. Yet with his grace of bearing was strangely united a certain awkwardness. "He would stumble in stepping across the floor of a drawing-room; he would trip himself up on a smooth-shaven grass plot, and he would tumble in the most inconceivable manner in ascending the commodious, facile, and well-carpeted staircase of an elegant mansion, so as to bruise his nose or his lip on the upper steps, or to tread upon his hands, and even occasionally to disturb the composure of a well-bred footman ; on the contrary, he would often glide without collision through a crowded assembly, thread with unerring dexterity a most intricate path, or securely and rapidly tread the most arduous and uncertain ways." He always dressed " like a gentleman," says Hogg, " handsomely indeed," yet he conformed to the fashion only as far as it did not interfere with his own pleasure, so that there was, " it must be admitted, something of singularity in his appearance. His throat was often bare, the collar of his shirt open, in days when a huge neckcloth was the mode. Other men's heads, like those of private soldiers, were then clipped quite close ; the poet's locks were long, which certainly was a singular phenomenon, and streaming like a meteor ; and the air of his little round hat upon his little round head was troubled and peculiar."

The friends often eschewed the four-o'clock dinner in hall, thus in part acquiring a reputation as unsocial and as affecting singularity. Shelley, it must be confessed, was deficient in true British devotion to the roast and boiled. His food " was plain and simple as that of a hermit, with a certain anticipation, even at this time, of a vegetable diet." He could have lived, says Hogg, thinking of a somewhat later time, " on bread alone without repining. When he was walking in London with an acquaintance, he would suddenly run into a baker's shop, purchase a supply, and breaking a loaf he would offer half of it to his companion. . . . Sometimes he ate with his bread the common raisins that are used in making puddings. . . . The common fruit of stalls, and oranges and apples, were always welcome to Shelley. Vegetables, and especially salads, and pies and puddings, were acceptable ; his beverage consisted of copious and frequent draughts of cold water, but tea was ever grateful—cup after cup—and coffee. Wine was taken with singular moderation, commonly diluted largely with water, and for a long period he would abstain from it altogether." But, observes Hogg, he retained his sweet tooth; "he would greedily eat cakes, gingerbread, and sugar; honey, preserved or stewed fruit, with bread, were his favourite delicacies; these he thankfully and joyfully received from others, but he rarely sought for them, or provided them for himself. The restraint and protracted duration of a convivial meal were intolerable; he was seldom able to keep his seat during the brief period assigned to an ordinary family dinner." At Oxford his fare, though temperate, was not meagre; he was, as Trelawny knew him in Italy, "like a healthy, well-conditioned boy." We find him vigorous, capable of enduring fatigue, and in the main happy; not troubled by nervous excitement or thick-coming fancies.

CHAPTER III.

OXFORD—*continued*.

THE year 1810, which opened joyously for Shelley, had a cloudy and troubled close. There was trouble at home with his father, trouble with the publisher Stockdale, and more grievous trouble in the discovery that his letters to Harriet Grove had alarmed both her and her parents by their energetic unorthodoxy, and that it was quick growing to a certainty that she could never be his. At the end of Michaelmas Term—towards the middle of December— Hogg left Oxford for a clergyman's house in Buckingham- shire, and Shelley returned to spend the Christmas vacation at Field Place. As to authorship, things had not gone altogether ill with him since the unfortunate affair of " Victor and Cazire." The courageous publishers who had given forty pounds for "Zastrozzi" were not inclined to repeat the experiment in the instance of a second romance ; but Stockdale had been induced to undertake the publica- tion, at the author's expense, of his new attempt—" St. Irvyne, or the Rosicrucian." " As it is a thing which almost *mechanically* sells to circulating libraries, etc.," writes Shelley, who at this time had a good knack of hoping, " I would wish it to be published on my *own* account." In the dark November and December days many longing thoughts travelled from University College to 41, Pall Mall. What compositors ever kept pace with a young author's desires? The question, "When do you suppose 'St. Irvyne' will be out?" changes in a fortnight to the plaintive cry, "When *does* 'St. Irvyne' come out?"

One morning, when Hogg had called at Shelley's rooms, the young author was discovered busily occupied in correcting and recorrecting with anxious care some proofs which lay before him. Suddenly throwing a paper on the middle of the table, he said, "in a penetrating whisper as he sprang eagerly from his chair, 'I am going to publish some poems.'" Hogg—sagacious critic—took the proofs and examined them; there were some good lines, some bright thoughts, but many irregularities and incongruities. The critic was faithful in pointing out errors and defects. "In their present form you do not think the poems ought to be published?" asked Shelley that evening, on waking from his after-dinner sleep. "Only as burlesque poetry," answered Hogg, who went on to show by an example how easily the poems would lend themselves to parody. A few strokes of the pen and he had effected the transformation of one piece. Shelley read it aloud in a ridiculous tone, was amused by the grotesque disguise, and abandoned his intention of publication. From day to day the pair of friends amused themselves in idle moments by making the poems "more and more ridiculous; by striking out the more sober passages, by inserting whimsical conceits;" and especially by giving them what they called a dithyrambic character. And now the poems seemed sufficiently absurd to present themselves abroad seeking the praise of folly. But what title should the collection bear? At times they thought of ascribing its authorship to some one of the chief living poets, or some grave man of learning and letters. Finally a bright idea flashed through the brain of Hogg. Peg

Nicholson, the mad washerwoman who had attempted to stab King George III. with a carving-knife, was still living in Bedlam. As Swift had killed the astrologer Partridge, so it was resolved that "that noted female," Margaret Nicholson, should depart this life, and that a nephew and administrator, John Fitz-Victor, should be created to serve as editor of his aunt's posthumous poetical fragments. "The idea," says Hogg, "gave an object and purpose to our burlesque—to ridicule the strange mixture of sentimentality with the murderous fury of revolutionists, that was so prevalent in the compositions of the day." The jest pleased the publisher, and in a few days a quarto pamphlet of verse, with noble type and ample margins, was for sale on Mr. Munday's counter; the name "John Fitz-Victor" stood illustrious on the title-page in those Old English characters which Southey had introduced on the title-page of "Thalaba." Shelley gazed in an ecstasy of delight at the superb form in which his jest rose glorified. Nobody, says Hogg, suspected or could suspect who was the author; the copies which remained, after "John Fitz-Victor" had presented a certain number to mystified friends were "rapidly sold"—a statement open to question—"at the aristocratical price of half a crown for half a dozen pages."

"When *does* 'St. Irvyne' come out?" sighed Shelley on the 2nd of December. After little more than one impatient fortnight his eyes were gratified with the sight of Stockdale's advertisement—probably the same which appeared later in the *Times*. "The University Romance.— This day is published, price only 5s., *St. Irvyne, or the Rosicrucian:* a Romance. By a Gentleman of Oxford University." "St. Irvyne" is perhaps less crude in style than "Zastrozzi," and is certainly less coherent in plot and incidents. Indeed, it readily falls asunder into two stories, feebly linked together by a paragraph at the close. This circumstance, together with various awkward turns of expression, which look like imperfect renderings from the German, has led Mr. Forman to conjecture that in "St. Irvyne" Shelley was less author than translator, and that two German tales are tacked together in the English romance. Whether translation or original, "St. Irvyne," together with "Zastrozzi," throws light upon the temperament and crude, excitable imagination of the Eton schoolboy and Oxford freshman. At all times what was strange and wonderful delighted Shelley; but in after years it was the wonder and strangeness of the beauty and terror which manifest themselves through sea and sky, through love and death, through the highest hopes and fears of humanity. As a boy he had but little sense of these finer, yet most real, springs of rapture and of awe; at the same time, he was unable to interest himself in the everyday, commonplace aspect of things; and thus he was driven to find food for his appetite for the marvellous in fantastic horrors and violent travesties of human passion. These, for the time being, were all in all to Shelley. His vision, grotesquely absurd though it might be, dominated him, and he had by him no standard of reality by which to measure its remoteness from the truth of nature.

"About this time," says the publisher, Stockdale, "not merely slight hints, but constant allusions, personally and by letters, . . . rendered me extremely uneasy respecting Mr. Shelley's religious, or indeed irreligious, sentiments." Possibly he was also not quite at ease with respect to the bill due to him for the publication of the "University Romance." He had been charmed by Shelley's frank, enthusiastic manner, joined with an unusual docility in profiting by suggestions as to the conduct of his tale; and he fully believed in Shelley's honour and integrity. But the young man was dependent on his father; and Mr.

Timothy Shelley, who appeared to Stockdale, in the few
conversations which took place in the shop, "not particularly bright," and "inclined to exercise the parental
authority with most injudicious despotism," declared that
his son was not of age, and "that he, his father, would
never pay a farthing" of the bill. It was Stockdale's
interest to keep on good terms, if possible, with the son;
but, even at the risk of a breach with "young Mr. Shelley,"
to keep on good terms with the elder Mr. Shelley, who
held the purse-strings, and seemed disposed to draw them
tight. If Stockdale could render an important service to
Mr. Timothy Shelley without doing a wrong to Mr. Percy,
all might be well. The youth was entering on dangerous
ways; he had spoken to Stockdale of the manuscript of
"a metaphysical essay in support of atheism, which he
intended to promulgate throughout the university;" and
of a novel in preparation "principally constructed to
convey metaphysical and political opinions by way of
conversation." What could be more dutiful than to warn
a father of the risks incurred by an amiable and enthusiastic
son; and how touching the appeal to a father's gratitude
and sense of justice if the son—a visionary youth, well-
meaning, but too easily led astray—were discovered, as
it were, placed between his good and evil angel on the right
hand and the left; his good angel Mr. Publisher Stockdale,
his worser spirit a certain college companion with a mind
"infinitely beneath that of his friend"—Mr. Jefferson
Hogg! Fortunately it was possible to gather evidence
against Hogg; for Mrs. Stockdale came from Lynnington
Dayrell, Buckinghamshire, where Hogg was spending his
Christmas vacation, and she could by letter play the part
of a female detective. The result of her inquiry was that
no doubt remained in the mind of the virtuous Stockdale
that if he did not "rush forward, and, however rudely,

pull " Shelley "from the precipice over which he was suspended by a hair, his fate must be inevitable."

"St. Irvyne" had scarcely appeared when the first note of alarm was sounded in Mr. Timothy Shelley's hearing. He forthwith despatched a letter from London to his son at Field Place, doubtless well meant, probably ill conceived and injudicious, one of those epistles of mingled tenderness and bluster, expressed in incoherent sentences where verbs helplessly appeal for nominatives, and nouns wander in search of verbs, such as we know through examples presented by Hogg. Shelley in an excited mood read his father's letter, and imagined that every man's hand, save his friend Hogg's, was against him. It would have been a consolation to Shelley if he could have turned in distress to his cousin Harriet, have shared his griefs and anxieties with her, and found a refuge from calamity in her affection. But she too had taken alarm, and was joined, as he conceived, with the rest against him. To troubles in his home circle were added the pangs of despised love. With Shelley the twofold misery of domestic strife and disappointed love sufficed to throw his whole nature into a state of nervous agitation ; and the letters to Hogg, which were written in rapid succession during the days of the Christmas vacation, tremble and palpitate and thrill with vehement and hectic feeling.

The conviction that all was over between himself and Harriet Grove did not come to Shelley in a moment, but forced itself gradually upon him. His sister Elizabeth attempted to plead his cause, but unsuccessfully. Harriet gave a discreet reply—how could she be certain that Shelley was in reality the exalted being whom his sister had fondly described ? Without doubt he had idealized herself, and only disappointment were in store for him if he should come to know her truly. At the close of the year 1810, Shelley seems to have sought and obtained a personal interview with his cousin, but the result was only a confirmation of his fears. "I am but just returned to Field Place from an inefficient effort," he wrote to Hogg on January 2. "Why do you, my happy friend, tell me of perfection in love? Is she not gone? And yet I breathe, I live! But adieu to egotism; I am sick to death at the very name of *self*." A few days later came the tidings that Harriet's promise of love and fidelity was already given to a Mr. Helyer. "She is gone! She is lost to me for ever! She married! Married to a clod of earth, she will become as insensible herself; all those fine capabilities will moulder. Let us speak no more of the subject. Do not deprive me of the little remains of peace which yet linger; that which arises from endeavours to make others happy" (January 11, 1811).

During these days of wintry cold without, and of fever at the heart, Shelley turned for support and consolation to his sister Elizabeth, and to his friend Hogg. And finding something to appease his spirit in "the endeavour to make others happy," he amiably resolved that Hogg should forthwith fall in love with Elizabeth, whom he had never seen, and that Elizabeth should be less unkind to his friend than Harriet Grove had proved to himself. "Believe me, my dear friend," he writes to Hogg (December 28, 1810), "that my only ultimate wishes *now* are for your happiness and that of my sisters." At this moment it was impossible to invite Hogg to Field Place, for Stockdale's representations had strongly prejudiced Mr. Timothy Shelley against his son's Oxford companion. But Shelley hoped that a meeting between the lovers designate might somehow or another soon take place; and meanwhile he informs his friend, "I read most of your letters to my sister. She frequently inquires after you,

and we talk of you often." To dissipate her melancholy
Shelley kept her "as much as possible employed in
poetry;" and her verses were duly despatched by her
brother to Hogg — verses as limp and incoherent as
Shelley's own of the same date (which is saying much),
and inspired by the like generous sentiments. Elizabeth's
admiration was no doubt claimed for the "extremely
beautiful" poetry written by Hogg — poetry which
"touches the heart," in which Shelley is metamorphosed
into an oak, and his faithless cousin into the ivy destroying
that hardy tree. Though the poetry sent by Hogg was
extremely beautiful, what Shelley especially desired was
that he should publish a tale. "I shall then give a copy
to Elizabeth, unless *you* forbid it." "I do not wish," he
writes, "to awaken her intellect too powerfully; this must
be my apology for not communicating all my speculations
to her." But to one of Hogg's talents and attainments
the guidance of her mind might be gratefully entrusted.

In truth, although Shelley at this period had departed
from the paths of traditional belief, he had not found for
himself an assured way. "Reason," to follow "reason"—
this was the watchword of his intellect; while at the same
time his imagination demanded the presence of a Spirit
of Life throughout the universe, and his heart craved
a communion with a Spirit of Love. "The word 'God,'"
he writes to Hogg (January 3, 1811), "a vague word, has
been, and will continue to be, the source of numberless
errors until it is erased from the nomenclature of
philosophy." But the soul of the universe, intelligent and
necessarily beneficent—"this it is impossible not to believe
in. I may not be able to adduce proofs; but I think that
the leaf of a tree, the meanest insect on which we trample,
are in themselves arguments more conclusive than any
which can be advanced, that some vast intellect animates

infinity. If we disbelieve *this*, the strongest argument in support of the existence of a future state instantly becomes annihilated. I confess that I think Pope's

'All are but parts of one stupendous whole'

something more than poetry." And he goes on to imagine as the future punishment of the vicious soul a thraldom in some prison-house as dull and cold as the body which it now inhabits ; and as the reward of the virtuous, love infinite in extent, eternal in duration, and for ever progressing in purity and passion.

"Do you find that the public are captivated by the title-page of 'St. Irvyne'?" asked Shelley of Stockdale, in a letter of January 11. It was the last friendly word uttered by Shelley to his publisher. Two or three days later he learnt that Stockdale had been making free with the character of his friend ; and at the same time Mr. Timothy Shelley arrived home from London, surprising his son with praises of Hogg. "Your principles," writes Shelley to his friend, "are *now* as divine as before they were diabolical. . . . [My father] has desired me to make his compliments to you, and to invite you to make Field Place your head-quarters for the Easter vacation."

On returning to Oxford, in January, 1811, Shelley resumed his close companionship with Hogg. They still kept in a great degree aloof from their fellow-students, and were preoccupied with their own ideas and their various literary projects. The piteous story of a certain Mary—a real person, known in her distress to Hogg—had been related by his friend to Shelley ; it had thrown him into a three weeks' "entrancement," and formed the occasion of a series of poems rapidly produced. The same story was treated in prose by Hogg, probably with considerable aid from Shelley, and the novel, to which they

E

gave the title "Leonora," was now in the hands of the Oxford publishers who had produced the "Posthumous Fragments of Margaret Nicholson." Shelley's printers were not slow to discover that "Leonora" was a novel with a tendency—the author "had interwoven his free notions throughout the work." Having earnestly, but without success, dissuaded him from publication, they declined to proceed with their task. The manuscript was thereupon placed in the hands of King, an Abingdon printer, who had nearly seen it through the press, when the abrupt termination of Shelley's Oxford career stopped its further progress.

This was but one of several literary enterprises, his own or those of others, in which Shelley was actively interested.

At this time his thoughts tended much in the direction of social and political questions. It will be remembered that Shelley had informed Stockdale, probably in December, 1810, or early in January, 1811, of his having completed "a metaphysical essay in support of atheism, which he intended to promulgate throughout the university." With his Oxford booksellers, Munday and Slatter, he was equally frank ; he would enter freely into conversation with them, and made no secret of his divergence from traditional beliefs. Partly as a convenient means of opening a correspondence with any distinguished contemporary on questions of religion, Shelley decided to print a "leaflet for letters," which should bear a startling title, "The Necessity of Atheism." "The mode of operation," writes Hogg, "was this: He enclosed a copy in a letter and sent it by the post, stating, with modesty and simplicity, that he had met accidentally with this little tract, which appeared, unhappily, to be quite unanswerable. Unless the fish was too sluggish to take the bait, an answer of refutation was forwarded to an appointed

address in London, and then in a vigorous reply he would
fall upon the unwary disputant." Hogg had called his
attention to the mystic virtue residing in the letters Q. E. D.
appended to the geometrician's proof of a proposition.
"If you ask a friend to dinner," exclaimed Shelley, smiling,
"and only put Q. E. D. at the end of the invitation, he
cannot refuse to come." If anything could decide a hesi-
tating champion of the faith to couch his lance, it would
be this calmly aggressive "quod erat demonstrandum" at
the end of the argument. The sting of the pamphlet was
to be in its tail.

After the Christmas vacation Shelley returned to
Oxford, envenomed against what he termed "intolerance"
and "bigotry," by the loss of his cousin's love, and of the
confidence of his own household. "I will crush Intolerance," he wrote to Hogg. "I will at least attempt it. To
fail even in so useful an attempt were glorious." Within
a fortnight after Shelley's return to college, in January,
1811, appeared in the *Oxford Herald* (February 9) an
advertisement of "The Necessity of Atheism," as speedily
to be published, and "to be had of the booksellers of
London and Oxford." The pamphlet, for which probably
Shelley had found it difficult to obtain a publisher, was
issued from a provincial press by the Phillipses, printers,
of Worthing, in Sussex. The author's name does not
appear upon the title-page, but the signature, *Thro'
deficiency of proof, An Atheist*, is appended to a brief
notice placed before the text, and attributed at the time
to Hogg, in which the author earnestly entreats those of
his readers who may discover any defect in his reasoning,
or may be in possession of proofs which his mind could
not obtain, to set forth the same "as briefly, as methodi-
cally, as plainly, as he has taken the liberty of doing."
Shelley's short and easy method with theists, starting from

a false premiss, "the senses are the source of all knowledge to the mind," briefly examines the evidence for the existence of a God derivable from the senses, from reason, and from testimony, and sets each aside as incompetent to establish a proof. It is free from passion, methodical in arrangement, clear and concise in style; but neither original in thought nor felicitous in expression. If Shelley's erroneous postulate—one common to many thinkers of the eighteenth century—that the senses are the sole source of human knowledge, be admitted as true, a logical mind will find it difficult to avoid arriving at Shelley's conclusion.

"The Necessity of Atheism" was advertised as for sale, and, we are assured, was actually on sale in Oxford, at least for twenty minutes. Without informing Messrs. Munday and Slatter, Shelley "strewed the shop-windows and counter" of their house with copies of the pamphlet, and instructed their shopman to sell them as fast as he could at the price of sixpence each. The Rev. John Walker, a Fellow of New College, having dropped in, was struck by the singular title, looked into the pamphlet, and immediately desired to see one or both of the principals. What was this poison they were vending? If they had any sense of propriety or any prudence, they would instantly destroy all the copies on which they could lay hands. The booksellers, surprised and alarmed, made haste to comply with the sensible advice, and at the fire of a back kitchen, while the Rev. John Walker, as chief inquisitor, looked on, an *auto-da-fe* of unshriven heretics took place. A request was at the same time sent by the booksellers to Shelley, to be allowed a few minutes' conversation with him at their house. He came without delay, and an eager dialogue ensued. On the one side, Mr. Munday, Mr. Slatter, and a certain Councillor Clifford (famous in the O. P. riots), who happened to be present, representing to Shelley the error of his ways, pleading, imploring, threatening ; on the other side, the unabashed and beardless boy, arguing in shrill tones, maintaining his right to think, and to declare his thoughts to others— to the last unconvinced and unpersuadable. He had done worse, he told them, than spread his net in the sight of callow Oxford birds—worse than shock the susceptibilities of a Fellow of New College ; he had sent a copy of his pamphlet to every bishop on the bench, to the Vice-Chancellor, to each of the heads of houses, and accompanying each copy was a pretty letter in his own handwriting, with the signature of "Jeremiah Stukeley," the latest avatar of Percy Bysshe Shelley, an incarnation assumed for this special occasion.

The date of these incidents is not precisely fixed. Shelley's authorship of "a prose pamphlet in praise of atheism" was noised abroad at least ten days before the college authorities were prepared to take public action. There were, doubtless, communications from dignitaries who had received copies of the pamphlet accompanied by the letter from Jeremiah Stukeley, the handwriting of which had been compared with that of Shelley, and found to agree with it, and big-wigs were laid together in consultation. Lady-Day came (March 25), a fine spring morning. Hogg called earlier than usual that morning at Shelley's rooms—they had agreed to lengthen their hours of reading. Shelley was absent. What followed shall be told in the words of Hogg. " Before I had collected our books he rushed in. He was terribly agitated. I anxiously inquired what had happened. 'I am expelled,' he said, as soon as he had recovered himself a little—'I am expelled ! I was sent for suddenly a few minutes ago. I went to our common room, where I found our Master and wo or three of the Fellows. The Master produced a copy of the little syllabus, and asked me if I were the author of it. He spoke in a rude, abrupt, and insolent tone. I begged to be informed for what purpose he put the question. No answer was given ; but the Master loudly and angrily repeated, 'Are you the author of this book ?' 'If I can judge from your manner,' I said, 'you are resolved to punish me if I should acknowledge that it is my work. If you can prove that it is, produce your evidence ; it is neither just nor lawful to interrogate me in such a case and for such a purpose. Such proceedings would become a court of inquisitors, but not free men in a free country.' 'Do you choose to deny that this is your composition ?' the Master reiterated in the same rude and angry voice. Shelley complained much of his violent and ungentle-manlike deportment, saying, 'I have experienced tyranny and injustice before, and I well know what vulgar violence is, but I never met with such unworthy treatment. I told him calmly, but firmly, that I was determined not to answer any questions respecting the publication. He immediately repeated his demand. I persisted in my refusal ; and he said furiously, " Then you are expelled, and I desire you will quit the college early to-morrow morning at the latest." One of the Fellows took up two papers and handed one of them to me ; here it is.' He produced a regular sentence of expulsion, drawn up in due form, under the seal of the college." "I have been with Shelley in many trying situations of his after-life," adds Hogg, "but I never saw him so deeply shocked and so cruelly agitated as on this occasion. . . . He sat on the sofa, repeating with convulsive vehemence the words, 'Expelled ! expelled !' his head shaking with emotion, and his whole frame quivering."

Hogg instantly addressed a note to the Master and

Fellows, who still sat deliberating. He regretted the treatment which Shelley had received at their hands, and expressed a hope that they would reconsider their sentence, since by a like procedure he or any other person might be subjected to the same imputation of guilt and the same penalty. A porter, after a brief delay, summoned him to the common room. The same questions were addressed to him which had been put to Shelley, and were met by the same refusal to answer them. He was ordered to retire, was hastily recalled, and, persisting in his refusal, received a formal sentence of expulsion, duly signed and sealed. While the conclave still sat and discussed the matter, hoping perhaps that, before the last act was performed and the deed irreversible, the rash youths might return and tender their submission, they perceived Shelley and Hogg walking up and down the quadrangle, and, so it seemed, flaunting their indifference to punishment in the face of the authorities. What more was needed? It was now towards the afternoon, and presently issued an official armed with the fatal edict—a large paper signed by the Master and Dean, bearing the college seal, and declaring that Thomas Jefferson Hogg and Percy Bysshe Shelley were publicly expelled from the college for contumacy in refusing to answer certain questions put to them, and for declining to disavow the obnoxious pamphlet. This was affixed to the hall door, and the deed was done.

At eight o'clock on the morning of March 26, 1811, the two friends mounted to the top of the coach which ran to London. Almost at the last moment information came that if it were inconvenient to them to quit the place so suddenly they might remain for a time, and that " if Shelley would ask permission of the Master to stay for a short period, it would probably be granted." Shelley was too indignant to petition for any favour; and so, while the coach-wheels whirled and the March breeze blew past them, they saw the towers and spires of Oxford sink in the distance, and felt that a new epoch of life had begun.

CHAPTER IV.

FIRST MARRIAGE.

It was in many ways unfortunate that Shelley should have been thrown abroad upon the world at the age of eighteen years and a half. He was an ardent student, and the seclusion of his college rooms was precious to him. The storing of his mind with wisdom and knowledge would have imposed checks upon his will of which he would have been scarcely conscious, and have given direction to his experimenting in real life which might have saved others and himself from much future suffering.

On reaching London and dismounting from the coach, Hogg and Shelley put up at a coffee-house near Piccadilly ; dined, and by-and-by sallied forth to take tea with Shelley's cousins, the Groves, in Lincoln's Inn Fields—" taciturn people," says Hogg, who held their peace while Bysshe told his story. There was also his cousin and former schoolfellow, Medwin, who must be informed of what had happened, the time chosen for this communication being the dark hour before the dawn of a March morning. " I remember," says Medwin, " as if it occurred yesterday, his knocking at my door in Garden Court, in the Temple, at four o'clock in the morning, the second day after his expulsion. I think I hear his cracked voice, with his well-known pipe—' Medwin, let me in ; I am expelled ! ' Here followed a sort of loud, half-hysteric laugh, and a repetition of the words, ' I am expelled,' with the addition of, ' for atheism.'" After breakfast there was a hunt for lodgings, and "never was a young beauty," declares Hogg, " so capricious, so hard to please," as the poet. At length they found themselves in lodgings, at Poland Street, Oxford Road,* with a quiet back sitting-room, its walls papered with trellised vine-leaves and clustering grapes. "We must stay here," whispered Shelley—"stay for ever." This "for ever" became afterwards a jest between the friends ; for all Shelley's movements, sudden and erratic as the starts of a meteor, were to conduct him to some resting-place where he should abide " for ever."

At the Poland Street lodgings the friends resumed, as far as might be, that life of study and companionship so rudely interrupted at University College. All would have been tranquillity were it not for the groundswell of disappointed love still aheave in Shelley's breast, and the inconveniences caused by a pair of afflicted and indignant fathers who threatened or implored. Mr. Timothy Shelley had instantly written to forbid Hogg's intended visit to Field Place, and despatched a troubled and not over-coherent missive, speedily followed by a second, to Mr. John Hogg, of Norton, Stockton-on-Tees, suggesting that he should come to London, where they might use their joint endeavours to separate the inseparable friends, each of the pair to be conveyed, if possible, to his own home —" your young man " to the far north, and " my young man " to his southern county. " These youngsters must be parted," wrote Mr. Shelley, " and the fathers must exert themselves. . . . They want to get into professions together. If possible they must be parted, for such monstrous opinions that occupy their thoughts are by no

* Now Oxford Street.

means in their favour." At the same time he addressed a letter from a Westminster hotel to his son in Poland Street, expressing sympathy with him in the misfortune resulting from his "criminal opinions and improper acts," and adding, what was due to his own character, his concern for his other children, and especially his feelings as a Christian, that if Bysshe looked for aid or protection from his father, he must instantly repair to Field Place, abstain for some considerable time from all communication with Hogg, and place himself "under the care and society of such gentleman as I shall appoint, and attend to his instructions and directions he shall give." Should these proposals be declined, Mr. Shelley felt bound to "with-draw himself" from his son, and leave that misguided youngster "to the punishment and misery that belongs to the wicked pursuit of an opinion so diabolical and wicked ' as that which he had "dared to declare." On the second Sunday (April 7) of the friends' sojourn in London, Mr. Shelley saw them at his hotel ; after some not unkindly bluster, with sudden and oddly veering flaws of temper, he proceeded, over a bottle of port, to demonstrate, by a short and easy method derived from "Paley's book," the existence of a Deity. "Paley's 'Natural Theology,'" he wrote to the elder Mr. Hogg, "I shall recommend my young man to read ; it is extremely applicable. I shall read it with him."

Their outlook on the future had now lost some of its first vagueness and confusion. Hogg's profession was already chosen. He designed himself for the bar, and was soon to enter a conveyancer's office in the city of York. Shelley loved the law and lawyers no better than he did a standing army, against which he would already declaim as he strolled or strode through St. James's Park ; and yet he was not without a portion of the debater's and orator's gift. Once about this time he went, with his cousin Charles Grove, to the British Forum, a speech-making club of fervid Radicals. " Bysshe made so good a speech," says his cousin,* " complimenting and differing from the previous orators, that when he left the room there was a rush to find out who he was, and to induce him to attend there again. He gave them a false name and address, not caring a farthing about the meeting or the subjects there discussed." Charles Grove had lately left the navy, and was now in town attending Abernethy's anatomical lectures. The profession of medicine, by its scientific bearings and its philanthropic aims, had a twofold attraction for Shelley. " The thought of anatomy," writes Charles Grove, ". . . became quite delightful to Bysshe." His mornings were usually occupied, with Hogg by his side, in writing. The writing ended, he would regularly set forth with his cousin for Abernethy's lecture at St. Bartholomew's Hospital, Hogg occasionally being one of the party. At this time Shelley seriously looked forward to becoming a physician.

He did not contemplate a flight from this old world, with its wrongs and sorrows ; but he could not view these calmly, and his intellect and imagination had been dazzled by the abstractions of French revolutionary thought, delivered with the air of a high philosopher by William Godwin. How was he to be just and sane at nineteen in such a time and with a philosophy which professed to reconstruct the world anew? " In theology," he wrote about this time to a friend—" inquiries into our intellect, its eternity or perishability—I advance with caution and circumspection. I pursue it in the privacy of retired thought or the interchange of friendship. But in politics —here I am enthusiastic. I have reasoned, and my reason

* John Grove : Hogg's " Life," vol. i. pp. 332, 333.

has brought me on this subject to the end of my inquiries. I am no aristocrat, nor '*crat*,' at all, but vehemently long for the time when men may dare to live in accordance with Nature and Reason—in consequence, with Virtue, to which I firmly believe that Religion and its establishments, Polity and its establishments, are the formidable though destructible barriers." It was a wild conclusion; but the times were wild, and Shelley was but an ardent boy.

Hogg's stay in London had been brief. Towards the middle of April he was off for a short holiday in Shropshire, previous to settling down to his legal training in York. It was arranged that Shelley should follow him to York before June, and that there they should recommence the pleasant student-life. A year later they were to return to London, and in London to remain together " for ever." " I quitted Shelley," says Hogg, " with mutual regret, leaving him alone in the trellised chamber . . . a bright-eyed, restless fox amidst sour grapes." In Hogg's absence the solitude deepened around Shelley ; thoughts of his lost love returned, and with these came at times a passion of despair, for which the effort to employ himself in writing poetry was not perhaps the fittest remedy. At the same time he was harassed by troublesome negotiations with his father. On leaving Oxford, Shelley had been obliged to borrow twenty pounds of his printers to take him on his way and meet his immediate needs. For a few weeks there was a community of goods between himself and Hogg, but on his friend's departure the pressure of want made itself painfully felt. Mr. Timothy Shelley would furnish no supplies to a son " undutiful and disrespectful to a degree." When Shelley, calling at Mr. John Grove's house, met his father in the passage and inquired after his health, the answer was a look " as black as a thunder-cloud," with a majestic " Your most humble

servant," in passing. "Father," he writes on April 29, " is
as fierce as a lion again. . . . He wants me to go to Oxford
to apologize to the Master, etc. ! No, of course." It
was Shelley's hope, though hardly a serious expectation,
that he might obtain from his father an allowance of two
hundred pounds a year, on condition of resigning all claim
to the entail, and consenting that the rest of the property
should be divided among his sisters. His son's request to
be disinherited only incensed Mr. Shelley, and, indeed, the
proposal was one which could not be carried into effect
until Bysshe had attained the age of twenty-one. Whether
his father would grant the allowance unconditionally,
remained in doubt : now, under the influence of John
Grove's soft persuasions, he seemed to yield ; and presently
he made haste to disavow anything of the nature of a
promise. "I am now at Grove's," wrote Shelley, on April
28. "I don't know where I am, where I will be. Future,
present, past, is all a mist ; it seems as if I had begun
existence anew under auspices so unfavourable. Yet no !
that is stupid."

Shelley's mother and sisters felt tenderly towards the
forlorn rebel, and were inclined to render him what service
they could, but dared not openly avow their feelings or
designs. A letter from Shelley to his father, which she
supposed might make the situation worse, was intercepted
by Mrs. Shelley. She urged her son to visit Field Place,
and enclosed a sum of money to meet his expenses ; but
he felt that to return home at this time would be equivalent
to accepting the intolerable conditions imposed by his
father, and therefore he declined his mother's gift, and sent
it back without delay. Aware of Bysshe's slender resources
or downright want, his sisters hoarded their pocket-money
for his sake, and from time to time sent him secretly, with
loving hearts, such small treasure as they could muster.

Elizabeth, the eldest, was now at home ; the younger girls were pupils in Mrs. Fenning's school, at Church House, Clapham—a mansion situated near the old town, on the north side of the common, directly facing Trinity Church. Shelley's sisters desired, as far as was in their power, to succour him in his distress; but who should they convey to him their little store of coin ? Two years older than the eldest of the schoolgirl sisters, and freer in her movements, as her parents lived in town, was Mrs. Fenning's pupil, Harriet Westbrook. Already she and Shelley were known to each other ; for early in January, when he went up to London from Field Place, in company with Charles Grove, he was the bearer of a letter of introduction and a present from his sister Mary to her friend Harriet. On January 11 he directed his publisher to send her a copy of " St. Irvyne ; " but, as if her address, 23, Chapel Street, Grosvenor Square, were not familiar to him, he gave, in his letter to Stockdale, a wrong number to the house. We meet the names of Shelley and his sisters, and Harriet Westbrook, in the list of subscribers to the little volume of " Poems " by Janetta Phillips—a list probably drawn up almost immediately after Shelley's departure from Oxford. Why should not Harriet Westbrook, his sisters' friend, his own acquaintance, be the bringer of good things from Church House, Clapham, to Poland Street ? On August 1, three days before Shelley's nineteenth birthday, Harriet would be sixteen years of age ; but she had a sister—Eliza—nearly twice as old, under whose conduct she moved, and who assumed in large measure the place of a mother towards her, although Mrs. Westbrook, seemingly an incapable person, was still living. Mr. John Westbrook, her father, known, from his swarthy looks and salient features, as " Jew Westbrook," had kept a " coffee-house "—in reality a tavern—in Mount Street. Having made sufficient means to enable him to retire from business, he was now enjoying the fruits of his toil, with one unmarried daughter at home, old enough to be skilled in the lore of life ; and one, still a schoolgirl, receiving a genteel education at Mrs. Fenning's seminary for young ladies.

The elder Miss Westbrook has obtained an evil memorial in the caricature drawn by Hogg's malicious pen. A figure meagre, prim, and constrained ; a face of dingy white, sadly scarred and seamed by disease, from which looked forth unintelligently a pair of dark lack-lustre eyes ; the whole over-topped by a mass of coarse hair, black and glossy— Miss Westbrook's peculiar pride ;—such are the features on which the limner dwells with rude insistence. " I remember her well," writes her nephew, a more trustworthy witness than Hogg, recalling her image in days long after —" I remember her well as a handsome, grand old lady, with dark front of hair, piercing dark eyes, and with a kind manner to children, but of whom we were somewhat afraid."*
Whether Eliza were a comely or uncomely maiden of thirty, it is certain that Harriet was all youthful freshness, fairness, bloom ; short of stature ; slightly and delicately formed ; light of foot and graceful in her movements ; with features regular and well proportioned ; her complexion bright and clear—" the tint of the blush rose," as Peacock puts it, " shining through the lily ; " her abundant hair light-brown and beautiful, says Miss Hellen Shelley, as " a poet's dream." She dressed, we are told by Peacock, with

* Rev. W. Esdaile. Her kindness to Harriet Shelley's daughter, Ianthe, is gratefully remembered by Mrs. Esdaile's children. Eliza Westbrook inherited her father's property, and married a gentleman whose name was originally Farthing (Somerset family of yeomen). He was a clerk in a London bank ; an old lady named Beauchamp fell in love with him, and left him all her property, on condition that he should change his name to Beauchamp. Thus Eliza Westbrook became Mrs. Beauchamp. Mr. Farthing Beauchamp's name appears with Mr. and Miss Westbrook's in the Chancery case of 1817-18.

taste and simplicity. "The tone of her voice was pleasant; her speech the essence of frankness and cordiality; . . . . her laugh spontaneous, hearty, and joyous."

The copy of "St. Irvyne" forwarded to Harriet in January by Shelley's direction probably led to some correspondence between its author and his new acquaintance. Her schoolfellows, we may suppose, were not slow to discover this, and the strange opinions of her young correspondent becoming known, it is easy to imagine how Harriet had to bear the playful sallies of the witty, and the averted looks, the warnings or reproaches, of the wise. Did she not receive letters from an atheist? "Atheist"—Harriet did not know precisely what was the meaning of the word, but felt certain that it must mean something dreadful. When they explained to her all its tremendous significance, she was appalled, and wondered that the earth did not gape to swallow him, or the lightning descend from heaven to strike him dead. In after days, when she had been Shelley's wife for some few months, and had caught, as by a feeble reflex, his manner of speech, Harriet gave in a letter to a female friend—Miss Hitchener—a sketch of her early life, her girlish feelings, and her first acquaintance with Shelley, in which there is much naïve self-betrayal which gives it a touching interest.

"I will tell you my faults, knowing what I have to expect from your friendship. Remember my youth; and, if any excuse can be made, let that suffice. In London, you know, there are military, as well as everywhere else. When quite a child I admired these red-coats. This grew up with me; and I thought the military the best as well as most fascinating men in the world—though at the same time I used to declare never to marry one. This was not so much on account of their vices as from the idea of their being killed. I thought, if I married any one, it should be a clergyman. Strange idea this, was it not? But being brought up in the Christian religion, 'twas this first gave rise to it. You may conceive with what horror I first heard that Percy was an atheist; at least so it was given out at Clapham. At first I did not comprehend the meaning of the word; therefore when it was explained I was truly petrified. I wondered how he could live a moment professing such principles, and solemnly declared that he should never change mine. I little thought of the rectitude of these principles, and when I wrote to him I used to try to shake them—making sure he was in the wrong, and that myself was right. Yet I would listen to none of *his* arguments, so afraid I was that he should shake my belief. At the same time I believed in eternal punishment, and was dreadfully afraid of his supreme Majesty, the Devil. I thought I should see him if I listened to *his* arguments. I often dreamed of him, and felt such terror when I heard his name mentioned. This was the effects of a bad education and living with Methodists. Now, however this is entirely done away with, and my soul is no longer shackled with such idle fears."

Alone in London, an outcast from his Oxford College, an exile from his father's house, Shelley was grateful to any one who might have courage to associate with him and take his hand in kindness. The elder Miss Westbrook, on her own part and as guide and guardian of her younger sister, showed the friendliest solicitude on behalf of the interesting misbeliever; wrote to him; called on him with Harriet; invited him to dinner when her father was from home; conducted him to church on Sunday; studied under his direction the graceless articles of Voltaire's "Dictionnaire Philosophique." During the Easter holidays, when Harriet was at home, Miss Westbrook made friendly incursions on Shelley's solitude; and when the vacation came to an end, and Mrs. Fenning's pupils were required to resume business, Miss Westbrook was so "condescending" as to invite the friendless youth to accompany her to Clapham in order to make inquiries after Harriet, who had not been looking well, and to take her for an airing on the common. "My little friend Harriet Westbrook," wrote Shelley to Hogg (April 24, 1811), "is gone to her prison-house. She is quite well in health; at least so she says, though she looks very much otherwise. I saw her yesterday with her sister, and walked about Clapham Common with them for two hours. The youngest is a most amiable girl; the eldest is really conceited, but very condescending."

A day or two later and Harriet was really ill, and once again at home. The elder sister, indefatigable and ever thoughtful, sent late in the evening for Shelley to minister comfort to the invalid; was herself more than commonly amiable in manner; began by discoursing on love; then led him to her sister, and finding that her own company was too much for the sufferer, withdrew. Mr. Westbrook was occupied with friends below, but saw Shelley, and was strangely civil. "[April 28, 1811.] My poor little friend has been ill; her sister sent for me the other night. I found her on a couch, pale; her father is civil to me, very strangely; the sister is too civil by half. She began talking about *l'Amour*. I philosophized, and the youngest said she had such a headache that she could not bear conversation. Her sister then went away, and I stayed till half-past twelve. Her father had a large party below he invited me; I refused." Shelley's visit certainly did not act injuriously on Harriet's nerves. "They [the sisters]," he continues, "are both very clever, and the youngest (my friend) is amiable. Yesterday she was better; to-day her father compelled her to return to Clapham whither I have conducted her, and I am now returned." Again a day or two and Shelley was sent for to accompany Miss Westbrook to Clapham; on the way she was more than ever clever and agreeable; but the pleasure of the visit was marred by learning how cruel the persecution of Harriet by her schoolfellows had grown—persecution endured for the sake of Shelley and of truth, and which she met with a noble disdain. All Shelley's envenomed hatred against "the wretch Intolerance" returned; here once more "the fiend" was poisoning the innocent joys of life. "She is called an *abandoned* wretch, and universally hated, which she remunerates with the calmest contempt. My third sister, Hellen, is the only exception. She, in spite of the *infamy*, will speak to Miss Westbrook, because she cannot see how she has done wrong.'

It was hard to bear cold looks and unfriendly words from former companions who had held her dear; for Harriet's gentle disposition had caused her to be generally beloved. But there was something yet more painful to endure. Some time previously—perhaps at the beginning of the year—Mrs. Fenning, now grown elderly, had transferred the care of the school to the younger hands of Miss Hawkes. One morning as she entered the schoolroom Miss Hawkes perceived Harriet Westbrook suddenly crumpling a letter in her hands as if to conceal it from view. The keen-eyed head-mistress instantly pounced upon the prize; the letter was signed by the Miss Shelleys' brother, and may possibly have been one of those designed to assist in adding Harriet "to the list of the good, the disinterested, the free." Miss Hawkes took the matter seriously; sent, it is said, for Mr. Westbrook and Mr. Timothy Shelley, announced the discovery, and even went so far (but this may be the exaggeration of rumour) as to dismiss Harriet from the school.

But it was not Eliza, or Harriet Westbrook, or little
Hellen, who occupied the first place in Shelley's thoughts;
that place was reserved for Elizabeth, his eldest sister,
already designated by him as bride-elect of Hogg. She
was now at Field Place, and to visit his home, save under
conditions not to be accepted, was forbidden to her brother.
It was grievous to reflect that while he was kept at a
distance, father, mother, friends, were near at hand under-
mining his influence, darkening her intellect, fettering her
free spirit, and rendering her unworthy of the devotion of
Hogg. Her letters showed, indeed, that already she was
tainted with intolerance. She talked of "duty to her
father—duty of all kinds,"—phrases which really signified
servility to the opinion of the world. Suddenly the letters
ceased. "She does not any longer permit a *philosopher*
to correspond with her," said Shelley, not aware at the
time that she had been stricken with a scarlet fever.

The hearty good will and friendly offices of one of his
kinsfolk opened a way for Shelley's return to Field Place.
Captain Pilfold, his maternal uncle, had fought with
Nelson, and commanded His Majesty's ship *Ajax* at
Trafalgar. He was now settled with his wife and children
at Cuckfield, a market town of Sussex some ten miles
distant from Shelley's birthplace. The good-humoured
captain had a liking for his nephew, recognized his amiable
qualities, was not greatly shocked by his theological heresies,
or alarmed by his rash adventurous spirit, and sincerely
desired to reconcile the father and the son. Shelley
probably made his advances on Field Place from the
vantage-ground of Cuckfield, and by the middle of May,
1811, aided by the intervention of the Duke of Norfolk, he
had come to terms with his father. Two hundred pounds
a year were henceforth to be his, unencumbered by conditions; he might choose his own place of abode, his own

friends. Two hundred pounds a year; it seemed to Shelley an ample allowance—" more than I can want," he wrote to Hogg; " besides, what is money to me ? What does it matter if I cannot even purchase sufficient *genteel clothes ?* I still have a shabby great-coat, and those whose good opinion constitutes my happiness would not regard me the better or the worse for this or any other conse- quence of poverty. Fifty pounds per annum would be quite enough." So excellent an uncle surely deserved all gratitude; and what better could Bysshe do for him than endeavour to enroll this worthy sea captain among the company of philosophers, and add him to the list of the disinterested and the free ? "[Sunday, May 19.] I am now with my uncle. He is a very hearty fellow, and has behaved very nobly to me, in return for which I have illuminated him. A physician named Dr. J—— dined with us last night, who is a red-hot saint ; the captain attacked him warm from ' The Necessity,' and the doctor went away very much shocked."

Once more at home, Shelley looked around, and thought it strange that he should have been exiled in the name of religion from such a home. "If a man is a good man, philosopher or Christian," said his mother, "he will do very well in whatever future state awaits him;" and the liberality of this expression of opinion pleased her son. His father, who, to gain Captain Pilfold's confidence in reference to Bysshe, had in private professed himself "a sceptic," was in reality, Shelley thought, neither Christian nor freethinker. "He is nothing, no *ist*, professes no *ism* but superbism and irrationalism." "It is most true," he wrote to Hogg, "that the mass of mankind are Christians only in name ; their religion has no reality. . . . Certain members of my family are no more Christians than Epicurus himself was ; but they regard as a sacred criterion the opinion of the world ; the discanonization of this saint of theirs is impossible until something more worthy of devotion is pointed out ; but where eyes are shut, nothing can be seen."

To a certain extent Shelley's intercourse with his sister Elizabeth was checked or disturbed by their father ; but it was evident that her feeling towards him was changed. Her illness had passed away ; her health was now perfect, and she had a girlish joy in the amusements and social gatherings of the summer days. To Bysshe—an earnest young evangelist—her spirits seemed but too frivolously gay ; casual pleasures, petty gratifications of her pride, came from day to day to fill her heart. It used not to be the character of my sister, said Shelley—" serious, contemplative, affectionate, enthusiastically alive to the wildest schemes ; despising the world. Now apathetic to all things except the trivial amusements and despicable intercourse of restrained conversation ; bowing before that hellish idol, the *world ;* appealing to its unjust decisions, in cases which demand a trial at the higher tribunal of conscience. Yet I do not despair ; what she *once was* she has a power to be again ; but will that power ever be exerted ? " Shelley feared that she had grown unworthy of Hogg ; feared that it was an idea of his own mind which he had loved and had named " Elizabeth." When he spoke seriously, she affected to pity the wildness of his brain, or broke away with a scornful exclamation—" You and your mad friend ! " When he attempted a liveliness like hers, to see if congeniality even in folly would effect anything, she became grave and fell into a silence. Matrimony—that most horrible of the means by which the world binds the noble to itself—was " the subject of her constant and *pointed* panegyric." Hogg, musing at a distance on the abstract idea of perfection, had pronounced it blasphemy to doubt Elizabeth's divine excellence. Shelley wished to believe that Hogg was right. Why should not the question be put to the test, and finally settled by Hogg's coming to Field Place, secretly and by night? From an honourable imprisonment in Shelley's study he could look out upon the lawn, and behold Elizabeth as King James of Scotland viewed his lady Joanna from the Windsor Tower. "[June 23, 1811.] Come, then, my dear friend. . . . You must content yourself to sleep upon a mattress; and you will be like a State prisoner. You must only walk with me at midnight for fear of discovery. My window commands a view of the lawn, where you will frequently see an object that will repay your journey—the object of my fond affections."

Hogg did not travel from York to Horsham to enjoy imprisonment with an occasional view of Miss Shelley on the lawn; and his friend was not slow to perceive the unreasonable nature of his proposal. It had, indeed, been partly suggested to him by his longing for some congenial companionship. Elizabeth was alienated from him; his father either absent in London, or if at home a disturbing element. His nights were sleepless, haunted by thoughts of his own disprized love—the time for Miss Grove's marriage was now approaching—and of the failure of his plans respecting Elizabeth and Hogg. A troubled gloom hung over his spirits. Now and again he would utter his feelings in verse—some complaint against lovers' perfidy, or musings in presence of the evening star. Or he would write a page of a kind of composite fiction, the work of himself and his friend Hogg, in which they intended to embody in the form of a series of letters much of their personal experience; or he relieved his heart in arguments or passionate meditations addressed to Hogg and destroyed as soon as written; or the letter would be one to Miss

Westbrook or her sister ; for before he had come to the country Shelley had spent much of his time in the company of the elder lady, finding her "amiable," though "not perhaps in a high degree," and had "arranged a correspondence" with each of the sisters. Letters from Miss Westbrook followed him to Cuckfield and Field Place, and still he found that she improved upon acquaintance ; "or is it," he questions doubtfully, "only when contrasted with surrounding indifference and degradation ? " In Harriet there was "something more noble, yet not so cultivated as the elder—a larger diamond, yet not so highly polished Her indifference to, her contempt of surrounding prejudice are certainly fine. But perhaps the other wants oppor tunity." At least it beguiled the time to write letters ana to receive letters in return, and to occupy the position of philosophic friend to gentle correspondents is an honour and a pleasure at nineteen.

But though Miss Westbrook, to please a friend, read Voltaire, she was to a certain extent an *esprit borné;* Harriet was but an interesting schoolgirl. Far different communion of spirit would Shelley enjoy, were he to meet a woman of ardent and aspiring feelings, high intellectual powers, and resolute will, who had made her way almost unaided toward the uplands and wide air of liberty and truth. What matter if in the eyes of worldlings her origin were humble ; what matter if she toiled with head or hand to win an honourable subsistence ? Such accidents as these would only tend to raise her in the scale of being, and enhance the dignity of her character. Such a woman Shelley now had found, or—for the alternative expresses a difference—supposed that he had found. While staying at Cuckfield with his uncle Pilfold, he had been introduced to Miss Hitchener, mistress of a school in Hurstpierpoint, a small neighbouring town. A daughter of Captain Pilfold's was among her pupils, and she had certainly gained the esteem of her pupil's parents. It was stated in a letter written by the Earl of Chichester in the following year that Miss Hitchener's father had been originally a smuggler, that his true name was Yorke, and that he had changed his name previous to entering into business as keeper of a public-house. Yorke had run his kegs of spirits ashore duty-free; Mr. Hitchener it was who legally vended liquor to thirsty dwellers near the Downs. Miss Hitchener owed little to father or mother; at nine years old she had been sent to school, and in the schoolmistress, Miss Adams, who, "having too much virtue for her age," was "ever an object of persecution," had found "the mother of her soul." Miss Adams, now old, was still toiling for her bread; and her grateful pupil entered on her profession with the hope of being able at some time to offer this aged friend a place of shelter and repose.

✓ Elizabeth Hitchener was now in her twenty-ninth year, but looked younger; she was exceedingly spare, and somewhat tall in figure; with well-formed Roman features; her complexion dark as that of a foreigner of the south; her face lit by eloquent black eyes; her black hair when uncoiled falling heavily and far. She was of quick, excitable spirits, and eager in uttering her thoughts; prone to melancholy, yet full of animation when her interest was aroused. Her kinsfolk and acquaintance termed her romantic, visionary, eccentric, conceited; and she, in turn, lamented that there was not one from whom she could "seek improvement," not one who "understood" her. Perhaps her opinions alienated them, for she was known to be a liberal *doctrinaire* in politics and religion. Yet she was not aggressive; would have named herself a Christian, if required to declare her faith; and would fain "tread lightly and cautiously," as she declares, "on what others consider sacred." Once, and probably only once, Shelley had met her, and their talk was doubtless about poetry, education of the young, virtue, truth, the existence of a God. On reaching home he despatched to Hurstpierpoint, under his father's frank, a letter—the first of many—proposing a "polemical correspondence," for as yet she had gone but half-way towards complete illumination, and there had halted. "If secure of your own orthodoxy," he writes, "you would attempt my proselytism; believe me, I should be most happy to subject myself to the danger."

Miss Hitchener in her isolation, with a pestering throng of thoughts and feelings which she dared not express to those who had already classed her and explained her by the epithets "romantic" and "visionary," found a happiness which she could not forego in the prospect of liberating her spirit in numerous sheets of letter-paper to one who, like herself, was an enthusiast, like herself a votary of Reason and of Truth.

It was Shelley's intention to quit Field Place early in July and join his friend Hogg in York. He ordered his lodgings, and looked forward with pleasure to the luxury of "unrestrained converse." Mr. Westbrook had, indeed, invited his daughters' friend and correspondent to accompany him and the Miss Westbrooks to Wales; they were about to spend part of the summer at Aberystwith. A previous invitation to Wales had come from Shelley's cousin, Mr. Thomas Grove, who had purchased an estate—ten thousand acres of wild hill and valley—five miles from Rhayader, in Radnorshire, and was now converting the waste into a paradise. Shelley had accepted his cousin's invitation, and intended, on leaving Mr. Grove's house, to meet the Westbrooks at Aberystwith. Yet his thoughts tended longingly towards Hogg; and when there seemed to be a chance that Hogg might become a secret visitor at Field Place, Shelley resolved that he would accompany his friend on his return journey to the north. The clandestine visit never took place. Now, however, the desire for renewed companionship with Hogg had grown paramount, and Shelley decided to reach Wales, after a week in London with "old Westbrook," by a circuitous route, which should include York upon the way. But a decree stood written in the books of fate that whenever Shelley announced his intention of steering to any one point of the compass he should find himself moving towards another. It had been arranged that he was to possess two hundred pounds a year, but his father still held the purse-strings ; and Mr. Timothy Shelley, whose opinion that the undutiful youngsters must be separated had not changed, informed his son that he might, if he pleased, go to York, but, should he do so, all expectation of money must cease. Shelley saw the imprudence of open warfare. It seemed best to accept his cousin's invitation to Cwm Elan. He would make but a brief halt in London ; transact some business there ; call on Miss Hitchener, who expected to be in town early in July ; then travel to Wales on foot, "for the purpose of better remarking the manners and dispositions of the peasantry ;" and, after his visit to Mr. Grove, strike northwards to his friend, dropping the name of Shelley and becoming for the nonce " Mr. Peyton," in whose movements his father, unless a rare diviner, could feel no special interest.

Cwm Elan, the glen of the Elan, lies to the south-west of Rhayader, among the most romantic mountains of Radnorshire. The Elan, a tributary of the Wye, descends through a narrow glen between mountains of slate and limestone, on whose sides mingle alder, and birch, and oak, and mountain-ash. Having crossed a wooden bridge some way up the glen, the traveller in Shelley's time would find

himself in Mr. Grove's lawn, which extended from the
house and followed the course of the river. The special
charm of the landscape lay in its union of wild loveliness
with the grace and ornament of human culture.

Shelley arrived at Cwm Elan in no condition to enjoy
its beauty. His days in London had been occupied with
" pressing and urgent business," the nature of which we
are left to conjecture. The July sun loaded the air with
fire ; sleepless nights made no protecting barrier between
day and day. The shock of his expulsion from University
College, the consequent struggle with his father, the money
embarrassments of the spring, the pains of disappointed
love, the failure—causing disappointment hardly less keen
—of his plans for Elizabeth's union with Hogg,—each and
all of these had told upon an organization high-strung,
and therefore delicate; and the journey to Wales, though
probably not on foot as at first intended, had sufficed to
exhaust energies already overtasked. A short but violent
nervous illness was the result. It was an additional cause
of vexation to learn on his recovery that his father, by
some mysterious means, had discovered all about the
proposed visit of Hogg to Field Place, and Shelley's intended journey with him to York. Mr. Shelley was highly
incensed at his son's undutifulness, presumption, and
manœuvring. Nor did the company of Mr. and Mrs.
Grove serve to divert Shelley's mind from its own broodings.
" I am now with people," he wrote, " who, strange to say,
never *think*. I have, however, much more of my own
society than of theirs." And to Hogg, " I am all solitude,
as I cannot call the society here an alternative of it. I
must stay here, however, to recruit my finances, compelled now to acknowledge poverty an evil." " I am
what the sailors call banyaning. I do not see a soul ;
all is gloomy and desolate. I amuse myself, however,

with reading Darwin, climbing rocks, and exploring this scenery."

Now for the first time Shelley was among mountain solitudes, and heard the voices of mountain torrents; but the power of hills was not upon him. The poet in Shelley at this time was trammelled and taken in the toils by the psychologist and metaphysician; and if he were to break loose and regain his freedom, it must be by vigorous action rather than by words or thoughts.

"I am more astonished at the grandeur of the scenery," Shelley wrote to Hogg towards the end of July, "than I expected. I do not *now* much regard it; I have other things to think of." Other and unexpected things indeed! Mr. Westbrook and his daughters had gone to their house at Aberystwith, some thirty miles from Rhayader. Eliza and Harriet did not quite forget that their interesting friend was among the mountains, and with no congenial companion at hand. Letters came more frequently than before from Harriet and Eliza. Hogg, who as early as May had arrived at an "odd conclusion" about Eliza Westbrook, which Shelley declined to accept, now gave broader licence to his mocking pen. "Your jokes on Harriet Westbrook," wrote Shelley, "amuse me: it is a common error for people to fancy others in their own situation, but, if I know anything about love, I am *not* in love. I have heard from the Westbrooks, both of whom I highly esteem." The esteem, however, soon was mingled with alarm and intense anxiety. His friends had returned from Aberystwith to London, and urgent letters came in quick succession from Harriet. She was wretched; persecuted in her own home; about to be compelled to return to school—a school where, as Shelley knew, the black badge was hung around the throat for a small misdemeanour, and where Harriet had been shunned by her schoolfellows

and styled "an abandoned wretch." She was happy only
when she could give her heart in love; it was misery to
live with no one near on whom her love could be bestowed.
She was of no use to herself or to others; would it be
wrong to make an end of her useless life? should she resist
her father and refuse to return to school? She would be
guided by Shelley's advice. Shelley was a philosopher,
but a philosopher of nineteen. A beautiful girl of sixteen,
the victim of oppression, chose him for her counsellor, and
placed her fate in his hands. As a philosopher he dis-
dained knight-errantry; but reason and gratitude required
that he should respond to her appeal. He wrote instantly
advising resistance, and at the same time addressed a letter
to Mr. Westbrook, commending gentler measures towards
his daughter. Mr. Westbrook, inexorable, refused to be
mollified. A despairing letter arrived from Harriet, in
which she threw herself upon Shelley's protection. She
would fly with him if he would but consent. Shelley
speedily took coach for London, but had time to anticipate
his arrival by a letter to his cousin Charles Grove, saying
that his decision was taken; that as for himself his own
happiness had been altogether blighted when he lost the
hope of his cousin's love, Charles's sister Harriet; that now
the only thing worth living for was self-sacrifice, and that
he therefore obeyed the summons of Harriet Westbrook,
which called him from his solitude in Wales. A postscript
ended the letter, adapted from the words of Macbeth when
the bell is struck which bids him to Duncan's murder—

> "Hear it not, Percy; for it is a knell
> That summons thee to heaven or to hell."

On arriving at London, Shelley lost no time in calling
on Harriet; he was shocked by her altered looks, and
ascribed them to the sufferings she had undergone from

domestic persecution. Harriet, shrinking from the avowal, yet could not choose but undeceive him; her pale face and woebegone aspect meant that he had grown too dear for her, and that she feared he never could return her love. Shelley, among many perplexing things, saw one thing clear—it was in his power to chase away grief from one who loved him, and bring joy in its place. He did not hesitate to place his hand in hers, or falter in the promise to make her his own.

When the first glow of chivalric enthusiasm faded, and Shelley came out into the common light of day, his pulse sank and the world looked grey. He intended soon to visit his uncle at Cuckfield, but waited for some days longer in London, and called now and again on Harriet. All her brightness had returned, while he had a certain depression to conceal from her. It was probably on one of these days that he replied to a letter from Hogg, in which it seems that his friend had urged the duty of a legal marriage, for sake of her who would be the chief sufferer if law and custom were disregarded. "My arguments," Shelley wrote, "have been *yours*. They have been urged by the force of the gratitude which this occasion excited. But I yet remain in Lon'on; I remain embarrassed and melancholy. I am now dining at Grove's. Your letter has just been brought in; I cannot forbear just writing this. *Your* noble and exalted friendship, the prosecution of your happiness, can alone engross my impassioned interest. This, I fear"—Shelley speaks of his devoting himself to Harriet Westbrook—"more resembles exerted action than inspired passion." And a little later, "The late perplexing occurrence which called me to town occupies my time, engrosses my thoughts. I shall tell you more of it when we meet, which I hope will be soon. It does not, however, so wholly occupy my thoughts but that you and your interests still are predominant." Once again Shelley's hopes for a union between his sister and his friend had revived ; but he was unwilling to raise unfounded expectations, remembering as he did the pain which he himself had felt on the loss of his cousin's love. "I know," he wrote, "how deep is the gulf of despair, and I will not, therefore, increase any one's height" (August 15).

Under the influence of arguments advanced by Hogg, Shelley now brought himself to contemplate without repulsion the idea of a marriage duly celebrated with legal ceremony. "Reputation and its consequent advantages," he said, "are rights"—rights not to be forfeited without sufficient cause. "How useless to attempt by singular examples"—so Shelley reasoned—"to renovate the face of society, until reasoning has made so comprehensive a change as to emancipate the experimentalist from the resulting evils, and the prejudice with which his opinion (which ought to have weight for the sake of virtue) would be heard by the immense majority!" Moreover, the social loss and suffering fell in a wholly disproportionate degree upon the woman. For his own part, he declared, he was indifferent to reputation ; but a woman's happiness is fragile, all too easily shattered, and therefore to be guarded against shock or stroke. Thus Shelley debated the question during the days of mid August. But on leaving London about this date for a visit to his uncle Pilfold, he asserted that he had little expectation of being speedily required to put his new opinions into practice. While at Cuckfield he saw Miss Hitchener for the second time—the press of business in July had prevented him from calling upon her when in town—and informed her that his present purpose was to devote himself to the study of medicine, and qualify himself for entering on the duties of a physician. He had

G

assured Harriet, before bidding her farewell, that she had
but to summon him and he would return to London.   Not
a week can have passed at Cuckfield and Field Place
before the summons came.   Her tormentors were still
resolved to force her back to school; she was helpless
and miserable without Percy.   In fulfilment of his promise
Shelley hastened to London; saw Harriet, and proposed
immediate marriage as the means of delivering her from
this relentless persecution.   At John Grove's house in
Lincoln's Inn Fields he arranged his plans, without the
knowledge of his cousin John, but with his cousin Charles
as aider and abettor.   From Lincoln's Inn Fields one
evening—it may have been Saturday, August 24—he
wended his way to a small coffee-house in Mount Street,
not far distant from Mr. Westbrook's house in Chapel
Street, Grosvenor Square; thence he despatched a letter
to Harriet, naming the hour at which he would be ready
with a hackney-coach at the coffee-house door to receive
her.   One short night, and it was the dawn of a memorable August day.   Mr. Grove's servant called a coach, into
which entered the cousins Bysshe and Charles; at the
Mount Street coffee-house, some time before the hour
appointed for Harriet's arrival, the coach drew up.   A
breakfast was ordered and was ended, and Harriet did
not yet appear.   While the bridegroom-designate waited
at the door he beguiled the time by flinging the shells of
the oysters on which they had breakfasted across the
street, with the words, "Grove, this is a *Shelley* business!"
Presently Harriet was seen tripping round the corner from
Chapel Street, and the coach-wheels rattled towards the
city inn from which the northern mails departed.   There
a livelong day of waiting was spent by the three—Harriet,
Bysshe, and Charles—for the Edinburgh mail did not
start until seven or eight in the evening.   At last arrived

the hour of departure, good-byes were said, and the fugitives were on the road for York.

A night and a day's rattling along the northern road brought the coach, in which were seated Shelley and Harriet Westbrook, to York; and while towards midnight they rested to change horses, Shelley found time to scribble a note to Hogg, which should be taken to his friend's lodging next morning. " I passed to-night with the mail," he wrote; " Harriet is with me. We are in a slight pecuniary distress. We shall have seventy-five pounds on Sunday, until when can you send ten pounds?" To take him on his way Shelley had borrowed a small sum from the elder Mr. Medwin, and he counted on soon receiving his quarterly allowance of fifty pounds, which probably became due on Sunday, September 1. An additional twenty-five pounds was expected by the wanderers, from what source we know not. Meanwhile there were the expenses of almost a week in Edinburgh to be provided for, and Shelley relied for succour from Hogg's good fellowship. And so in darkness the fugitives bade farewell to the sleeping city, and bowled northwards still, until in the grey of a third morning the coach drew up before the post-office in Edinburgh. A resting-place was found by the travellers, and then with as little delay as the circumstances permitted, in regular form, and with such ceremony as the Scottish law required, they joined hands as husband and wife. In the books of the Register House, Edinburgh, the entry may be seen—" August 28, 1811. Percy Bysshe Shelley, farmer, Sussex, and Miss Harriet Westbrook, St. Andrew Church Parish, daughter of Mr. John Westbrook, London." The united ages of bride and bridegroom made thirty-five.

CHAPTER V.

WANDERINGS.

WHEN Shelley, in the coach with Harriet, reached Edinburgh, his scanty resources were exhausted. In a handsome house in the new-built George Street, on the side
next to Princes Street, he found excellent ground-
floor rooms, and was fortunate in alighting on a good-
humoured landlord, to whom he explained his position
—his present need, his expectation of speedy relief,
and the object of his journey to Scotland. Would he
take them in, Shelley asked, advance them money to get
married, and supply their wants until a remittance came?
The landlord cheerily assented on one condition — that
Shelley should treat himself and his friends to a supper
in honour of the wedding. In the mail-coach Shelley had
happened to meet a young Scotch advocate, to whom he
confided the motive of his flight, and from whom he ascertained the proper steps to take with a view to a speedy
celebration of marriage. All things, therefore, were easily
arranged and satisfactorily accomplished; and while the
host, with his North British companions, made merry with
friendly cracks and tales and bumpers of Scotch drink,
Shelley and his bride were content to be alone.
   Shelley's bride was young, beautiful, of a sweet and

pliable disposition; strength of intellect and strength of character were lacking to her. She had received the education of a schoolgirl of sixteen, but as regards true culture in any direction was still a child. She was docile, and submitted her mind to such influences as were brought to play upon it, so that she soon caught up the words and phrases which Shelley used, and could even array her own thoughts in the shadows or simulacra of his. He spoke of reason, and truth, and freedom, and equality, and perfectibility; and she, with some uncertainty in dealing with these airy sounds, could also utter the terms of enchantment, and produce the cabala of revolution on her lips or with her pen. She loved to read, and especially to read aloud in her sweet, clear, equable voice. She had heard much about virtue from Bysshe, and liked best those books which frequently discoursed of virtue. She sang pleasingly; and could scribble such *graffiti* as may be found in schoolgirls' copy-books, which, if sufficiently suggestive of humanity, they dignify with the name of caricatures. She was bright of temper, yet had known occasional moods of gloom and deep depression. Though gentle and amiable, she might be rash or she might be obstinate. From the first Shelley was, doubtless, not insensible to her sweetness and brightness of nature; now he saw, or thought he saw, that she could be moulded into the form of gracious womanhood.

How to live upon love was a problem which Shelley found himself immediately required to solve. His quarterly allowance of fifty pounds, counted on as due by September 1, never came. Mr. Timothy Shelley had heard of Bysshe's flight, and was in towering indignation. Some of his over-wrought feelings found relief in accusations against Mr. Medwin, who had lent the fugitive twenty-five pounds, but, in lending it, was wholly unaware of the purpose to

which the money should be applied; some escaped in
troubled communications with the elder Mr. Hogg—for
it was conjectured that Bysshe, having " set off for Scotland with a young female," might " make York on the
way," and God only knew what might happen if " my
young man " and "your young man " were to meet. But
an afflicted father could at least cut off all supplies, and
try whether starvation would bring the runaway to reason.
It was the first time that Shelley, with another now depend-
ing upon him, felt the humiliations of penury. He wrote
to his father with more vehemence of tone than he had
hitherto allowed himself. He was here four hundred miles
from any friend, exposed to all the insults of fortune, his
allowance cut off, although it had been promised without
proviso or limitation, and on the faith of that promise he
had incurred obligations. Had it not been for jovial Uncle
Pilfold, the days in Edinburgh would have been days of
heart-corroding anxiety. Cheerful, generous letters and
a bank-post bill came from the captain. " My uncle,"
Shelley afterwards wrote from York, " is a most generous
fellow. Had he not assisted us we should still have been
chained to the filth and *commerce* of Edinburgh. Vile as
aristocracy is, commerce — purse-proud ignorance and
illiterateness—is more contemptible." At a later date he
learnt to think more justly of the grey metropolis, and was
drawn back to Edinburgh by its culture and its recognition
of intellect.

But all the days and hours of this singular honeymoon
were not unhappy. On receiving Shelley's note, left at
the inn as he passed through York, Hogg was about to
start on a holiday excursion. Why not take the coach,
and follow the fugitives to Scotland ? One morning, early
in September, a knock was heard at the door in George
Street, a visitor was ushered into the front parlour, and

Shelley had the joy of welcoming his friend, whose intended arrival had been announced by letter, and of introducing him to his bride. " Lovely," she appeared to Hogg— " bright, blooming, radiant with youth, health, and beauty." The college companions had not seen each other since they parted last April ; now they were to renew the days of their inseparable comradeship and never to part again. A bedroom was found for Hogg at the top of the house. The morning was bright and breezy, so they would all visit Holyrood together, whence Shelley might return, if he pleased, to write letters, while his friend escorted Harriet to the summit of Arthur's Seat. It was a day of glee sunshine, and rejoicing.

When the first tumult of spirits had subsided, the wedded pair and their new associate settled down to a regular way of living. Each morning before breakfast Bysshe would start off to obtain his letters at the post-office. Breakfast over, some hours of study would follow. A treatise of Buffon especially interested Shelley, and he occupied his mornings with translating it into English with a view to publication. Harriet, by his side, was similarly engaged ; the novels of Madame Cottin, then of recent date, and distinguished by their sensibility united with a moral purpose, had caught her fancy, and morning after morning she advanced steadily with a version of the affect- ing tale " Claire d'Albe," designed by its authoress as a warning against the fatal consequences of a woman's first fault. After dinner the three friends went forth for an afternoon ramble, returning at dusk to tea. The little maid who waited on them had quickly discovered that the unvarying element among their daily wants was tea ; and after many ringings of the bell she would suddenly appear —intruding at the door a small untidy head—with the exclamation, " Oh ! the kittle !" in unmusical northern

accent, from which Shelley shrank in agony. " Send her
away, Harriet," he would cry, rushing wildly into a corner
and covering his face with his hands. " Oh! send her
away ; for God's sake send her away ! " Tea being ended,
Harriet would begin to read aloud in her clear sweet voice,
and would not readily leave off. " Morality," says Hogg,
with amused superciliousness, " was her favourite theme ;
she found most pleasure in works of a high ethical tone ;
Telemachus and Belisarius were her chosen companions."
Bysshe had a fatal tendency to drowsiness about the hour
when in his college rooms he would coil himself upon the
hearthrug in a sweet and mighty oblivion. " His innocent
slumbers," declares his friend, "gave serious offence, and
his neglect was fiercely resented ; he was stigmatized as
an inattentive wretch." Before bedtime the three companions would perhaps stroll out once again, to view from
Princes Street the comet, nightly increasing in brilliancy,
and to enjoy the cool air beneath the stars.

Five weeks in Edinburgh amply sufficed to weary
Shelley : he was impatient to be gone, and as Hogg must
return to his conveyancer's chambers in York, Shelley and
Harriet must needs accompany him to that ancient city,
there to reside for a year, at the end of which period " we
were all," says Hogg, " to remove to London and to dwell
there together 'for ever,' writing, reading, and being read
to." To render the journey more agreeable to Harriet
they travelled in a post-chaise, and halted for a night at
Belford and for a night at Darlington. October mists and
rains enveloped them as they drove. But Harriet was
superior to accidents of the weather ; some novels by
Holcroft lay at her side, from which, as the chaise
rolled on, she read aloud "almost incessantly." Bysshe,
who hated the closeness and confinement, became at
times restive, and pleaded pathetically, but in vain, for a

relaxation of the rigorous law of perpetual Holcroft. If the carriage drew up, and Hogg, the man of affairs, went bustling about luggage, Shelley would have vanished before boxes and trunks had been counted. "Once at Berwick," writes his friend, "when Harriet had taken her seat and all was ready, Bysshe was missing; but he was retaken on fresh pursuit, being captured by myself, as he was standing on the Walls in a drizzling rain, gazing mournfully at the wild and dreary sea, with looks not less wild and dreary." The third evening—close of a dull autumnal day—brought the travellers in rain and mire to York. Lodgings were sought in spite of the dimness and the mist, and were found at the Miss Dancers', No. 20, Coney Street — "a dismal and poverty-stricken house," within hearing of the river which the back garden over looked; "the dingy dwelling," so Hogg describes it, "of certain dingy old milliners."

Had Shelley's imagination dwelt lovingly in the past, he would have found much to interest him in the winding streets of York, in its venerable relics of antiquity, above all in its majestic minster. But Reason was a pedant who thought scorn of history, and the noble cathedral appeared to him to be but a huge erection of unreason, a waste of barbaric pomp. Hogg was in York, and that was much. It was Shelley's hope that his other friend—dearer, if possible, than Hogg—Miss Hitchener, might soon become their guest; but the words of his invitation do not sound as if he possessed a superfluity of joy: "How happy should I be to see you! There is no need to tell you this; and my happiness is not so great that it becomes a friend to be sparing in that society which constitutes its only charm."

Anxiety about the means to live again harassed Shelley. The captain's bounty was exhausted; Mr.

Timothy Shelley was still indignant, refused all aid, and
even commanded that his son's name should never be
mentioned in his presence.   Ten days or more had passed
in York, and the need of some regular provision grew
urgent.   Shelley resolved to hasten south, to make his
uncle's house at Cuckfield a resting-place for a couple of
nights, and thence seek an interview with his father in
order to urge in person his claims.   It was arranged that
Harriet's sister Eliza should accompany Bysshe on his
return to York.   The journey was not wholly without a
prospect of pleasure ; for although his stay in Sussex was
to be brief, he was determined not to leave Cuckfield
without having seen Miss Hitchener.

Three days' travelling on the outside of the coach
brought Shelley, alert and bright-eyed in spite of sleepless
nights, to his uncle's house at Cuckfield.   The kindly
captain made haste to invite Miss Hitchener to dine
with his nephew on Tuesday, October 22.   What talk
of virtue, disinterestedness, freedom, equality, there must
have been that evening, when Elizabeth Hitchener arrived
expecting a sympathetic debate on these high themes !
Meanwhile Bysshe had "tried the force of truth" on
"that mistaken man," his father.   It is not certain
whether the father and son actually met, or whether the
negotiation was conducted wholly in writing ; in either
case the immediate result was the same—nothing was to
be obtained from Mr. Shelley.   Disappointed and unsuc-
cessful, Shelley hastened through London, and was again
in York before October closed, having been absent little
more than a week.

Eliza Westbrook had not waited for Shelley's escort,
and was already installed in the place of supreme authority
at York.   It was Harriet's misfortune—one natural and
almost inevitable—to lean much upon her elder sister, and

defer in most matters to her judgment. For the careless freedom of the earlier days in York a strict *régime* was substituted. It had not previously been suspected that Harriet possessed any nerves; now, says Hogg, "we heard of little else. . . . The house lay, as it were, under an interdict; all our accustomed occupations were suspended; study was forbidden; reading was injurious—to read aloud might terminate fatally; to go abroad was death, to stay at home the grave. Bysshe became nothing; I," adds the narrator, "of course very much less than nothing—a negative quantity of a very high figure." Eliza's own authority with the young people was very great; backed by an appeal to the highest of sanctions, "What would Miss Warne say?" it became irresistible. Miss Warne— an august but impalpable presence—overawed all exercise of private judgment. "The poor poet," declares Hogg, "was overwhelmed by the affectionate invasion; he lay prostrated under the insupportable pressure of our domiciliary visit."

Such, in miniature, is Hogg's picture of the state of things at York on Shelley's arrival from Sussex. It must be taken with reserve, for Miss Westbrook desired—not without cause—to stand between the bride of sixteen and her husband's friend. She necessarily took up the position of guardian to Harriet, of antagonist to Hogg; and that such a person should be a successful antagonist was insufferable. She might, in truth, have found Harriet's nerves disturbed, and have been of opinion that walks with Hogg and readings aloud, even of such tranquillizing and edifying works as Telemachus and Belisarius, would not tend to promote Harriet's happiness. "My dear friend Hogg, that noble being, is with me," Shelley had written to Miss Hitchener, "and will be always." On leaving for the south he had placed his young wife with entire trust

in his friend's care. He had not long returned before
he perceived with pain that Harriet's behaviour towards
Hogg was greatly altered, and that she now regarded
him with aversion. When he touched on the subject, she
replied with dark hints of Hogg's unworthiness, which
filled Bysshe with vague alarms. Pressing his inquiry, he
heard with dismay that the friend whom he had looked on
as the realized ideal of upright and generous manhood,
yielding to ignoble passion, had betrayed the trust reposed
in him—had declared to Harriet that he "loved" her, had
implored her to permit his "love." The first advances,
he was told, had been made immediately on their arrival
at York from Edinburgh. Harriet had forbidden the
intruder on her peace ever to mention the subject again,
and, hoping to hear no more of it, had preferred to leave
Shelley ignorant of what had occurred. During his
absence in Sussex the odious importunity had been
renewed. Harriet had appealed to her persecutor's sense
of right, and seemingly not without effect, for he admitted
the error of his conduct, and proposed, as the only expia-
tion in his power, to inform Bysshe by letter of the whole.
Fearful of the effects of such a communication on Shelley's
mind while he was far from her, Harriet had forbidden
this; and it was on the following day—sooner than had
been expected—that Shelley reached York.

Shelley's first feeling on receiving this disclosure was
not indignant wrath and the pride of wounded honour,
but that shock of mind which attends a shattered ideal—
a sense of wreck and ruin which would have approached
despair, had he not believed it possible that his friend
might rise from this lamentable fall. If Hogg were base,
what was to be thought of human nature in general?
If that countenance "on which," says Shelley, "I have
sometimes gazed till I fancied the world could be reformed

by gazing too," were but a mask concealing unworthy
thoughts and desires, what hope could there be for mankind? But no—he would think of his friend as dreadfully
mistaken, the victim of prejudice, yet not wholly lost. In
such a temper Shelley sought an explanation with Hogg.
"We walked to the fields beyond York," he tells Miss
Hitchener; "I desired to know fully the account of this
affair. I heard it *from him,* and I believe he was sincere.
All I can recollect of that terrible day was that I pardoned
him—fully, freely pardoned him; that I would still be a
friend to him, and hoped soon to convince him how lovely
virtue was; that his crime, not himself, was the object of
my detestation; that I value a human being not for what
it has been, but for what it is; that I hoped the time
would come when he would regard this horrible error with
as much disgust as I did. He said little; he was pale,
terror-struck, remorseful."

The discovery of Hogg's unfaithfulness had two consequences of importance. Harriet Shelley rose in her
husband's esteem, though she still occupied but a secondary
place; and now that he could no longer expend the wealth
of his idealizing imagination on one friend, he poured all
its extravagant treasures around the other, his heroine
of a daydream, Elizabeth Hitchener. Shelley's feeling
towards her did not compete with his affection for
Harriet; it moved in a different and higher plane.
Harriet was a gentle being to protect and cherish;
Elizabeth Hitchener was his "Veiled Glory of this lamp-
less Universe!" She was the "Spirit of Intellectual
Beauty," clothed in the accidents of humanity, whom in
one form or another he was for ever to pursue, and lose
and pursue again. "Oh, it is terrible!" he wrote to Miss
Hitchener. "This stroke has almost withered my being.'
Friendship with Hogg seemed to be a thing of the earth,

earthy; friendship with his imagined lady of light was felt to be boundless as the heavens, to partake of their eternity, and thus to be a pledge of endless existence.

The residence at York now hastened to a close. It became clear that, for the sake of Harriet's happiness, they must live at a distance from Hogg, and Shelley, caring little at this moment whither they should bend their steps, left the choice of a place of abode to his wife and her sister. Their decision was in favour of Keswick, and Shelley acquiesced. Probably in order to avoid a scene of heated argument and expostulation, they did not inform Hogg of the time of their intended departure. One afternoon, early in November, he discovered with surprise that the lodgers in Blake Street had flown. It was a situation worthy of the "Sorrows of Werther." Shelley, with his professed superiority to passion, seemed to Hogg as cold and insensible as Goethe's Albert; Harriet had all the grace and freshness of a Lotte. What less could the forsaken Werther do than despatch letter after letter in pursuit of his friends, announcing in the first of these that he would have Harriet's forgiveness or would blow his brains out at her feet? "Think not," Shelley wrote in reply,* "that I am otherwise than your friend; a friend to you now more fervent, more devoted than ever, for misery endears to us those whom we love. You are, you shall be, my bosom friend. You have been so but in one instance, and there you have deceived yourself. Still let us continue what we have ever been. I will remain unchanged; so *shall* you *hereafter*. Let us forget this affair; let us erase from the memory that ever it had being. Consider what havoc one year, the last of our lives, has made in memory. How can you say that good will not come; that we shall not again be what we were?"

* Evidently Shelley's, but transformed to a "Fragment of a Novel" by Hog

Hogg begged earnestly to be permitted to be once more
inmate of the same home with his friends; but to this
Shelley resolutely refused to accede. Frequent letters
went to and fro between York and Keswick for some
five or six weeks. In one of these Hogg hinted the
possibility of a challenge and duel, to which Shelley
replied that nothing which his friend could do or say
would induce him to accept a challenge—he had no right
to take another's life or to expose his own. Hogg's
answer was apologetic, dwelling on his quick passions, his
high sense of honour. To this Shelley seems to have
made no response, and from December onwards for many
months intercourse between the Oxford comrades and
confederates ceased.

Travelling through the Yorkshire Richmond, the wanderers reached Keswick in the dull November days. They
obtained lodgings in the town, and were soon happy in
having secured, for a moderate rent, a small furnished
house. Chesnut Cottage, which may still be seen, is a
low, one-storied house, standing upon the side of the
umbrageous road which runs down the south-western slope
of Chesnut Hill. It looks forth upon the fertile grounds
which connect the lakes of Derwentwater and Bassen-
thwaite. Both lakes are visible from the garden—a garden
of old-fashioned shrubs cut in the Dutch fashion.

Were it not for the disturbing letters which came from
Hogg, and certain troubles connected with ways and means,
these days of the declining year would have been bright
with inward happiness. Shelley's affection for his young
wife had strengthened with his growing sense of protectiveness towards her. Eliza Westbrook was with them, and
her presence added to Harriet's satisfaction in her new
home. "Words," wrote the younger sister, "can never
sufficiently express her goodness and kindnes to me. She

is my more than mother." To Shelley at this time his sister-in-law seemed "a woman rather superior to the generality"—prejudiced, yet with prejudices which he did not consider unvanquishable; "indeed," he adds, "I have already conquered some of them." "Eliza," he wrote some weeks later, "is a very amiable girl. Her opinions are gradually rectifying." It was pleasant to have within arguing range a victim of intolerance who was not unwilling to be illuminated. But a far higher pleasure lay in anticipating the arrival at Chesnut Cottage, in the Christmas holidays, or at latest in the following midsummer, of one who needed no illumination, one who was herself all light and love—Elizabeth Hitchener. Even now to wander alone among the mountains, musing on Miss Hitchener and human nature, was no mean delight. "[November 23, 1811.] I have taken a long *solitary* ramble to-day. These gigantic mountains piled on each other, these waterfalls, these million-shaped clouds tinted by the varying colours of innumerable rainbows hanging between yourself and a lake as smooth and dark as a plain of polished jet—oh, these are sights attunable to the contemplation! . . . I have been thinking of you and of human nature. Your letter has been the partner of my solitude—or, rather, I have not been alone, for you have been with me."

Various literary enterprises occupied Shelley during the months at Keswick, and were pursued with so much zeal that Harriet feared lest the strain might over-tax his strength. Early in December he had in contemplation a poem designed to set forth his vision of the future golden age, presenting as in a picture "the manners, simplicity, and delights of a perfect state of society." "Will you assist me?" he asked Miss Hitchener. "I only thought of it last night. I design to accomplish it and publish. After, I shall draw a picture of Heaven. I can do neither without some hints from you. The latter I think you ought to *make.*" Shelley's early design found a partial fulfilment in those sections of "Queen Mab" which tell of the happier life of man in ages yet to come, and a nobler fulfilment in that impassioned prophecy which leads the "Prometheus" to its close.

A second of the Keswick projects occupied Shelley longer, and was nearly brought to a successful issue ; he purposed to collect and publish his shorter poems, which he valued less for their literary merits than for their moral and political tendency. "I think it wrong," he said, "to publish anything anonymously, and shall annex my name and a preface, in which I shall lay open my intentions, as the poems are not wholly useless.

"I sing, and Liberty may love the song."

In his retirement among the mountains Shelley did not find it easy to negotiate with printers or publishers ; he prepared his manuscript, and on leaving Keswick for his mission to Ireland he took with him this sheaf of poems.

In his seclusion of Chesnut Cottage Shelley saw little of the general society of Keswick. The Duke of Norfolk, whose seat of Greystoke was close to Penrith, had written, we are told, to some gentlemen among his agricultural friends, "requesting them to pay such neighbourly attentions to the solitary young people as circumstances might place in their power." But Shelley's solitude was not often invaded by these rural gentry. The tenants of Chesnut Cottage may have appeared to some of them little better than a pair of strayed children. "Was the garden let with your part of the house?" asked a member of the Southey family. "Oh no," replied Mrs. Shelley—a matron who was still almost a schoolgirl—"the garden is not ours ; but then, you know, the people let us run

H

about in it, whenever Percy and I are tired of sitting in the house." The straitened means of the household did not favour a needless hospitality ; and Shelley's strange ways and his absence on Sundays from church were enough to suggest that his acquaintance might be one of questionable advantage.

Before leaving York, Shelley, acting on the advice of his cousin, Charles Grove, had written to the Duke of Norfolk, requesting his Grace to use his influence to restore friendly relations between his father and himself. The duke took the matter up in the kindliest spirit ; wrote in a guarded manner to Shelley, not wishing to raise expectations which might not be fulfilled ; wrote also to Shelley's father, proposing to visit Field Place, and there confer with him " on the unhappy differences with his son." The conference with Mr. Timothy Shelley, as the duke had feared, led to no results immediately favourable. Returning to the north, his Grace learnt that the young folk had quitted York, and were now residing near Keswick. His kind offices did not cease, and he wrote, when November was in its wane, inviting Shelley, with his wife and sister-in-law, to Greystoke. With empty pockets, and a heart not over full of hope, Shelley, accompanied by Harriet and Eliza, reached the mansion. From December 4 the visit extended itself probably to the 8th or 9th, and Shelley was not unfavourably impressed by his host. If only he were a man and not a duke ! If only the courtiers in attendance were a little less obsequious or acquiescent ! When, once more at ease in his mountain nook, he could unbosom his spirit to his republican friend and philosopher, Elizabeth Hitchener, a long sigh of relief escaped his lips. " Your letters, my dearest friend, are to me an exhaustless mine of pleasure. Fatigued with aristocratical insipidity, left alone scarce one moment by those senseless monopolizers

of time that form the court of a duke, who would be very
well as a man, how delightful to commune with the soul
that is undisguised, whose importance no arts are necessary
nor adequate to exalt ! "

The duke's intervention in behalf of the young exile
from Field Place had certainly set Mr. Timothy Shelley
and old Sir Bysshe a-thinking.   Shelley's grandfather,
whose cherished purpose was to hand down a great property to his descendants, had already taken measures to
restrain the wild boy, who had just celebrated a runaway
marriage with a coffee-house keeper's daughter, from breaking up or encumbering the family estates.   Perhaps he
or Mr. Timothy Shelley had heard of the young man's
intention of dividing the property, whenever he might
enter into possession of it, with his sisters and the sister
of his soul, Miss Hitchener.   Not many days had gone
by after Shelley's return from Greystoke, when rumours
reached him through Captain Pilfold of a scheme by which
he might at once pass from penury to wealth, if only he
would consent to entail the estate on his eldest son, or, in
default of issue, on his brother.   Old Bysshe feared his
grandson's wild ways, and desired at any cost to bind him
from parcelling out the family property.   To Shelley, with
his revolutionary conception of basing life wholly upon
reason, the ties of kindred and tradition seemed little better
than bonds of evil custom.   Considerations of justice and
honour, as he conceived them, peremptorily forbade his
accepting the bribe of £2000 a year, which Captain Pilfold
declared was about to be offered for his acceptance, when
this was coupled with the condition of entailing a great
property, the equivalent of a vast command over labour,
on one who might be a vicious man or a fool.   The anticipated proposal was in anticipation indignantly rejected.

" I have heard from Captain P[ilfold]," wrote Shelley

to Miss Hitchener. "His letter contains the account of a meditated proposal, on the part of my father and grandfather, to make my income immediately larger than the former's, in case I will consent to entail the estate on my eldest son, and, in default of issue, on my brother. Silly dotards! do they think I can be thus bribed and ground into an act of such contemptible injustice and inutility? that I will forswear my principles in consideration of £2000 a-year? that the good will I could thus purchase, or the ill will I could thus overbear, would recompense me for the loss of self-esteem, of conscious rectitude? And with what face can they make me a proposal so insultingly hateful? Dare one of them propose such a condition to my face—to the face of any virtuous man—and not sink into nothing at his disdain? That I should entail £120,000 of command over labour, of power to remit this, to employ it for beneficent purposes, on one whom I know not—who might, instead of being the benefactor of mankind, be its bane, or use this for the worst purposes, which the real delegates of my chance-given property might convert into a most useful instrument of benevolence! No! this you will not suspect me of."

Two days previously, Shelley, in ignorance of the meditated proposal, had written to his father, on the advice of the Duke of Norfolk, a letter which is admirable in temper, conciliating, yet firm and frank when dealing with points as to which he could make no concession.

Shelley to Mr. Timothy Shelley.

Keswick, Cumberland, December 13, 1811.

My dear Sir,

I have lately returned from Greystoke, where I had been invited by the Duke of Norfolk, that he might speak with me of the unhappy differences which some of my actions have occasioned. The result of his advice was that I should write a letter to you, the tone of whose expression should be sorrow that I should have wounded the feelings of persons so nearly connected with me. Undoubtedly I should thus express the real sense of my mind, for when convinced of my error no one is more ready to own that conviction than myself, nor to repair any injuries which might have resulted from a line of conduct which I had pursued.

On my expulsion from Oxford you were so good as to allow me £200 per annum; you also added a promise of my being unrestrained in the exercise of the completest free agency. In consequence of this last I married a young lady whose personal character is unimpeachable. This action (admitting it to be done) in its very nature required dissimulation, much as I may regret that I had descended to employ it. My allowance was then withdrawn; I was left without money four hundred miles from one being I knew, every day liable to be exposed to the severest exile of penury. Surely something is to be allowed for human feelings, when you reflect that the letters you then received were written in this state of helplessness and dereliction. And now let me say that a reconciliation with you is a thing which I very much desire. Accept my apologies for the uneasiness which I have occasioned; believe that my wish to repair any uneasiness is firm and sincere. I regard these family differences as a very great evil, and I much lament that I should in any wise have been instrumental in exciting them.

I hope you will not consider what I am about to say an insulting want of respect or contempt; but I think it my duty to say that however great advantages might result from such concessions, I can make no promise of concealing my opinions in political or religious matters. I should consider myself culpable to excite any expectation in your mind which I should be unable to fulfil. What I have said is actuated by the sincerest wish of being again upon those terms with you which existed some time since. I have not employed hypocrisy to heighten the regret which I feel for having occasioned uneasiness. I have not employed meanness to concede what I consider it my duty to withhold. Such methods as these would be unworthy of us both. I hope you will consider what I have said, and I remain, dear father, with sincerest wishes for our perfect right understanding,

Yours respectfully and affectionately,

P. B. SHELLEY.

To this letter Mr. Timothy Shelley replied in a tone of conciliation. There was also good tidings from Harriet's father. Possibly the visit to the seat of the Duke of Norfolk, with hardly a guinea in the pockets of the three guests, had made an impression on Mr. Westbrook. It was not becoming that his daughter should pay her respects at ducal castles in a state of entire destitution; henceforth he would allow her £200 a-year. The same sum was granted by Mr. Timothy Shelley.

"By-the-by," wrote Shelley a month later to Miss Hitchener, "my father has allowed me £200 per annum, attended with the compliment that he did it to *prevent my cheating strangers*." Thus, although nothing more was heard of the rumoured proposal by which Shelley was to be made a wealthier man than his father, by the beginning of the year 1812 he was relieved from distress, and the household at Chesnut Cottage could count upon an income, independent of Eliza Westbrook's means, of £400 a-year.

It was in Mr. William Calvert's house at Windybrow that Shelley first met Robert Southey. To dwell in the neighbourhood of a poet, whose genius had been as that of a master with his imagination, was doubtless one of the attractions to Keswick; but during some of the earlier days of Shelley's residence at Chesnut Cottage Southey was absent from home. "The scenery here is awfully beautiful," Shelley wrote on November 14, ". . . but the object most interesting to my feelings is Southey's habitation. He is now on a journey; when he returns I will call on him." Christmas had almost come when the meeting at Calvert's house took place. The elder poet resembled the younger in the natural ardour and sensibility of his temperament, and in the fact that his youth had been haunted by visions of human perfectibility, and of a golden age of equality and innocence and joy. But Southey, an Arab steed, had long been serving as a beast of burden ; he had dutifully, cheerfully trained himself to control his excessive sensibility, and as he advanced to mature years his early hopes and visions had taken a sober colouring. In Shelley he fancied that he beheld the image of his own ardent youth revived from the past. "Here is a man at Keswick," he wrote, "who acts upon me as my own ghost would do. He is just what I was in 1794. . . . He is come to the fittest physician in the world. At present he has got to the Pantheistic stage of philosophy, and in the course of a week I expect he will be a Berkeleyan, for I have put him upon a course of Berkeley. It has surprised him a good deal to meet, for the first time in his life, with a man who perfectly understands him, and does him full justice. I tell him that all the difference between us is that he is nineteen and I am thirty-seven ; . . . God help us ! The world wants mending, though he did not set about it exactly in the right way."

With characteristic kindness, Southey at once set him-self to be of service to his young acquaintance ; invited him, with his wife and sister-in-law, to Greta Hall ; lent him books ; induced Shelley's landlord, Mr. Dare, to reduce the weekly charges at Chesnut Cottage ; supplied the Cottage, in order to effect this reduction, with linen from Mrs. Southey's store ; took privately such indirect means as were in his power of assuring Shelley's father that, erroneous as his son's conduct might have been, his heart would bring him right, and that everything might be hoped from his genius and his virtues. Differences of opinion, which quickly discovered themselves, did not alienate the elder from the younger man. He recognized Shelley's generosity of temper, and made allowances for the illusions of an intellect eager for truth, but immature and imperfectly trained. Shelley responded to this kindness ; told Southey the story of his life, and communicated to him, with vivid interest, all his thoughts concerning things past, present, and to come. "Southey," he assured Miss Hitchener, "though far from being a man of great reasoning powers, is a great man. He has all that characterizes the poet ; great eloquence, though obstinacy in opinion, which arguments are the last things that can shake. He is a man of virtue. He will neve• belie what he thinks ; his professions are in compatibility with his practice. More of him another time."

A copy of Berkeley was procured from Lloyd, the friend of Coleridge and of Lamb. What most deeply impressed Shelley in the volume was not Berkeley's chain of reasoning, but a comment pencilled by Charles Lloyd in the margin—a comment which leads one to surmise that Lloyd had not penetrated far into the thoughts of Berkeley : "Mind cannot create, it can only perceive."

To be the object of a young idealist's enthusiasm is not a piece of unmingled good fortune for man or woman. Shelley's early idols were all sooner or later dethroned, and, ceasing to be divinities, did not always obtain from him their just rights as human beings. So it had been with Hogg ; so it was to be with Elizabeth Hitchener ; so to some extent it was now with Southey. Shelley's loyalty was constantly given to his own ideals ; but he had a certain infirmity of vision. The figures of men and women, standing out from a luminous background, seemed to him to be surrounded with a nimbus of glory. He advanced ; the splendour receded to the horizon's bound, and his divinity stood on the common earth, shorn of the aureole.

It needed but a few days to discover that Southey was an erring mortal, of stature not wholly heroic. " I do not think so highly of Southey as I did. It is to be confessed that to see him in his family, to behold him in his domestic circle, he appears in a most amiable light. I do not mean that he is or can be the great character which once I linked him to; his mind is terribly narrow compared to it. *Once* he was this character,—everything you can conceive of practised virtue. Now he is corrupted by the world, contaminated by custom : it rends my heart when I think what he might have been ! "

If Southey could not remain on the heights of admiration, it was inevitable that his descent must be extreme and swift.

Another influence than that of Southey, and a far different one, which had long been dominant with Shelley's intellect, was now to clothe itself in humanity, and to utter itself not merely with the voice of abstract reason, but with a personal force and living authority. We do not find it difficult at the present time to point out fallacies and inconsequence in the revolutionary theory and argument of William Godwin; but to many minds at the close of the last and the opening of the present century his "Political Justice" seemed to sum up the truths of the great intellectual and political movement in France, divested of all that was temporary or accidental, and all that might cause violence and terror. The philosophy of Godwin was as if expressly framed to impose itself with authority on the intellect of a youth of ardent temperament and aspiring moral views ; it seemed to be at once victory and law ; it promised to quell all dissonance of passion, and inspire a regulated enthusiasm of virtue, reason, benevolence ; it knew not fear nor favour ; it scorned the limitations of concrete fact ; its conclusions were sanguine as the hopes of a lover, yet seemingly exact as the calculations of a sage. In "Political Justice" Shelley had found a doctrine and a rule of life, into harmony with which he had brought his opinions and conduct in ardent discipleship. If ever he subjected the bonds of kindred and of filial duty to the criticism of reason, he was only acting out the principles of his master ; if he spoke of vicious inclination as "prejudice," or a criminal as one labouring under a mistake, it was because he had learnt from Godwin that all vice is error ; if he resolved to divide his inheritance with strangers or friends in the common faith of equality and freedom, he could justify the resolve by proving from " Political Justice " that property belongs of right to those who can best use it for the public good.

Godwin's treatise had been published while his future disciple was a babe in arms. In 1812 his influence was largely spent ; he had already entered into "the twilight of a doubtful immortality." To Shelley he was a spiritual presence, a great legislator of the past, whose mind still moved over the turbulent waters of society to evolve order from their chaos. While at Keswick Shelley learnt, towards the close of December, 1811, that the lawgiver and prophet even now trod this earth. He was profoundly moved by the discovery. Hardly daring to hope for an answer, he hastened to despatch a letter to the shrine of truth and virtue—it seemed no less to him—at Skinner Street, London, laying bare his soul before the eyes of William Godwin, and craving a blessing — such a blessing as philosophers may bestow—at his hands. " The name of Godwin," thus ran his letter (January 3, 1812), " has been used to excite in me feelings of reverence and admiration. I have been accustomed to consider him a luminary too dazzling for the darkness which surrounds him. From the

earliest period of my knowledge of his principles, I have
ardently desired to share on the footing of intimacy that
intellect which I have delighted to contemplate in its
emanations. Considering, then, these feelings, you will
not be surprised at the inconceivable emotions with which
I learnt your existence and your dwelling. I had enrolled
your name in the list of the honourable dead. I had felt
regret that the glory of your being had passed from this
earth of ours. It is not so. You still live, and I firmly
believe are still planning the welfare of human kind. I
have but just entered on the scene of human operations,
yet my feelings and my reasonings correspond with what
yours were. My course has been short but eventful. I
have seen much of human prejudice, suffered much from
human persecution, yet I see no reason hence inferable
which should alter my wishes for their renovation. The
ill treatment I have met with has more than ever impressed
the truth of my principles on my judgment. I am young :
I am ardent in the cause of philanthropy and truth. Do
not suppose that this is vanity. . . . I shall earnestly await
your answer."

Godwin immediately replied to Shelley's letter, confessing that his unknown correspondent was for the present
a figure in the vague, an abstraction of ardent youthfulness
rather than an actual man. Shelley's second letter, which
reviews his past life, is of much biographical interest, but
we must bear in mind that the writer, who had only a faint
interest in the history of nations, was one of those men
for whom the hard outline of facts in their own individual
history has little fixity ; whose footsteps are for ever
followed and overflowed by the wave of oblivion : who
remember with extraordinary tenacity the sentiment of
times and of places, but lose the framework of circumstance
in which the sentiment was set ; and who, in reconstructing

an image of the past, often unconsciously supply links and lines upon the suggestion of that sentiment or emotion which is for them the essential reality.

Shelley to Godwin.

Keswick, January 10, 1812.

. . . I am the son of a man of fortune in Sussex. The habits of thinking of my father and myself never coincided. Passive obedience was inculcated and enforced in my childhood. I was required to love, because it was *my duty* to love : it is scarcely necessary to remark that coercion obviated its own intention.   I was haunted with a passion for the wildest and most extravagant romances.   Ancient books of chemistry and magic were perused with an enthusiasm of wonder, almost amounting to belief.   My sentiments were unrestrained by anything within me ; external impediments were numerous, and strongly applied ; their effect was merely temporary.

From a reader I became a writer of romances ; before the age of seventeen I had published two, "St. Irvyne" and "Zastrozzi," each of which, though quite uncharacteristic of me as now I am, yet serves to mark the state of my mind at the period of their composition. I shall desire them to be sent to you : do not, however, consider this as any obligation to yourself to misapply your valuable time.*

It is now a period of more than two years since first I saw your inestimable book of " Political Justice ; " it opened to my mind fresh and more extensive views ; it materially influenced my character, and I rose from its perusal a wiser and a better man. I was no longer the votary of romance ; till then I had existed in an ideal world—now I found that in this universe of ours was enough to excite the interest of the heart, enough to employ the discussions of reason. I beheld, in short, that I had duties to

* Shelley's statement that he had *published* " St. Irvyne " and "Zastrozzi " before he was seventeen is untrue. He seems to wish to prove that they belong to a period of boyhood before the great event of his becoming a student of " Political Justice.

perform. Conceive the effect which the "Political Justice" would have upon a mind before jealous of its independence, and participating somewhat singularly in a peculiar susceptibility.

My age is now *nineteen;* at the period to which I allude I was at Eton. No sooner had I formed the principles which I now profess than I was anxious to disseminate their benefits. This was done without the slightest caution. I was twice expelled, but recalled by the interference of my father. I went to Oxford. Oxonian society was insipid to me, uncongenial with my habits of thinking. I could not descend to common life: the sublime interest of poetry, lofty and exalted achievements, the proselytism of the world, the equalization of its inhabitants, were to me the soul of my soul. You can probably form some idea of the contrast exhibited to my character by those with whom I was surrounded. Classical reading and poetical writing employed me during my residence at Oxford.

In the mean time I became, in the popular sense of the word "God," an atheist. I printed a pamphlet avowing my opinion and its occasion. I distributed this anonymously to men of thought and learning, wishing that Reason should decide on the case at issue: it was never my intention to deny it. Mr. Copleston at Oxford, among others, had the pamphlet: he showed it to the Master and the Fellows of University College, and *I* was sent for. I was informed that in case I denied the publication, no more would be said. I refused, and was expelled.

It will be necessary, in order to elucidate this part of my history, to inform you that I am heir by entail to an estate of £6000 per annum. My principles have induced me to regard the law of primogeniture an evil of primary magnitude. My father's notions of family honour are incoincident with my know ledge of public good. I will never sacrifice the latter to any consideration. My father has ever regarded me as a blot, a defilement of his honour. He wished to induce me by poverty to accept of some commission in a distant regiment, and in the interim of my absence to prosecute the pamphlet, that a process of outlawry might make the estate, on his death, devolve to my younger brother. These are the leading points of the history of the man before you. Others exist, but I have thought proper to make some selection, not that it is my design to conceal or extenuate any part, but that I should by their enumeration quite outstep the bounds of modesty. Now it is for you to judge whether, by permitting me to cultivate your friendship, you are exhibiting yourself more really useful than by the pursuance of those avocations, of which the time spent in allowing this cultivation would deprive you. I am now earnestly pursuing studious habits. I am writing " An Inquiry into the Causes of the Failure of the French Revolution to Benefit Mankind." My plan is that of resolving to lose no opportunity to disseminate truth and happiness.

I am married to a woman whose views are similar to my own. To you, as the regulator and former of my mind, I must ever look with real respect and veneration.

To this letter Godwin replied promptly, expressing a deep and earnest interest in Shelley's welfare, warning him against indulging anger towards his father, and endeavouring to repress his youthful enthusiasm for the reform of the world until wisdom and knowledge should have qualified him to become a teacher. Shelley felt a happy pride in submission to his philosophic master, yet he retained the conviction that he had ascertained truths which the world needed to understand, and that it could not be doing ill if he were to become the organ or mouthpiece of these truths.

Shelley to Godwin.

Keswick, January 16, 1812.

. . . You mistake me if you think that I am angry with my father. I have ever been desirous of a reconciliation with him, but the price which he demands for it is a renunciation of my opinions, or, at least, a subjection to conditions which should bind me to act in opposition to their very spirit. It is probable that my father has *acted* for my welfare, but the manner in which he has done so will not allow me to suppose that he has *felt* for it unconnectedly with certain considerations of birth; and feeling for these things was not feeling for me. I never loved my father—it was not from hardness of heart, for I have loved and do love warmly.

You say, " Being yet a scholar, I ought to have no intolerable itch to become a teacher." I have not so far as any publications of mine are irreconcilable with the general good, or so far as they are negative. I do not set up for a judge of controversies, but into whatever company I go I have introduced my own senti-ments, partly with a view, if they were any wise erroneous, that unforeseen elucidations might rectify them; or, if they were not, that I should contribute my mite to the treasury of wisdom and happiness. I hope in the course of our communication to acquire that sobriety of spirit which is the characteristic of true heroism. I have not heard without benefit that Newton was a modest man : I am not ignorant that vanity and folly delight in forwardness and assumption. But I think there is a line to be drawn between affectation of unpossessed talents and the deceit of self-distrust, by which much power has been lost to the world ; for

> " Full many a flower is born to blush unseen,
> And waste its sweetness on the desert air."

This line may be called " the modesty of nature." I hope I am somewhat anxious not to outstep its boundaries. I will not again crudely obtrude the question of atheism on the world. But could I not at the same time improve my own powers and diffuse true and virtuous principles? Many with equally confined talents to my own are by publications scattering the seeds of prejudice and selfishness. Might not an exhibition of truth, with equal elegance and depth, suffice to counteract the deleterious tendency of their principles? Does not writing hold the next place to colloquial discussion in eliciting and classing the powers of the mind? I am willing to become a scholar—nay, a pupil. My humility and confidence, where I am conscious that I am not imposed upon, and where I perceive talents and powers so certainly and un-doubtedly superior, is unfeigned and complete. I have desired the publications of my early youth to be sent to you. You will perceive that " Zastrozzi " and " St. Irvyne " were written prior to my acquaintance with your writings; the " Essay on Love," a little poem, since. I had, indeed, read "St. Leon" before I wrote "St. Irvyne;" but the reasonings had *then* made little impression.

In a few days we set off to Dublin. I do not know exactly where we shall be; but a letter addressed to Keswick will find me. Our journey has been settled some time. We go principally to *forward as much as we can* the Catholic Emancipation.

Southey the poet, whose principles were pure and elevated once, is now the paid champion of every abuse and absurdity. I have had much conversation with him. He says, "You will think as I do when you are as old." I do not feel the least disposition to be Mr. S.'s proselyte.

In the summer we shall be in the north of Wales. Dare I hope that you will come to see us? Perhaps this is an unfeasible neglect of your avocations. I shall hope it until you forbid me.

The period of Shelley's residence at Keswick was now nearly at an end. It had been on the whole a season of happiness—of growing affection for Harriet; of delight in mountain and vale and lake; of study and aspirant authorship; of eager hopes for the improvement of society; of delighted communion with his friend at Hurstpierpoint; and the acquaintance formed now for the first time with eminent men—Godwin and Southey—made these months an epoch in Shelley's life. Not many days before Shelley's departure from Chesnut Cottage occurred a disturbing incident, which bears some resemblance to a strange event, afterwards to be recorded, that brought to a close his subsequent residence at Tanyrallt. The winter of 1811-12 was a time when marauders had multiplied in consequence of commercial distress, lack of employment, and the disturbed state of the country. During the dark nights of January several attempts at robbery had been made in or near Keswick. About seven o'clock on the night of Sunday, January 19, Shelley, alarmed by an unusual noise, went to the door of his cottage, opened it, and instantly received a blow which struck him to the ground, where he remained for a time senseless. Mr. Dare, his landlord, who was at hand, hearing the disturbance, rushed into the house, and the assailants, perceiving that he was armed, fled immediately.* Such is the account given by the local newspaper, and supported by statements of Shelley and Harriet. But certain residents at Keswick were sceptical respecting the reality of the supposed robber, and spoke of the affair, apparently with no sufficient reason, as a dream or hallucination of Shelley's brain.

For some time past Shelley's thoughts and hopes had tended towards Ireland. There, more than elsewhere, was being fought out, as he conceived, the struggle for political independence and religious liberty. With his desire to translate his ideas at once into action, and his passion for reforming the world, Shelley longed to be a banner-bearer where the strife was thickest and the cries of battle were most clearly uttered. When first he came to reside at Keswick he looked forward to settling before long in some picturesque, retired corner of his native county—somewhere, perhaps, in St. Leonard's Forest. But Harriet was much pleased with Keswick, and for a time there was a charm in Southey's conversation. Ireland was thought of as a remote rather than an immediate field of action ; there was a long summer in prospect which should be enjoyed at the Lakes, with all its delights enhanced to rapture by the presence of Elizabeth Hitchener. Invigorated and inspired to high achievement by close communion with that great spirit, veiled in the form of woman, Shelley

---

* Both Harriet and Shelley speak of this attack in letters to Miss Hitchener. I follow the account in the *Cumberland Pacquet*, January 28, 1811. Shelley had been suffering from "nervous complaints," and had taken a quantity of laudanum ; but it must be noted that in a letter written shortly before the date of the assault he tells Miss Hitchener that he is now "quite recovered."

might visit Ireland in the autumn, and illuminate the
unhappy land by a beam of the light of Godwin's philosophy. When, however, January arrived, Keswick was
fast losing its attraction. Shelley was daily obtaining
clearer evidence that Southey was a hireling who had
prostituted his talents in the service of tyranny, and that
the people of Keswick generally were detestable. It was
decided that a party, consisting of Percy, Harriet, and
Eliza Westbrook, should start for Dublin early in February.
There would be no want of funds, for Captain Pilfold was
sending fifty pounds, and the Duke of Norfolk would
perhaps lend a hundred ; besides, money was to be made
in Ireland by the publication of Shelley's poems and moral
essays—money which should all be squeezed out of the
rich. One thing alone was wanting to complete the happiness of the little party—the addition of Miss Hitchener to
its number. Why should she not join them at once ? " If
two hearts, panting for the happiness and liberty of mankind, were joined by union and proximity, as they are by
friendship and sympathy, what might we not expect ! . . ."
" I look up to you," he writes, " as a mighty mind. I
anticipate the era of reform with the more eagerness as
I picture to myself *you* the barrier between violence and
renovation." Harriet joined her entreaties to the more
impassioned appeal of her husband. But Miss Hitchener
was not to be moved ; her duty to some young American
pupils, little " nurslings of liberty," kept her from an
adventure across the Channel ; and it was not without
tremors that she thought of Shelley a central figure amid
Government spies and Irish assassins, perhaps facing from
the dock a hostile judge or languishing alone in a felon's
cell. The meeting with Miss Hitchener, though impossible
at present, was, however, only postponed. A paradise was
to be opened when May arrived, in the wild of North

Wales. Thither might come Miss Hitchener and her pupils, with Mrs. Adams, the "mother of her soul;" thither also the venerable Godwin. "We shall then meet in Wales. I shall try to domesticate in some antique feudal castle, whose mouldering turrets are fit emblems of decaying inequality and oppression, whilst the ivy shall wave its green banners above like liberty, and flourish upon the edifice that essayed to crush its root. As to the ghosts, I shall welcome them, though Harriet protests against my invoking them. But they would tell tales of times of old; and it would add to the picturesqueness of the scenery to see their thin forms flitting through the vaulted charnel. Perhaps the captain will come, and my aunt and the little things; perhaps you will bring the dear little Americans and my mother, Mrs. Adams. Perhaps Godwin will come, I shall try to induce him. These castles are somewhat aërial at present; but I hope it is not a crime in this mortal life to solace ourselves with hopes. Mine are always rather visionary. In the basis of this scheme, however,—if you and I live—we will not be disappointed."

The last week in Cumberland was spent with the Calverts at Greta Bank, a residence within a short distance of Keswick, on the Penrith road. Mr. Calvert strenuously opposed the Irish project; Southey also expressed his regret on hearing of the intended departure of his young friends. From Godwin came a letter of advice and warning, accompanied by an introduction to J. Philpot Curran, now Master of the Rolls in Ireland. Shelley's philosophic Mentor had informed his pupil that he felt in a measure responsible for his conduct, and was interested in him as a young man possessing extraordinary powers, and as one whose family and fortune gave him the means of being "extremely useful to his species." A few days before leaving Keswick, Shelley wrote to assure Godwin that he was no firebrand about to kindle strife in Ireland, and that as to his father he harboured no feelings of resentment or hostility.

Early in February—probably on Sunday, February 2—Shelley with his wife and sister-in-law left Keswick. It was with regret that they parted from the little mountain town which had given them harbourage for three months ; but although Shelley had bade farewell to Southey in a friendly manner, promising to write to him from Ireland, the central charm of Keswick was gone for him when he ceased to venerate and admire the presiding intellectual presence of the place. At a later date Shelley rediscovered something of Southey's true character, and looked back with pleasure to the kindness with which he had been received in the hospitable circle of Greta Hall. On February 3 the travellers were at Whitehaven, eagerly waiting for nightfall, when they might escape from a "filthy town and horrible inn." The wind which was to blow their ship to the Isle of Man was fresh and favourable. Strong in hope and nerve, Shelley looked forward to his work as an evangelist in Ireland. It is probable that February gales kept the ship for some days weather-bound in Douglas harbour. When at length they set sail in a slate-galiot, a storm whirled them quite to the north of Ireland. For eight and twenty hours they tossed in their little barque ; and it was not till the night of February 12 that the wanderers found themselves safe, after perils by sea and a weary journey by land, in Dublin city.

CHAPTER VI.

WANDERINGS—*continued.*

IRELAND—WALES—DEVON. FEBRUARY, 1812, TO AUGUST, 1812.

SHELLEY at nineteen years old was possessed by an inextinguishable hope for the world and an enthusiasm of humanity which never ceased to inspire his deeds and words. Of Irish parties and internal politics he knew but little; he was not the first or last of his countrymen who fancied that by a promenade in Ireland he could restore order from the chaos. But though Shelley had no close grip of concrete facts, he held in his hand a gospel—the gospel of reason and charity, of virtue and freedom, of William Godwin and Political Justice; and he believed that amid the rival bigotries of Irish religions and the fierce strife of contending interests there was a need for such a gospel. Shelley came to tell the Irish people that Catholic Emancipation was good, but chiefly as a pledge or promise of the ultimate victory of reason over all intolerance and all superstition, including Catholicism itself; that the repeal of the Union was better, for it would at once bring some relief to the overburdened poor, and restore wealthy proprietors who had deserted the country to a sense of their duties and privileges at home: but that there was something far beyond either of these occasional or temporary benefits towards which men should look with eyes of ardent hope—a far-off millennium of freedom, virtue, equality, happiness; that this could not be attained by sudden or violent measures; that it involved a great moral and intellectual change; that moral effects were to be looked for in the future as the result of moral causes put in operation to-day; that what Irishmen, therefore, needed before all else was not the emancipation of Catholics, not even the repeal of the Union, but sobriety, regularity, knowledge, thought, peace, benevolence—in a word, virtue and wisdom; "when you have those things," he said, "you may defy the tyrant."

In first-floor rooms at No. 7, Sackville Street, a house belonging to Mr. Dunne, a woollen-draper, Shelley and his party speedily found lodgings. Standing on the balcony outside his windows, he could see, and almost hear, the Liffey gliding under its bridges, and survey the widest avenue of Dublin—an unbroken vista from the Rotunda, at its northern end, to the late Houses of Parliament, beyond the river, to the south. Having breakfasted, and devoured with greater eagerness his letters from Miss Hitchener, Shelley sallied forth to put into a printer's hand the manuscript of an "Address to the Irish People," which he had written before leaving Keswick. It was intended for the poor, and at first Shelley's wish had been that it should be "printed in large sheets to be stuck about the walls of Dublin." He secretly hoped that it might be followed by other pamphlets, designed "to shake Catholicism on its basis, and to induce Quakerish and Socinian principles of politics, without objecting to the Christian religion, which would do no good to the vulgar just now, and cast an odium over the other principles which are advanced." The language of the pamphlet had purposely been "vulgarized" to adapt it to the humblest capacity among readers. The plan of printing the address as a broadsheet was abandoned, and the price of the pamphlet, of which fifteen hundred meanly printed copies were struck off, was fixed at the modest sum of a five-penny bit. Harriet and their friend at Hurstpierpoint had feared that Shelley was deliberately preparing for himself a reception in one of his Majesty's prisons ; but the writer of the pamphlet had no such apprehension. He felt that he came to Ireland more as the preacher of moral and intellectual reform than as a political agitator ; that he pleaded for order rather than for revolution ; or if for revolution, for one remote and vast, undertaken in the name of order, and to be approached solely by a moral and intellectual advance. He had now in hand a second pamphlet, offering proposals for an Association of Philanthropists desirous to accomplish the regeneration of Ireland. The association might regard Catholic Emancipation and the repeal of the Union as its immediate objects, but these only occupied the foreground of a prospect wide and deep. The means of operation were to be discussion and debate, with such united effort for carrying reform into effect as might be free from violence and disorder. There was no necessity to define precisely the remoter objects of the association ; it would always aim at the spread of knowledge and the promotion of virtue ; it would form a bond of union between men of benevolence and men of ideas. " The endeavours of the truly virtuous necessarily converge to one point, though it be hidden from them what point that is." In a word, Shelley's proposed association was to be an association for making men better ; it was to be primarily moral, and as such it was to deal with politics ; for politics, Shelley argued, are but a department of morals. Here had been the cause of the failure of the French Revolution. It had been preceded by a brilliant intellectual movement ; that in itself was well, for " knowledge is incompatible with slavery." " Before the restraints of

government are lessened," said Shelley, addressing the
Irish people at a time when restraints were many and
strict, "it is fit that we should lessen the necessity for
them." "I cannot," he said, "expect a rapid change. . . .
We can expect little amendment in our own time, and . . .
must be contented to lay the foundation of liberty and
happiness by virtue and wisdom." A "cautious awe" is
the temper of mind in which we ought to gaze forward and
advance towards the future golden age of freedom and
of love.

Whether such principles as these are important truths,
cheap truisms, mere revolutionary fallacies, or a mixture of
all these, they were certainly the principles which Shelley,
at the age of nineteen, put forward in his Irish pamphlets.
Until some days after the appearance of his "Address,"
on February 25, he had lived in comparative seclusion,
occupied in drawing up his second pamphlet. He could
not ally himself unreservedly to any political party. "Good
principles," he wrote, "are scarce here. The public papers
are either oppositionist or ministerial; one is as contemptible and narrow as the other. I wish I could change
this. *I*, of course, am hated by both these parties. The
remnant of United Irishmen, whose wrongs make them
hate England, I have more hopes of. I have met with no
determined Republicans, but I have found some who are
democrat*ifiable.*"

On arriving in Dublin, Shelley, bearing in his hand
Godwin's letter of introduction, had called at Curran's
house; but Curran was not at home, and though Shelley
repeated the call more than once, the result was still the
same. The incorruptible young reformer began to discover
that Curran, like Southey, was a hireling, and to dislike
him for having accepted the office of Master of the Rolls.
Though few visitors came, the days went by quickly and

not unhappily in the Sackville Street lodgings. Great
things might soon be expected, when the pamphlet should
make its appearance. Harriet sympathized with her
husband in his mission, and had suddenly been transformed
into a patriotic Irishwoman. Eliza Westbrook's opinions,
which had been gradually rectifying, were now almost
purified to proof. Two important works engaged her
thoughts—a red cloak, offspring of her artistic fancy, and,
when this should be complete, a collection of the "useful
passages" from the writings of Tom Paine. Has it been
recorded of the great prophet of Islam or any other
inspired teacher that he ever converted his sister-in-law?
Eliza, the eldest of the party, had, moreover, evidently
been assigned the position of sense-carrier to the others,
and as such she held the common purse.

"Eliza," writes Shelley, "keeps our common stock of
money for safety in some hole or corner of her dress, but
we are not all dependent on her, although she gives it out
as we want it." Fortunately as yet afflicted patriots had
not begun to prowl about the lodgings and sniff for the
spoils hidden near Miss Westbrook's heart.

Nor was the other Elizabeth forgotten by her friends
in Dublin. While Shelley penned his second pamphlet,
the spiritual presence of Miss Hitchener leant over him
and smiled approval. "I ought to count myself a favoured
mortal," he wrote to her, "with such a wife and friend
(these human names and distinctions perhaps are necessary
in the present state of society)." He was not sure but that
the agents of Government might inspect his letters to her,
but he would continue to write as freely as from Keswick.

When Miss Hitchener spoke of the duty of earning
her bread, and of her unwillingness to be dependent on
her friend's generosity, he flung himself against her frail
barriers of defence in words such as these : "You may not,

when among us, procure your own subsistence : how much
nobler a task to procure the happiness of those who love
you ! *Even* if this were all ! Besides your writings, which,
if they do not bring money, will at all events be *useful.* I
am, too, now incapable of writing compared to what I shall
be when I personally am enlightened with the emanations
of your genius, and invigorated by the deductions of your
reason. . . . Let us mingle our identities inseparably, and
burst upon tyrants with the accumulated impetuosity of
our acquirements and resolutions." The laboured sobriety
of Shelley's pamphlets and his letters to Godwin were
perhaps oppressive to a philosopher of nineteen, and he
obtained the desired relief in such outbreaks as these. To
Godwin spoke the dialectician ; to his imagined Cythna,
the poet.

That Miss Hitchener must join them in Wales, bringing
with her, if she should please, " the dear little Americans,"
was not to be questioned. One difficulty, and only one,
presented itself—how should she be named by them when
she came ? " for Eliza's name," observed Shelley, " is ' Eliza,'
and ' Miss Hitchener ' is too long, too broad, and too deep."
" Do, dear—dear—what am I to call you ? " exclaims
Harriet—" hasten your departure for us." The republican
schoolmistress pondered this weighty matter, and resolved
in favour of the name of Cato's daughter, and Brutus' wife
—the Roman *Portia.* But innocent Harriet was taken
aback by a style so lofty and classical. " I do not like the
name you have taken ; but, mind, only the name. You
are fully worthy of it ; but, being a name so much out of
the common way, it excites so much curiosity in the mind
of the hearer. This is my only reason for not liking it. I
had thought it would have been one more common and
more pleasing to the ear." * The objection was timidly

* March 14, 1812.

offered, and *Portia* was a name clinging too close to the
consciousness of Miss Hitchener to be laid aside on account
of Harriet's childish scruples.

Not quite a fortnight had passed in Dublin when the
" Address," duly advertised in an evening paper, made its
appearance. Shelley's hands at once were full of business,
scattering the good seed on the winds of spring. " For
two days," he informed Miss Hitchener, to whom he had
already despatched the first sheet of his pamphlet, " I have
omitted writing to you, but each day has been filled up
with the employment of disseminating the doctrines of
philanthropy and freedom. I have already sent four hundred of my little pamphlets into the world, and they have
excited a sensation of wonder in Dublin ; eleven hundred
yet remain for distribution. Copies have been sent to
sixty public-houses. No prosecution is yet attempted.
I do not see how it can be. Congratulate me, my friend,
for everything proceeds well. I could not expect more
rapid success." If only the patriot party in Ireland could
see that morality, not expediency, was the true principle of
politics ! But of this Shelley hoped to convince them.
" To expect that evil will produce good, or falsehood gene-
rate truth, is almost as rational as to conceive of a patriot
king or a sincere lord of the bedchamber." Would that
Elizabeth Hitchener were by his side, to share with him
" the high delight of awakening a noble nation from the
lethargy of its bondage," and by the resources of her
powerful intellect to mature and organize his undeveloped
schemes ! " For expectation is on the tiptoe. I send a
man out every day to distribute copies, with instructions
how and where to give them. His accounts correspond
with the multitudes of people who possess them. I stand
at the balcony of our window, and watch till I see a man
who looks likely ; I throw a book to him. On Monday

[March 2] my next book makes its appearance. This is addressed to a different class, recommending and proposing associations. I have in my mind a plan for proselytizing the young men at Dublin College." What might not be done when Miss Hitchener and he should unite their forces a few weeks hence in Wales? Might not associations, similar to that started in Dublin, be extended all over England, and the country be thus quietly revolutionized? "My *youth*," Shelley adds, "is much against me here. Strange that truth should not be judged by its inherent excellence, independent of any reference to the utterer. To improve on this *advantage*, the servant gave out that I was only fifteen years of age. The person who was told this, of course, did not believe it." But youth has its pleasures as well as its afflictions, and Harriet at least entered into the work of evangelization with a certain sense of girlish frolic. " I am sure," she wrote in Percy's letter to Miss Hitchener, while her husband was called away by business, "you would laugh were you to see us give the pamphlets. We throw them out of window, and give them to men that we pass in the streets. For myself I am ready to die of laughter when it is done, and Percy looks so grave. Yesterday he put one into a woman's hood of a cloak ; she knew nothing of it, and we passed her. I could hardly get on, my muscles were so irritated."

The day following that on which this letter was written was a day of political stir and excitement in Dublin. It had been decided that on February 28 an aggregate meeting of the friends of Catholic Emancipation should be held in Fishamble Street Theatre, to consider the drafts of an address to the Prince Regent, and a petition to both Houses of Parliament. Hither, at one o'clock on February 28, 1812, came Lord Fingall, the dignified and trusted leader of the Catholic cause ; hither a train of noblemen and commoners, representing the wealth and influence of almost every county in Ireland ; hither Mr. O'Connell, the burly tribune, whose large utterance was to sway the crowd that day ; and hither also came "Mr. Shelley, an English gentleman," already known by his ardent pamphlet—a slender youth, with a look of high aspiration and resolve on his sensitive lips and in his wide blue eyes. Address and petition were read and adopted. O'Connell spoke at length, reviewing the late proceedings against the Catholic committee, grasping lightly and firmly a handful of telling facts, manipulating them with incomparable force and skill, and calling forth, with easy ascendency over his audience, indignation, laughter, or resolve. A vote of thanks had been proposed to " the distinguished Protestants who have this day honoured us with their presence." In response to this resolution, Shelley rose and spoke for more than an hour. He was an Englishman, he told his hearers ; and when he reflected on the crimes committed by his nation on Ireland, he could not but blush for his countrymen, did he not know that arbitrary power never failed to corrupt the heart of man. He had come to Ireland for the sole purpose of interesting himself in the misfortunes of the country, and impressed with a full conviction of the necessity of Catholic Emancipation, and of the baneful effects which the union with Great Britain had entailed upon Ireland.

Chief Baron Woulfe, an Irish judge, recalling to mind, after an interval of many years, the meeting of February 28, 1812, spoke of Shelley's mode of address as cold and precise ; he paused ever and anon, and delivered his slow sentences as so many disconnected aphorisms. A maiden-speech is seldom characterized by spontaneous movement or easy force. Shelley may in general have studiously avoided appeals to passion, and, compensating for his extremely youthful appearance by an excess of gravity, have given play to the moralist and dialectician within him rather than to the orator. It can hardly be supposed that Shelley's speech gave satisfaction to Lord Fingall and the chief leaders of the movement; they did not care to embarrass their position by attacks upon the Union with Great Britain; they were aristocrats, not republicans or humanitarian dreamers; while urging their grievance, they desired to conciliate the Government by professions of loyalty. But they seem to have been patient with the young enthusiast—possibly they did not take him over-seriously.

After the meeting of February 28, Shelley remained for more than a month in Dublin. For a few days there may have been a lull of excitement, while he waited for the appearance of his second pamphlet; but it cannot have been of long duration. On March 7 appeared in the Dublin *Weekly Messenger*, an article headed "Pierce Byshe Shelly, Esq," which pointed out the young English gentleman as "a missionary of truth," devoted to "social benevolence." Naturally, after this, Mr. Shelley had visitors, and we can imagine that No. 17, Grafton Street, to which he had lately moved from his Sackville Street lodgings, became a kind of Hibernian cave of Adullam. "My brain has hardly time to consult my heart," he wrote to Miss Hitchener on March 10, "or my heart to consult my brain; yet with the remaining nature, with thee who constitutest the Trinity of my Essence, I will converse. I cannot recount all the horrible instances of unrestricted and licensed tyranny that have met my ears, scarcely those which have personally occurred to me." "I am sick," proceeds Shelley, "of this city, and long to be with you and peace. The rich grind the poor into abjectness, and then complain that they are abject. They goad them to famine, and hang them if they steal a loaf." It

was with a certain desperation that Shelley now clung
to his project of illuminating and elevating the Irish
people. "The association proceeds slowly, and I fear will
not be established. Prejudices are so violent, in contra-
diction to my principles, that more hate me as a freethinker than love me as a votary of freedom. . . . I have
at least made a stir here, and set some men's minds afloat.
I *may* succeed, but I fear I shall not, in the main object
of associations. . . . I have daily had numbers of people
calling on me; *none* will do. The spirit of bigotry is
high."

Some interesting acquaintances Shelley had made
during his residence in Dublin, which was now drawing
to a close. Curran, after long delay, called, and Shelley
twice dined at his house; but in 1812 the genius of Curran
was in its decline. The fire which animated his mean and
decrepit person was sinking; the light had faded from his
eye; his face looked yellow, wrinkled, and livid; he fell
into fits of melancholy silence. Of the contrast, however,
between Curran's earlier and later self, Shelley could be
no judge, and on the occasion of his visits Curran was
animated. What struck Shelley most and impressed him
unfavourably, was the lack of elevation in Curran's table-
talk. He had expected something different from the
advocate of the United Irishmen. The weary Master of
the Rolls, escaped from his official work, sought relief
in easy conversation, witty turns of speech, and tales
of drollery. Shelley had hoped to find him not un-
interested in freedom, virtue, wisdom, and humanity.
More to Shelley's liking than Curran was Curran's
devoted admirer, Mr. Lawless, a well-known Irish politician and a member of the Catholic Board. "Honest
Jack Lawless," though he confessed that he regarded
Shelley's ultimate hopes for society as visionary, was

believed by his young friend to be of sound republican principles; he was ardent and energetic; more zealous, perhaps, than discreet; gifted with a certain eloquence, which served the purpose of agitation, but too flighty to be trusted for organizing, sustaining, or directing a great movement. In him and his wife, Shelley and Harriet found their most intimate Dublin friends. He it probably was who wrote the article in the *Weekly Messenger* setting forth Shelley's virtues and beneficence.

We catch a glimpse of another Irish friend of the Shelleys from a letter of Harriet to Miss Hitchener, dated March 18. "My dear Portia," she wrote, " . . . I believe I have mentioned a new acquaintance of ours, a Mrs. Nugent, who is sitting in the room now and talking to Percy about virtue." Catherine Nugent, who was now more than twice as old as Harriet or Percy, and in old-fashioned style had changed the "Miss" to "Mrs.," was a woman of no ordinary character and intellect. Small of person and plain of feature, she yet charmed and attached those who rightly knew her by her energy of mind, by the vivacity of her conversation, and by the warmth and generosity of her heart. Though born a Catholic, she did not hold strictly by the creed or practices of her religion. "She has felt most severely the miseries of her country," wrote Harriet to Miss Hitchener, "in which she has been a very active member. She visited all the prisons in the time of the Rebellion to exhort the people to have courage and hope." Miss Nugent in 1812 earned her living as assistant in a furrier's shop in Grafton Street—"there she is every day," says sympathetic Harriet, "confined to her needle." A poor man had offered her Shelley's pamphlet for a few pence, stating that a bundle of such papers had been given him by a young gentleman with directions to get what he could for them—at all events to distribute them. "Inquiry was made at Shelley's lodgings to ascertain the truth of the vendor's story. He was not at home, but when he heard of it he went to return the visit, and kindly acquaintanceship thus arose." At this time Shelley, his wife, and sister-in-law were recent converts to the principles of vegetarianism. "You do not know," wrote Harriet to Miss Hitchener on March 14, "that we have forsworn meat, and adopted the Pythagorean system. About a fortnight has elapsed since the change, and we do not find ourselves any the worse for it. . . . We are delighted with it, and think it the best thing in the world." But, although in the fervour of a new faith, they were not intolerant, and when Miss Nugent, after her day's work, would come to discourse with Percy or Harriet about virtue, they relaxed for her benefit the severity of their code, and, pitying her infirmity, presented for their friend's dinner a murdered fowl.

To confirm Shelley's growing apprehension that little good was to be done by him in Ireland, came letters of warning—almost of condemnation—from Godwin. On the appearance of his first pamphlet he had forwarded a copy to his philosophic friend, announcing at the same time a second pamphlet, in which he was about to recommend "the institution of a philanthropic society." Shelley had to meet the general objection of Godwin, that he, whose age disqualified him, should have come forward as a teacher of men; and a special objection to his scheme of an association, such banding together of men for political purposes having been expressly condemned by the author of "Political Justice." "No *unnatural unanimity*," argued Shelley, "can take place, if secessions of the minority on any question are invariably made. It might segregate into twenty different societies, each coinciding generically, though differing specifically." And as to the

K

position which he had prematurely assumed of preacher
or teacher : " In the first place, my physical constitution
is such as will not permit me to hope for a life so long as
yours ;—the person who is constitutionally nervous, and
affected by slight fatigue at the age of nineteen, cannot
expect firmness and health at fifty. I have therefore resolved to husband whatever powers I may possess, so that
they may turn to the best account. . . . My publications
will present to the moralist and metaphysician a picture
of a mind, however uncultured and unformed, which had
at the dawn of its knowledge taken a singular turn ; and
to leave out the early lineaments of its appearance, would
be to efface those which the attrition of the world had
not deprived of right-angled originality. Thus much for
egotism."

Southey had afflicted Shelley by foreclosing discussion
with the words, " When you are as old as I am you will
think with me." Godwin gazed down on his young disciple
from a yet higher elevation of years. " As far as I can
yet penetrate into your character," he wrote, " I conceive
it to exhibit an extraordinary assemblage of lovely qualities,
not without considerable defects. The defects do and
always have arisen chiefly from this source—that you are
still very young, and that in certain essential respects you
do not sufficiently perceive that you are so."

" Your letter," replied Shelley in a humble strain, though
as yet unconvinced, "affords me much food for thought ;
guide thou and direct me. In all the weakness of my
inconsistencies bear with me ; the genuine respect which
I bear for your character, the love with which your virtues
have inspired me, is undiminished by any suspicion of
externally constituted authority ; when you reprove me,
Reason speaks ; I acquiesce in her decisions. I know that
I am vain, that I assume a character which is perhaps

unadapted to the limitedness of my experience, that I am
without the modesty which is so generally considered an
indispensable ornament to the ingenuousness of youth. I
attempt not to conceal from others or myself these defici-
encies, if such they are. That I have erred in pursuance of
this line of conduct I am well aware : in the opposite case
I think that my errors would have been more momentous
and overwhelming. 'A preponderance of resulting good
is imagined in every action.' I certainly believe that the
line of conduct which I am now pursuing will produce a
preponderance of good ; when I get rid of this conviction
my conduct will be changed." Will truth alone convert
the world, without generous advocates of the truth united
to press its claims upon an unheeding generation ? It is
nearly twenty years since " Political Justice " was first
published. "What has followed? Have men ceased to
fight ? Have vice and misery vanished from the earth ?
Have the fireside communications which it recommends
taken place ? . . . I think of the last twenty years with
impatient scepticism as to the progress which the human
mind has made during this period. I will own that I am
eager that something should be done."

One more letter of remonstrance from Godwin, and
Shelley, now discovering on his own account that the
scheme of an association had proved impracticable, was
reduced to submission. " Political Justice," its author
admitted, had not converted the world in the course of a
couple of decades ; but what of that ? " Oh that I could
place you on the pinnacle of ages, from which these twenty
years would shrink to an invisible point ! It is not after
this fashion that moral causes work in the eye of Him
who looks profoundly through the vast and, allow me to
add, venerable machine of human society. But so reasoned
the French revolutionists. Auspicious and admirable

materials were working in the general mind of France;
but these men said as you say, 'When we look on the last
twenty years we are seized with a sort of moral scepticism
—we must own we are eager that something should be
done.' And see what has been the result of their doings!
He that would benefit mankind on a comprehensive scale,
by changing the principles and elements of society, must
learn the hard lesson—to put off self, and to contribute by
a quiet but incessant activity, like a rill of water, to irrigate
and fertilize the intellectual soil. Shelley, you are preparing
a scene of blood!"

On the same day on which Shelley wrote his last letter
from Ireland to William Godwin, he packed the remaining
copies of his pamphlets in a box, which was addressed to
Miss Hitchener, and forwarded to her by the Holyhead
packet. Beside the pamphlets the box contained copies
of a "Declaration of Rights," printed in the form of a folio
poster or broadside. In thirty-one brief aphorisms Shelley
set forth his political creed. Government has no rights;
it exists only by the consent of those who delegate to it
certain powers reclaimable at will; the rights of man are
liberty and an equal participation of the commonage of
nature; liberty includes the right to think, the right to
express one's thoughts, and the right to a certain degree of
leisure; these rights are universal; the only use of government is to repress the vices of man;—these, and other
principles in harmony with them, are announced with clearness, decision, and an absoluteness of thought and phrase.
Among the contents of the large deal box was a letter
from Harriet to her "dear Portia," written on St. Patrick's
Night, when "the Irish always get very tipsy." " Disperse
the declarations," she advises Miss Hitchener; " Percy says
the farmers are very fond of having something posted upon
their walls. . . . All thoughts of an association are given

up as impracticable. We shall leave this noisy town on
April 7, unless the Habeas Corpus Act should be suspended,
and then we shall be obliged to leave *as soon as possible.*
Adieu." Shelley's consignment of "inflammable matter,"
as Harriet styles it, was inspected by the Surveyor of
Customs at Holyhead, and Harriet's letter was found and
read. Without delay the Secretary of State, the Secretary
of the Post Office, and the Irish Secretary, Mr. Wellesley
Pole, were informed of the notable discovery; but these
high officials were less disturbed by the tidings than were
their agents at Holyhead. No action in the matter seems
to have been taken further than that the authorities resolved
to have an eye on Miss Hitchener, and on that extraordinary young man, the son of the member for New
Shoreham.

After a visit which had lasted seven weeks, Shelley
with his wife and sister-in-law set sail from Dublin to
Holyhead at two o'clock in the afternoon of Saturday,
April 4. They tacked against a baffling wind to get clear
of land; the whole of Sunday they struggled against the
breeze; and at length, two hours past midnight, reached
Holyhead in a drenching mist. Lighted by the sailors'
lanterns, they scrambled for a mile over the rough way
and having tasted no food since leaving Dublin, and being
much exhausted by the voyage, they forgot that they were
Pythagoreans, and fell to with exceeding good will upon a
supper of meat—the abhorred thing. It was Shelley's
intention, when leaving Dublin, to settle, if possible, in
Merionethshire; the beauty of the district had been vividly
described in Godwin's novel "Fleetwood," and here it
might be Shelley's happiness to receive the venerable
author of "Fleetwood" as his guest. Having rested for
a day at Holyhead, the travellers started on Tuesday for
the south; but no house of suitable size and suitable rent

could they hear of within range of the scene of Fleetwood's early life. From Barmouth, with its sands and terraced rock, they set off in an open boat for Aberystwith, thirty miles distant by water. Here Harriet and Eliza had spent part of the last summer; but neither in the "sweet shire of Cardigan" could they discover a dwelling-place to their liking. At length, after a week's wandering, Shelley with his companions found himself (April 14) once more close to Cwm Elan, where his cousin Thomas Grove had his summer residence, and where he himself—not, as now, happy in the society of a wife and illuminated sister-in-law —had passed some weeks of the preceding July and August. Nantgwillt, named after the "wild brook" which flowed near, was an old and roomy house, beautifully situated a little above the junction of the Elan and Clearwen, and was distant about a mile or a mile and a half from the residence of Mr. Grove. It seemed in every respect a desirable place in which to settle. As yet they could obtain possession of only a portion of the house, but when it was wholly in their hands, what should hinder them from receiving in this romantic retreat their venerable friend Godwin with his wife and family; their adored Portia with her little nurslings of liberty; and perhaps her father, to whom the management of the farm would be an amusement, while his daughter and her friend might occupy themselves in promoting by their writings the highest interests of humanity? Some of the feelings which had possessed Shelley during his visit to the Irish capital now took form in verse. Here, perhaps, was written a short unpublished poem entitled "The Tombs," expressing a faith in the immortality of

> "Courage and charity and truth
> And high devotedness,"

even in presence of the mouldering clay of the patriot's

brain and heart, and amid the mournful emblems of the grave. To Nantgwillt also may belong the unpublished verses "On Robert Emmet's Grave"—a piece of seven stanzas, which thus reaches its close:—

" No trump tells thy virtues—the grave where they rest
    With thy dust shall remain unpolluted by fame,
Till thy foes, by the world and by fortune carest,
    Shall pass like a mist from the light of thy name.

" When the storm-cloud that lowers o'er the day-beam is gone,
    Unchanged, unextinguished its lifespring will shine ;
When Erin has ceased with their memory to groan,
    She will smile through the tears of revival on thine."

The metre was perhaps a reminiscence from Campbell's "Wounded Huzzar."

As late as 1878 a tourist to Cwm Elan, who loved the poetry of Shelley and knew the story of his life,* came at Nantgwillt upon an old woman who remembered a visitor at Mr. Grove's house when she was a little girl and carried the post-bag—"a very strange gentleman," one who on week-days wore a little cap, and had his neck bare, but went on Sundays in a tall hat, and so nice-looking, with the family to church ; who bought for her at the sale at Nantgwillt House the little brass kettle on which she had set her heart—"him that put the five-pound note on the boat." Who could the strange gentleman have been but Shelley ? and in the memory of old Elizabeth Jones probably reminiscences of Shelley's visits of 1811 and 1812 had run together. He loved, she said, to sail in the rapid mountain-streams a wooden boat about a foot in length, and would run along the banks, using a pole to direct his craft and keep it from shipwreck on the rocks. On one memorable occasion a banknote served as sail, and little

* My friend, Mr. W. J. Craig.

Elizabeth wished that it had been hers. Once the young gentleman provided a captain or coxswain for his boat in the person of a cat; and she remembered his wild peals of laughter—for he was full of fun—when the cat, proving an unwilling sailor, leaped from shallop to rock, and then again from one rock to another, until the bank was reached.

One literary acquaintance, who afterwards became a friend, Shelley is said to have met for the first time while staying during this spring and summer in the neighbourhood of Rhayader. Thomas Love Peacock, in 1812, was in his twenty-seventh year—older by seven years than Shelley—and was already known as the author of several pieces of verse possessing a character and distinction of their own. He was a lover of Welsh landscape, and was drawn towards Carnarvonshire by a peculiar attraction, for there resided Miss Jane Gryffydth, who afterwards became his wife. In person, as well as in gifts of the mind, he was no ordinary man—tall and handsome, with a profusion of bright brown hair, extravagant in its disarray; eyes of fine, dark blue; massive brow; shapely features; graceful, laughing lips; and complexion as fair as a girl's. His way of thinking was that of easy liberality. His conversation sparkled with keen, ironic wit; he told a good story, and brought out its points with vivacity. He viewed all things from a certain mundane point of view, mocking at the follies, affectations, and extravagances around him; yet he never became a mere man of the world. Something of the poet was curiously allied in him to the laughing philosopher. He was well read in Greek and Latin authors, had some knowledge of ancient art, and had already seen something of life and of society. Through Peacock's introduction it is probable that Shelley came into communication with Peacock's publishers, the Hookhams, of Bond Street.

The happiness of the April days at Nantgwillt was soon

dashed by anxieties and annoyance. Harriet, before the
month had ended, was seriously ill, with a feverish gastric
attack, which left her so weak that she could not walk
across the room without assistance; it was deemed necessary to send for the nearest physician, at a distance of forty
miles. Shelley was himself harassed with legal vexations,
for the proprietor of Nantgwillt House refused to accept
his new tenant without satisfactory security for the payment
of rent, and this Shelley found himself unable to procure.
Moreover, letters came in quick succession from Miss
Hitchener, informing him of odious and scandalous reports
current at Hurst and Cuckfield and Horsham with respect
to him and her, and the visit which she proposed to pay to
him and Harriet at midsummer. A flush of indignation
mounted from Shelley's heart to his head. These slanders,
he believed, were the mischievous inventions of Mrs.
Pilfold, who feared that if Miss Hitchener left Sussex her
children might lose the services of an admirable teacher.
But neither Mrs. Pilfold nor Mr. Hitchener, who had forbidden his daughter to visit the Shelleys, should dash the
cup of happiness from the lips of those about to drink.
This short period of anxiety and distress was but "the
probationary state" before they should "all enter the
heaven of virtue and friendship." Shelley instantly and
impetuously wrote to Captain Pilfold and to Mr. Hitchener.
Could the captain credit such malicious calumnies? And
who was Mr. Hitchener that he should refuse an invitation
addressed to his daughter? Who made him her governor?
"You have agitated her mind until her frame is seriously
deranged. Take care, sir; you may destroy her by disease,
but her mind is free; *that* you cannot hurt. . . . Adieu.
When next I hear from you I hope that time will have
liberalized your sentiments."

Shelley's excitement and vexations were followed by a

sharp feverish attack.   Nantgwillt House could not be had without offering security for a considerable sum.   " These accidents," said Shelley to Godwin, " are unavoidable to a minor."   It became evident that they must seek a home elsewhere.   It would be desirable to find some modest place of abode ; and from Godwin they had heard of a cottage which might suit them at Chepstow, within reach of Tintern Abbey and the woods and cliffs of Piercefield. They had thought of pushing on to Ilfracombe, but if the cottage at Chepstow proved to be attractive, they would settle there—leave Eliza in possession of it, and make their way across country to Hurst, to bear off Miss Hitchener from the enemies who now compassed her around.

Perhaps Miss Hitchener discouraged Shelley and Harriet in this enterprise, which certainly was not carried into effect.   On a late day in June the travellers saw the last of Cwm Elan, and journeyed south towards Chepstow, with which they were already, as it were, connected by the waters of the Wye.   But after the wild loveliness of Cwm Elan and Nantgwillt, the scenery of Chepstow, exquisite though it be, seemed tame and uninteresting.   The cottage was unfinished, and unfit for the reception of tenants ; besides, it was too small for their requirements.   Accordingly they decided to carry out their original intention of visiting Ilfracombe ; and, perhaps crossing the Severn by the Beachley ferry, they made their way through Somerset, with its leafy lanes, to the coast of North Devon.   Descending on foot or horseback the precipitous path—hardly then a road—which dropped from Countisbury westwards, and drew towards the sea, they saw before and beneath them a fairy scene—little Lynmouth, then some thirty cottages, rose-clad and myrtle-clad, nestling at the foot of the hills. It was enough.   Why should they wander farther, if by good fortune one of these straw-thatched cottages might be theirs?

And by good fortune one—and only one—was to be had. Before it lay the summer sea; behind rose the summer hills, broken into coombes, through which the twin streams, which give its name to the village, leaped and foamed and flashed, or coiled in quiet pools amid a landscape of sylvan loveliness. "Shelley often expressed to me," wrote Hogg, "the most lively admiration of the Valley of Rocks . . . and this picturesque valley made an indelible impression upon his memory. It was not less lasting than forcible, for during the whole of his too brief life, even until its disastrous and too early termination, it was his habit to sketch or scrawl, almost unconsciously, with his pen upon the fly-leaves of books, on the backs of letters, and in note-books, and occasionally even upon the wall or wainscot, points, spires, and pinnacles of rocks and crags as recollections and memorials of the fascinating spot."

By the end of June Shelley and his household were settled in Mrs. Hooper's lodgings at Lynmouth. The rooms were tiny, but their number in some degree compensated their size. One was already assigned, in delighted anticipation, to Miss Hitchener: might not Godwin and his wife and daughters occupy the others? But while Shelley's pen was running on to the invitation, Harriet interposed—the rooms were no better than servants' rooms, the beds were coarse as those of peasants, and Godwin's health was delicate; better wait until they should own a house in London, when their friend of Skinner Street and his family might come and live with them for ever. Meanwhile could not Fanny Godwin—the daughter of Mary Wollstonecraft by her first husband, Imlay—be persuaded to visit them at Lynmouth? If their venerated friend, knowing what to expect, chose to accompany her, their happiness would be thereby enhanced; but he should be prepared for a republican plainness of living. On Fanny's behalf Godwin declined the invitation—he must make their personal acquaintance before his daughter could be their guest; an idle excuse—so thought Shelley and Harriet—for were they not perfectly acquainted with the author of "Political Justice," although they had never beheld his face? But from Godwin that might well be borne which, coming from another, would have been occasion of offence. "I should regard it as my greatest glory," Shelley wrote (June 11), "should I be judged worthy to solace your declining years; it is a pleasure the realization of which I anticipate with confident hopes, and which it shall be my study to deserve. I will endeavour to subdue the impatience of my nature, so incompatible with true benevolence." To temper Shelley's revolutionary zeal, Godwin had tried to win him to the study of history, and hoped that the age of chivalry, by its heroic ideals and charms for the imagination, might attract him and bind him in loyalty to the past; and Shelley was at least docile in disposition. "I yet know little of the chivalric age. The ancient romances, in which are depicted the manners of those times, never fell in my way. I have read Southey's 'Amadis of Gaul' and 'Palmerin of England,' but at a time when I was little disposed to philosophize on the manners they describe. I have also read his 'Chronicle of the Cid.' It is written in a simple and impressive style, and surprised me by the extent of accurate reading evinced by the references. But I read it hastily, and it did not please me so much as it will on a reperusal seasoned by your authority and opinion."* A little later, sharing some of his wife's and daughters' surprise and disappointment that Shelley had not settled in the house which they had recommended at Chepstow,

* June 11, 1812.

Godwin took it upon him to read his young friend a
lecture, mildly severe, on the duty of a plain, philosophic,
republican way of life, and the wickedness of pampering
selfish whims or accumulating personal luxuries. For all
that Godwin knew, the Chepstow house might indeed be
"of the dimensions of a pig-sty." "Nor is it my habit,"
he added, "to reason directly to a particular case; the
bent of my mind's eye is always towards a general
principle." With admirable temper and the grace of
perfect manners, Shelley replied. A letter already on
its way would explain to Godwin that he was trying to live
modestly on a modest income, rather than burden his
patrimony by raising money on his expectations, and that
if he was an heir "panting for twenty-one," his hopes and
desires were of no selfish kind. "My letter, dated the
5th, will prove to you that it is *not* to live in splendour,
which I hate; *not* to accumulate indulgences, which I
despise, that my present conduct was adopted." His
Lynmouth cottage was no home of luxury; it was more
like a peasant's dwelling. Were he to work at the loom,
or his wife engage in culinary business, would that add to
their usefulness? "See my defence. Yet, my esteemed
and venerated friend, accept my thanks; consider yourself
as yet more beloved by me for the manner in which you
have reproved my suppositionary errors, and ever may
you, like the tenderest and wisest of parents, be on the
watch to detect those traits of vice which, yet undiscovered,
are marked on the tablet of my character, so that I pursue
undeviatingly the path which you first cleared through
the wilderness of life." Godwin's young disciple would
seem to have gained already some of that mild and
equable benevolence which his counsellor had recommended, and to have found unexpected occasion for putting
it to use.

The Lynmouth cottagers were now eagerly expecting the arrival of Miss Hitchener. Shelley had bespoken for her a kind reception from William Godwin, as she passed through London on her way to Devon. So introduced, she was kindly received. On July 14 she supped and slept at Godwin's house ; next morning she took her leave, bearing a letter from him to Shelley, and, after a brief interval of time, her presence must have irradiated the rose and myrtle embowered cottage by the sea. " I have much to talk to you about," wrote Shelley, in anticipation of her arrival—" innate passions, God, Christianity, etc." And when the tall, dark, thin, foreign-looking lady, with the long black hair and Roman features, had recovered from her fatigue, doubtless there were eager and eloquent debates on things terrestrial and things celestial. She brought her friends interesting, yet not wholly satisfactory news of William Godwin, who had seemed to her to regard himself with too fond an admiration, and who held himself strangely aloof from his own domestic circle. It was agreed between the ladies that the name " Portia " should be dropped, and the simpler " Bessy " take its place ; and soon Bessy, when not talking, or laughing, or languishing, was eagerly engaged in reading Shelley's manuscript passages from Irish history, or writing at his instigation in the service of humanity.

These days of July and August which went by on the Devon coast were probably among the happiest days of Shelley's early life. His love for Harriet was ardent and unmarred by fleck or flaw ; in his relations with Miss Hitchener he had not yet passed from enthusiasm to disillusion ; welcome letters arrived now and again from Godwin ; parcels of books, to be read and discussed with Bessy, were ordered from London ; and Shelley's mind was vigorously occupied with a new prose pleading on behalf of liberty of speech, and with enterprises of pith and moment in English verse.

"You must know," Shelley had written from Dublin to Godwin, "that I either am, or fancy myself, something of a poet." Several unpublished pieces would seem to have been inspired by the beauty, not untouched by awe and terror, of wild Wales.* The poetical mood was not likely to pass away when Shelley found himself at Lynmouth, still amid hills and rushing brooks, and now in presence of the ever-changing sea. It was certainly at Lynmouth, and in August, 1812, that Shelley, stirred to creation by the mystery and music of the waves, wrote a fragment of some three hundred lines—still in manuscript—entitled "The Voyage." Here also on the Devon coast was probably written "A Retrospect of Times of Old"—a rhymed piece, also unpublished, having much in common with those earlier pages of "Queen Mab," which picture the fall of empires, and celebrate the oblivion that has overtaken the old rulers of men and lords of the earth. Now, too, Shelley was actually engaged on "Queen Mab." Whether or not it had been conceived long before, we cannot for certain tell; at Nantgwillt, Cwm Elan, and Lynmouth it probably began to take its present shape. In form "Queen Mab" agrees with "The Voyage;" in substance it has kinship with "A Retrospect of Times of Old."

Shelley's private happiness did not dull his sensibility to the wrongs and sorrows of the world. Of all those "rights of man" of which his broadsheet "Declaration" spoke, he probably valued most highly the right to freedom of thought and speech. In March, 1812, Daniel Isaac Eaton, a bookseller of Ave Maria Lane, was prosecuted in the Court of King's Bench for publishing, at his

---

* Some of these, however, may belong to Shelley's visit in 1811.

" Ratiocinatory, or Magazine for Truth and Good Sense," a blasphemous and profane libel on the Holy Scriptures entitled " The Age of Reason : Part the Third. By Thomas Payne." The jury, guided by a vigorous charge from Lord Ellenborough, did not long delay in finding Eton guilty, and he was sentenced on May 8 to eighteen months' imprisonment in Newgate, and during the first month to stand in the pillory for an hour in the Old Bailey. On May 26, amid the waving of hats and cheering of the crowd, Eaton, a man upwards of sixty years of age, underwent his public punishment, and not a voice or arm was raised against him. Popular sentiment had outrun the law, and whether it was in sympathy with Tom Paine's audacities or not, condemned the last relic of the fire-and-fagot system of suppressing heresy. In the solitude of Lynmouth, perhaps with Miss Hitchener as sympathetic listener to the pleading, " A Letter to Lord Ellenborough " was completed, and Shelley entrusted his manuscript to Mr. Syle, a well-known printer and bookseller of Barnstaple, the little metropolis of North Devon, distant some eighteen miles from Lynton. It is said that Shelley ordered a thousand copies to be printed, and that the printer, taking alarm at an incident presently to be related, after perhaps a tenth of this number had been delivered into the author's hands, suppressed and destroyed the remaining sheets The " Letter to Lord Ellenborough," written before Shelley was twenty years old, has clearness and vigour, and is certainly superior in style to anything which he had previously written. It was legal, Shelley admits, that Mr Eaton should suffer punishment because he denied the divinity and resurrection of Jesus Christ ; it may even have been politic ; but was it just? was it moral? was it in accordance with the principles of reason, or even with the teaching of Jesus Christ Himself?

By July 29 Shelley had received the pamphlet from his printer, for on that day he forwarded twenty-five copies to his acquaintance in Old Bond Street, Thomas Hookham; a parcel of fifty copies followed the twenty-five on August 18; and single copies were despatched to Lord Sidmouth, Sir Francis Burdett, and some private friends of the author. He was eagerly desirous to impress his opinions on others, and at the same time, bearing in mind Eaton's pillory and imprisonment, was apprehensive of drawing down a prosecution on any over-hardy publisher who should venture to set forth his dangerous wares. These were now accumulating on his hands. Copies of the Irish pamphlets were in his possession, copies of the "Letter to Lord Ellenborough," copies of the broadside "Declaration of Rights," and copies of a broadside ballad entitled "The Devil's Walk"—a satire on Church and State, poor in verse and poor in wit, modelled on that well-known piece in which Southey and Coleridge had laid their heads together, and which, in one of its forms, bore the same title as Shelley's extravaganza. This last had been composed in Dublin, and was perhaps printed by Mr. Syle, of Barnstaple. It was certainly inconvenient to be in possession of so much "inflammable matter," as Harriet had termed it, now accumulating in certain heavy chests, and yet to find it so difficult to inflame the world, or even one small fishing-village of Devon. But the author of these papers was a poet, and could negotiate with higher powers than those of Paternoster Row or Old Bond Street. The winds and the waves were publishers against whom no Attorney-General could file an information; even my lord Ellenborough could not condemn the summer gales, or the surge and rollers of the Atlantic to pillory and imprisonment. Already, as an Eton schoolboy, Shelley had learnt how to send a fire-balloon on its errand to the sky; lately, at

L

Nantgwillt, he had delighted in sailing his rough toy-boat upon the mountain-stream. Why should not a fire-balloon be the emissary of freedom, and bear a "Declaration of Rights" or a "Devil's Walk" across the midnight sky, to be found next morning, perhaps, by some Welsh husbandman or Devon milkmaid in field or farmyard? The "Devil" would also submit to be bottled, like the Arabian Afreet in the jar, and might float away on the August waves, possibly to be drawn to shore in the net of some unsuspecting fisherman or coastguard needing illumination. For the more important "Declaration of Rights" there might be constructed a little box, covered with bladder, well resined and waxed to keep out the water, with lead below to maintain it in an upright position, and a tiny mast and sail above to attract attention at sea. Thus fitted out, his craft might sail to unknown coasts— might catch the eye of some patriot on the Irish shore, or might be drawn on board some passing vessel, to sustain and encourage that generosity and love of freedom commonly found among seafaring men in trading brigs, or to startle the crew of some king's ship from the apathy of their servitude. Accordingly, we discover Shelley—a boyish figure—in the August days, alone or accompanied by a tall, foreign-looking female (taken by some for a maidservant), on the Lynmouth beach, pushing certain small boxes, each with its mast and sail, from the rocks ; or watching from his boat a little flotilla of dark green bottles, tightly corked, which rise and sink as the waves sway them seawards. Or we see him in the twilight launching his fiery craft, laden with truth and virtue, into the evening air.

Sea and air had been invaded by Shelley's envoys, and the element of fire was his servant ; it remained to operate somehow on this solid earth. Might it not be

possible to send the "Declaration of Rights" from hand
to hand among the inhabitants of Devonshire, or to exhibit
the broadside in some public place where all might read?
The "Declaration," Shelley had written from Nantgwillt
to Miss Hitchener, "would be useful in farmhouses; it
was by a similar expedient that Franklin promulgated his
commercial opinions among the Americans." Best of all
it would be if North Devon could be attacked at its heart
and centre—Barnstaple. And happily Shelley had by
his side an ally and minister, less radiant and spiritual
than the genius of fire, but better suited for operating in
the streets of a country town. One treasure Shelley had
brought with him from Dublin to Wales, and had never
since relinquished—an honest, blundering Irishman; short,
thick-set, and hard-featured. It was Dan Healey, who, to
enhance the fame of his young master's political achievements, had given out in Dublin that he was but fifteen
years old; it was blundering Dan who had despatched
Shelley's packets, containing pamphlets to be forwarded
to Godwin and Miss Hitchener, by post instead of by
coach, thereby causing the impecunious philosopher to
pay a charge of £1 1s. 8d., for which injury his young
friend duly received a mild rebuke. Dan was warmly
attached to his master—ready, he declared, "to go through
fire and water" for Shelley. For his part Shelley, though
bearing a friendly feeling to Dan, found him somewhat of
a superfluity at Lynmouth; it was difficult to make him
useful; he was certainly not ornamental. Shelley feared
that he must part with Dan; then, as if to discover a use
for him, thought of sending him to Dublin to look after
the poems in the Irish Stockdale's hands. Now, however,
the Irishman's opportunity had come! he was to wake
and find himself famous, at least in Barnstaple, and was to
be heard of even by high officials of the State.

On the evening of Wednesday, August 19, a man was observed distributing and posting up certain papers about Barnstaple—papers which bore the heading "Declaration of Rights," and began with the formidable words, "Government has no rights." It was felt in Barnstaple that if Government has no rights it has at least duties, and one obvious duty was to arrest this sower of sedition. On being brought before the mayor the prisoner stated that his name was Daniel Hill (why should Dan bring the honourable family of Healey to shame before the Sassenach?), and that he was servant to P. B. Shelley, Esq., now residing at Lynmouth. Asked how he became possessed of these seditious papers, Hill replied that on his road from Lynton he had met a gentleman in black who begged him to take the papers to Barnstaple and post and distribute them, the unknown gentleman giving him five shillings for his trouble. As for himself, Hill did not know how to read, and was ignorant of the deadly contents of the documents of which he was the bearer. Not satisfied with Dan's story of the gentleman in black, the mayor made inquiries about the man's master, and learnt that Mr. Shelley was viewed with suspicion at Lynmouth and Lynton on the ground of his unusually large correspondence. Who but a conspirator could want to write sixteen letters of a day, including one addressed to that notorious patron of the discontented, Sir Francis Burdett? Moreover, Mr. Shelley had been frequently observed to drop bottles into the sea, and once was watched while wading, bottle in hand, into the water, on which occasion his consignment to the waves had drifted to shore, and, being captured, was found to be as full of sedition as an egg is of meat. Thus fortified in his ill opinion, the loyal mayor of Barnstaple made haste to convict honest Daniel in ten penalties of twenty pounds each, for publishing and dispersing printed papers without the printer's name affixed ; in lieu of payment, the prisoner should undergo confinement for six months in the common gaol of the borough. On the day after Healey's arrest Shelley arrived from Lynmouth to look after his servant, and if possible obtain his discharge. To pay such a sum as two hundred pounds for Dan's freedom was not in his master's power, but it was arranged that for a weekly fee of fifteen shillings the prisoner should be granted certain immunities and privileges, and this provision for his relief Shelley was prepared to make.

These important events formed the subject of communication between the town-clerk of Barnstaple and Lord Sidmouth, then Secretary of State for the Home Department ; and again between the Barnstable post-master, the secretary of the Post Office, and the Earl of Chichester, joint Postmaster-General with the Earl of Sandwich. Lord Chichester had already some acquaintance with the " Declaration of Rights," for a copy had been forwarded to him from Holyhead in April, when the chest of papers addressed from Dublin to Miss Hitchener had there been opened by the surveyor of customs. At his seat in Sussex—Stanmer Park—he had heard of Mr. Timothy Shelley's troubles with his son ; and he shook his head over the young man who was disgracing his family. The Home Secretary was informed that the connection between Shelley and the seditious bill-posting had now been clearly established, for a small box as well as a bottle had been drawn at Lynmouth from the sea, and each was discovered to contain one of the two papers—" Declaration " and " Devil's Walk "— found in Daniel Hill's possession. A legal opinion was sought as to whether any steps could with propriety be taken against Mr. Percy Shelley in consequence of his " very extraordinary and unaccountable conduct," with the result that no prosecution was advised, but it was recommended that some person should be instructed to observe his future behaviour, and to transmit any information respecting him to head-quarters; to which effect instructions were sent to the mayor of Barnstaple. Thus Mr. Percy Shelley, though unmolested by a paternal government, was placed under observation, and perhaps for some time, as he moved hither and thither, was provided in each locality with an attendant in the person of a spy.

In these August days Shelley doubtless had a feeling that there was thunder in the upper regions. The quiet happiness of the Lynmouth cottage was over and gone. Shelley had loved to stand on the slope before his door, engaged in the delightful pastime of blowing soap-bubbles, and would watch the gleaming aërial voyagers until they suddenly broke and vanished. The radiant summer hours seemed to have disappeared like so many bright bubbles borne away. He was impatient to be gone from Devon, and to find a refuge across the British Channel, somewhere in his beloved Wales, possibly northwards in the Vale of Llangollen, where, before these Barnstaple troubles, he had planned to make his abode at least for the coming winter It was Shelley's design to sail from Lynmouth to Swansea, a distance of about twenty-five miles, but the winds of heaven refused to aid his flight.

Unwilling to remain longer at Lynmouth, he journeyed, with his household party and Miss Hitchener, towards the close of August, some ten days after his servant's arrest, to Ilfracombe, and thence with little or no delay passed over to Swansea.

A few days later the town-clerk of Barnstaple proceeded to Lynmouth to obtain further information for Government respecting Mr. Shelley. But Mr. Shelley was nowhere to be found; he had vanished, he and his grand

armada of bottles and boxes, and his large chests supposed
to contain sedition, and so heavy that scarcely three men
could lift them—a marvel to the village ; for the Lynmouth
fishermen probably had had few previous opportunities of
estimating the weight of Milton's Prose Works, Hartley on
Man, Davy on Chemistry, together with a hundredweight
or two of materialistic French philosophers.

Henry Drake, town-clerk, was not the only visitor to
Lynmouth, this September, who was surprised and disappointed to learn that Shelley had flitted beyond his ken.
William Godwin, though not much given to running about
the world for pleasure, ordinarily refreshed his spirits with
an autumn holiday ; and this year the excursion should be
to Devonshire, where a meeting between him and his young
disciple might take place as affecting as that, in his own
novel, between Casimer Fleetwood and the venerable
Ruffigny. On the same day on which Drake was reporting
to Lord Sidmouth the result of his visit of espionage to
Lynmouth, Godwin started from London for Bristol.
Having visited Chepstow and Tintern Abbey, and spent
some time with Cottle and other friends in Bristol, he left
that city on a windless afternoon, about mid-September, in
a small and crazy vessel overcrowded by her fourteen pas-
sengers. Tiding it for six hours, and lying at anchor for
six, they slowly dropped down the Severn ; next morning
in a rainy squall, tossed to and fro, and, before night, putting over to the Welsh coast, the travellers found shelter in
a roomy barn—a cruel reverse to Godwin, who had looked
for welcome and repose in the pleasant Lynmouth cottage.
It was three or four o'clock on the afternoon of Friday,
September 18, when by favour of the captain the weary
voyager was put ashore in a small boat at Lynmouth,
instead of being taken fifteen miles further, to Ilfracombe.
He had eaten nothing since Wednesday's dinner, and had

slept but little. There was a moment's trial for his temper when, on landing, he was informed that the Shelleys had flown ; but, accepting the situation with as much equanimity as he could command, Godwin was not ill pleased to find his feet on solid earth and to be able to obtain a comfortable dinner. On his return from a solitary ramble to the Valley of Rocks, or perhaps next morning, he found Shelley's landlady, good Mrs. Hooper, and was "delighted" with her. She "quite loved the Shelleys," declares Godwin, in a letter to his wife ; and for Godwin himself, in his disappointment, she had some cheering news, assuring him that within a fortnight, that is, early in October, the Shelleys would be in London. "This," he writes, "quite comforts my heart."

CHAPTER VI

IT seems to have been Shelley's intention, on leaving
Devon, to seek for a house in the Vale of Llangollen; then
to hasten to London, and after a brief visit to return to
Wales, there to spend the winter, and perhaps the greater
part of the ensuing year. To this plan, in its general outline, he still adhered; but from Llangollen, where perhaps
no suitable house was to be found, he was drawn away by
the attractions of sea-shore, mountain, and valley, on the
south coast of Carnarvonshire. The little town of Tremadoc,
in 1812, was a recent marvel of human contrivance and
energy, impressive even amidst the old and greater wonders
of Nature in her giant play. Mr. W. Alexander Madocks,
member of Parliament for Boston, had conceived the
design of rescuing from the sea a large tract of land on the
western side of the estuary, known as the "Traeth mawr,"
or "great sand." By the year 1800 he had reclaimed
nearly two thousand acres of excellent land, which soon
produced luxuriant crops of barley, wheat, and clover.
Tremadoc, named after its founder, rose on this land
rescued from the sea—a little town built in quadrangular
form, provided with its market-house, assembly-rooms, and
church. It was backed by a craggy height, and at a short

distance from the town, perched upon a rock amid flourishing young plantations, and standing out from the mountain-buttresses behind, was Mr. Madocks' new villa residence, Tanyrallt, a residence elegant in design and commodious. Encouraged by the success of his first enterprise, the creator of Tremadoc formed a plan to recover some five thousand acres more—the greater part of the drowned lands within the Traeth mawr. A vast embankment was to be constructed from side to side of the estuary. Its length when complete would be nearly a mile; its width could not be less than a hundred feet at the base. By September, 1810, the embankment had been carried from each extremity to within one hundred yards of the centre; but here was the critical point of the whole work, for through this chasm the tide ran with amazing force, and swept away or disturbed the barriers which the workmen had placed to oppose its onset. When Shelley arrived in September, 1812, the embankment was still unfinished; a fortune had been already spent upon it, and just as the great enterprise approached completion—so Shelley was given to understand—Mr. Madocks found it necessary to slacken his efforts to carry it to a successful issue. Charmed by the beauty of the neighbourhood—the encircling mountains, the sea, the valley, with its stream and hanging cliffs, leading upwards to Pont Aberglaslyn and Beddgelert—and deeply interested by the great experiment here being made, which should prove the pre-eminence of mind over matter, and of beneficent enterprise over the rude forces of nature, Shelley fixed upon Tremadoc as his place of abode. On inquiring for a house, he ascertained from Mr. Madocks' agent—John Williams—that Tanyrallt, the beautiful villa, alone upon its rocky perch, was now vacant. The number of rooms was more than sufficient for all his needs, and the landlord could afford to wait for his rent until payment was convenient. Immediately Shelley closed with the offer, and was in possession of Tanyrallt.

All his thoughts and hopes and fears were at once given to the enbankment. Its promise of beneficent results, its display of human contrivance on a great scale, its position as a centre around which the energies and lives of many men had gathered, were enough to excite Shelley's ardour and activity. The work must not be allowed to languish. Once again the tide had rolled fiercely against the embankment, and borne part of it away. Shelley instantly resolved to put his own hand to the work, and to endeavour to induce others to follow his example. In company with Mr. Madocks' agent he visited the gentry of the county, to urge upon them the duty of aiding a great public enterprise. It was proposed to call a meeting and raise a subscription, Shelley at once giving in his own name for one hundred pounds. Thus some two or three thousand pounds were in good time obtained, and workmen were once again active in repairing the sea-breach and endeavouring to render the defences secure against future invasion. A chief object of Shelley's visit to London in October was to solicit further subscriptions, which should help to carry the great sea-walls forward impregnably to the point of junction.

By Sunday, October 4, Shelley, with his wife, his sister-in-law, and Miss Hitchener, had arrived in London, and found rooms at Lewis's Hotel, St. James's Street. To meet Godwin face to face had been looked forward to as one of the chief happinesses of this visit to London, and the first eager meeting was but one of many. The philopher was all sweetness and benignity ; delighted with his young disciple, and for his sake willing to be put out of his habitual ways. And while he sat and conversed with Percy on high themes—matter and spirit, atheism, utility

and truth, the clergy, Church government, or the charac
teristics of German thought and literature—Harriet would
listen and look on with admiration, discovering a likeness
in aspect between Godwin and the great master of antiquity
from whom Plato had learnt to discourse of knowledge,
virtue, and beauty. Throughout October and the early
part of the following month two days rarely went by
without a meeting between the friends. Now it was a call
from Godwin at the hotel; now a walk with Shelley,
enlivened by animated discussion; now a dinner at Godwin's house, to which Miss Hitchener or Eliza Westbrook
would be invited, together with Harriet and Percy; and
now the dinner would be given in return by Shelley
and his wife, who would receive, in company with their
philosophic friend, the second Mrs. Godwin, and Mary
Wollstonecraft's gentle daughter Fanny. During these
days of early intercourse the Godwin household was viewed
by the Shelleys through the rosiest veil of mist. Mrs.
Godwin, who eleven years since had caught her illustrious
husband in gross and palpable meshes of the flatterer's
net, is known to have had an imperious temper and a most
mendacious tongue. "She is a very disgusting woman,"
broke out Charles Lamb in 1801, "and wears green
spectacles." But when she came to Lewis's Hotel, arrayed
perhaps in her black velvet dress, and looking very short
and very stout, her young acquaintances of 1812, whose
spectacles were rose-coloured, found her to be chiefly
distinguished by a sweet resoluteness and magnanimity of
soul. They reflected with admiration, not wholly un-
deserved, on the gallant struggle she was making to
carry on the Juvenile Library in Skinner Street. In her
nine-years-old son they discovered an unfledged philosopher,
worthy of such a father, though as yet capable only of
chirping wisdom from a callow throat. Fanny Godwin

(the name Imlay, if ever in use, had given place to that of Godwin) could not fail to interest any one who loved modesty, good sense, and sweetness of disposition ; she was now in her nineteenth year, and through the plainness of her face beamed somewhat timidly the light of a heart not strong and joyous, but ever gentle and sympathetic. Of Jane Clairmont, daughter of Mrs. Godwin by her first marriage, we hear nothing on this occasion ; during the visit of the Shelleys to London she was for not more than two nights at home. Godwin's only daughter, named Mary Wollstonecraft, after the mother who died at her birth—the child of love and grief, bearing the promise of so rare a heritage of intellectual strength and genius of the heart—had been absent since June with her father's friends, the Baxters of Dundee, sent to them from London that she might drink the invigorating Scottish air, and race about the Forfar woods and hills in company with her girl-friends and comrades Isabel and Christy Baxter ; for Mary had been ailing in the early summer. On August 30 had come her fifteenth birthday, while she was still in Scotland ; by November 10 Christy Baxter and Mary Godwin had arrived in London from the north ; and when Shelley, with Harriet and Eliza Westbrook, dined next day at Godwin's house—the last occasion of the kind before his hasty departure for Tremadoc—it is possible that his eyes may have lighted on the fair face and girlish figure of one who was to influence his life so profoundly in after years. But no record remains of any such meeting between Shelley and Mary in this autumn of 1812.

On November 5 Percy and Harriet, with Miss Hitchener, were at dinner with Godwin and his wife. Little William, the nine-years-old boy, announced that he was going to let off fireworks with his friend, young Newton, hard by Mr.

Newton's house in Chester Street, Grosvenor Place. " I will go with you," said Shelley to little William, and went ; and when the gunpowder had blazed and cracked itself into smoke and smell, Shelley, again yielding to his impulse, and following young Newton, walked upstairs and introduced himself to the family circle at Chester Street. Thus began an important and interesting acquaintance with a household of unusual charm and refinement—an acquaintance which also served to introduce Shelley to Mrs. Newton's relatives the De Boinvilles, of whom we shall afterwards hear. If Shelley had not previously been aware of the fact, he probably learnt from Godwin, before proceeding to Chester Street, that Mr. Newton was zealous in the vegetarian faith, and had published two years previously an essay entitled " The Return to Nature," being a defence of the vegetable regimen. Since 1809 the household in Chester Street, consisting of Mr. and Mrs. Newton, a nurse, and four young children, had strictly adhered to a vegetarian diet ; the children, said Shelley, " are the most beautiful and healthy creatures it is possible to conceive ; the girls are perfect models for a sculptor ; their dispositions are also the most gentle and conciliating." And we are assured that if Shelley delighted in the Newton children, the delight was not all on his side ; they rejoiced when the tall, slight figure of their new friend appeared in Chester Street, and would fly downstairs from the nursery to meet him at his entrance. Hogg, with his characteristic play of satire, tells of a visit with Bysshe in the year 1813 to a house in London, which surely must have been that in Chester Street. It was considered by Mr. Newton, according to Hogg's account, to be a desirable part of the return to nature that the little ones should occasionally expose their bodies to the action of air and sunlight, unimpeded by clothing even of vegetable texture, or, as it was expressed in a single word, that they should at convenient seasons "nakedize." Ascending the steps hastily about five o'clock of a summer Sunday afternoon, Bysshe delivered at Mr. Newton's door one of his superb bravura knocks. When the door was thrown open and Hogg, as being the stranger, stood prepared to enter first, a singular spectacle presented itself—there were five naked childish figures in the passage advancing rapidly to welcome their friend, the teller of wonderful stories "As soon as they saw me," writes Hogg, "they uttered a piercing cry, turned round and ran wildly upstairs, screaming aloud. The stairs presented the appearance of a Jacob's ladder, with the angels ascending it, except that that they had no wings, and they moved faster and made more noise than the ordinary representations of the patriarch's vision indicate."

Shelley's visit to London in October and November 1812, is memorable as the occasion on which he renewed the acquaintance with Hogg, so unhappily interrupted at York a year since. In the interval Hogg had removed to London, entered as a student in the Middle Temple, and become the pupil of a special pleader. "I had returned from the country," he writes, "at the end of October, 1812, and had resumed the duties of a pleader. I was sitting in my quiet lodgings with my tea and book before me ; it was one evening at the beginning of November, probably about ten o'clock. I was roused by a violent knocking at the street door, as if the watchman was giving the alarm of fire ; some one ran furiously upstairs, the door flew open, and Bysshe rushed into the middle of the room. . . . He looked, as he always looked, wild, intellectual, unearthly ; like a spirit that had just descended from the sky ; like a demon risen at that moment out of the ground." Shelley could not nourish resentment against his old

college friend; he had always assured Hogg that he was
prepared to forgive and forget the past, if indeed the
harmful passions of the past did not live on into the
present.   Now all was forgotten in the happiness of friendship renewed, and the exchange of recollections which
should fill the gap of time during which the friends had
suffered estrangement.   It was late at night when Shelley
departed.   Before parting, Bysshe had invited his friend
to dine with him and Harriet at the hotel in St. James's
Street.   There at six o'clock, in a sitting-room high above
the street, Hogg was received by Eliza Westbrook, who
smiled faintly upon him in silence, and by Harriet, radiant
and blooming as ever, with much cordial handshaking.
To beguile the time Harriet produced a broadside sheet
containing a report of Robert Emmet's speech before his
judges, with a portrait of the unhappy young man at the
top, standing at the bar and addressing the bench; but
the hard-hearted Hogg refused to be touched or interested
by the pathos of the woodcut.   " Presently Bysshe came
thundering upstairs from the street like a cannon-ball, and
we had dinner.   After dinner the poet spoke of Wales
with enthusiasm.   I was to come and see it.   He talked
rapturously of the waterfalls, walking about the room and
gesticulating as he described them. . . . Soon after tea
Eliza said they must go and pack up; they were to set
out for Wales early next morning, and she trembled for
dear Harriet's nerves.   A few shabby, ill-printed books,
productions of the Irish press, were lying about the room;
they treated of the history of Ireland and of the affairs of
that country."   But of his Irish expedition Shelley refrained
from speaking; nor does he seem to have been disposed to
be more confidential about his manner of life in London, for
Hogg was not informed of his acquaintance and almost
constant intercourse with William Godwin.

To regain an old friend was well ; to be rid of a new friend who had grown insupportable, was a matter of yet livelier rejoicing. The Elizabeth Hitchener of Shelley's dream-world, the Roman Portia of the correspondence, had disappeared for ever, and in her place stood a mere mortal woman—tall, lean, brown-visaged, glorified by no peculiar nimbus, and having parts and passions as obnoxious to comment and criticism as those of any ordinary human creature. Her opinions, theological and political, were sadly tainted by the spirit of compromise. Her temper was variable, and it is probable enough that soon the poor Sussex schoolmistress had cause for sinkings of the heart, as she came to feel how difficult and delicate was her position. It is hardly conceivable that Eliza Westbrook and Harriet should long have accepted with complacency the presence of one their superior in intellect, the chosen partner of Shelley's spirit in his higher strivings and aspirations. Harriet was stung by expressions which implied that the girl-wife must take up a humbler position of service towards Percy than that held by the elect sister of his soul, and she believed that Miss Hitchener's aim was to separate her from her husband, whose love had in truth grown closer and fonder since the marriage-flight to Scotland. Shelley's very extravagance of idealization had prepared the way for a revulsion of feeling. Elizabeth Hitchener had been so much above humanity that it was now the less difficult for her to become a supernatural being of a different species ; she was no longer " Portia," or even " Bessy," but was now known to the circle of her non-admirers as the " Brown Demon." In London, probably, the crisis came ; and affairs would seem to have been managed with a certain decency. Perceiving that he had done Miss Hitchener a material injury when he persuaded her to abandon her school and expose herself

M

to the cruel gossip of her neighbours, Shelley undertook
to make good that injury as far as was possible, promising
her an annuity, for how long or short a period we know
not, of one hundred pounds. Whether she ever actually
accepted such compensation we cannot be quite certain.
However this may have been, she consented to take her
departure. It was a Sunday, and Hogg appeared that
morning at the hotel. Shelley had an engagement elsewhere ; Harriet suffered from a headache. It was proposed
to Hogg that he should take Miss Westbrook and Miss
Hitchener for an airing, and because he consented, if he
ever sinned as man or biographer, his sins must be forgiven.
" With the brown demon on my right arm and the black
diamond on my left," writes Hogg in his derisive way,
" we went forth into St. James's Park, and walked there
and in the neighbouring parks for a long time, a very
long time. ' These were my jewels,' as Cornelia proudly
exclaimed." Dinner passed off quietly ; when evening
came a coach was called, and Miss Hitchener took a
courteous leave of her altered friends. A weight seemed
to be lifted from the spirits of all as soon as the coach was
fairly out of sight.

" The Brown Demon, as we call our late tormentor
and schoolmistress, must receive her stipend "—so Shelley
wrote to Hogg (December 3). " I pay it with a heavy
heart and an unwilling hand ; but it must be so. She
was deprived by our misjudging haste of a situation where
she was going on smoothly ; and now she says that her
reputation is gone, her health ruined, her peace of mind
destroyed by my barbarity ; a complete victim to all the
woes mental and bodily that heroine ever suffered ! This
is not all fact ; but certainly she is embarrassed and poor
and we being in some degree the cause, we ought to
obviate it." Whereupon follows an outbreak of unmitigated

and fantastic vituperation, and then the acknowledgment of his own lack of discernment and discretion. "My astonishment at my fatuity, inconsistency, and bad taste was never so great as after living for four months with her as an inmate. What would Hell be were such a woman in Heaven?" In later years, when the pain and the shame of his indiscretion had died down into the past, Shelley could look back and tickle his fancy with a glance at the grotesque points of the situation. Miss Hitchener had maintained the rights of woman, and once attempted an ode celebrating the emancipation of her sex. According to Medwin, Shelley, when in Italy, would sometimes recite, laughing till the tears ran down his cheeks, the opening line, which struck the key-note of the whole—

"All, all are men—women and all!"

The "Brown Demon," though wounded and sore with a sense of unmerited dishonour, seems to have cherished a gentler feeling towards Shelley. "I saw her after her return, at the house of her father," wrote an acquaintance of Shelley's who in happier days had been the bearer of messages from him to her, "sitting alone, with one of Shelley's works before her. Her fine black eye lighted up, her well-formed Roman countenance was full of animation, when I spoke of Shelley." In 1822, the year of Shelley's death, appeared a blank-verse poem by Miss Hitchener, entitled "The Weald of Sussex," which proves that its author, though not a poet, was a woman of some culture and vigour of mind. Let us take farewell of Miss Hitchener, not in her character of "Brown Demon," but in that of a woman useful and respected. In later days she and her sister conducted a girls' school at Edmonton with credit and success. "The school-days I passed at Edmonton," writes a former pupil, "under the kind and judicious teaching of Miss Hitchener, were some of the happiest in my life. . . . I consider her to have been a high-principled, clever woman, with a remarkable capacity for teaching. I think all her pupils loved her. Both she and her sister will be cherished in my memory as long as it lasts."

During his six weeks' visit to London Shelley exerted himself vigorously on behalf of the subscription for completing the embankment at Tremadoc; but the result of his efforts was not encouraging. He had heard from Mr. Madocks' agent, Williams, that the men were now working with a will, and that some real progress had been made. If, therefore, the means of paying wages could be procured all might be well. Too often the labourer had toiled for nothing better than a promise of his hire, and when evening came had attempted to obtain some subsistence for his family by cultivating under the moonlight a small patch of sterile ground. It was a disappointment to Shelley to find that he could effect so little ; he was still a minor, and could not raise money on his expectations without paying a ruinous interest ; his friends and acquaintances were strangely apathetic about the great enterprise in North Wales. "The Duke of Norfolk," he wrote to Williams,* "has just returned to London. I shall call upon him this morning, and shall spare no pains in engaging his interests, or perhaps his better feelings, in ours and our country's cause. I see no hope of effecting, on my part, any grand or decisive scheme until the expiration of my minority ; . . . but in the meanwhile my fervid hopes, my ardent desires my unremitting personal exertions (so far as my health wil allow), are all engaged in that cause, which I will desert *but with my life.*"

The last days in London were days of " embarrassments qualms, and fluctuations," caused we know not by what

* St. James's Coffee Room, November 7, 1812.

unless it were difficulties about money. The date of departure for Wales, first fixed for November 12, had been postponed, and an invitation to dinner for Friday, the 13th, was given to Godwin ; but on that day, submitting, says Shelley, "to a galling yet unappealable necessity," he quitted London hastily with Harriet and Eliza Westbrook, too much pressed for time even to make a farewell call on Godwin's household. Passing through Oxford, the travellers rested for the night at Stratford-on-Avon, among memories the most sacred to a poet. Having proceeded, by way of Birmingham and Shrewsbury, to Capel Curig, they wound thence in their chaise under the heights of Snowden towards Tremadoc.

In the bitter winter of 1812 the toilers at the Tremadoc embankment, ill-paid or unpaid, suffered many hardships. " I have often heard Mr. Madocks dilate," writes Medwin, "on Shelley's numerous acts of benevolence, his relieving the distresses of the poor, visiting them in their humble abodes, and supplying them with food and raiment and fuel during the winter." " He was very generous and kind-hearted," declared Mrs. Williams, when recalling what she had learnt from her husband respecting Shelley at Tremadoc ; and she went on to tell how on one occasion, when there was talk in Shelley's presence of the straitened means of a poor widow in the neighbourhood, he said nothing, but next morning a five-pound note—his gift—was in the needy creature's hands. In Wales, as in London, he seemed to see mankind unnaturally divided into two races —the well-to-do, protected from painful sympathy with their fellows by a thick, non-conducting web of comfort, prejudice, pride ; and the indigent, ever toiling yet ever on the edge of beggary, helpless, hopeless, inured to submission by long years of crouching and piteous shambling towards the grave.

The affairs of the embankment now pressed heavily on Shelley, and were felt as a serious inconvenience, for important poetical designs claimed his undivided care, and the difficulties connected with Mr. Madocks' great enterprise teased him out of all poetry. There is ground for believing that Shelley and Harriet, as they came to know more of the circumstances of Tremadoc, lost faith, at least for a time, in Mr. Madocks and his disinterested patriotism; that they questioned whether on the whole he had not done more harm than good to the Welsh people; and that the daily sight of an unprofitable waste of sand, through which the sea-water still soaked and oozed, grew a fatigue to their eyes, and filled them, when they thought of the human effort expended upon its reclamation, with indignant despair. It was the history of the expedition to Dublin repeated in another shape; and hopes as ardent as those which sank in the quicksands of Irish politics now were swallowed in the estuary of the Traeth mawr.

But at home with Harriet her husband was "the happiest of the happy." Harriet's thoughts still took their colour, as by a pale reflection, from his, and she repeated his phrases about virtue, benevolence, equality, wisdom, with sufficient aptitude. Her voice when she sang lent a charm to the winter evenings, and it was old and plain melodies that she best loved, especially the ancient airs of Ireland. Under Shelley's guidance, and probably in part at least to give him pleasure, she worked at the study of Latin, could already read some Odes of Horace, and was even projecting a Latin epistle to Hogg. Beside these indoor sources of pleasure during the winter of 1812-13, there was ever present the happiness of a new hope and a new care, for Shelley and Harriet expected that when summer came a child would be in their arms. His annual income, indeed, without the presence of this new crier for gold, had been proving itself insufficient to meet the varied demands of travel, household expenses, and charity ; but every month brought nearer the date of his majority, when it would be possible to raise money on reasonable interest —a knowledge of which fact might convince his father that it was impolitic to be tight-fisted. Acting on the advice of Hogg, Shelley wrote in December to the Duke of Norfolk, begging that his Grace's kind offices might be used on his behalf with Mr. Timothy Shelley ; and on the opening of the new year he had himself addressed his father, stating the difficulties of his position, and adding kind inquiries and good wishes for all at Field Place. Mr. Shelley returned the good wishes tenfold, hoping that his son would have many and more happy years, but responded to the appeal for money only by pointing out that a truer kind of wealth might be obtained from a wise contemplation of Welsh landscape. "I lament exceedingly that there should be cause for the present difficulties. I hope the mountains in Wales will produce reflections that you will know would be congenial to my own sentiments as well as those of your mother." "I have as yet received no answer from the Duke of Norfolk," wrote Shelley to Hogg on December 27 ; "I hardly expect one. I do not see that it is the interest of my father to come to terms during my nonage ; perhaps even not after. Do you know, I cannot prevail upon myself to care much about it. Harriet is very happy as we are ; and I am very happy."

When affairs of the embankment did not trouble him, the solitude around Shelley was deep and delightful. Yet newspapers and letters from friends in London kept open his communications with the great world. When, in January, 1813, the execution of fourteen of the riotous framebreakers known as Luddites took place at York, Shelley and Harriet heard of it before long, and were eager to start a subscription in London for the destitute widows and orphans of the victims. A month earlier John and Leigh Hunt, as printer and editor of the *Examiner*, had been convicted of publishing a libel, intended to traduce and vilify his Royal Highness the Prince Regent, whom they had described as a violator of his word, a libertine over head and ears in disgrace, a despiser of domestic ties, a companion of gamblers and demireps, and, hardly less libellously, as a corpulent gentleman of fifty. Brougham spoke on behalf of the defendants, and was grossly described by Lord Ellenborough in his charge as having been inoculated with all the poison of the libel. To Shelley the professional glosses and shifts of the advocate seemed hardly worthy of the cause, and he desired a bolder and plainer kind of language, backed by more strenuous moral force. When, in February, 1813, the Hunts were sentenced to two years' imprisonment in separate gaols, with a fine of five hundred pounds each, Shelley's indignation flamed forth in a letter to Hookham, and he longed to bring speedy succour, as far as was possible, to men whom he regarded as the distressed champions of liberty of speech. "I am boiling with indignation at the horrible injustice and tyranny of the sentence pronounced on Hunt and his brother ; and it is on this subject that I write to you. Surely the seal of abjectness and slavery is indelibly stamped upon the character of England. Although I do not retract in the slightest degree my wish for a subscription for the widows and children of those poor men hung at York, yet this £1000 which the Hunts are sentenced to pay is an affair of more consequence. Hunt is a brave, a good, and an enlightened man. Surely the public, for whom Hunt has done so much, will repay in part the great debt of obligation which they owe the champion of their liberties and

virtues; or are they dead, cold, stone-hearted, and insensible
—brutalized by centuries of unremitting bondage? However that may be, they surely may be excited into some
slight acknowledgment of his merits. While hundreds of
thousands are sent to the tyrants of Russia, he pines in a
dungeon, far from all that can make life to be desired.
Well—I am rather poor at present ; but I have £20 which
is not immediately wanted. Pray begin a subscription for
the Hunts ; put my name [down] for that sum, and when
I hear that you have complied with my request, I will
send it you. Now, if there are any difficulties in the way
of this scheme of ours, for the love of liberty and virtue
overcome them. Oh ! that I might wallow for one night
in the Bank of England ! " Shelley's twenty pounds sped
on their way to Hookham, but the difficulty of applying
the sum to its intended use was insuperable—the Hunts
magnanimously refused to let their friends or the public be
taxed in order that they might possess the privilege of
rash speaking. We may surmise that Shelley wrote direct
to Hunt in prison, offering to pay either the whole or a
great part of the fine. " He wrote to me," says Leigh
Hunt, " making me a princely offer ; " but whatever this
offer may have been, it was promptly and decidedly
declined.

While Shelley thus sprang forward to support the
cause which he regarded as that of truth and freedom, a
certain moderation and tolerance with respect to those
who honestly differed from him were growing up within
him. To Hogg he protested against the supposition that
the wide severance between their moral and political
creeds could cause any shadow of alienation on his part.
" You misinterpret my feelings on the state of the moral
world," he wrote (December 3), " when you suppose that
the bigotry of commonplace republicanism or the violence

of faction enters into them at all. I am certainly a very resolved republican (if the word applies) and a determined sceptic ; but although I think their reasoning very defective, I am clearly aware that the noblest feelings might conduct some few reflecting minds to aristocracy and Episcopacy. Hume certainly was an aristocrat, and Locke was a zealous Christian." And again, to Hogg, in February, 1813, " I need not say that your letters delight me, but all your principles do not. The species of pride which you love to encourage appears to me incapable of bearing the test of reason. Now, do not tell me that Reason is a cold and insensible arbiter. Reason is only an assemblage of our better feelings—passion considered under a peculiar mode of its operation. . . . Perhaps you will say that my republicanism is proud ; it certainly is far removed from pot-house democracy, and knows with what smile to hear the servile applauses of an inconstant mob. But though its cheeks could feel without a blush the hand of insult strike, its soul would shrink neither from the scaffold nor the stake, nor from those deeds and habits which are obnoxious to slaves in power. My republicanism, it is true, would bear with an aristocracy of chivalry and refinement before an aristocracy of commerce and vulgarity ; not, however, from pride, but because the one I consider as approaching most nearly to what man ought to be." In such utterances we recognize some growth towards maturity of intellect and temper.

From Godwin letters came now and again to Shelley at Tremadoc. Six weeks' personal intercourse with the author of " Political Justice " had somewhat abated or qualified the enthusiasm with which the Shelley household had at first regarded him. Godwin exacted from those who approached him a degree of deference which made it difficult to be at ease in his company ; and his influence seemed to be chiefly exerted to check and chill the ardour of spirits younger and more impassioned than his own. Still, a thinker so eminently useful, a veteran in persecution, a votary of freedom and virtue, though now in his decline, justly claimed their respectful consideration. Of Fanny Godwin a happier impression seems to have remained with her new friends. A little while after his arrival from London, Shelley wrote to her in a tone of pleasant *cameraderie*, with touches of playfulness not common in his early letters. She had blamed him for his hurried flight to Wales, as sudden and mysterious as the proceedings of the hero of a modern novel, and used words which implied that she looked upon Harriet as "a fine lady;" to which Shelley good-humouredly responds, "How is Harriet a fine lady? You indirectly accuse her in your letter of this offence—to me the most unpardonable of all. The ease and simplicity of her habits, the unas- suming plainness of her address, the uncalculated connec- tion of her thought and speech, have ever formed, in my eyes, her greatest charms; and none of these are com- patible with fashionable life, or the attempted assumption of its vulgar and noisy *éclat*."

The summer, autumn, and winter which went by while Shelley resided at Lynmouth and at Tremadoc had been a period of earnest study, of many literary plans and pro- jects, and of important poetical achievement. At an age when, if Shelley had pursued his career at Oxford, he might have been nourishing his spirit with the wisest thoughts and the high ideals of beauty to be found in classical antiquity, he turned away from these impatiently, and maintained, in spite of Godwin's arguments in favour of classical learning, that "the evils of acquiring Greek and Latin considerably overbalance the benefit." Not one of the truths of "Political Justice"—thus he pleaded in support of his opinion—rests on the excellence of ancient literature. The governments of republican Rome and of some states of Greece were as oppressive and arbitrary as the government of Great Britain under George III. As for the Greek and Roman poets, Godwin himself had admitted that "they are fit for nothing but the perpetuation of the noxious race of heroes." Lucretius forms, perhaps, the single exception. Throughout the whole of ancient literature honour and fame, or public opinion, are set above virtue. The politics of the old world were corrupt because their morals were corrupt. "They are our masters in politics," said Shelley, "because we are so immoral as to prefer self-interest to virtue, and expediency to positive good." Why spend the best years of youth in learning *words*—words which eminently contribute to the growth of prejudice—when the same years might be profitably employed in the study of *things?* "I should think," Shelley went on, "that natural philosophy, medicine, astronomy, and, above all, history, would be sufficient employments for immaturity. . . . Of the Latin language, as a grammar, I think highly. It is a key to the European languages, and we can hardly be said to know our own without first attaining a complete knowledge of it. Still, I cannot help considering it as an affair of minor importance, inasmuch as the science of things is superior to the science of words." The vindicators of ancient learning—excepting Godwin, who was willing to subject his opinions to reason—were no better than vindicators of a literary despotism, tracers of a circle which was intended to shut out from real knowledge all who do not breathe the air of prejudice.

In 1812 the chosen masters of Shelley's intellect were lights of the modern world—heralds of revolution, the leaders of the "illumination" in France. Of Kant he had heard, and was desirous to study his writings through a translation into Latin; if Shelley at this period read German at all, he read it imperfectly and with difficulty. From Hookham he obtained a copy of Spinoza's "Tractatus Theologico-Politicus," and perhaps a copy of the "Opera Posthuma;" but although Shelley afterwards worked at a translation of the "Tractatus" at three several times, we find no evidence that he received in youth any adequate or profound impression, as Goethe did, from one of the purest and loftiest spirit among philosophical seekers after God. Of far greater influence with Shelley than Spinoza or Kant were those arrogant thinkers who prepared the soil of France for the ploughshare of revolution. With eager curiosity and wistful longing he followed upon their traces. "Do you know anything," he wrote to Hookham, "of the famous French Encyclopédie composed by Voltaire, D'Alembert, etc.? It is a book I should much wish to have. Is it to be obtained? Could you obtain it? . . . There is a work by a French physician, Cabanis, that I wish you also to send." Already he had read Helvétius. But the work which at this time, more than any other, contributed to his patchwork system of thought was the celebrated "Système de la Nature"—the extreme philosophical outcome of eighteenth-century materialism. Holbach's book, which gave Goethe as a youth, a distaste for all philosophy, so highly delighted Shelley, that, while still ignorant of its authorship, he resolved to render it into English. Reading the work in his solitudes at Nantgwillt and Lynmouth, he was struck by it as "a book of uncommon powers, yet too obnoxious to accusations of sensuality and selfishness." At a later date he looked back upon the intellectual teachers of his youth with a sense of the injury he had suffered at their hands. "The doctrines of the French and material philosophy," he wrote in the year of his death, "are as false as they are pernicious. And in the prose fragment "On Life," written perhaps about 1819, "The shocking absurdities of the popular philosophy of mind and matter, its fatal consequences in morals, and their violent dogmatism concerning the source of all things, had early conducted me to materialism. This materialism is a seducing system to young and superficial minds. It allows its disciples to talk, and dispenses them from think:ng. But I was discontented with such a view of things as it afforded. Man is a being of high aspirations, 'looking before and after,' whose 'thoughts wander through eternity,' disclaiming alliance with transience and decay ; existing but in the future and the past ; being not what he is, but what he has been and shall be." When these words were written, matter and motion had disappeared as ultimate realities from Shelley's spiritual vision ; he perceived no existence except that of universal mind and its phenomena.

In no sense was he at this period an independent thinker. Deeply dissatisfied with the condition of society around him, and with the traditional creeds and doctrines, which had been presented to him in forms lacking true vitality, he caught up the opinions of those teachers who made the largest and loudest promises for the happiness of man ; he attempted to weld these into a self-consistent whole, and failed in the impossible attempt. But at least he coloured them with the hues of his own sentiment and imagination. Atheist he would doubtless have named himself; yet he sang the praises of a universal Spirit of nature, acting necessarily, but forwarding the ends of wisdom and of righteousness. A disciple of French materialism, he yet looked forward not merely to a happier earth for future generations of men, but dared to expect an immortality for the individual soul. A utilitarian in

creed, his ethics were passionately disinterested. It is
deserving of note that notwithstanding his arguments
against classical studies addressed to Godwin, and his
regard for such writers as Holbach and Helvétius, among
the books ordered from Hookham during Shelley's residence at Tanyrallt are Marcus Aurelius, Seneca, and
Plato.

The study of history—English, Greek, and Roman—
and that of our elder poets and prose writers, had been
earnestly recommended to Shelley by William Godwin.
He did not propose to feed his disciple with abstract
doctrines or philosophies of history ; his trust was that
Shelley might make acquaintance with what is most noble
and admirable in human character and human achievement. To see this in act and in example, he writes, "is
perhaps superior to all the theories and speculations that
can possibly be formed." The great writers of the Eliza-
bethan age he commended to Shelley's attention because
they were thinkers—"every line is pregnant with sense,
and the reader is inevitably put to the expense of thinking
likewise."   " *You,*" said Godwin, who had read in manuscript a portion of "Queen Mab," "have what appears to
me a false taste in poetry. You love a perpetual sparkle
and glittering, such as are to be found in Darwin, and
Southey, and Scott, and Campbell." Shelley's interest in
history was faint ; he conceived it in a series of visions—
visions which were thrown before him, as it were, by the
phantasmagoria of his own imagination. Empires rose
and fell as if by the power of earthquakes, and anarchs
stalked huge across the scene, and priests were banded in
dark conclaves, and patriot martyrs endured the agony ;
and then the series was exhausted, and the same pictures
were shown over again. " Facts," Shelley afterwards said,
in a beautiful and characteristic passage, " are not what we

want to know in poetry, in history, in the lives of individual men, in satire or panegyric. They are the mere divisions, the arbitrary points on which we hang, and to which we refer those delicate and evanescent hues of mind, which language delights and instructs us in precise proportion as as it expresses." But, under the influence of Godwin's authority, Shelley determined to toil against the current of his genius, and to strive to attain at least some general knowledge of past events. Almost immediately on receiving Godwin's letter of advice Shelley wrote to Hookham, requesting him to send a selection from the books recommended by his philosophic guide, together with certain others of his own choice. The place of honour was given to metaphysics. The works of Edmund Spenser were included, as representative of what is best in the poetry of that age towards which Godwin had specially directed his attention. " Subjoined is a list of books," wrote Shelley, " which I wish you to send me very soon. I am determined to apply myself to a study that is hateful and disgusting to my very soul, but which is above all studies necessary for him who would be listened to as a mender of antiquated abuses. I mean that record of crimes and miseries—history. You see that the metaphysical works to which my heart hankers are not numerous in this list. One thing you will take care of for me—that those standard and reputable works on history, etc., be of the cheapest possible editions. With respect to metaphysical works I am less scrupulous." The names of Kant and Spinoza stand at the head of Shelley's list, which also includes Hume's " Essays," and Darwin's " Zoonomia." Herodotus, Thucydides, Xenophon, and Plutarch, recommended by Godwin, and of which Shelley desired to have translations into Latin or English, as well as the original texts, are supplemented by Gillies' " History of

Greece," and Vertot's "History of Rome." Gibbon's "Decline and Fall of the Roman Empire" would serve as a broad viaduct between the ancient and modern worlds. For a narrative of events in our own country, Shelley was content to rely on Hume, with Adolphus's "History of England from the Accession of George III. to 1783" for the more recent period. Here were resources and equipment for a vigorous raid into the alien territory of history. Shelley's list, which did not omit to specify the "Faerie Queene," closes with some miscellaneous works of interest —Count Rumford "On Stoves," Moor's "Hindu Pantheon," and Southey's "History of Brazil."

The months thus occupied with various studies and with generous effort on behalf of the embankment scheme and of the suffering poor were not fruitless of literary enterprise and endeavour, in bringing which to a successful issue Shelley looked for help from his new friend, the publisher Hookham. On August 18 he forwarded to Hookham copies of the two Irish pamphlets, acknowledging that they had but partial success in Ireland (no publisher having had an interest in their sale), and requesting Hookham's opinion as to the probable result of publishing them in London as one pamphlet, with an explanatory preface, and certain "suggestions" for forming associations which during his residence in Ireland had been drawn up in manuscript. "I shall, if possible," goes on Shelley, still addressing Hookham, "prepare a volume of essays, moral and *religious*, by November; but all my manuscripts now being in Dublin, and from peculiar circumstances not immediately obtainable, I do not know whether I can." The manuscripts were, in fact, in the hands of the Dublin publisher, Stockdale; he had undertaken to publish a volume of Shelley's verse, and perhaps a portion of this collection of short poems had been

N

put into type. Stockdale, on Shelley's quitting Ireland, demanded to be paid in advance—a demand with which it was not convenient to comply, and which appeared unreasonable to Shelley, for surely publishers are accustomed to wait for payment until an author's profits have come in. Such was not the opinion of Stockdale, who would neither proceed with his commission nor deliver up the author's manuscripts. It was not until December that Shelley heard that the long-lost manuscripts were on their way to London, whence he desired Hookham to forward them to Tremadoc.

In Shelley's letters of 1812–13 several references occur to a prose manuscript intended to have been published as a little volume, bearing the title " Biblical Extracts." We cannot be certain, but it seems not unlikely that Shelley's design was to exhibit the moral and spiritual teaching of Jesus, apart from theological dogma and the record of miracles. For a brief space of time — certainly while preparing the notes of " Queen Mab "—Shelley was led to regard the founder of Christianity as an impostor. At a later date Jesus Christ appeared to him to be the most important of all religious teachers, abiding in closest harmony with that Spirit of energy and wisdom which is the ruling Power of the universe ; a poet and a thinker, interpreting to us the highest truths ; the enemy of falsehood and oppression ; of meek and majestic demeanour ; calm in danger ; of natural and simple habits ; beloved to adoration by his adherents ; unmoved, solemn, and severe ; yet gentle and benign. In 1812 he could not set forth the moral teaching of the Gospels without guarding his reader at the same time from what he deemed to be the mythology and immorality of the Bible. This, it would seem, he proposed to do by a preface. The whole would make a tiny volume about the size of Godwin's " Essay on Sepulchres."

Shelley's quarrel with historical Christianity, which he regarded as the fruitful parent of persecutions, wars, superstitions, frauds, intolerance, and ignoble asceticism, was intensified by his conviction that the Christian ethics are not purely disinterested, and that heaven and hell are put forward as a bribe and a threat to determine conduct which ought to be determined solely by an incorruptible love of virtue. By the close of January, 1813, he was expecting to find printed copies of the " Biblical Extracts " in a box which Hookham had promised to forward. Whether the manuscript was ever placed in a printer's hands we cannot tell ; that it never issued from the press seems almost certain.

We have seen that during the spring and summer Shelley was engaged upon " Queen Mab." Some lines of the ninth section of the poem occur in a letter addressed from Dublin to Miss Hitchener ; a considerable fragment was sent in August by way of specimen from Lynmouth to the publisher Hookham ; on the last day of October, 1812, Godwin made the entry in his diary, " Queen Mab, pp. 44," signifying, probably, that he had read by that day forty-four pages of Shelley's manuscript. Although the affairs of the embankment absorbed much of Shelley's time during part of the year 1813, he still worked at " Mab," when it was possible, and hoped soon to have his poem at an end. " I expect," he wrote to Hookham on January 16, " to have ' Queen Mab ' and the other poems finished by March. ' Queen Mab ' will be in ten cantos, and contain about 2600 lines. The other poems will contain probably as much more. The notes to ' Q. M.' will be long and philosophical. I shall take that opportunity, which I judge to be a safe one, of propagating my principles, which I decline to do syllogistically in a poem. A poem very didactic is, I think, very stupid." And on

February 7, to Hogg: "'Mab' has gone on but slowly, although she is nearly finished. They have teased me out of all poetry. With some restrictions I have taken your advice, though I have not been able to bring myself to rhyme. The didactic is in blank heroic verse, and the descriptive in blank lyrical measure. If an authority is of any weight in support of this singularity, Milton's ' Samson Agonistes,' the Greek choruses, and (you will laugh) Southey's 'Thalaba' may be adduced." " Since I wrote the above," the letter goes on towards its close, " I have finished the rough sketch of my poem. As I have not abated an iota of the infidelity or cosmopolicy of it, sufficient will remain, exclusively of innumerable faults, invisible to partial eyes, to make it very unpopular. . . . I mean to subjoin copious philosophical notes." A few days later (February 19) Shelley informed Hookman that the poem was finished and transcribed. " I am now preparing the notes, which will be long and philosophical. You will receive it with the other poems. I think that the whole should form one volume ; but of that we can speak hereafter."

" Queen Mab," disclaimed by its author in 1821, when a pirated edition was given to the public, and described by him in a letter of that date "as villanous trash," is noteworthy as the first serious attempt of Shelley's intellect and imagination to work together. Hitherto they had stood apart, and criticized each other. " Queen Mab,' which is very far from being a great poem, is also far from being villanous trash. A certain moral shallowness, indeed, makes the poem comparatively uninteresting (and the same remark applies to many of its author's later writings), a moral shallowness arising from the view of evil as having existence less in human character than in institutions, laws, governments, and generally in things

external to the conscience and the will. That Shelley
had crude notions about the history of the world, the
origin of civil institutions, of religions, and much beside,
is obvious on the hastiest survey ; that he had taken a
merely one-sided and therefore a flagrantly unjust view
of the Jewish and the Christian religions is equally obvious ;
and it is not difficult to show that his own theory of the
universe is fatally cracked and rent by internal flaws and
fissures. Nevertheless the poem has value even when regarded as an imaginative setting forth of important truths.
Seldom before in English poetry had the unity of nature
and the universality of law—the idea of a cosmos—been
expressed with more precision or a more ardent conviction.
Seldom before in poetry had the vast and ceaseless flow
of Being—restless yet subject to a constant law of evolution and development—been so vividly conceived. Nature,
or, as Shelley preferred to say, the Spirit of Nature, acting
necessarily, and at present producing indifferently good
and evil, giving birth alike to the hero, the martyr, the
bigot, the tyrant, poisonous serpent and innocent lamb,
yet tends unconsciously upward to nobler developments,
purging itself of what is weak and base. His faith in the
possibility of a better life of man did not die away ; it
inspires the " Hellas " and " Prometheus ; " it is the faith
which has inspired the saints and martyrs and confessors
of our century. The good man, according to Shelley in
" Queen Mab," is he who co-operates with nature, and has
a share in its forward tendency ; he is resolute yet meek
gentle but of unalterable will ; he commands not nor
obeys, but steers right on towards his goal, impelled by
" a quenchless desire of universal happiness," an enthusiasm
of humanity. This conception remained with Shelley,
and was embodied in his " Laon " and his " Prometheus."
That his ideal of the future golden age may be smiled at

by common sense as impracticable and impossible, need give us small offence. It is more difficult to understand how Shelley, who did not willingly give pain to a worm, should eagerly wound devout religious spirits in their tenderest part. The explanation is that he could not, at this period, hold two truths together in his head, or two feelings together in his heart. Christianity, whence sprang wars, persecutions, bigotries, hypocrisies, intellectual tyranny, appeared to him to be an impious worm; it must be for the happiness of men that he should strive to wound the evil thing to the death. To all the noble and gentle lives, all the sweet and heroic deaths which had clasped to their breasts the cross of Christ, Shelley, who could see but one side of things, was blind.

"You will receive 'Queen Mab' with the other poems," Shelley wrote to Hookham on February 19, 1813; "I think that the whole should form one volume.' In mid-December he had been preparing the manuscript of these poems, which would contain, he reckoned, some two thousand and six hundred lines of verse. No poem written before "Alastor" can be expected to add to Shelley's poetical glory; but it is well that his years of nonage should be rightly conceived as a period of gradually expanding powers, and of progressive education in his art. Happily his manuscript book containing the pieces intended for publication in the spring of 1813 is in existence, and the history of Shelley's imagination from the days at Oxford to the days at Tremadoc is no longer a blank. Of the shorter poems several may be described as occasional. Several are direct inspirations—never transcripts—from external nature, and seek to render into words some of the emotion caused by its beauty, or wonder, or terror. Or Shelley is alone amid the desolation of the hills, and would fain confront the awful Spirit of the wild, waste

places. Or he wanders forth on the sabbath morning,
away from the church and church-goers, through a "mountain labyrinth of loveliness," meditating on the worship
and religion of " the man sincerely good," to whom every
day is a sabbath day.   Or he bends over a poison-berried
plant, fair in leaf and stem, and moralizes it into many
meanings.   Or the sea-wind blows on his breast and in
his hair, and he prolongs his pleasure by transmuting it
into the gladness of an imagined lover waiting for the
breeze to blow her true-love to her arms.   Other poems
express the ardour of his affection for Harriet, and in
these there is a spiritual quality not always to be found
in poetry which tells of the passion of boy and girl.   We
trace in these early poems influences, in various degrees,
derived from Southey, Campbell, Wordsworth, Scott.
The collection, which is introduced by the dedication to
Harriet afterwards prefixed to " Queen Mab" (and here
given with differences of phrasing), opens with a series of
poems in unrhymed stanzas, the use of which Shelley had
learnt from Southey's early volumes.   Such lines as those
to Liberty—

> " And the spirits of the brave
> Shall start from every grave,
> Whilst from her Atlantic throne
> Freedom sanctifies the groan
> That fans the glorious fires of its change "—

are a direct reminiscence from " Ye Mariners of England "
and " The Battle of the Baltic."   Beside the dedication,
one other poem was transferred to " Queen Mab " from
this manuscript book—the dialogue between Falsehood
and Vice, which Shelley gave in a note to " Queen Mab,"
intimating that it was there printed because it expressed
strongly his abhorrence of despotism and falsehood, and

no other opportunity would probably occur of rescuing it from oblivion.

Shelley's residence at Tremadoc was suddenly and strangely brought to a close. On the night of Friday, February 26, as stated by Shelley and Harriet—a night of storm and rain—the lonely house of Tanyrallt was entered by some villain bent on outrage. Shelley, hearing a noise, descended, pistols in hand, from his bedroom. Shots were fired, and a hand-to-hand struggle ensued, which ended with the escape of Shelley's antagonist. Later in the night—towards the wild March morning—a second attempt at assassination was made, from which Shelley escaped unhurt in life or limb, but much shaken in nerves. Next day Shelley, Harriet, and Eliza quitted Tanyrallt, and took shelter with friends—the Nanneys —at seven miles' distance. For some days Shelley was seriously indisposed. By March 6 he, with his wife and sister-in-law, was at Bangor Ferry on his way to Ireland, where he hoped by change of scene to dissipate the painful impressions left by the night of peril and excitement.

On the day after the nocturnal attack, Shelley endeavoured to address a letter to Hookham ; but, having written a line or two, he was unable to continue, in consequence of nervous excitement. He desired to receive back for his immediate needs the £20 intended to have been applied to Leigh Hunt's benefit. A postscript by Harriet confirmed his statement respecting the attempted assassination.

Shelley to Hookham.

My dear Sir,
          I have just escaped an atrocious assassination. Oh . send the £20 if you have it. You will perhaps hear of me no more,
                                        friend,
                                             Percy Shelley.

[*Postscript by Harriet Shelley.*]

Mr. Shelley is so dreadfully nervous to-day from having been up all night, that I am afraid what he has written will alarm you very much. We intend to leave this place as soon as possible, as our lives are not safe so long as we remain. It is no common robber we dread, but a person who is actuated by revenge, and who threatens my life and my sister's as well. If you can send us the money, it will greatly add to our comfort.

Sir, I remain your sincere friend,
H. SHELLEY.

Immediately Hookham sent the much-desired succour, and Shelley's heart, wounded by doubts and unfriendly suspicions among the Tremadoc folk whom he had sought so earnestly to serve, overflowed in gratitude and gladness.

"The ball of the assassin's pistol (he fired at me twice) penetrated my night-gown," Shelley writes, "and pierced the wainscot. He is yet undiscovered, though not unsuspected, as you will learn from my next."

From Dublin, a few days later, Harriet Shelley communicated to Hookham the promised details.

[Dublin, March 11.]—"On Friday night, the 26th of February, we retired to bed between ten and eleven o'clock. We had been in bed about half an hour, when Mr. S. heard a noise proceeding from one of the parlours. He immediately went downstairs with two pistols, which he had loaded that night, expecting to have occasion for them. He went into the billiard-room, where he heard footsteps retreating; he followed into another little room, which was called an office. He there saw a man in the act of quitting the room through a glass window which opens into the shrubbery. The man fired at Mr. S., which he avoided. Bysshe then fired, but it flashed in the pan. The man then knocked Bysshe down, and they struggled on the ground. Bysshe then fired his second pistol, which he thought wounded him in the shoulder, as he uttered a shriek and got up, when he said these words : ' By God, I will be revenged !   I will murder your wife ;

I will ravish your sister! By God, 'I will be revenged!' He
then fled—as we hoped for the night. Our servants were no
gone to bed, but were just going, when this horrible affai
happened. This was about eleven o'clock. We all assembled in
the parlour, where we remained for two hours. Mr. S. the
advised us to retire, thinking it impossible he would make a
second attack. We left Bysshe and our manservant, who ha
only arrived that day, and who knew nothing of the house, to si
up. I had been in bed three hours when I heard a pistol go off
I immediately ran downstairs, when I perceived that Bysshe'
flannel gown had been shot through, and the window-curtain
Bysshe had sent Daniel to see what hour it was, when he hear
a noise at the window. He went there, and a man thrust hi
arm through the glass and fired at him. Thank Heaven! th
ball went through his gown and he remained unhurt. Mr. S
happened to stand sideways; had he stood fronting, the ball mus
have killed him. Bysshe fired his pistol, but it would not go off
he then aimed a blow at him with an old sword, which we foun
in the house. The assassin attempted to get the sword from him
and just as he was pulling it away, Dan rushed into the room
when he made his escape.

"This was at four in the morning. It had been a most dread
ful night; the wind was as loud as thunder, and the rai
descended in torrents. Nothing has been heard of him: and w
have every reason to believe it was no stranger, as there is a ma
of the name of Leeson, who the next morning that it happene
went and told the shopkeepers of Tremadoc that it was a tal
of Mr. Shelley's to impose upon them, that he might leave th
country without paying his bills. This they believed, and non
of them attempted to do anything towards his discovery.

"We left Tanyrallt on Saturday, and stayed, till everything wa
ready for our leaving the place, at the Solicitor-General of th
county's house, who lived seven miles from us. This Mr. Leeso
has been heard to say that he was determined to drive us out o
the country. He once happened to get hold of a little pamphl
which Mr. S. had printed in Dublin; this he sent up to Gover
ment. In fact, he was for ever saying something against u
and that because we were determined not to admit him to o

house, because we had heard his character ; and from many acts
of his we found that he was malignant and cruel to the greatest
degree."

The Tanyrallt outrage has been a perplexity to Shelley's
biographers. Was the assassin real, or a creation of the
brain ? Or was the first attack real, and the second a
delusion ? It is certain that on more than one occasion
Shelley was the victim of his own overwrought sensibility,
and suffered from the persecution of phantasies. In the
present instance there can be no doubt that Shelley's mind
was to a certain degree unhinged ; but we cannot now
determine whether this was the cause of a train of fantastic
illusions, or the consequence of an actual struggle for life
with a desperate assailant. " I was in North Wales in the
summer of 1813," wrote Peacock, "and heard the matter
much talked of. Persons who had examined the premises
on the following morning had found that the grass of the
lawn appeared to have been much trampled and rolled on,
but there were no footmarks on the wet ground, except
between the beaten spot and the window; and the impression of the ball on the wainscot showed that the pistol
had been fired towards the window and not from it. This
appeared conclusive as to the whole series of operations
having taken place from within." * Of a struggle out of
doors upon the grass, Harriet's letter to Hookham gives
no information ; but the information needed to render
Peacock's statement intelligible is supplied by Mrs. Williams,
writing in 1860 from a recollection of her husband's talk of
forty years before. " My husband has often talked to me
about ' Shelley's ghost,' as it used at the time I married, in
1820, to be the topic of conversation among strangers who
used to visit this place. . . . To me he often said that he

---

* This last argument, as has been observed, is far from conclusive, for
three shots are said to have been fired, one by Shelley himself.

believed that there was no attempt at burglary, or was there anything like an apparition at Tanyrallt at the time alluded to ; it was all produced by heated imagination. . . . Mr. Williams was sent for, and found Mr. Shelley in a sad state of distress and excitement ; he had fancied that he saw a man's face on the drawing-room window ; he took his pistol and shot the glass to shivers, and then bounced out on the grass, and there he saw leaning against a tree the ghost, or, as he said, the devil ; and to show Mr. Williams what he had seen, he took his pen and ink and sketched the figure on the screen, where it *is* at this moment, showing plainly that his mind was astray. . . When I add that Mr. Shelley set fire to the woods to burn the apparition (with some trouble they were saved), you may suppose it was not all right with him." There is enough here to convince us that either as cause or consequence of the horror of the night Shelley's thick-coming fancies painfully oppressed him. The sense of a terrible reality however, was not transitory with him ; in after years he ascribed the spasms of physical agony from which he suffered to an injury caused by the pressure on his body of the Tanyrallt assassin's knee ; and Mrs. Godwin, alleging Jane Clairmont as her informant, declared that there were days on which he believed that he was still dogged by Leeson, his Tanyrallt enemy, and feared in consequence to walk out alone. On the night of alarm, Shelley retired to bed, as Harriet mentions in her letter to Hookham, with loaded pistols, expecting to have need of them before morning. We may well suppose that Shelley's Irish man servant, Dan Healey, who had arrived at Tanyrallt a few hours previously, after having completed his six months imprisonment in Barnstaple gaol, was in a communicative mood ; and it is not improbable that questions had been put to him respecting his master which suggested to Dan

what was indeed the fact, that Shelley was regarded in the
little Devonshire town as a dangerous criminal, and had
been under the observation of the authorities. Shelley
may have thought it probable that Dan had been tracked
from Barnstaple to Tremadoc by some emissary of the
authorities. Dark suspicions with regard to Leeson might
revive under the influence of Dan's rumours and reports.
For Leeson, at least, was no phantom of the brain. Leeson,
an eminently loyal and disagreeable Englishman, who had
learnt in the early Tremadoc days from Williams or Miss
Hitchener of Shelley's authorship of a seditious pamphlet,
and the risk of a Government prosecution; "an envious,
unfeeling sort of man," declares Mrs. Williams, "not very
particular what he said of any one," and who had charged
Shelley to the face with his utterance of sedition—what
might not Leeson attempt against an enemy of the Government, perhaps with secret encouragement from those in
power? And it is really not impossible that Leeson, with
his officious loyalty, may have been in communication with
Government respecting Shelley, as were the mayor and
town-clerk of Barnstaple—may have been directed to keep
an eye on the dangerous young man, and may have done
some amateur espionage on a neighbour whom he disliked.
If the assassin were one of flesh and blood, and other than
a common burglar—and the burglar at that date did a
fairly brisk business all over England during the winter
nights—may we not accept in a modified form Shelley's
theory as not wholly improbable? May not some sturdy
loyalist in Leeson's employ, whose attention had been
directed towards the treasonable occupant of Tanyrallt,
have overstepped the bounds of his commission, and,
tempted by the boisterous weather and the lonely situation
of the house, have thought to enrich a true king's man at
the expense of his country's enemy, whose possession of

wealth had lately been demonstrated by the promise of a liberal subscription to the embankment fund? The villain it is true, was seen by no one except Shelley ; but flesh-and-blood burglars have a modesty which generally hinders them from presenting themselves before an assembled company. Unless ingeniously awkward or deliberately fraudulent, Shelley could hardly have pierced his night-gown with the ball of his own pistol; and Harriet's state-ment throughout has an air of sincerity. Miss Westbrook " often in after years," it is said, " related the circumstance as a frightful fact." Leeson's cruel assertion that Shelley invented the entire story as an excuse for escaping from his creditors in Tremadoc, is sufficiently disproved—if disproof were needed—by the state of nervous excitement in which Shelley was found next morning by Williams, and by his account of the ghost or demon on the lawn, a feature of the tale obviously tending to discredit all the rest with persons of sober judgment.

Adrift once more, like a cloud anchored for a time to the Welsh mountain-height and suddenly loosened from its anchorage, whither should Shelley now be blown? Why not westward across the Irish Sea? To settle in London, near Godwin and the Newtons, would indeed have been a happy arrangement; but at present Shelley needed complete change, and was not disposed for a little while to settle anywhere. Harriet still remained enthu-siastically Irish in her sympathies, and she had friends in Dublin whom she desired to see. Perhaps already, although no hint of this was given in letters to Hogg, they had some notion of a possible visit to the lakes of Killarney. Their movements hitherto had been largely influenced by a craving for beauty of landscape; they had seen something of Scotland, the lakes of Cumberland, North and South Wales, the romantic sea-coast of Devon.

Why should not Killarney, with its enchantment of lake and island and mountain, draw them towards itself? Hitherto in Ireland they had seen only the decaying grandeurs and living squalor of Dublin; now, having rested for a while with friends in the Irish capital, they were to journey southward on no political mission, but merely in search of beauty and of joy.

In Cuffe Street, Stephen's Green, now a dingy byway, but inhabited in 1813 by sufficiently well-to-do citizens— barristers, proctors, and attorneys—resided Shelley's friend, "honest Jack Lawless," and from the house of Lawless Harriet's letter to Hookham is dated. Perhaps Shelley stayed with Mr. and Mrs. Lawless, or found lodgings in the same street. Before starting for Killarney he was himself able to write to Hookham, and to forward the complete manuscript of "Queen Mab," the printing of which he hoped might proceed while he was engaged in preparing the notes.

Of Shelley's second visit to Ireland little is known. On Tuesday, March 9, he reached Dublin; some ten days or a fortnight later he was in Killarney, and may have arrived there somewhat earlier. He hired a cottage, situated, according to Hogg, on one of the islands of the lake. He gathered his books about him, which were needed for the preparation of the notes to "Queen Mab." We do not find that the purple reeks, or Innisfallen with its ivied ruins, or the fantastic legends of the lakes, suggested to Shelley a single line of verse; yet Shelley was not insensible to the loveliness which lay around him. Long afterwards, when wandering by the shores of the fairest of Italian lakes, his memory travelled back to Ireland in search of something more beautiful than aught else on which his eyes had rested. "Since I last wrote to you," he told Peacock, in April, 1818, "we have been to Como, looking for a house. This lake exceeds anything I ever beheld in beauty, with the exception of the arbutus islands of Killarney."

At Tanyrallt Shelley had looked forward with pleasure to a visit from Hookham, and a visit from Hogg. The invitation had been accepted by Hogg for the month of March, and having brought his mind to contemplate a journey to Carnarvonshire, it seemed a small matter to extend his travel a little further, and follow his friends to Dublin. But on inquiring for Shelley at No. 35, Cuffe Street, he learnt to his surprise and chagrin that the whole party—Bysshe, Harriet, Eliza, and a servant (probably the faithful Dan)—had taken flight, and were now at a distance of some nine score miles—Irish miles to be measured over rough Irish roads. Having heard of Hogg's arrival in Dublin, and perhaps having failed to persuade him to advance into the wilds, Shelley with quick remorse bade farewell to lakes and woods and arbutus islands on the evening of Monday, March 29, and, accompanied by Harriet, reached Cork on the following afternoon, just in time to catch the mail for Dublin. Six and twenty hours of jolting and rattling brought the jaded travellers to their destination. Now, however, it was their turn to suffer disappointment; for Hogg, having spent a week or ten days in Dublin, and heard loud praises of Mr. Percy Shelley, but having never seen his face, decided to return from whence he came, and had sailed the day before in the Post-office Packet for Holyhead. Shelley resolved to follow him to London with all possible speed. A brief delay was inevitable, for he had not wherewithal to pay his way. "I must by some means raise money for the journey here," thus he wrote to Hogg; "but I am no one," he added, "to stick at difficulties." Probably in order that no question as to rent might be immediately raised Eliza Westbrook, with the servant, had remained at Killarney. Shelley, rejoicing, if Hogg's account be true, to have escaped from the irksome presence of his sister-in-law, was once more upon the wing, and, having quickly vanquished all difficulties, again crossed the Irish Channel—now for the last time in his life—pressed forward, and on some evening early in April—probably on Monday, the fifth of the month—with Harriet by his side, entered the door of Mr. Westbrook's house in Chapel Street, Grosvenor Square.

O

CHAPTER VIII.

LONDON, BRACKNELL, EDINBURGH, AND WINDSOR
(APRIL TO DECEMBER, 1813).

WHEN Hogg called on Shelley and his wife, a few days
after their arrival in London, he found them not in Mr.
Westbrook's house, but at Cooke's Hotel, Albemarle
Street, Piccadilly. "They were both well, and in good
spirits," he writes; "the lady was as bright, blooming, and
placid as ever." Not a word was said of the outrage at
Tanyrallt, but they were "brimful of the recollections of
discomforts and miseries endured at Killarney," and complained bitterly of the fatigue, expense, and imposition
from which they had suffered. In an incredibly short
time, says Hogg, Eliza reappeared—"mute, smiling, and
languishing as before"—and resumed her sovereign
functions. "Whether she lived constantly with them I
was not exactly informed; it seemed rather that she went
and came in a hushed, mystical manner." Harriet had
not lost her old love of reading aloud, and she was in
excellent voice. "She promptly seized every opportunity
of indulging her taste; she took up the first book that
came to hand as soon as I entered the room, and the
reading commenced. Sir William Drummond's 'Academical Questions,' Smith's 'Theory of Moral Sentiments,'
some of Bishop Berkeley's Works, Southey's 'Chronicle

of the Cid,' had taken the place of Telemachus, Belisarius, Volney's 'Ruins,' and the other works which she had formerly read to me. Whenever Eliza made a descent upon us, silence was immediately proclaimed, and the book was carried away;" for Harriet was soon to be a mother, and must not exhaust her nervous power with the exercise of reading. As for Eliza herself, books were not an essential part of her daily existence; indeed, unless it might be Sir James Lawrence's edifying "History of the Nairs," declares Hogg, she never read anything.

The hotel in Albemarle Street suited Shelley for several reasons. If Harriet should require her sister's attendance, and Eliza were not actually on the spot, she might easily come and go in her hushed, mystical manner, for her father's house in Chapel Street was near at hand. Still closer was the house of Shelley's good friend Hookham, the publisher of Old Bond Street, in whose hands he had placed, a few weeks since the manuscript o 'Queen Mab." An easy walk from Piccadilly, by the Green Park and Grosvenor Place, would bring Shelley to the delightful household in Chester Street—the Newtons —among whom he found the charms of kindred enthusiasm, refinement, affection, and gentle manners. Godwin and his family were, indeed, at a distance from Shelley's present place of abode; but something like a temporary estrangement had taken place between the returned wanderers and the household in Skinner Street. Mrs. Godwin was discovered in her true colours; she had made herself intolerably disagreeable to Harriet Shelley, having failed perhaps to "manage and economize her temper," as Godwin had long since recommended to her. Bysshe, with characteristic frankness, had explained to her husband how matters stood. On a day early in June Mrs. Godwin called on Shelley, and from that date friendly intercourse was renewed, although we do not now read of invitations accepted by Harriet to dinners at Skinner Street, or of dinners at the hotel graced by the presence of Mrs. Godwin.

To pay his travelling expenses to London, Shelley had raised a small sum before leaving Ireland. His purse was slenderly provided ; and some debts had been incurred at Tremadoc. From his cousins, the Groves, he seems to have heard that his mother and sisters were anxious to welcome him and Harriet to Field Place, and, on his cousins' earnest entreaty, he resolved to address a letter of conciliation to his father. The hotel was a convenient place for conducting a friendly negotiation ; the Duke of Norfolk had lately called, and expressed an interest in his affairs. Shelley's twenty-first birthday was drawing near, and possibly Mr. Shelley might perceive that it was his interest to come to terms with a son who might soon have it in his power to encumber the property with *post-obit* bonds. "My dear father," he wrote from Albemarle Street on May 4, "I once more presume to address you to state to you my sincere desire of being considered as worthy of a restoration to the intercourse with yourself and my family which I have forfeited by my follies. . . . I hope the time is approaching when we shall consider each other as father and son with more confidence than ever, and that I shall no longer be a cause of disunion to the happiness of my family." Shelley was conscious that he had been in some ways wanting in consideration for his father's feelings ; he would willingly now place matters on a better footing, if that were possible. But Mr. Timothy Shelley, with characteristic wrongheadedness, must choose a test of Bysshe's filial obedience to which it was impossible for him to submit. Shelley could not disavow his convictions ; he could not declare to the authorities o

University College that he was now a sincere and dutiful son of the Church. "What regards your avowed opinions," wrote his father, "are in my judgment the most material parts of character requiring amendment. And as you now avow there is no change effected in them, I must decline all further communication or any personal interview until that shall be effected ; and I desire you will consider this as my final answer to anything you may have to offer." Not without reason might Bysshe write to the Duke of Norfolk (May 28, 1813), "I was prepared to make to my father every reasonable concession, but I am not so degraded and miserable a slave as publicly to disavow an opinion which I believe to be true. Every man of common sense must plainly see that a sudden renunciation of sentiments seriously taken up is as unfortunate a test of intellectual uprightness as can possibly be devised. I take the liberty of enclosing my father's letter for your Grace's inspection."

Letters of Shelley, from May 4 to July 6, are dated from Cooke's Hotel ; we know that by July 27 he was in occupation of a country house at Bracknell, in Berkshire. It is not easy to bring into agreement with these facts the statement of Hogg, that after a few days had been spent at the Albemarle Street Hotel, Harriet "took lodgings in Half-Moon Street, accounting the situation fashionable," where, he declares, Shelley and his wife stayed for several months. The statement is precise. "There was a little projecting window," writes Hogg, " in Half-Moon Street, in which Shelley might be seen from the street all day long, book in hand, with lively gestures and bright eyes ; so that Mrs. Newton said he wanted only a pan of clear water and a fresh turf to look like some young lady's lark, hanging outside for air and song." We are forced to suppose either that Shelley's residence in Half-Moon

Street was for a brief period in April, or a still briefer period in some later month, or else that he dated his letters from the hotel, though not actually living in it, the Half-Moon Street lodgings, at no great distance from Dover and Albemarle Streets, being possibly in connection with the hotel. Harriet, in whom Fanny Godwin had discovered "a fine lady," now aspired, according to Hogg, to be fashionable. While expecting the birth of a child, she could not trudge the London streets, and Bysshe ventured—he to whom the confinement of carriage-driving was odious—to set up a carriage for his wife.

In the Half-Moon Street lodgings, Bysshe, says Hogg, was happy and comfortable—"comfortable according to his own peculiar scheme of life." The little sitting-room on the first floor, with its projecting window, soon grew into a miniature library; books were "arranged in rows on the floor, in the recesses on each side of the fireplace; and they were piled in disorder on tables and chairs, and heaped up under tables in confusion." Here, when Hogg would call, Harriet was to be found "bright, blooming, calm, and composed as heretofore;" and here she would read aloud, in her clear, equable voice, from Scott's last poem, "Rokeby," which had appeared in January. "Bysshe was sometimes able to give his attention for a little while to the reading, which flowed on easily in a continuous, unbroken stream; . . . he then suddenly started off, and returned, and heard a little more"—an unsatisfactory auditor to a reader who would fain have strict fealty shown to the new quarto volume.

Soon after their return from Ireland, when his intimacy with the Newtons was renewed, Shelley and Harriet resumed strictly vegetarian habits; but to an unconverted guest like Hogg meat-offerings of flesh were presented. If it were proposed to Shelley that he should order dinner he stood aghast, says Hogg, in speechless trance ; when recovered from the outrage to his feelings, " Ask Harriet," he would cry, with a desponding, supplicating mien. " The good Harriet herself was no proficient in culinary art ; she had never been initiated in the mysteries of house-wifery. ' Whatever you please,' was her ordinary answer." " Whatever you please " did not produce a dainty *menu*. A leg of coarse mutton boiled to rags, with no sauce and half-raw turnips ; or some impregnable beef-steaks, with potatoes worthy of the beef-steaks and mutton, followed by uneatable cheese—the memory of these lived painfully with Hogg during half a century. " I have dropped a word, a hint about a pudding ; a pudding, Bysshe said dogmatically, is a prejudice." To regular meals Bysshe, who did not submit to the bondage of times and seasons, was supremely indifferent. He ate only when hungry, said Trelawny of Shelley in the last year of his life, "and then like the birds, if he saw something edible lying about. . . . His drink was water, or tea if he could get it ; bread was literally his staff of life ; other things he thought superfluous." He made his meal of bread luxurious by the addition of common pudding raisins, and these he carried loose in his waistcoat-pocket. Tea remained Shelley's favourite luxury to the close of his life. " Spirituous liquors he never tasted ; beer rarely. He never called for, purchased, or drew wine for his own drinking ; but if it came in his way, and the company was not disagreeable to him, he would sit at table a while after dinner, and take two or three glasses of any white wine, uniformly selecting the weakest." " We luxuriated, ran riot," says Hogg, " in tea and coffee, and sought variety occasionally in cocoa and chocolate. Bread and butter and buttered toast were eschewed ; but bread-cakes, plain seed-cakes, were liberally divided amongst the faithful."

Honey, and especially honeycomb, were dear to the poet's lips ; he did not think scorn of radishes ; and one addition to the vegetable dietary seems to have been all his own— in country rambles he would pick the gummy drops from fir-tree trunks and eat them with a relish, or "in walking through a pine wood, he would apply his tongue to a larch, and lick it as it oozed in a liquid state from the bark."

As to costume, for a time Shelley was careful to avoid the use of any material formed from the wool or hide of beasts, and his long black coat was made of jean. " I never remember," Hogg writes, "to have seen Bysshe in a great coat or cloak, even in the coldest weather. He wore his waistcoat much or entirely open ; sometimes there was an ellipsis of his waistcoat ; it was not expressed but understood. Unless he was compelled to cover it by main force, he had his throat bare ; the neckcloth being cast aside, lost, over the hills and far away, and the collar of his shirt unbuttoned. In the street or road he reluctantly wore a hat, but in fields or gardens his little round head had no other covering than his long, wild, ragged locks." These wild locks upstared more wildly when Shelley, having dipped his head, with much splashing like a bird, in a basinful of cold water, a ceremony repeated several times each day, would thrust his fingers through the dripping, brown hair, setting it on end. A vegetarian diet and abundance of cold water were less likely to affect Shelley's health injuriously than was the intellectual excite-ment which set in with him at hours when other mortals are struck and strewn by the leaden mace of slumber. Shelley's drowsy fit came on early, and when it had passed away, he was as a skylark saluting the new day, but at midnight. Sometimes Hogg would sit up with him all night, reading, conversing, drinking tea, playing at chess.

A little later, when at Bracknell, Shelley confessed to his friend Cornelia Turner that he lingered late, conversing with her, because he dreaded the visions which pursued him when alone at night. " He never was inclined," says Hogg, who loves a fantastic exaggeration, "to go to bed ; it may be truly affirmed that he never went to bed. He was sent to bed, taken to bed, put to bed, but he never retired to rest of his own accord and voluntarily." Although Shelley, by turning night into day, may have been preparing nervous disorders for himself, as yet his health was not seriously impaired. Already, indeed, he suffered from a pain in the side and chest, which afterwards caused him acute and sometimes prolonged anguish. He coughed, and had a nervous apprehension that he was consumptive. " He suffered occasionally from certain painful infirmities," says Hogg ; "but his stamina were sound, his constitution and general health good."

The early summer of 1813 had been bleak and churlish ; flowers opened timidly and late, and fruits were harsh and crude. But before June was over a new brightness had entered the year for Shelley and Harriet—a little, fair, blue-eyed babe was born. By the twenty-eighth of the month the young mother was rapidly recovering. They named the blue-eyed girl Ianthe—" violet-blossom "—a comer to redeem the broken promises of spring ; the name, known to readers of Ovid, was also that given by Shelley to the first daughter of his imagination, the violet-eyed lady of " Queen Mab." They added the name Elizabeth. It doubtless pleased Harriet that the child should be called after her sister, and Shelley's favourite sister was an Elizabeth. " This accession to his family," says Hogg, " did not appear to afford Shelley any gratification or to create an interest. He never spoke of his child to me." And Harriet, Hogg goes on to say, was

unwilling to let him see the little one, because the child
suffered from some trivial blemish in one of her eyes ; and
the mother, herself a beauty, could not bear that it should
be known that one so nearly connected with her was not
perfectly beautiful. From which we learn that Shelley
and Harriet did not turn to Hogg—"a pearl within an
oyster-shell"—for sympathy in their new joy. We know
that Harriet delighted in the babe's azure eyes, and that
Shelley had a father's happiness in fondling and cherishing
his fragile blossom of humanity. "He was extremely
fond of his child," writes Peacock, "and would walk up and
down a room with it in his arms for a long time together,
singing to it a monotonous melody of his own making,
which ran on the repetition of a word of his own making.
His song was 'Yáhmani, Yáhmani, Yáhmani, Yáhmani.
It did not please me, but, what was more important, it
pleased the child, and lulled it when it was fretful. Shelley
was extremely fond of children. He was pre-eminently
an affectionate father."

It was Hogg's impression that Ianthe was born at a
small house in some quiet back street in Pimlico, where he
called several times to inquire for the mother and daughter.
There, he says, they remained not above a month. It is
certain that by July 27 Shelley and his wife had moved
to Bracknell, in Berkshire. The motive for the change
of residence, according to Hogg, was that they might be
nearer to some new and charming acquaintances, the
Boinvilles, whom they had probably first met at the house
of Mr. and Mrs. Newton. In this acquaintance the attraction was mutual, for Shelley was formed to be an ever
fresh delight to those with whom he found himself in
sympathy.

"So you know the Boinvilles," Shelley wrote from
Rome to Peacock, in the year 1819. "I could not help

considering Mrs. Boinville, when I knew her, as the most admirable specimen of a human being I had ever seen. Nothing earthly ever appeared to me more perfect than her character and manners. It is improbable that I shall ever meet again the person whom I so much esteemed, and still admire. . . . Cornelia, though so young when I saw her, gave indications of her mother's excellences ; and certainly less fascinating, is, I doubt not, equally amiable and more sincere. It was hardly possible for a person of the extreme subtlety and delicacy of Mrs. Boinville's understanding and affections to be quite sincere and constant." In 1813 Shelley's acquaintance with the Boinville household had all the charm of radiant newness ; it was the entrance into a world more amiable and exquisite than he had yet known. Mrs. Newton and her sister Mrs. Boinville (or Madame de Boinville, if the French form of the name should be preferred) were the daughters of Mr. Collins, a wealthy proprietor of plantations and negroes in Saint Vincent, who resided in England. He had travelled on the Continent, was a good French scholar, and had imbibed the new sentiments and ideas of his time which gathered around the enchanted word "liberty." In his house came and went many of the constitutional emigrants from France, who had helped to lead the Revolution through its earlier stages, and had been driven abroad by the proscription and bloodshed of its later days. The eldest daughter of the family, a beautiful creature, eager for ideas and full of generous enthusiasm, had caught the political fervour of the day. To Mr. Collins's house, while the French Revolution was still pursuing its bloody way, was introduced a distinguished foreigner, tall and handsome, some thirty-seven years of age, who had played no insignificant part in the affairs of France. M. de Boinville, born at Metz in 1756, had been a *fermier-général* under the old *régime.* He had married early, and after the birth of one child had lost his wife by consumption. In the brilliant society of pre-Revolution days he was distinguished by Lafayette's special confidence and esteem, and naturally attached himself to the liberal-constitutional party in politics. While in England, engaged on a political mission to Philippe Égalité, his name was entered by the revolutionary government on the list of *émigrés,* and his property was confiscated. He dared not at this time return to France ; and it was now, while penniless in London, that he made the acquaintance of Mr. Collins and his household. His distressed condition doubtless would make him all the more an object of interest to an enthusiastic girl ; and when he avowed his love, Miss Collins resolved that her father's objection to a bridegroom who could not support a wife should be no bar between them. She had two hundred a-year of her own, and it should be his. One day, while Mr. Collins was absent, the lovers fled northwards ; they were married by the blacksmith of Gretna Green, and a second time according to the rites of the Church of England. Mr. Collins's resentment did not last long, and their first child, named Cornelia, was born in his house in 1795. Under the Consulate M. de Boinville returned to France, and his wife following him, and by special permission entering Paris, had the pleasure of being introduced to Lafayette, for whose freedom, when he was an Austrian prisoner, she and her husband had eagerly exerted themselves. When Napoleon entered on the disastrous Russian campaign, M. de Boinville accepted a valuable appointment in the Commissariat department of the Grand Army. Mortally stricken, like so many others, by the frost during the retreat from Moscow he died, calling on his daughter Cornelia, in the hospital at Wilna, on February 7, 1813. It was not long before

this date that Mr. Collins had died. Thus in the same
year in which Shelley made the acquaintance of the
Boinville family, a cloud of sorrow had overshadowed
them. Though her face retained a certain youthful beauty,
already the hair was white as snow on Madame de
Boinville's forehead. Shelley remembered the mysterious
spinner, Maimuna, in his favourite poem of " Thalaba,"
who sang by the pinewood fire, in sweet low tones, an
unintelligible song—

> " The pine-boughs were cheerfully blazing,
>   And her face was bright with the flame ;
>   Her face was as a damsel's face,
>   And yet her hair was gray."

This, then, was Maimuna, and Shelley was indeed caught
in an almost invisible thread spun around him, but unconsciously, by this subtle and benignant enchantress.

The weaker side of the Boinville enthusiasms and
sentiment was that which chiefly caught Hogg's amused
glances. Mrs. Boinville was "too much of the French
school " to be quite agreeable to one who did not choose
ever to desert the substantial realities of the world for the
sake of airy principles or fine feelings. "The greater part
of her associates," says Hogg, " were odious. I generally
found there two or three sentimental young butchers, an
eminently philosophical tinker, and several very unso-
phisticated medical practitioners or medical students, all
of low origin and vulgar and offensive manners. They
sighed, turned up their eyes, retailed philosophy, such as
it was, and swore by William Godwin and 'Political
Justice,' acting, moreover, and very clumsily, the parts of
Petrarchs, Werthers, St. Leons, and Fleetwoods. . . . I
bore with the rabble rout for a little while, on account of
my friend, and because I could there enjoy his precious

society ; and they had made him believe that their
higgledy-piggledy ways were very right and fine, and
conducive to progress and perfectibility."

The intimacy between the Boinville and Shelley households did not lessen when both migrated to the quiet little
village of Bracknell, where Shelley found himself at no
great distance from scenes with which he had been familiar
as an Eton schoolboy. The small house which he obtained
as a temporary residence bore a name—" High Elms "—
promising greenery and cool refreshment after the July
streets. Hither, as a visitor to the Shelleys, came Mrs.
Newton, pleased to be near her sister, and Mr. Newton to
taste the Berkshire roots and fruits, sip distilled water,
and brood on the mysterious significances of the signs of
the Zodiac. Hogg had now gone northwards for his
vacation ; but Peacock was just returned from Wales, and
when Shelley begged that he would visit Bracknell, he
was not slow to accept the invitation. To Peacock, with
his keen, ironic good sense, High Elms seemed like his
own Crotchet Castle seen in a pure, anticipated cognition.
" At Bracknell," he says, " Shelley was surrounded by a
numerous society, all in a great measure of his own
opinions in relation to religion and politics, and the larger
portion of them in relation to vegetable diet. But they
wore their rue with a difference. Every one of them
adopting some of the articles of the faith of their general
Church, had each nevertheless some predominant crotchet
of his or her own, which left a number of open questions
for earnest and not always temperate discussion. I was
sometimes irreverent enough to laugh at the fervour
with which opinions utterly unconducive to any practical
result were battled for as matters of the highest importance to the well-being of mankind. Harriet Shelley was
always ready to laugh with me, and we thereby both

lost caste with some of the more hot-headed of the party."

Harriet, if we may conjecture, was finding her true self, and was being freed from that vague and luminous mist into which she had for a time been caught as Shelley's girlish disciple, zealous if without knowledge. We may suppose that Harriet's laughs with Peacock were not recognized by Shelley as a sign that they were growing closer each to the other in sympathy. A more positive source of annoyance was that Harriet had delegated the nursing of her child to a servant, and that Eliza Westbrook, whom Shelley now vehemently disliked, was for ever advising, directing, superintending, hovering as guardian angel over the cradle. "I have often thought," wrote Peacock, "that if Harriet had nursed her own child, and if this sister had not lived with them, the links of their married love would not have been so readily broken." A few days after the arrival of the Shelleys at Bracknell Harriet completed her eighteenth year. Twelve months ago, at Lynmouth, Shelley had celebrated the anniversary in a sonnet bright in its confidence of ever-enduring love. Now, as the sun sank on the last evening of July, he thought wistfully, fondly, yet almost fearfully of his happiness with Harriet, whose birthday was on the morrow, and he expressed his feeling in a sonnet. In spite of its words of cheer, there is something in it of the strangeness and sadness of sunset ; in the tone of its closing lines one detects already the little rift within the lover's lute :—

Evening. To Harriet.

O thou bright Sun ! beneath that dark blue line
Of western distance that sublime descendest,
And gleaming lovelier as thy beams decline,
Thy million hues to every vapour lendest,

And over cobweb lawn and grove and stream
Sheddest the liquid magic of thy light,
Till calm Earth, with the parting splendour bright,
Shows like the vision of a beauteous dream ;
What gazer now with astronomic eye
Could coldly count the spots within thy sphere ?
Such were thy lover, Harriet, could he fly
The thoughts of all that makes his passion dear,
And turning senseless from thy warm caress
Pick flaws in our close-woven happiness.

As yet, however, if there was a speck upon Shelley's
happiness, it was no more than a speck ; nor had Harriet
cause for discontent. "Very blooming and very happy,"
she seemed to Mrs. Newton during the visit of the
Newtons to High Elms. "Ianthe," adds that lady in a
letter to Hogg, "was grown surprisingly ; and Miss Westbrook ever smiling and serene."

The hurry of life in London and Ianthe's birth had
probably brought to an end the lessons in Latin given by
her husband to Harriet. From a teacher Shelley now
became a pupil. Mrs. Boinville and her young married
daughter, Cornelia Turner, incited him to enter a new and
exquisite province—that of Italian poetry. These Italian
studies, commenced in London, with Hogg for his fellow-
student, were pursued further in the quiet of the country.
Bysshe, says Hogg, "had always at his command a short
and royal road to knowledge." While reading Tasso, the
two friends advanced at an even pace, side by side ; but
when they came to their second author, Ariosto, Shelley
could not restrain his ardour, and Hogg found himself left
far behind. Ariosto had excited and fascinated Shelley ;
he eagerly devoured the "Orlando Furioso," returning to
it again and again. "He spoke of the unparalleled poem
with wild rapture during our walks," says Hogg, "and

read aloud to me detached passages with energy and enthusiastic delight." In 1813 Dante was left unattacked; but towards Petrarch the two students were drawn by the special interest taken in that poet by a fair acquaintance— perhaps Mrs. Boinville's daughter, Cornelia. She was, says the mocker, Hogg, a prey to a kind of sweet melancholy arising from causes purely imaginary; she required consolation, and found it in the poetry of Petrarch. " Bysshe entered at once fully into her views, and caught the soft infection, breathing the tenderest and sweetest melancholy as every true poet ought." There may have been, as Hogg intimates, a touch of sentimental unreality in this cult of Petrarch; but if Cornelia Turner was priestess in this worship, it is but just to add that Petrarch was honoured by a woman of noble and generous nature.

In June, when Mr. Timothy Shelley abruptly broke off negotiations with his son, tidings reached Shelley that his mother wished to see him. He had not been long settled at Bracknell when she begged him, during an absence of his father and the three youngest children, to visit his home once more. Shelley determined to walk across the country to Horsham, a distance of some thirty miles, arriving in the twilight of a long summer's day. When within a few miles of Field Place, a farmer gave him a seat in his cart, and amused his unknown companion with grievous information respecting Master Shelley, who seldom went to church. A young officer, Captain Kennedy, then quartered at Horsham, and receiving hospitality from the Shelley family, has left a record of this last, strange, clandestine visit of a son to his father's house :—

"As it was not desirable that Bysshe's presence in the country should be known, we arranged that walking out he should wear my scarlet uniform, and that I should assume his outer garments. So he donned the soldier's

P

dress and sallied forth. His head was so remarkably small that, though mine be not large, the cap came down over his eyes, the peak resting on his nose, and it had to be stuffed before it would fit him. His hat just stuck on the crown of my head. He certainly looked like anything but a soldier. The metamorphosis was very amusing; he enjoyed it much, and made himself perfectly at home in his unwonted garb. We gave him the name of Captain Jones, under which name we used to talk of him after his departure; but with all our care Bysshe's visit could not be kept a secret."

While residing at Bracknell Shelley attained his majority. He was in sore straits for money, and there was an accumulation of debts which, to one whose income was large, would have seemed inconsiderable, but which pressed heavily on him, who still received from his father only two hundred pounds a-year. Early in August he was in town, endeavouring to procure the means of subsistence, while Harriet, with Eliza Westbrook, remained at High Elms, with a slenderly provisioned purse. Negotiations were reopened with Mr. Timothy Shelley, and an amicable meeting took place between father and son. While lawyers were consulting and drawing up opinions on disputed points, Shelley ran some risk of being arrested for debt; and it is stated that his father, without informing him, took means to avert this indignity. Shelley's mother privately acquainted him with all that went on, and Harriet received friendly letters from her husband's sisters. To live on hopes deferred, however, was impossible, and at length, in October, Shelley found himself compelled, chiefly with a view to paying his debts, to resort to the ruinous mode of raising money by post-obit bonds. A bond for two thousand pounds procured for his pressing needs precisely one-fourth of that sum.

When Shelley took up his abode at High Elms it was

his intention to remain at Bracknell, at least until the following spring. But by autumn his thoughts had begun to turn once more towards the Welsh mountain vale in which Harriet and he had spent some happy days after his first visit to Ireland. If only Nantgwillt house were to be had! In such a delightful retreat they might indeed find rest for ever. Meanwhile it was arranged that he should have another interview with his father in November, and therefore, however it might be with Harriet, he could not himself remain long absent from London. October was now come, with its misty splendours and fading glory of the woods. Two years since, in the dull November days, they had arrived at Keswick, and had found it even then a region of delight. Why should they not forthwith hasten to the southern district of the English lakes, and make acquaintance with the beauty of Windermere? The carriage, which Shelley had rashly procured some months since, might now render them a useful service, for in so easy a conveyance Harriet and little Ianthe would suffer but slight fatigue. There would be room for Eliza West-brook—the inevitable sister-in-law—for Shelley, with a light equipment of luggage, and yet a seat for one more traveller. For reasons of his own it suited Peacock to be absent from London at this time ; he, then, should be the fourth in their carriage, and except to chosen friends their whereabouts should remain a secret.

By October 6 the party of four, with little blue-eyed Ianthe for a fifth, were at Warwick on their way to the Lakes. A few days later they had taken rooms at Lowood Inn, and were looking for a house ; but no house to suit them could be found. And if the people of Carnarvon-shire were all aristocrats and saints, the good folk of Westmoreland were, if possible, more intolerant and intolerable. It was decided that the travellers should

push on to Edinburgh, there perhaps to spend the winter.
The literary reputation of the Scottish capital stood high
—and justly so—in these palmy days of the *Edinburgh
Review*, and where there was an intellectual atmosphere
there must be a spirit of tolerance. By mid-October, or
perhaps a little later, the wanderers had reached Edinburgh. The child had borne the journey well, and Harriet
was happy. Shelley found in Peacock a companion who,
if too little ardent to be wholly sympathetic, was yet full
of interest in things of the mind—a man of keen intellect
and refined culture. At Lynmouth he had read certain of
Peacock's poems, finding in them imaginative genius, wide
learning, and beauty of versification, while at the same
time he lamented the objects to which Peacock applied his
powers. It was a happy characteristic of Shelley that he
could enjoy the society of persons whose temper and
disposition were widely different from his own. He was
to a certain extent aware that Peacock could dwell only
in the suburbs of his affections, yet he did not for this
reason despise the pleasure of his company. " He is a
very mild, agreeable man," Shelley wrote from Edinburgh
to Hogg, " and a scholar. His enthusiasm is not very
ardent nor his views very comprehensive ; but he is neither
superstitious, ill-tempered, dogmatical, nor proud."

Shelley's negotiations with his father had not prospered.
Between persons so alien in character and opinions it was
almost idle to look for a perfect understanding. Towards
the close of November Mr. Timothy Shelley was ill, and
the interview arranged for that month had not yet taken
place. Shelley thought of leaving Harriet with Ianthe
and Eliza Westbrook in Edinburgh, and of coming to
London alone. " My evenings," he wrote to Hogg, " will
often be spent at the Newtons, where I presume you are
no infrequent visitor." But when, early in December, he

returned to London, his wife and sister-in-law, with the infant, accompanied him. Entries in Godwin's diary lead one to conjecture that Shelley, though lately obliged for his own necessities to raise money on unfavourable terms, was at this time endeavouring to aid the needy Skinner Street household in their distress. On arriving in London, he saw much of Godwin and of his friends the Newtons ; but before the year was at an end he had left the town, and was settled at Windsor in a furnished house, which he had taken for two or three months, thus finding himself in the midst of his schoolboy haunts, and at no great distance from Bracknell, where the Boinvilles still resided.

The outcome of Shelley's philosophical studies and reflections appeared early in 1814, in the form of an argumentative essay on religion, thrown into the form of a dialogue, and printed under the title, "A Refutation of Deism." It follows, with considerable vigour and subtlety of reasoning, the lines of thought indicated in the notes to "Queen Mab." The book may be regarded as the last development of that contentious, argumentative side of Shelley's nature which found expression at an earlier time in the letters addressed by him under feigned names to eminent champions of orthodoxy, and in the pamphlet which led to his expulsion from University College. The title-page, borrowing a word from Pindar, announces that the dialogue is not for the many, but for the understanding few—Συνετοισι—and in his preface the anonymous author explains that it has been printed in a costly form, "with a view of excluding the multitude from the abuse of a mode of reasoning liable to misconstruction on account of its novelty." The multitude seem to have been effectually excluded. We do not know whether the "Refutation of Deism" was ever offered for sale ; if it were, we may question whether a single copy found a buyer.

CHAPTER IX.

PARTING FROM HARRIET (JANUARY—JULY, 1814).

IN the early part of the year 1814 Shelley was a frequent
visitor at Bracknell, where he found a resting-place in the
home of Mrs. Boinville—and of her daughter, Mrs. Turner.
On one occasion Hogg arrived at Bracknell late at night,
and stayed with Bysshe's friends ; but Bysshe was away in
London. In Shelley's bedroom was much to remind Hogg
of its recent occupant ; clothes were scattered about ; there
were books on every side—"wherever a book could be laid,
was an open book, turned down on its face to keep his
place." Three charming ladies entertained the mocker
with cups of tea, late hours, Wieland's "Agathon," sighs
and smiles, and the celestial manna of refined sentiment.
" Such," he says, "were the delights of Shelley's paradise
in Bracknell." Next day a French youth was his guide
to the neighbouring points of interest—among these to
Shelley's former residence, High Elms, and the brook in
which, as the story was told, Bysshe had stealthily gone to
sea, embarking on board such a vessel as that of Wordsworth's "Blind Highland Boy"—

> "A Household Tub, like one of those
> Which women use to wash their clothes"—

and "rowing or punting his frail bark with a stick used in
washing, until the bottom came out." "He then," the

faithful chronicler goes on, "freely took possession of another vessel until the whole fleet of tubs had suffered shipwreck." These nautical adventures served to diversify Italian studies in which Shelley obtained some assistance from Cornelia Turner.

"I lament to inform you," Shelley wrote from Bracknell to his father on March 13, "that the posture of my affairs is so critical that I can no longer delay to raise money by the sale of post-obit bonds to a considerable amount. I trust that the many expedients which I have employed to avoid this ruinous measure will testify the reluctance with which my necessities compel me at length to have recourse to it. I need not urge the vast sacrifices which money-lenders require, nor press upon attention that I put it out of my power to resettle the estate in any manner by conceding to their demands. Upon your good wishes and consoling assurances I rely with the most entire confidence. I know that you do not lack the will but only the power of doing everything which I could reasonably expect. But surely my grandfather must perceive that his hopes of preserving and perpetuating the integrity of the estate will be frustrated by neglecting to relieve my necessities; he knows that I have the power, which, however reluctantly, I shall be driven to exert, of dismembering the property should I survive himself and you. I do not take the liberty of frequently addressing you, but I hope the urgency of the occasion will be thought sufficient to excuse the present exercise of the licence you permitted." Old Sir Bysshe was now in the last year of his life, although he had, once and again, shown himself friendly towards his grandson in former days, the old man's temper did not err through excess of amiability, and this appeal of Shelley's, if it reached him, fell on deaf ears. It was stated by Shelley's lawyer, in a letter dated April, 1814, that his family could not assist him during his grandfather's life, and that he had "used the utmost of his endeavours" to raise money on the entailed property for the payment of his debts, but "without success." Probably, in the course of these negotiations with money-lenders, a question as to the validity of Shelley's marriage, celebrated in his minority according to the rites of the Church of Scotland, had been raised; and in order to obviate all possible doubts he decided to act in the same manner as M. de Boinville, who, on returning from Scotland after his less formal and regular marriage at Gretna Green, had confirmed the ceremony by re-marriage in an English church. To Shelley it was now essential that no question should exist as to the legitimacy of any son who might be born to him. Godwin had doubtless been consulted on this matter, and Godwin's views respecting marriage were altered much since the first edition of ʻ Political Justice" had proclaimed his revolutionary creed. On March 22 he accompanied Shelley to Doctors' Commons to obtain the licence, and two days later Percy Bysshe Shelley and Harriet Shelley were re-married in St. George's Church by Edward Williams, curate, in the presence of Harriet's father, Mr. John Westbrook, and another witness.

But before this second marriage was solemnized, Shelley's tranquillity had been racked by other anxieties and troubles than those connected with money. His content in his home had seriously suffered, although he did not yet despair of possible healing and recovery. In recording the events which lead up to the parting of Shelley and his first wife, Hogg strikes the note of change on reaching the autumn of 1813. If we may trust Hogg—our only witness who descends from generalities to particulars — the dream of intellectual sympathy between Shelley and his wife was dissolving, or was already dissolved. We can readily conceive how she had grown from the ardent schoolgirl into a woman, possessing a definite sense of certain realities which make up no inconsiderable part of any ordinary woman's life. When Shelley set up a carriage and made a considerable purchase of plate, it was certainly not to gratify his own taste. Harriet could not dwell for ever in a golden mist of liberty, equality, and fraternity, feeding on roots and fruits, and sipping distilled water. Debts and duns were sorry accompaniments of the theory of human perfectibility. She was recovering from the dream and the illusion — for such they were to her — and was able to perceive her husband's infirmities. And he could perceive hers. With Shelley intellectual sympathy—sympathy with his ideal aspirations in the case of a companion who ought to be the nearest and dearest—counted for much, counted for almost all. When in 1812, on her first birthday since she had placed her hands in his, Shelley uttered vows for their future happiness, it was his chief longing that she might retain her enthusiasm of heart even when time should destroy the beauty of face and form. What if now her soul should appear to Shelley to be sinking under the influence of the world? We cite Hogg to bear his testimony such as it is: "The good Harriet had fully recovered from the fatigues of her first effort of maternity, and in fact she had taken it easily. She was now in full force, vigour, and effect; roseate as ever, at times, perhaps, rather too rosy. She had entirely relinquished her favourite practice of reading aloud, which had been formerly a passion. I do not remember hearing her read even once after the birth of her child; the accustomed exercise of the chest had become fatiguing, or she was weary of it. Neither did she read much to herself; her studies, which had been so constant and exemplary, had dwindled away to nothing, and Bysshe had ceased to express any interest in them, and to urge her, as of old, to devote herself to the cultivation of her mind. When I called upon her, she proposed a walk if the weather was fine, instead of the vigorous and continuous readings of preceding years. The walk commonly conducted us to some fashionable bonnet-shop."

While Harriet, if we may believe Hogg, was thus falling away from her interest in things of the mind, Shelley was advancing with eager strides into regions of thought and feeling where she could not be his companion; was absorbed in Laplace, or Homer, or Tacitus; or studied in a translation the dialogues of Plato; or made acquaintance with the poetry of Tasso, Ariosto, and Petrarch in the Italian. In the society of Mrs. Newton, Mrs. Boinville, and Cornelia Turner he found a refinement of perception, a degree of culture, and an enthusiasm for art and literature which he vainly looked for in his own home. By Shelley's connection with his friends at Bracknell his subsequent conduct, in Hogg's opinion, was much influenced. His delight in their society might naturally have been a cause of uneasiness or heartache to Harriet; even if his affections were not drawn away from her—and this she may have believed to be the case—he must needs read her intelligence in the light of theirs.

Still the good, common things of life—precious as daily food, or air and sunlight—establish a basis for wedded love and happiness more solid and enduring, perhaps, than can ever be found in our rarer trances of thought and mountings of the mind. The pleasures of the fireside, mingled memories, and kindred hopes and fears, a blue-eyed babe to fondle and sing to sleep,—these at least remained for Shelley and his wife. Unhappily Shelley's satisfaction in these was now infected with a subtle poison. Peacock has told us how passionately he resented the introduction into his home of a nurse to suckle the infant. Hogg would have us believe that Harriet was lacking in the warmth and

quickness of a mother's love, and he relates how, during
some surgical operation performed upon Ianthe, Harriet
stood by narrowly observing all that was done, but, to the
astonishment of the operator, betraying not the smallest sign
of emotion. We must not infer from this that Harriet did
not feel, but we learn that those about her could believe
her to be hard and insensible. If words of tender affection
and motherly pride addressed to her Irish friend, Miss
Nugent, prove the reality of love, then undoubtedly she
loved her firstborn child. And should Harriet ever assume
an air of pride and hardness towards her husband, it was
surely his part to press forward and discover the tenderness which lay concealed under her seeming indifference.
Unhappily it was impossible in such circumstances to deal
with Harriet alone ; the inevitable elder sister—we speak
from Shelley's point of view—was constantly by her side
as counsellor, guide, and guardian. When Shelley fled to
Scotland in August, 1811, he supposed that he was wedding
a solitary girl, persecuted in her father's home, and turning
to him for protection. How was it then that she had another
protector—an ever-present custodian, in whom she trusted
as the embodiment of feminine wisdom ? How was it that
he had wedded along with Harriet this Eliza Westbrook,
whose touch was upon everything, and who seemed to
Shelley to contaminate everything by her touch ? We
know how swiftly a fever of dislike could inflame Shelley's
blood, could infect his whole nature, and, rising to detestation and abhorrence, could render every nerve a seat of
throbbing anguish. That he put constraint upon himself,
and checked the "overflowings of his abhorrence," was well ;
but such self-control, with one whose reserve of strength
was quickly exhausted under excitement, must result at
last in extreme fatigue of heart. We know Eliza Westbrook at this date too exclusively through coloured mediums

to pronounce independent judgment on her character and conduct; but we know that Shelley now and ever afterwards regarded her with horror, and it is certain that Shelley's friends, though differing on various other matters, agreed in believing that her influence on Harriet was used with most injurious effect.

Shelley, heir to a baronetcy and a great fortune, was now of age; it was natural that his wife's relatives should desire a settled position for Harriet, and the ease and elegance suitable to her rank and prospects. She was married—as it happened—to a poet and a man of genius, for whom a fashionable life meant a living death. And Harriet's greatest charm in Shelley's eyes had been, as he informed Fanny Godwin, when defending his wife from the accusation of being a fine lady, that in all her tastes and habits and ways of thought and feeling she was simple, natural, and plain. What if now she had set her desires on elegant apartments, a carriage, silver plate, and masterpieces of the milliner's art? It is well to cite the statement of Thornton Hunt, who wrote with full knowledge of the views of Leigh Hunt, his father. "There can be no doubt," he says, "that one member of the [Westbrook] family had hoped to derive gain from the connection with himself [*i.e.* Shelley], as a person of rank and property. . . . Poor, foolish Harriet had undoubtedly formed an attachment to Shelley, whom she had been allowed to marry; but she had then suffered herself to become a tool in the hands of others, and the fact accounted for the idle way in which she importuned him to do things repugnant to his feelings and convictions. She thus exasperated his temper and lost her own. . . . Too late she became aware how fatal to her interests had been the intrigues of which she had been the passive instrument."

However the mischief may have been wrought, it is certain

that some cause or causes of deep division between Shelley and his wife were in operation during the early part of the year 1814. To guess at the precise nature of these causes, in the absence of definite statement, were useless. We may rest content with Shelley's own words, in a paper drawn up in 1817, for use in connection with the Chancery suit which deprived him of his children. "Delicacy," he wrote, "forbids me to say more than that we were disunited by incurable dissensions." A week before the ceremony of re-marriage to Harriet in St. George's Church, Shelley wrote to Hogg, from Mrs. Boinville's house at Bracknell, as follows :—

[March 16, 1814.]—I have been staying with Mrs. B[oinville] for the last month ; I have escaped, in the society of all that philosophy and friendship combine, from the dismaying solitude of myself. They have revived in my heart the expiring flame of life. I have felt myself translated to a paradise, which has nothing of mortality but its transitoriness ; my heart sickens at the view of that necessity, which will quickly divide me from the delightful tranquillity of this happy home,—for it has become my home. The trees, the bridge, the minutest objects, have already a place in my affections.

My friend, you are happier than I. You have the pleasures as well as the pains of sensibility. I have sunk into a premature old age of exhaustion, which renders me dead to everything but the unenviable capacity of indulging the vanity of hope, and a terrible susceptibility to objects of disgust and hatred.

My temporal concerns are slowly rectifying themselves ; I am astonished at my own indifference to their event. I live here like the insect that sports in a transient sunbeam, which the next cloud shall obscure for ever. I am much changed from what I was. I look with regret to our happy evenings at Oxford, and with wonder at the hopes which in the excess of my madness I there encouraged. . . . Eliza is still with us,—not here !—but will be with me when the infinite malice of destiny forces me to depart. I am now but little inclined to contest this point. I certainly hate her with all my heart and soul. It is a sight which awakens an inexpressible sensation of disgust and horror, to see her caress my poor little Ianthe, in whom I may hereafter find the consolation of sympathy. I sometimes feel faint with the fatigue of checking the overflowings of my unbounded abhorrence for this miserable wretch. But she is no more than a blind and loathsome worm, that cannot see to sting.

I have begun to learn Italian again. I am reading " Beccaria dei delitti e pene." His essay seems to contain some excellent remarks, though I do not think that it deserves the reputation it has gained. Cornelia assists me in this language. Did I not once tell you that I thought her cold and reserved? She is the reverse of this, as she is the reverse of everything bad. She inherits all the divinity of her mother.

What have you written? I have been unable even to write a common letter. I have forced myself to read Beccaria, and Dumont's Bentham. I have sometimes forgotten that I am not an inmate of this delightful home—that a time will come which will cast me again into the boundless ocean of abhorred society.

I have written nothing but one stanza, which has no meaning, and that I have only written in thought—

> Thy dewy looks sink in my breast ;
> 　Thy gentle words stir poison there ;
> Thou hast disturbed the only rest
> 　That was the portion of despair !
> Subdued to Duty's hard control,
> 　I could have borne my wayward lot :
> The chains that bind this ruined soul
> 　Had cankered then, but crushed it not.

This is the vision of a delirious and distempered dream, which passes away at the cold clear light of morning. Its surpassing excellence and exquisite perfections have no more reality than the colour of an autumnal sunset.

Four days after writing this letter Shelley was at Doctors' Commons, to procure the licence for his marriage with Harriet according to the rites of the English Church. This incident of ceremonious marriage altered little, if at all, the position of affairs. In April Shelley was once more at Bracknell, and Harriet was elsewhere. "Shelley," wrote Mrs. Boinville to Hogg (April 18), "is again a widower; his beauteous half went to town on Thursday with Miss Westbrook, who is gone to live, I believe, at Southampton." That Eliza Westbrook had taken her departure was something gained, but the gain came too late. The beautiful "Stanzas," dated "April, 1814," read like a fantasia of sorrow, the motives of which are supplied by Shelley's anticipated farewell to Bracknell, and his return, at the call of duty, to a home which seemed to him loveless.

Stanzas: April, 1814.

Away! the moor is dark beneath the moon,
Rapid clouds have drunk the last pale beam of even :
  Away! the gathering winds will call the darkness soon,
  And profoundest midnight shroud the serene lights of heaven.
Pause not! the time is past! Every voice cries, "Away!"
Tempt not with one last tear thy friend's ungentle mood :
Thy lover's eye, so glazed and cold, dares not entreat thy stay :
Duty and dereliction guide thee back to solitude.

Away, away! to thy sad and silent home ;
  Pour bitter tears on its desolated hearth ;
  Watch the dim shades as like ghosts they go and come,
  And complicate strange webs of melancholy mirth.
The leaves of wasted autumn woods shall float around thine head,
  The blooms of dewy Spring shall gleam beneath thy feet :
But thy soul or this world must fade in the frost that binds
    the dead,
Ere midnight's frown and morning's smile, ere thou and peace, may
    meet.

The cloud-shadows of midnight possess their own repose,
For the weary winds are silent, or the moon is in the deep ;
  Some respite to its turbulence unresting ocean knows :
Whatever moves or toils or grieves hath its appointed sleep.

Thou in the grave shalt rest :—yet, till the phantoms flee
  Which that house and heath and garden made dear to thee
    erewhile,
Thy remembrance and repentance and deep musings are not free
From the music of two voices, and the light of one sweet smile.

Early in May Shelley left London. He did not yet despair of reconciliation with Harriet, nor had he ceased to love her. His feelings find record in a poem addressed by Shelley to Harriet in May, 1814. It is the first of a few short pieces added in Harriet's handwriting to the manuscript collection of poems prepared by Shelley for publication in the early days of the preceding year. In this appeal Shelley declares that he has now no grief but one—the grief of having known and lost his wife's love ; if it is the fate of all who would live in the sunshine of her affection to endure her scorn, then let him be scorned above the rest, for he most of all has desired that sunshine ; let not the world and the pride of life harden her heart ; it is better that she should be kind and gentle ; if she has something to endure, it is not much, and all her husband's weal hangs upon her loving endurance ; let her not cure his malady by the fatal way of condemning him to exile beyond all hope or further fear ; let her trust no erring guide, no unwise counsellor, no false pride ; rather learn that a nobler pride may find its satisfaction in and through love ; or if love be for ever dead, at least let pity survive in its room.

To Harriet : May, 1814.

Thy look of love has power to calm
  The stormiest passion of my soul ;
Thy gentle words are drops of balm
  In life's too bitter bowl ;
No grief is mine, but that alone
These choicest blessings I have known.

Harriett! if all who long to live
    In the warm sunshine of thine eye,
That price beyond all pain must give
    Beneath thy scorn to die—
Then hear thy chosen own too late
His heart most worthy of thy hate.

Be thou, then, one among mankind
    Whose heart is harder not for state,
Thou only virtuous, gentle, kind,
    Amid a world of hate ;
And by a slight endurance seal
A fellow-being's lasting weal.

For pale with anguish is his cheek,
    His breath comes fast, his eyes are dim,
Thy name is struggling ere he speak,
    Weak is each trembling limb;
In mercy let him not endure
The misery of a fatal cure.

O trust for once no erring guide !
    Bid the remorseless feeling flee ;
'Tis malice, 'tis revenge, 'tis pride,
    'Tis anything but thee ;
O deign a nobler pride to prove,
And pity if thou canst not love.

Cook's Hotel.

It is evident that in May, 1814, Harriet had assumed an
attitude of alienation towards her husband, who pleaded
with almost despairing hope for the restoration of her love.

How Harriet responded to this appeal we cannot tell.
As far as we can ascertain, a fatal misunderstanding existed
between husband and wife. We are assured by Thornton
Hunt that Harriet of her own accord left Shelley. When
next we can discover her place of residence—in the

Q

beginning of July—we find her at Bath, whereas Shelley, save from a brief interval between June 8 and June 18, had remained in London since the latter days of May. Harriet, perhaps, had not ceased to love her husband; but it seems certain that, whatever may have been the cause, she maintained an appearance of hardness, and refused to meet his advances of affection. The sense of what seemed to him a cruel and unconquerable hardness certainly was present with Shelley at this time, and the memory of it lived on with him into later years. In the copy of "Queen Mab" given by him to Mary Godwin in July, 1814, under the dedication of that poem to Harriet he wrote the words, "Count Slobendorf was about to marry a woman who, attracted solely by his fortune, proved her selfishness by deserting him in prison." It was Shelley's veiled comment on the words of that dedication in which he had addressed Harriet as "his purer mind," "the inspiration of his song"— a comment penned in bitterness of spirit, and perhaps with some of the injustice of such bitterness. He had married a woman who, as he now persuaded himself, had never truly loved him, who loved only his fortune and his rank, and who proved her selfishness by deserting him in his misery—

> "The cage
> Of fettered grief that dares not groan."

These words of the dedication to Harriet were precisely the words in the volume which he could not bear that Mary should read as expressing his present mind; but his comment should be intelligible only to one who could interpret a riddle. "I believe," wrote Shelley to Mary on October 28, 1814, "I must become in Mary's hands, what Harriet was in mine. Yet how differently disposed—how devoted and affectionate—how beyond measure reverencing and adoring the intelligence that governs me!" And

three years later, after Harriet's piteous death, he still felt
her hardness towards him, though he would not now permit
himself to give utterance to the feeling. In the sixth
stanza of the dedication of "The Revolt of Islam," two
lines which stand thus in the printed text—

> " Yet never found I one not false to me,
> Hard hearts and cold like weights of icy stone ! "—

were originally written with obvious allusions to his cousin
Harriet Grove and his first wife—

> " One whom I found was dear but false to me,
> *The other's heart was like a heart of stone.*"

Yet Harriet Shelley's heart was indeed no heart of stone,
but a frail heart of woman, capable of love, of grief, and of
despair.

In May, Shelley's prayer to his wife had been that in
mercy she should save him from "The misery of a fatal
cure." Now it seemed as if there might be no cure but
this fatal one—to free himself for ever from the past. In
a volume dedicated to Harriet he had declared his views
as to the conditions under which wedded union and its
mutual obligations may cease, little imagining at the time
that such words could have an application to his own case.
"What law," he asks, "ought to specify the extent of the
grievances which should limit the duration of the union of
wife and husband ? " And he answers in accordance with
the revolutionary creed which he had learnt from Godwin's
writings : "A husband and wife ought to continue so long
united as they love each other. . . . The present system of
constraint does no more, in the majority of instances, than
make hypocrites or open enemies. Persons of delicacy
and virtue, unhappily united to one whom they find it
impossible to love, spend the loveliest season of their life

in unproductive efforts to appear otherwise than they are, for the sake of the feelings of their partner, or the welfare of their mutual offspring; those of less generosity and refinement openly avow their disappointment, and linger out the remnant of that union which only death can dissolve, in a state of incurable bickering and hostility. The early education of their children takes its colour from the squabbles of the parents; they are nursed in a systematic school of ill-humour, violence, and falsehood. Had they been suffered to part at the moment when indifference rendered their union irksome, they would have been spared many years of misery; they would have connected themselves more suitably, and would have found that happiness in the society of more congenial partners which is for ever denied them by the despotism of marriage. They would have been separately useful and happy members of society, who, whilst united, were miserable, and rendered misanthropical by misery." To discuss this matter in the abstract was easy. Human hearts, however, are not framed of doctrines and opinions; they are sensitive to strain and shock, and may bleed inwardly.

Since the day after Shelley's errand, in company with Godwin, to procure the licence of marriage, he had not once called at Godwin's house until early in May, when he came from Bracknell to London. His pecuniary affairs, though they had been slowly mending, as he informed Hogg in March, were still in a condition far from satisfactory; but Godwin was sunk even deeper in distress. With characteristic generosity, Shelley resolved that he would put forth all his powers to raise a sum sufficient to place above present anxiety the friend towards whom he felt a reverential attachment, and whose teaching had been for him—as he believed—an inspiring moral force. The sum was necessarily a large one—three thousand pounds,

it is said—and to procure this in Shelley's present circumstances would be difficult, if, indeed, it did not prove
impossible.   In the course of monetary negotiations,
Shelley's intercourse with Godwin was drawn closer.
During the month of May and the first week of June the
friends met usually twice a week, and when, after an
interval of ten days (Shelley perhaps being absent from
London for that period), they were again together, it seems
to have been arranged that Shelley should henceforth join
the Skinner Street household each day at dinner.   In one
of these calls at Skinner Street, in May or early June,
Shelley's eyes first rested with interest on Godwin's
daughter Mary, now just returned from a long visit to the
Baxters in Scotland—a girl in her seventeenth year, with
shapely golden head, a face very pale and pure, great forehead, earnest hazel eyes, and an expression at once of
sensibility and firmness about her delicately curved lips.
It is possible that Shelley may once have seen her as a
child in 1812; in the following summer when he was in
London, Mary was away at Dundee.   Whether he saw
her or not on previous occasions, certainly now for the
first time he felt her rare attraction.   The daughter of
Godwin and Mary Wollstonecraft had gifts of heart and
mind such as Shelley had never hitherto known in woman.
"She is singularly bold, somewhat imperious, and active in
mind"—so Godwin described Mary at the age of fifteen;
"her desire of knowledge is great, and her perseverance in
everything she undertakes almost invincible."   From her
father she had inherited clearness and precision of intellect,
firmness of will, and a certain quietude of manner, which
sometimes gave way before an outbreak of strong feeling;
for under this quiet bearing lay her mother's sensibility
and ardour, with an imaginative power which quickened
and widened her sympathies.   Though of a temper naturally

more conservative than that of Godwin or her mother, Mary had breathed during her entire life an atmosphere of free thought ; she could not live in Godwin's house and meet Godwin's friends without insensibly learning to consider the facts of life from the rationalist or critical point of view. Her father she regarded with a fond reverence and devotion ; and cherished with peculiar attachment the memory of the mother who died when she was born. but whose face, winningly sweet and sad, looked down upon her from Opie's portrait hanging in her father's study. The second Mrs. Godwin had not made her home a happy one for Mary ; and it was Mary's custom on fine days, book in hand, to turn her steps northward until she reached the churchyard of old St. Pancras, then partly surrounded by meadow-land and pasturage, and there by her mother's grave to sit and read.

If Shelley had never met a woman who united in herself so many high attractions as Mary, assuredly Mary had never known a being composed of elements so fine and rare as those which made up the nature of Shelley. It was easy to divine that some restless grief possessed him ; Mary was herself not unlearned in the lore of pain. His generous zeal in her father's behalf, his spiritual sonship to Godwin, his reverence for her mother's memory, were guarantees with Mary of his excellence. The new friends could not lack subjects of discourse, and underneath their words about Mary's mother, and " Political Justice," and " Rights of Woman," were two young hearts, each feeling towards the other, each trembling in the direction of the other. On June 8, the eve, it would seem, of Shelley's departure from London for ten days, he called at the Juvenile Library, Skinner Street. Hogg accompanied him, and on that occasion saw for the first time Shelley's future wife. " I followed him," writes Hogg, " through the shop, which was the only entrance, and upstairs. We entered a room on the first floor; it was shaped like a quadrant. In the arc were windows; in one radius a fire-place, and in the other a door, and shelves with many old books. William Godwin was not at home. Bysshe strode about the room, causing the crazy floor of the ill-built, unowned dwelling-house to shake and tremble under his impatient footsteps. He appeared to be displeased at not finding the fountain of Political Justice. 'Where is Godwin?' he asked me several times, as if I knew. I did not know, and, to say the truth, I did not care. He con-tinued his uneasy promenade; and I stood reading the names of old English authors on the backs of the venerable volumes, when the door was partially and softly opened. A thrilling voice called, 'Shelley!' A thrilling voice answered, 'Mary!' And he darted out of the room, like an arrow from the bow of the far-shooting king. A very young female, fair and fair-haired, pale indeed, and with a piercing look, wearing a frock of tartan, an unusual dress in London at that time, had called him out of the room. He was absent a very short time—a minute or two; and then returned. 'Godwin is out; there is no use in waiting.' So we continued our walk along Holborn. 'Who was that, pray?' I asked; 'a daughter?' 'Yes.' 'A daughter of William Godwin?' 'The daughter of Godwin and Mary.' This was the first time . . . that I beheld a very distinguished lady, of whom I have much to say hereafter. It was but the glance of a moment, through a door partly opened. Her quietness certainly struck me, and possibly also, for I am not quite sure on this point, her paleness and piercing look."

Before the close of June it was known and felt by Mary and Shelley that each was inexpressibly dear to the other; but though their hearts were one, they did not yet dare to think that the closest of unions was possible for them. Even this stage in their mutual approach had been reached by degrees. Shelley had put a certain constraint upon his feelings ; had shrunk from a confession. And it would seem that Mary's pity, through some betrayal of agitation or of tears, had involuntarily manifested itself as but the veil of a deeper feeling, before they dared to lay heart to heart in what still was named friendship, but a friendship now without reserve. The fragmentary poem addressed to Mary Wollstonecraft Godwin, in June, 1814, is the record of the hopes and fears, and joy and sorrow, of this brief period.

To Mary Wollstonecraft Godwin : June, 1814.

I.

Mine eyes were dim with tears unshed ;
   Yes, I was firm—thus wert not thou ;—
My baffled looks did [yearn *], yet dread,
   To meet thy looks—I could not know
How anxiously they sought to shine
With soothing pity upon mine.

II.

To sit and curb the soul's mute rage
   Which preys upon itself alone ;
To curse the life which is the cage
   Of fettered grief that dares not groan,
Hiding from many a careless eye ·
The scorned load of agony.

V.

We are not happy sweet! our state
   Is strange, and full of doubt and fear ;

* Evidently the word "fear" which stands here is wrong.

More need of words that ills abate ;—
   Reserve or censure come not near
Our sacred friendship, lest there be
No solace left for thee or me.

VI.

Gentle and good and mild thou art,
   Nor can I live if thou appear
Aught but thyself, or turn thy heart
   Away from me, or stoop to wear
The mask of scorn, although it be
To hide the love thou feel'st for me.

Although now Shelley was coming to believe that his
wedded union with Harriet was a thing of the past, he had
not ceased to regard her with affectionate consideration ;
he wrote to her frequently, and kept her informed of his
whereabouts. Unhappy Harriet, residing at Bath, had
perhaps never desired that the breach between herself
and her husband should be irreparable and complete. And
when four days passed at the beginning of July, and no
letter from Shelley reached her, she reflected on his strange
and sudden ways, until her anxieties and fears, as to what
might have happened, grew intolerable, and she determined
to apply to Hookham for a resolution of her doubts.

Harriet Shelley to Hookham.

6, Queen's Square, Bath [postmark July 7, 1814].

MY DEAR SIR,
     You will greatly oblige me by giving the enclosed to
Mr. Shelley. I would not trouble you, but it is now four days
since I have heard from him, which to me is an age. Will you
write by return of post, and tell me what has become of him, as
I always fancy something dreadful has happened if I do not hear
from him. If you tell me that he is well, I shall not come to
London ; but if I do not hear from you or him, I shall certainly

come, as I cannot endure this dreadful state of suspense. You are his friend, and you can feel for me.

                    I remain yours truly,

                                        H. S.*

Harriet, as we may conjecture from this pathetic letter, would now gladly have retraced her steps. She feared that her husband might do some rash and desperate deed, and this she could not bear to contemplate. But the time to retrace her steps was now past. Her friend, her guardian, Shelley might still be, but never again her husband. From an assurance that she had ceased to love him, Shelley— we are told—had passed on to a conviction that she had

---

* To avoid embarrassing the text, I relegate an important matter to this note. It has been stated as certain "that letters from Harriet are or were in existence, written in moving terms . . . proving that Shelley at some time disappeared from her cognizance without making proper arrangements, or giving any warning or explanation of his intentions." The writer of these words will rejoice to learn that he is in error. I have traced out this assertion to its source, and I find that it arose from a mistaken interpretation of the letter from Harriet to Hookham printed above. The witness alluded to as authority for the statement saw indeed a series of letters addressed to Hookham —those from Shelley, with one or two from Harriet, letters written in their happy days; but he saw only one letter of a date subsequent to the commencement of troubles between husband and wife, viz. the letter printed above. It was hastily assumed that this letter had been written after some sudden disappearance of Shelley from Harriet's cognizance; but Harriet wrote from Bath, and Shelley, as Godwin's diary shows, had been in London since June 18. He corresponded with Harriet, and it was the cessation of his letters which caused her, after an interval of four days, to address herself to Hookham. I may add, and it is important, that I have also traced back further than any other biographer the statement that Harriet on some occasion of supposed desertion by Shelley "had for herself and her child only fourteen shillings of ready money." The alleged fact was communicated to Mr. Rossetti by a correspondent reporting a conversation in which one of the speakers related a conversation of many years earlier with the bookseller Hookham. On my applying to Robert Browning, whose conversation was reported to Mr. Rossetti, he declared that he was not the authority for this statement. Thus a conflict of testimony arises before we reach Hookham, whose statement, if ever made, may or may not be trustworthy. There is decisive evidence to prove that Shelley, when leaving England, was very careful to see that Harriet was provided with money.

given her heart to another, and had linked her life to his. An Irish gentleman, named Ryan, had been intimate with Shelley and Harriet in the summer of 1813. On May 21 of that year he had dined with them at Cook's Hotel; on June 22 he was still in town, and he saw them from time to time. We may feel the most absolute assurance that at this date Harriet loved her husband, and loved him alone. Of Ryan we do not hear again until the summer of 1814. In a note to her transcript of letters addressed by Mrs. Godwin to Godwin's friend, Lady Mountcashell, Miss Clairmont writes as follows: "He [Shelley] succeeded in persuading her [*i.e.* persuading Mary Godwin to elope with him] by declaring that Harriet did not really care for him; that she was in love with a Major Ryan; and the child she would have was certainly not his. This Mary told me herself, adding that this justified his having another attachment. I spoke to my mother and to the Boinvilles on this point in after years. Neither had ever seen or heard of any such person as Ryan." A Mr. Ryan, however, was undoubtedly known to both Shelley and Harriet; he was known also by Mary to be a veritable man and no shadow, a few months after her flight with Shelley.* "Letter from . . . Ryan," she notes in her journal for January 4, 1815. "Shelley had staid at home till two to see Ryan; he does not come" (January 6); "Ryan calls, but I do not see him" (January 7). It is certain that Shelley at a later date wholly abandoned the supposition that Harriet's second child—Charles Bysshe—was not his true and lawful son. But it seems to be equally certain that in later years he believed that Harriet was false to him before he placed his hand in that of Mary Godwin.

I am well aware that Shelley's judgment was in a

* From the Army List it appears that an Irish Matthew Ryan became a major in June, 1813.

peculiar degree liable to err. Shelley himself virtually
admitted over and over again that he had erred in disclaiming the parentage of his second child. Yet evidence
exists which makes one hesitate before asserting that
Harriet had not, at least through indiscretions, if not
through graver error, given occasion for her husband's
belief that she was untrue to him. "The late Mrs.
Shelley," wrote Godwin to Mr. William T. Baxter on
May 12, 1817, some months after Harriet's death, "had
turned out to have been a woman of great levity. I know
from unquestionable authority, wholly unconnected with
Shelley (though I cannot with propriety be quoted for
this), that she had proved herself unfaithful to her husband
before their separation. . . . Peace be to her shade!"
Godwin, whose condemnation of Shelley for his flight with
Mary had been unfaltering, was no partisan, although,
undoubtedly, a motive existed for his seeking to soften the
world's harsh judgment of Shelley's conduct; he had continued in friendly relations with Harriet after her husband's
separation from her. In January, 1817, he had communicated to Shelley the statement made by his unnamed
informant; and Shelley had found no difficulty in accepting the statement as true. "I learn just now from Godwin,"
Shelley wrote to Mary on January 11, "that he has evidence
that Harriet was unfaithful to me *four months* before I
left England with you." In later years Mary made no
explicit statement to any one; but she wrote as follows
on December, 28, 1825, to Leigh Hunt, who had placed in
her hands a manuscript article on Shelley's life, intended
for the *Westminster Review*—"You may remember that
immediately on reading your manuscripts concerning our
Shelley, I wrote to you thanking you for it, and pointing
out a few mistakes or omissions to be rectified or made,
and I sent it back to Mr. Bowring with my approval. . .

I afterwards found that Peacock had it, and he mentioned to me a circumstance which I wondered had not struck me before, but which is vital. It regards Shelley and Harriet—where you found your reasoning on a mistake as to fact. They did not part by mutual consent, and Shelley's justification, to me obvious, rests on other grounds ; so that you would be obliged to remodel a good part of your writing." They did not part by mutual consent, therefore either Harriet refused to return to her husband (but this Harriet herself declared was not the case), or Shelley refused to receive her as his wife ; and in the opinion of Mrs. Shelley, writing in 1825, he was justified—at least to his own conscience—in his refusal. In 1839 Mary Shelley still maintained that in all he did, Shelley, even when in error, had acted according to the dictates, not of egoistic desire, but of his conscience. "I abstain from any remark on the occurrences of his private life," she wrote in the preface to the collected edition of Shelley's poems, published in that year, "except inasmuch as the passions which they engendered inspired his poetry. No account of these events has ever been given at all approaching reality in their details, either as regards himself or others ; nor shall I further allude to them than to remark that the errors of action, committed by a man as noble and generous as Shelley, may, as far as he only is concerned, be fearlessly avowed by those who loved him, in the firm conviction that, were they judged impartially, his character would stand in fairer and brighter light than that of any contemporary." And in her note on "Alastor : " "This is neither the time nor place to speak of the misfortunes that chequered his life. It will be sufficient to say that in all he did, he, at the time of doing it, believed himself justified to his own conscience."

It was in fact, however, not only in 1814 that Shelley

believed himself justified in what he did. Six years later, in 1820, when he was residing at Pisa, he wrote to Southey, inquiring whether his old entertainer and friend of the Keswick days were the author of an article in the *Quarterly Review*, which had spoken in cruel terms of his domestic calamities. Southey, in a reply kindly in purpose but unrelenting in the cruelty of its kindness, entreats Shelley to review his past life, and judge whether his pernicious opinions have not brought misery upon others, and guilt all but irremediable on himself. With solemn earnestness Shelley responds to that appeal, and it is thus that he writes—

"With what care do the most tyrannical Courts of Judicature weigh evidence, and surround the accused with protecting forms, with what reluctance do they pronounce their cruel and presumptuous decisions, compared with you! You select a single passage out of a life otherwise not only spotless, but spent in an impassioned pursuit of virtue, which looks like a blot, merely because I regulated my domestic arrangements without deferring to the notions of the vulgar, although I might have done so quite as conveniently had I descended to their base thoughts—this you call *guilt*. I might answer you in another manner, but I take God to witness, if such a Being is now regarding both you and me, and I pledge myself, if we meet, as perhaps you expect, before Him after death, to repeat the same in His presence—that you accuse me wrongfully. I am innocent of ill, either done or intended; the consequences you allude to flowed in no respect from me. If you were my friend, I could tell you a history that would make you open your eyes; but I shall certainly never make the public my familiar confidant."

Thus it is evident that when Shelley parted finally from Harriet, he did so as it were under a judicial decree issued —issued, as I believe, rashly—by himself as judge in his own cause. He had in May sought a reconciliation; now he had persuaded himself that Harriet, although she still might claim from him the duties of a certain guardianship and watchful solicitude, could never again be his true and loyal wife.

It is no part of this biography to justify Shelley. The biographer's duty is rather to show precisely what his words and deeds were, leaving the reader to pronounce such judgment as may seem just. Still less is it the part of Shelley's biographer to cast a shadow upon the memory of Shelley's first wife. Harriet herself declared that she had never ceased to love her husband; that her heart was devoted to him. " I feel it due to the memory of Harriet," wrote Peacock, "to state my most decided conviction that her conduct as a wife was as pure, as true, as absolutely faultless, as that of any who for such conduct are held most in honour." "There is not a trace of evidence or a whisper of scandal against her before her voluntary departure from Shelley," wrote Thornton Hunt. "I was assured," Trelawny writes, "by the evidence of the few friends who knew both Shelley and his wife—Hookham, who kept the great library in Bond Street, Jefferson Hogg, Peacock, and one of the Godwins—that Harriet was perfectly innocent of all offence." It is right that such testimony as this should be set over against Shelley's persuasion, and the evidence of the unnamed informant of Godwin in 1817, whom we can neither cite as a person of authority nor cross-examine. No one who was not a rash partisan would assert that Harriet was not innocent.

On July 7, the day on which Hookham received Harriet's distracted letter from Bath, Godwin accompanied Shelley to Bond Street. On the following day he had a serious talk with Mary, after which he wrote to Shelley. Mary's explanations and assurances seem to have been satisfactory to her father, but Shelley now ceased to dine at Godwin's house. So surrounded with difficulties apparently insurmountable was Shelley's position, that even in July Mary did not believe it possible that their union could ever be other than that "sacred friendship" of which Shelley's poem had spoken ; or if love—and now they could not doubt the nature of their feeling—it must be love denied the happiness of lives made one. The copy of "Queen Mab" presented by Shelley to Mary bears an inscription, written hastily in pencil inside the cover in Shelley's handwriting, "Mary Wollstonecraft Godwin, P. B. S.," and inside the second cover, also hastily written in pencil, the words, "You see, Mary, I have not forgotten you." The flyleaf at the end of the same volume has an inscription in Mary's handwriting, which is dated July, 1814: "This book is sacred to me and as no other creature shall ever look into it I may write in it what I please—yet what shall I write —that I love the author beyond all powers of expression and that I am parted from him dearest and only love—by that love we have promised to each other although I may not be yours I can never be another's. But I am thine exclusively thine

> 'By the kiss of love, the glance none saw beside,
> The smile none else might understand,
> The whispered thought of hearts allied,
> The pressure of the thrilling hand.'

I have pledged myself to thee and sacred is the gift. I remember your words—you are now Mary going to mix with many and for a moment I shall depart but in the solitude of your chamber I shall be with you—yes you are ever with me sacred vision—

> 'But ah! I feel in this was given
> A blessing never meant for me;
> Thou art too like a dream from heaven
> For earthly love to merit thee.'"

It is evident that when these words were written no plan

for effecting their union had been contrived by Mary and Shelley.

Godwin's talk with Mary on July 8, and his subsequent letter—this discussion of affairs by a person outside the charmed circle and the dream of love—probably determined Shelley to take a decisive step towards attaining the end at which he now consciously aimed. He could never again give a husband's heart to Harriet; he could not pretend to do this, and believing that she too would willingly accept freedom from the bondage of their recent wedded death-in-life, he resolved to propose to her a formal separation. Harriet—so he hoped—making no wifely claim upon his life or love, might yet accept what he could still give—such care and such advantages as should belong to one towards whom he acknowledged a peculiar duty. At least he would proceed openly, and lay his proposal before her. Accordingly he wrote to Harriet, begging her to come to London, where she arrived on July 14. What followed we know but imperfectly. According to Harriet's own account, the shock and agitation of Shelley's disclosure brought on an illness, alarming to one who looked forward to the birth of a baby in December, during which Eliza Westbrook was constant in attendance, and Shelley was by her side beseeching her to return to life and health. With a common womanly instinct, in which there is an injustice which men, the gainers by it, treat as excusable, Harriet's indignation pressed less heavily against her husband than against Mary Godwin. Shelley was depraved and debased—no longer the man whom she had known; but it was Mary who by her arts had wrought this change; she it was who had ensnared Shelley by her witchcraft, by her sentimental raptures at Mary Wollstonecraft's grave, by her avowals of love; she alone had done this wrong, unaided save by the pernicious lessons which Shelley had

R

derived from Godwin's philosophy. That Harriet consented to a separation, or yielded to it as inevitable,
recognizing the fact that it would be final, we may reasonably doubt. In the account which she gave of these events
to Peacock, it was implied that no separation by mutual
:onsent had ever taken place ; and there is some reason
:or supposing that Harriet, even after Shelley's departure
for France with Mary Godwin, was not without expectation that her husband would tire of the stranger who had
displaced her in his affections, and would return to herself.
It was when the certainty gradually forced itself upon her
at a later date that all was over between her and Shelley,
that he was indeed Mary's and not her own—it was then,
in the solitude and dull constraint of her father's house,
that unhappy Harriet's anguish grew to a height, and that
she became willing to try to forget it in excitement and
change. But in July, 1814, the very expectation that
Shelley would return to her might have induced her to
appear compliant. We know that Shelley, acting with
frankness and a certain deliberation, went through necessary formalities, obtained legal advice, and directed that a
settlement should be drawn up for Harriet's benefit. We
know that he departed for France with the assurance that
his action appeared to her not cruel or harsh, but the
action of one who still had a sincere concern for her
interests and her happiness. So little of a breach was
there between them, as he conceived, that, with blind
ignorance of a woman's heart, he hoped that Harriet might
settle somewhere on the Continent in his neighbourhood.

The last days in London were days of anxiety and
distraction to Shelley. Suffering physically from sharp
spasms of nervous pain, he sought relief, as he had formerly
done at Keswick, in excessive doses of laudanum. I
would seem that he was excluded from Godwin's house

although the latter, apparently desirous to restore happy relations between Shelley and Harriet, now and again wrote to one or the other. Perhaps it was at this time or somewhat earlier that Shelley begged Peacock, on coming to London from the country, to call upon him. "Nothing that I ever read in tale or history," writes Peacock, "could present a more striking image of a sudden, violent, irresistible passion than that under which I found him labouring. . . . Between his old feelings towards Harriet, from whom he was not then separated, and his new passion for Mary, he showed in his looks, in his gestures, in his speech, the state of a mind 'suffering, like a little kingdom, the nature of an insurrection.' His eyes were bloodshot, his hair and dress disordered. He caught up a bottle of laudanum, and said, 'I never part from this.' He added, 'I am always repeating to myself your lines from Sophocles—

> "Man's happiest lot is not to be;
> And when we tread life's thorny steep,
> Most blest are they who earliest free
> Descend to death's eternal sleep." ' "

Yet, notwithstanding his physical sufferings and mental agitation, Shelley acted with a purpose and with circumspection. If he could not meet Mary Godwin at her father's house, there was always that place, on the outskirts of the town, where her mother's body lay, and where on one eventful day Bysshe had poured forth his griefs, his hopes, his love, and she had placed her hand in his. The daughter of Godwin and Mary Wollstonecraft was not restrained from uniting her lot with one whom she regarded as pure and noble and sorrowful, by scruples as to legality or by dread of public opinion. The ceremony of marriage was desired by both Shelley and Mary, but it was impossible, and they did not hold it to be necessary.

Mary, like Shelley, believed that she inflicted no wrong upon another; if she erred, the error was that of a girl who had not yet reached the close of her seventeenth year. Her first and ruling thought was to deliver from weakness and misery the man whose life—measurelessly dear to her —seemed to be placed in her hands to save or to destroy. Shelley believed that, in endeavouring to remain a careful guardian of Harriet's interests, he did all that was now possible for him to do. "In me," he wrote to her, with almost incredible blindness, a few days after his departure to the Continent, "you will at last find one firm and constant friend, to whom your interests will be always dear— by whom your feelings will never wilfully be injured. From none can you expect this but me." * Had Shelley and Mary perceived that through self-denial, practised even for a season, a truer union of hearts could have been attained, it may be that they would have found the reward of such strenuous self-denial in moral safety or diminished risk for Harriet.

By July 27, 1814, arrangements, unknown to Godwin and his wife, had been made for the departure of Shelley and Mary early next morning for Dover on their way to the Continent.

* I may here point out, what has hitherto escaped attention, that some important passages of biography, transmuted for the purposes of fiction, may be found in Mrs. Shelley's novel "Lodore," published in 1835. In it may be found an almost literal transcript from her life and that of Shelley during the weeks of distress and separation in London, which followed soon after the return from the Continent in 1814. In it may be found, in a transmuted form, the story of Emilia Viviani. In it also may be found a version of the story of Shelley's marriage with Harriet Westbrook, and his parting from her. No suggestion of infidelity to her marriage vow by Harriet is made in this piece of veiled biography.

CHAPTER X.

WHEN, between four and five o'clock on the morning of July 28, 1814, Mary Godwin stepped across her father's threshold, Mary Jane Clairmont, daughter of her father's second wife by a former marriage, was at her side. Two months before—on May 23—Mary's sister Fanny had left the house in Skinner Street for a long visit to relations in Wales. Her maturer years, her gentle, unadventurous temper, her anxious, almost humble, conscientiousness, would have made Fanny a prudent monitor had she been at home during June and July, and had she been entrusted with the secret that lay nearest to Mary's heart. Jane Clairmont was of a different temperament and character. A dark-haired, dark-eyed, olive-checked girl, a few months younger than Mary—born on April 27, 1798—she was quick to observe, to think, to feel; of brilliant talents; ardent, witty, wilful; a lover of music and poetry, gifted with an exquisite voice in song; romantic in disposition, yet with a lively sense of reality; of untrained temper, yet at times affecting the girl-philosopher; making eager demands on life, with a capacity for sore fretting against the bars of fate; pleasure-loving, at times indolent, yet able to undergo much irksome toil; possessed of generous qualities, and of qualities dangerous to her own happiness and that of others. How far Mary may have taken Jane Clairmont into her confidence we cannot for certain say. It was stated by Jane that she left the house in Skinner Street on the morning of July 28, believing that no more was intended than an early walk, and that on meeting Shelley at the corner of Hatton Garden, she was pressed by him and Mary to enter the post-chaise and accompany them to France, because she was skilled in the language of that country, with which they were unfamiliar.

For the weeks on the Continent which followed Shelley's flight we have two chief sources of information—the journal of Shelley and Mary, and the journal, in parts fuller of details, kept by Jane Clairmont. Each of these journals exists, in whole or in part, in two forms—the rough original manuscript, and a later recast or revision. The "History of a Six Weeks' Tour," published in 1817, with a preface by Shelley, follows sufficiently closely, with certain omissions and some additions and amplifications, the earlier pages of that journal begun by Shelley on the day of his union with Mary Godwin, written afterwards by Mary or Shelley as was most convenient, continued finally by Mary until death parted her from her husband, and resumed occasionally at later dates. Jane Clairmont's revision of her journal is but a fragment written late in her life, and is remarkable chiefly for inserted comments and conversations of Shelley, reproduced from memory, or perhaps more largely created from hints of memory by her imagination after a lapse of half a century. This we may set aside as of necessity less trustworthy than the other records. We turn to the first page of Shelley's journal and seek in it his story of the events of the long July day, which opened for the wanderers in the London streets, before London was yet awake, and closed amid the moonlit waters and rising gales of the Channel.

"*July* 28.—The night preceding this morning, all being decided, I ordered a chaise to be ready by four o'clock. I watched until the lightning and the stars became pale. At length it was four. I believed it not possible that we should succeed; still there appeared to lurk some danger even in certainty. I went; I saw her; she came to me. Yet one quarter of an hour remained. Still some arrangement must be made, and she left me for a short time. How dreadful did this time appear; it seemed that we trifled with life and hope; a few minutes passed; she was in my arms—we were safe; we were on our road to Dover.

" Mary was ill as we travelled, yet in that illness what pleasure and security did we not share ! The heat made her faint; it was necessary at every stage that she should repose. I was divided between anxiety for her health and terror lest our pursuers should arrive. I reproached myself with not allowing her sufficient time to rest, with conceiving any evil so great that the slightest portion of her comfort might be sacrificed to avoid it.

" At Dartford we took four horses, that we might outstrip pursuit. We arrived at Dover before four o'clock. Some time was necessarily expended in consideration—in dinner—in bargaining with sailors and custom-house officers. At length we engaged a small boat to convey us to Calais; it was ready by six o'clock. The evening was most beautiful; the sands slowly receded; we felt safe; there was little wind, the sails flapped in the flagging breeze. The moon rose, the night came on, and with the night a slow heavy swell and a fresher breeze, which soon became so violent as to toss the boat very much. Mary was much affected by the sea; she could scarcely move. She lay in my arms through the night; the little strength which remained in my own exhausted frame was all expended in keeping her head in rest on my bosom. The wind was violent and contrary. If we could not reach Calais the sailors proposed making for Boulogne. They promised only two hours' sail from the shore, yet hour after hour passed and we were still far distant when the moon sunk in the red and stormy horizon, and the fast-flashing lightning became pale in the breaking day. We were proceeding slowly against the wind, when suddenly a thunder-squall struck the sail and the waves rushed into the boat; even the sailors believed that our situation was perilous; the wind had now changed, and we drove before a wind, that came in violent gusts, directly to Calais.

"Mary did not know our danger; she was resting between my knees, that were unable to support her; she did not speak or look, but I felt that she was there. I had time in that moment to reflect and even to reason upon death; it was rather a thing of discomfort and of disappointment than horror to me. We should never be separated, but in death we might not know and feel our union as now. I hope, but my hopes are not unmixed with fear for what will befall this inestimable spirit when we appear to die.

"The morning broke, the lightning died away, the violence of the wind abated. We arrived at Calais, whilst Mary still slept; we drove upon the sands. Suddenly the broad sun rose over France."

Exhausted as Mary was with sickness and fatigue, she yet had a young traveller's pleasure in hearing for the first time the speech of a strange country, and in observing the novel costumes. The day passed not disagreeably, while the fugitives, weary from their excitement and the night of anxiety, awaited the arrival of their boxes by the packet from Dover. When packet and boxes, detained for several hours by contrary winds, at length arrived towards night, Mrs. Godwin, who on the preceding day had followed the fugitives to the sea-coast, also arrived, full of desire that Jane should separate herself from her dangerous associates and return to the shelter of Godwin's house.

"In the evening Captain Davison came and told us that a fat lady had arrived, who had said that I had run away with her daughter; it was Mrs. Godwin. Jane spent the night with her mother.

"*Saturday, July* 30.—Jane informs us that she is unable to withstand the pathos of Mrs. Godwin's appeal. She appealed to the municipality of Paris—to past slavery and to future freedom.

I counselled her to take at least an hour for consideration. She returned to Mrs. Godwin and informed her that she resolved to continue with us. . . . At six in the evening we left Calais, and arrived at Boulogne at ten.   We slept there."

Travelling in a cabriolet, drawn by three horses running abreast, and urged by a queer, upright little postillion, with long pigtail and cracking whip, they pressed forward with all possible haste, for Mary's health suffered from the intense heat, and they were desirous to have the journey to Paris quickly over.   For a few hours they slept at Abbeville; then, with no other halt, drove forward by night and day, until, winding through the narrow streets and beneath the many-storied houses of Paris, they drew up about two o'clock on the afternoon of Tuesday, August 2, at the entrance to the Hôtel de Vienne.   The hot August days in Paris were for Shelley and Mary made up of mingled happiness and vexations.   Money was needed to pursue their intended journey to Switzerland, and the supply expected from Hookham did not arrive.   Fortunately Shelley could turn with some hope of obtaining relief to Tavernier, a French man of business, whose office was in Paris.

Early on the morning of August 8, Shelley was up and abroad.   Accompanied by Jane, he visited the ass-market to purchase an ass; for Mary not being strong might need to ride, and a portmanteau containing necessaries must be taken with them, while the heavier luggage went by diligence.   To fare on foot from Paris to Lucerne was, in 1814, an adventure which called for courage; an army had lately been disbanded, and reckless men might lurk in solitary places.   The hostess of the Hôtel de Vienne set before the young wanderers a lively vision of the dangers of the way—" les dames seroient certainement

enlevées ;" but their spirits were high, and they were not
to be deterred from a delightful enterprise by imaginary
terrors. When evening came they bade farewell to hostess
and hotel, drove to the barriers, the ass following their
fiacre, and in the summer twilight began the march to
Charenton. Unhappily their beast of burden was fit
rather to be carried than to carry. " We set out to Charenton in the evening," wrote Mary in her journal, " carrying
the ass, who was weak and unfit for labour, like the
' Miller and his Son.' "   " We were, however, merry
enough, and thought the leagues short. We arrived at
Charenton about ten."

To replace the unserviceable ass in the morning they
found a mule. " We sell our ass," Shelley records in the
journal, " and purchase a mule, in which we much resemble
him who never made a bargain but always lost half." And
so along roads level and dusty, between fields bright and
waving with the golden harvest, advance the little troop—
Mary in her black silk dress, seated on the mule, which
Shelley led at first ; Jane, also in black silk dress, following, until, grown weary and footsore, she in front would
manage the mule, while Mary and Shelley brought up the
rear. A small basket containing the bread and fruit for
their noonday meal was borne by Shelley. The French
skies and fields had not often looked upon a blither group
of wanderers.

Yet a journey on foot and muleback across France in
the year 1814 was not without its discomforts and inconveniences. Coarse fare, rancid bacon, and sour bread, beds
" infinitely detestable ;" rats which, Jane declared, put their
cold paws upon her face at night; in the daytime, white
roads inch-deep with dust, swarms of persecuting insects, a
cloudless heaven and the wide oppressive glare ;—such
were some of the trials and hardships of the way. The

squalor, ignorance, and rudeness of the inhabitants of some of the villages through which they passed surprised and shocked the travellers.   The wreck of recent invasion strewed the soil of France.   On the fifth day of wayfaring Shelley, having sprained his leg, was obliged to mount the saddle; the road lay across a white expanse of barren country; while his companions towards evening stepped wearily by his side, Shelley beguiled the tedium of the way by telling the tale of the Seven Sleepers.   That night was spent at Troyes, in rooms odiously unclean.   A carriage being henceforth a necessity, they bought an open *voiture* for five napoleons, and, selling their mule, hired another with a driver to convey them to Neuchâtel.   Before setting out for Switzerland, which they expected to reach within a week, Shelley wrote to Harriet a letter, begging her to follow them by the Geneva route, and assuring her that her best interests were still dear to him, though now their lives had moved apart.

Shelley to Harriet.

Troyes, 120 miles from Paris on the way to Switzerland,
August 13, 1814.

My Dearest Harriet,

I write to you from this detestable town; I write to show that I do not forget you; I write to urge you to come to Switzerland, where you will at last find one firm and constant friend, to whom your interests will be always dear—by whom your feelings will never wilfully be injured.   From none can you expect this but me—all else are either unfeeling or selfish, or have beloved friends of their own, as Mrs. Boinville, to whom their attention and affection is confined.

I will write at length from Neufchatel, or you direct your letters " d'étre laissé à la Bureau de Poste Neufchatel "—until you hear again.   We have journeyed from Paris on foot, with a mule to carry our baggage; and Mary, who has not been sufficiently well to walk, fears the fatigue of walking. We passed through a fertile country, neither interesting from the character of its inhabitants nor the beauty of the scenery. We came 120 miles in four days; the last two days we passed over the country that was the seat of war. I cannot describe to you the frightful desolation of this scene; village after village entirely ruined and burned, the white ruins towering in innumerable forms of destruction among the beautiful trees. The inhabitants were famished; families once independent now beg their bread in this wretched country; no provisions; no accommodation; filth, misery, and famine everywhere. (You will see nothing of this on your route to Geneva.) I must remark to you that, dreadful as these calamites are, I can scarcely pity the inhabitants; they are the most unamiable, inhospitable, and unaccommodating of the human race. We go by some carriage from this town to Neufchatel, because I have strained my leg and am unable to walk. I hope to be recovered by that time; but on our last day's journey I was perfectly unable to walk. Mary resigned the mule to me. Our walk has been, excepting this, sufficiently agreeable; we have met none of the robbers they prophesied at Paris. You shall know our adventures more detailed if I do not hear at Neufchatel that I am soon to have the pleasure of communicating to you in person, and of welcoming you to some sweet retreat I will procure for you among the mountains. I have written to Peacock to superintend money affairs; he is expensive, inconsiderate, and cold, but surely not utterly perfidious and unfriendly and unmindful of our kindness to him; besides, interest will secure his attention to these things. I wish you to bring with you the two deeds which Tahourdin has to prepare for you, as also a copy of the settlement. Do not part with any of your money. But what shall be done about the books? You can consult on the spot. With love to my sweet little Ianthe, ever most affectionately yours,

S.

I write in great haste; we depart directly.

On August 19, as the travellers approached Neuchâtel, the snow-clad Alps hung on the far horizon, cloud-like

dazzling, and of visionary splendour. At the Neuchâtel
post-office no letters ; no letters, indeed, to be expected
for another week. The sixty pounds obtained in Paris
had now nearly disappeared, and something should be
done. "Shelley," the journal informs us, "goes to the
banker's, who promises an answer in two hours. At the
conclusion of the time he sends for Shelley, and, to our
astonishment and consolation, Shelley returns staggering
under the weight of a large canvas bag full of silver.
Shelley alone looks grave on the occasion, for he alone
clearly apprehends that francs and écus and louis d'ors
are like the white and flying cloud of noon, that is gone
before one can say 'Jack Robinson.'" Two days more
in a voiture, of which they were now heartily tired—
Shelley's weariness, however, assuming the form of a
"jocosely horrible mood"—brought them within a short
distance of Lucerne, and by the forenoon of August 23—a
most divine day—they were advancing in a small boat
along the waters of the lake, with its majestic mountain-
heights, and rock, and pine-forest, and verdant pastoral
slopes around them. At Brunnen, in sight of William Tell's
Chapel, a resting-place was found, and, as the mountains
darkened in the twilight, they lingered by the shores of the
lake, musing, conversing, and drinking in the freshness of
the quickening breeze.

When morning dawned a furious south-wind blew, and
the waters were in wild commotion. To remain in their
present abode could not be thought of with comfort, for its
uncleanliness had been "terrible" to Mary ; to proceed by
water to Flüelen was impossible. Finding that they could
not obtain a house at Brunnen, the wanderers resolved to
content themselves with two unfurnished rooms in the big,
ugly "Château," and these they hired for six months at a
guinea a month. Beds were moved into the empty rooms ·

a stove, lit with difficulty, diffused its unwholesome heat ;
and while cold rains fell without, Shelley beguiled the
hours by dictating to Mary the opening pages of a
romance. On the preceding afternoon Mary and Shelley
had walked to the shore of the lake, and read the description of the siege of Jerusalem in Tacitus. With the siege
of Jerusalem the romance of " The Assassins " opens.

Shelley with his young companions, had fled from
London to this solitude among the mountains, outlaws—
innocent outlaws, as they held, who refused submission to
the social rule, yet shaped their conduct according to the
conclusions of the reason and the legitimate dictates of the
heart. His imagination, wandering through dim centuries
and distant lands, found a spiritual kinship between his
small household, isolated from the great world by lake and
snowy peaks, and certain ancient exiles from Jerusalem,
who pitched their tents in the valley of Bethzatanai among
"mountains of everlasting snow "—a tribe known by the
dreaded name of " Assassins," yet gentle and benign, who
" acknowledged no laws but those of God," and " modelled
their conduct towards their fellow-men by the conclusions
of their individual judgment on the practical application of
these laws ; " who " esteemed the human understanding to
be the paramount rule of human conduct ; " who with a
religious temper united " an intrepid spirit of inquiry as to
the correctest mode of acting in particular instances of
conduct that occur among men ; " who fled to the solitudes
of Lebanon to escape the " poison of a diseased civilization "—" they would no longer owe their very existence to
the vices, the fears, and the follies of mankind. Love,
friendship, and philanthropy would now be the characteristic disposers of their industry ; " who in a community
falsely named " civilized " should upon principle wage war
against the impious laws of society, and must themselves

become the "victims of calumny and persecution;" but who in their Lebanonian vale might love and be beloved. Full of courage and of active virtue, living for the highest service of man, they might here find God—learning to identify this mysterious friend and benefactor "with the delight that is bred among the solitary rocks, and has its dwelling alike in the changing colours of the clouds and the inmost recesses of the caverns;" "they were already disembodied spirits; they were already the inhabitants of Paradise;" and here Albedir and Khaled might watch their children grow, and the very snakes—those wronged outcasts of creation—might be the loving playfellows of the Arabian boy and girl.

From his dream of "The Assassins," brought face to face with the wrongs and sorrows of the world in the person of the Wandering Jew, Shelley was rudely awakened by the discomforts of residence at the Château, and by the serious considerations that only twenty-eight pounds remained in his purse, that no addition to this slender store of money could be counted on before December, and that he was here many hundreds of miles from his basis of supplies. The rooms in the Château had been engaged until the following January; the old Abbé—not too well received—and the Médecin had called to pay their respects to the new-comers; but on August 27 a surprise awaited the good folk of Brunnen—the six months' residence had suddenly shrunk to one of forty-eight hours; at seven o'clock on the morning of that day the young English people took boat in a downpour of rain, and bade farewell to Schwytz and Uri, directing their boatmen to row westward toward Lucerne.

Shelley had decided that immediate return to London was unavoidable, and after his late experiences of voiture and muleback, he judged that the least costly mode of travel was by water. Having rested at Lucerne, where Shelley read " King Lear " aloud, and continued his romance of " The Assassins," the travellers were at early morning on the green waters of the Reuss, descending through rocks and rapids, in the public conveyance— *diligence par eau*—to Lauffenburg. The rain fell ceaseless, and their fellow-voyagers — " uncleanly animals " who smoked prodigiously, and were " exceedingly disgusting " —were an oppressive presence, spoiling some of the delight in rocky bank and breaking wave, and the swift shoot of the boat from watery height to hollow. The brutal rudeness of the fellows angrily contesting for seats " provoked Shelley to knock one of the foremost down. He did not return the blow, but continued his vociferations until the boatmen interfered, and provided us with other seats."

At six or seven o'clock in the evening of August 29, the Rhine bore them, cold and comfortless, under the high roofs and spires of Bâle. The descent of the Rhine from Bâle to Cologne, accomplished in a week, now in a slight canoe borne forward by the steadfast current, now in the ungainly public boat, was an adventure the delights of which more than compensated the inconveniences. Their companions changed as they went along from the Strassburg students — " Schwitz, a rather handsome, goodtempered young man ; Hoff, a kind of shapeless animal with a heavy, ugly German face ; and Schneider, who was nearly an idiot "—to less agreeable smoking and drinking and swaggering Teutons ; but the English party sufficiently maintained its independence. " We read Shakespeare," Mary's journal records. " Our companions in voyage are tolerable. We frightened from us one man who spoke English, and whom we did not like, by talking of cutting off kings' heads." On two successive nights they slept in the boat with the luxury around them of the cool September air.   " I have sailed down mighty rivers," wrote Shelley, in the preface to the "Revolt of Islam," " and seen the sun rise and set, and the stars come forth, whilst I have sailed night and day down a rapid stream among mountains."   And Mrs. Shelley, recalling the beauty of hill and river between Mayence and Bonn, declares that memory, taking all the dark shades from the picture, presented this part of the Rhine to her remembrance "as the loveliest paradise on earth."

To escape the companionship of "the canaille," they decided to quit the Rhine route at Cologne, and advance by carriage or land diligence.   At Bonn seats were taken for Clêves in the lumbering diligence—"the most detestable of things," as it seemed to Mary, "being five times slower than a snail's walk ; that is to say, rather more than a mile an hour."   Wearied and impatient, they posted the remainder of the way from Clêves, through sandy roads, between verdurous autumn fields, by endless canals, past endless lines of willow trees, past countless windmills, past neat Dutch houses and gardens bright with marigolds, over flying bridges, until Rotterdam was reached (September 8).   Shelley, the purse-bearer, was now possessor of twenty crown pieces—coins too quick to disappear ; but with the guineas the journeying was also almost at an end. "We reflected with wonder," Mary writes, "that we had travelled eight hundred miles for less than thirty pounds." Having arranged the terms of their passage to London with an English captain, and endured a tedious delay at Marsluys, while west winds blew, and the breakers tumbled in the bar—an interval of time used by Shelley to continue his romance, while Mary began her tale entitled " Hate," and Jane her "Idiot" (designed "to develop the workings and improvements of a mind which by common people was deemed the mind of an idiot, because it conformed

S

not to their vulgar and prejudiced views " *)—at length
they found themselves clear of sands, among tossing waves
and sporting shoals of porpoises.　After a night of restless
discomfort, with the crash overhead of a breaking boom
came morning clear and calm, with the Suffolk coast in
sight.　"We remain on deck nearly the whole day," the
journal records; "Mary recovers from her sickness; we
dispute with one man upon the slave trade."　On the
following morning (September 13) the ship lay moored at
Gravesend, and the trouble with custom-house officer
over, Mary, Jane, and Shelley, who had with difficulty
prevailed on the captain to trust them for the passage
money, were on their way up the Thames by boat to
Blackwall, whence stage and hackney coach brought the
returned wanderers back into the rush of city streets.

* Jane's journal.　Nothing further is known of "Hate" or "The Idiot."

CHAPTER XI.

POVERTY IN LONDON.

THE months which passed between Shelley's return to England in September, 1814, and the death of his grandfather in January, 1815, were of a kind to blur, or else to brighten by contrast, the memory of those six weeks of free delight in the harvest-fields of France, in pine wood and mountain glen, on lake and rushing river, which had now come to a close. Never before or after were his miseries as a wealthy heir, harassed by debts and unable to meet the demands of eager creditors, so keen or so incessant. The cause lay in part in Shelley's temperament and habits. Though personally no lover of luxury or ostentation, he was ill fitted for holding tight the reins of domestic economy, month after month and year after year. He had gratified Harriet in costly indulgences, to which, however his prospects may have seemed to warrant the extravagance, his present resources were wholly inadequate. To rescue Godwin from his ever-present, ever-increasing embarrassments, Shelley had used his utmost exertions in the early summer, and when November came—although the indignant father now refused to hold communications with him except through an attorney—he was at work endeavouring to meet a bill for two hundred pounds, which, he had been informed, would come due on December 1, and which it was feared might cause bankruptcy to the little publishing house in Skinner Street.

And so in the October and dark November and December days much time and strength and vital spirits were consumed in miserable negotiations with lawyers, insurance agents, money-lenders ; and if relief were obtained, it came with the prospect of twofold or treble future loss. "Shelley goes with Peacock to the lawyers', but, as usual, does not succeed" (October 18) ; "Shelley is out all the morning at the lawyers', but nothing is done" (October 22) ; "Shelley goes to Lambert's place, proposes a *post-obit* for Godwin's debt" (November 22) ; "After breakfast Shelley is as badly off as I am with my work, for he is out all day with those detested lawyers" (November 30) ; "Shelley out among the bad all morning" (December 2) ; "Shelley goes to Pike's, to the insurance offices, and the lawyers' ; an agreement entered into for £3000 for £1000" (December 21). Such are some entries in the journal during these days of discomfort and anxiety, telling of weary hours in the city, which sent Shelley home at evening exhausted in body and mind—sometimes fit only to unburden himself of the load of fatigue in one of those slumbers resembling a deep lethargy which Hogg had observed with surprise long since during the winter evenings at Oxford.

With Godwin's household a half-surreptitious communication was kept up through Charles Clairmont, Jane's brother, a young man now in his twentieth year, who might assert some independence of action, and in a shy and furtive way through Fanny Godwin, whose affections were with Shelley and Mary, but whose sense of duty to Godwin restrained her from entering into direct relations with those who had offended him so deeply. Fanny's aunts, Everina Wollstonecraft and Mrs. Bishop, conducted with credit

school in Dublin ; it was their intention that Fanny should
succeed them as proprietress of the school ; therefore her
character and conduct must be clear from all possible
imputation of blame, and her associates must be above
reproach. Mrs. Godwin, writing to Lady Mountcashell—
the pupil and friend of Mary Wollstonecraft—now in Italy,
represented herself as not only robbed of her daughter
Jane, but unable to communicate with her, and as ignorant
for a time of the unhappy child's whereabouts. But here
Mrs. Godwin, with her fine gift of mendacity, lied. Three
days after his return from the Continent, Shelley wrote
to Godwin, and received a letter—" very prejudiced," says
Jane, in her journal—in reply ; on September 16 Mrs.
Godwin, accompanied by Fanny, paid a visit to the window
of the lodgings of the returned wanderers (56, Margaret
Street, Cavendish Square), but refused to speak to Shelley
when he went out to her ; in the month of November Jane
Clairmont, on the occasion of an alleged illness of her
mother, returned for a time to the house in Skinner Street.
Thus a certain irregular communication was kept up
between Godwin's household and that of Shelley, while
Godwin himself remained indignant, and yet found it
possible to accept important pecuniary favours from the
man whose offence against virtue was past forgiveness.
When recording in her journal her father's resolve to hold
no intercourse with Shelley except through an attorney,
Mary, in wonder at the strange inconsistencies of the
vanity of virtue, might well utter her exclamation, " *Oh,
philosophy !* "

Shelley's relations with Harriet, though at times they
wore a friendly appearance, could hardly be sound or
happy at heart. From the Continent he had written to
her as though each of the now-divided pair might be
sincerely regardful of the other's interests ; and, if we may

trust Miss Clairmont, he had sent from Calais or Paris, through Harriet, directions to his bankers to honour her calls for money as far as his account permitted. On landing penniless from Rotterdam, Shelley drove to his bankers', and ascertained that all his money had been drawn. Failing elsewhere to procure the means of paying for his passage and the smaller charges of waterman and coachman, he applied, says Miss Clairmont, to Harriet, and not without success, although to the twenty pounds which she handed to him were added the reproaches of an injured wife. On the next day and the next following, Shelley called upon Harriet, whose "strange behaviour" is noted in Jane's diary. On September 16 she sent him certain books which he desired to possess, with a "curious and weak letter," followed, at a brief interval, by another letter "mean and worldly" (the epithets are those of Jane's diary). It is evident that no true and wholesome understanding was possible, although Shelley may have desired to add nothing to the difficulties of the situation. As to Harriet, we can credit Mrs. Godwin's statement that she was not even yet convinced that her husband's heart had been finally alienated from her; "love affairs," she was told by every one, "last but a little time, and her husband will be sure to return to her." Such speeches, it was perceived by Mrs. Godwin, were cheering to Harriet, though she took it as cruel that one who had loved her long and tenderly should leave her for another at a time when she looked forward to the birth of a second child. "Letter from Harriet, very civil;" "Have a good-humoured letter from Harriet," are entries in Mary's journal for days of early October. The good-humoured letter had been written after a night of considerable anxiety, when Harriet had sent to inform Shelley of what she imagined to be a dangerous illness. Shelley lost no time in communicating with her, and in calling on her physician for trustworthy advice as to her state. Such concern manifested on her behalf was grateful to Harriet; yet it could hardly be hoped that any truce between the two could end in settled peace. Before a fortnight was over came tidings—whether true or false we cannot tell—that Harriet had been at work to injure Godwin; he whose "Political Justice" had corrupted Percy's heart, whose daughter Mary had determined to secure Percy (so Harriet phrased it) at every hazard, was the author of all her woes; and just now he was threatened with arrest; if only she could induce Hookham the bookseller to refuse to offer bail! "We talk over Harriet's plan of ruining papa," Jane enters in her journal on October 30. Nor by the close of the year had matters mended, when Harriet wrote, threatening Shelley with her lawyer (December 20). By January 2, 1815, Mary's patience had reached its limit, so grievous was this New Year's gift of hungry creditors, and her vexation has its outbreak in the journal: "Harriet sends her creditors here; nasty woman. Now we must change our lodgings."

At nine o'clock on the evening of November 30, 1814— a day on which Shelley had been for weary hours engaged with "those detested lawyers"—Harriet Shelley gave birth to an eight-months' child, a boy, very like his father, she afterwards declared. A week passed before Shelley was informed of the event, which is chronicled by Mary in her diary, with a bitter sense of Harriet's claim to occupy a different position from her own, and perhaps some indignant scorn at her charge of desertion now advanced against Shelley. "*Tuesday, December 6.*—Very unwell. Shelley and Clara [*i.e.* Jane Clairmont *] walk out, as usual, to

---

* It was apparently about this time that Jane Clairmont adopted the name *Clara*, *Clare*, or *Claire*, by which we shall henceforth know her. Her full name was Clara Mary Jane Clairmont.

heaps of places. . . . A letter from Hookham, to say that Harriet has been brought to bed of a son and heir. Shelley writes a number of circular letters of this event, which ought to be ushered in with ringing of bells, etc., for it is the son of his *wife*. A letter from Harriet confirming the news, in a letter from a *deserted wife ! !* and telling us he has been born a week." Next day Shelley called on Harriet, but the interview left husband and wife each embittered against the other. It was Harriet's complaint that Shelley viewed the new-born babe with mercenary eyes; the boy would "make money cheaper;" while Shelley, on his part, reported on his return that he had been met by insulting selfishness. " *Wednesday, December 7.* —Clara and Shelley go out together; Shelley calls on the lawyers, and on Harriet, who treats him with insulting selfishness; they return home wet and very tired." Charles Bysshe they named the boy; and it is in relation to him that the latest mention of Harriet occurs in Mary's journal In April, 1815, Shelley being concerned in a Chancery case promoted in order to determine certain doubtful questions respecting the family property, considered it expedient to produce his son in court. "Shelley passes the morning with Harriet, who is in a surprisingly good humour," write Mary in her journal of April 10; and some days late (April 21): "Shelley goes to Harriet to procure his son who is to appear in one of the Courts;" (April 22) "Shelley goes to Harriet about his son. Work. Fanny comes talk. Shelley returns at four; he has been much tease with Harriet." Unhappily, the journal from mid-May 1815, to July of the following year, has been lost, and from that date onwards no reference to Harriet Shelley occur until the day on which a letter from Hookham brough Shelley, when at Bath, the tidings of her death.

Solitude, unharassed by debts and duns, with Mary

companionship, the society of a few friends, and the delights of study and of authorship, would have made these winter months to Shelley months of unusual happiness and calm. But friends had fallen away ; Godwin was incensed, not without just cause ; when Mrs. Boinville wrote, her letter seemed "cold and even sarcastic ; " and the Newtons were either absent or held aloof. Peacock, indeed, was friendly and helpful, and his friendship and help were grateful in this season of cold and dearth. And after a time Hogg, whose first response to a letter from Shelley (October 17) had been far from sympathetic, renewed his intimacy somewhat on the old Oxford footing. We smile as we observe how the genial cynic, the worldling and the wit, yet with genuine admiration for an ideal of character remote from his own, at once repelled and attracted Shelley and Mary, and how by degrees the attraction proved the stronger force. "I saw Hogg last night," Shelley wrote, early in November; "I am disappointed in him, though my expectations were very moderate." A few evenings later (November 14) Hogg called for the first time at his friend's lodgings in Nelson Square. Shelley is now the diarist : " Mary is unwell. Receive a note from Hogg. . . . In the evening Hogg calls ; perhaps he still may be my friend, in spite of the radical differences of sympathy between us ; he was pleased with Mary ; this was the test by which I had previously determined to judge his character." If Mary returned Hogg's liking, it was at first with grave reserves. When he jested, he was amusing ; but when he discussed serious matters, his opinions were far astray — "quite muddled" about virtue, and "condemned in the courts of philosophy " for his respect for established opinions, "un enfant perdu," yet better liked on each successive visit.

So the old friendship renewed itself, with jest and

anecdote and argument, as in the days of University College; New Year's Day brought a note and present from the friendly cynic to Mary; and by-and-by Jefferson (Hogg's familiar Christian name now appearing in the journal) would accompany Clara and "the Maie" (Shelley's pet name for Mary) to the bonnet-shop; or, indoors, would read "Rokeby" aloud for them; or would listen while Mary—now a student of Latin—construed her lesson from Ovid. For a time, in the spring of 1815, Hogg lodged under the same roof with Shelley, Mary, and Clara Clairmont.

Jane, or Clara as she now chose to be called (a form of the name afterwards altered to "Clare" or "Claire"), with brilliant talents and some generous instincts, was yet hardly framed to be herself happy or to make happy those with whom her lot was cast. Nervous, excitable, with a changeful temper, and a capacity for brooding resentment, she already found at times that life went hard with her. Mrs. Godwin desired her daughter's return to Skinner Street; but Skinner Street, after the weeks of wandering on lake and river, had a narrow and saddened air, and, partly influenced by Shelley's advice, Clara was not inclined to yield submission to a mother who, though wife to Godwin, was not a philosopher or, indeed, moderately enlightened. Yet it became now and again apparent that, where she was, her presence was not desired—not desired certainly by Mary, and that through Mary it might be to Shelley also a source of discomfort. At first, indeed, all went well. All three were eager for knowledge, indefatigable readers for profit or for pleasure, and under Shelley's instruction both girls were soon zealously at work upon Latin translation and the Greek grammar. "Mary receives her first lesson in Greek," is noted in the journal a few days after they had settled in their Margaret Street lodgings. "Mary reads Greek and

' Rasselas,' " " Study Greek," " Read two odes of Anacreon before breakfast," are entries of Mary on days of September; while Clara is learning "four tenses of the verb *to strike*," and, having mastered the Greek characters, is able to dignify her diary with a mention of εἰμί.

The students of Greek were also students of philosophy, and gave their mornings, sometimes together, sometimes singly, to Godwin's " Political Justice ; " for the indignant father was still, through his writings, a philosophic guide to Shelley. With deep and peculiar affection Mary cherished her mother's memory, read and read again her mother's books ; and when she would peruse Godwin's " Essay on Sepulchres," made the little volume her companion as she sat now once more by the pillared tomb of Mary Wollstone-craft in old St. Pancras churchyard. When the sense grew upon her that an unborn life was bound up with her own, Mary became less frequently Shelley's companion in his weary walks to the lawyer's, insurance-agents', and money-enders' offices, and Clara took her place ; Shelley did not choose to be alone, and, if we may trust Miss Clairmont's account given in later years, was haunted by an appre-hension of sudden attack from Leeson, the supposed assassin of Tanyrallt, which he believed that the presence of a companion and witness by his side would avert. Sometimes, after these dull fatigues of business, Shelley would return with some new volume of poetry, and a delightful hour, during which he or Mary read aloud, would efface the perplexities and sordid cares of the day. "We read," Shelley enters in the diary (February 15, 1815), and are delighted with ' Lara,' the finest of Lord Byron's poems. Shelley reads ' Lara ' aloud in the evening." Or he would leave the present for the past, and lose himself in the enchanted region of Spenser's " Faerie Queene," or listen to the moral pleadings of the lady captive in Comus's

magic chair ; or he would try his spirit and those of his
hearers with the severer beauty of the " Paradise Regained."
Or it might be that poetry gave place to prose—that of
some elder writer, as Browne's remote and lofty meditation
in the "Religio Medici ;" or, perhaps, Gibbon's incomparable Memoir ; or, opulent in pseudo-passion and the
coarsely marvellous, Lewis's romance of "The Monk ;" or
the Abbé Barruel's strange history of Illuminati and secret
arch-conspirators ; or Godwin's novels, with their stronger
texture of logic supporting the plot interest ; or the tales of
Godwin's American disciple in romance, Charles Brockden
Brown. "Brown's four novels," says Peacock, "Schiller's
'Robbers,' and Goethe's 'Faust,' were, of all the works
with which he was familiar, those which took the deepest
root in Shelley's mind, and had the strongest influence in
the formation of his character." During the early months
of their union Mary's reading and Shelley's went on in the
main side by side ; a few Latin authors, with a volume or
two of travels, were alone unshared by Mary ; but gradually
—while much remained for them as a common possession
—their studies diverged. Both could speed on wings
through an author that interested them ; both could plod
at a slower pace when this was desirable. Twelve hundred
pages which Shelley sets down as the amount of his reading during seventeen days of January and February, 1815,
was no immoderate dose, though many of the pages were
in Latin. Clara, a little later, presented him with a copy
of Seneca, and Mary's entry in the journal is—"Shelley
reads Seneca ;" "Shelley reads Seneca every day and
all day."

In the evening, if Shelley were not reading aloud, or
playing chess with Mary, or Clara, or Hogg, he might be
engaged on one of his pieces of delicate untutored drawing
in which trees and fantastic rocks grew under his pen ; or

the time would pass in chemical experiments ; or he would
be off and away to hear " Garnerin's lecture on electricity,
the gases, and the phantasmagoria ; " or on some rare
occasion, accompanied by Mary and Clara, he would sit a
spectator in the theatre.   Shelley had a prejudice against
theatres, Peacock tells us, and he often talked of the
" withering and perverting spirit of comedy."   His keen
sense of pity caused him to feel that the grotesque in
humanity is too often the result of human suffering, of the
distortions of mental pain, or the stunted growth of mental
starvation.   " Society grinds down poor wretches into the
dust of abject poverty," he said, " till they are scarcely
recognizable as human beings ; and then, instead of being
treated as what they really are, subjects of the deepest
pity, they are brought forward as grotesque monstrosities
to be laughed at."   But if comedy offended Shelley, neither
did tragedy as represented on the stage satisfy his imagination or commend itself to his moral sense.   " With the
exception of [Milman's] 'Fazio,' " says Peacock, " I do not
remember his having been pleased with any performance
at an English theatre."   In 1814 Edmund Kean, appearing for the first time on the boards of Drury Lane, took
the town by storm.   It will be remembered how deep and
ardent was Keats's delight in the Shakesperian impersona-
tions of that extraordinary actor.   On October 13, 1814,
some sudden alarm, possibly in connection with creditors,
determined Shelley, with Mary and Clara, to quit London
instantly, and from Hookham was procured the sum of
five pounds to take them on their way.   As suddenly as
the resolution was formed it was altered, and the respited
fugitives deeming it sufficient precaution to move from
their lodgings to a hotel, decided to pass the evening in
one of the boxes at Drury Lane Theatre.   That evening
Kean appeared in " Hamlet ; " but when the curtain fell

on the second act, Shelley could endure no more and left
the house.   His feelings, no doubt, are truly interpreted by
the entry in Mary's diary : " Go to the play. The extreme
depravity and disgusting nature of the scene ; the inefficacy
of acting to encourage or maintain the delusion.   The
loathsome sight of men personating characters which do
not and cannot belong to them.   Shelley displeased with
what he saw of Kean."

Shelley's walks, when not determined elsewhere, often
tended in the direction of a pond at no great distance from
Primrose Hill, very proper for the delectable amusement
of sailing paper boats ; or in that of the Serpentine or the
Surrey Canal, where the same pleasure could be pursued
with a more daring spirit of adventure. In his poetry
Shelley often delightedly imagines some frail bark, instinct,
as it were, with spirit, and self-moved, or borne forward by
the pressure of some mighty wind. If fire were a joint
minister of his will with winds and water, Shelley's ecstasy
touched a rarer point ; and that must indeed have been a
fortunate day (October 3) on which he and Peacock, having
in the morning "set off little fire-boats" on the Primrose
Hill pond, after dinner made the darkness illustrious with
fireworks. Sometimes before he started on his walk a tiny
fleet would have been constructed by Mary's fingers ;
sometimes by edge of pond or river Shelley would himself
enact the naval architect. " On the Serpentine," writes
Hogg, " he would sometimes launch a boat, constructed with
more than usual care and freighted with halfpence. He
delighted to do this in the presence of boys, who would
run round to meet it, and when it landed in safety and the
boys scrambled for their prize, he had difficulty in restraining himself from shouting as loudly as they did."

In all these diversions and cares and studies Clara
Clairmont had a part. But there were times when

everything seemed to go wrong, when Mary seemed harsh, when even Shelley seemed unkind ; and then Clara would wander away alone, or retreat to her bedroom, or sit silent for the day, suffering from her own wrathful feelings, until soothing explanatory words were spoken, and the moody fit rolled off. "Charles Clairmont comes in the evening," Shelley enters in the journal of December 19 ; "a discussion concerning female character. Clara imagines that I treat her unkindly. Mary consoles her with her all-powerful benevolence. I rise (having already gone to bed) and speak with Clara ; she was very unhappy ; I leave her tranquil." And Mary, writing on November 26, "Work in the evening. Shelley reads 'Rights of Man.' Clara in an ill humour. She reads 'The Italian.' Shelley sits up and talks her into reason." "November 9 : Jane gloomy ; she is very sullen with Shelley. Well, never mind, my love ; we are happy." "November 10 : Jane is not well, and does not speak the whole day. . . . Go to bed early. Shelley and Jane sit up till twelve, talking. Shelley talks her into a good humour." "Shelley explains with Clara," "Shelley and Clara explain, as usual," are entries which signify that a misunderstanding was over and gone, and Clara, for her part, the chief sufferer from her own humours, makes piteous penitent resolutions in her diary, and tells how she hates her own bitterness, and likes " good, kind, explaining people." "Mary says things which I construe into unkindness. I was wrong. We soon become friends, but I felt deeply the imaginary cruelties I conjured up " (October 19).

It was not only imaginary cruelties that Clara's fancy could conjure up ; she suffered also from paroxysms of imaginary fear, and horrors of the supernatural, which Shelley sometimes regarded with sympathetic interest and half-belief ; sometimes with amused scepticism ; while by

Mary, with her calmer temper and maturer judgment, they were viewed with something like disdain. The usual reading aloud or game of chess being ended, Shelley, according to his wont, would sink into a deep and delightful slumber, from which if he were roused the pain was like that of one returning to life from the drowning trance. The like happy gift for slumber was possessed by Clara. By the hour of their awaking, Mary had retired to rest, and with "The Monk," or "Zastrozzi," or the Abbé Barruel for companion, the silence of midnight would sometimes begin to tingle for Clara's ears, and supernatural wonders would thicken the air. "I go to bed soon," writes Mary in the journal (October 18), "but Shelley and Jane sit up, and for a wonder do not frighten themselves."

These days, so teased and tangled with cares and anxieties respecting debts, and loans, and the sale of reversions, and annuities, and post-obit bonds, were little favourable to authorship. Some effort was made by Shelley (October 19) to continue his romance of "The Assassins," begun in Switzerland, and the portion already written was read aloud for the publisher, Hookham; but circumstances continued unpropitious for a high imaginative enterprise. Shelley's zeal relaxed, and "The Assassins" remains a fragment. This, as far as we can ascertain, was the sole production of the second half of the year 1814, if we except an article commending and criticizing Hogg's imaginary "Memoirs of Prince Alexy Haimatoff," which Shelley contributed to the *Critical Review* for December. His friend's philosophic-fantastic tale, neglected on its appearance and now buried ten fathoms deep in the waters of oblivion, appeared to its too-generous reviewer to be a work almost unsurpassed for boldness of thought and delicacy of imagination. Yet he indicates in no undecided way what seemed to him to be its errors of opinion and imperfections of style. Perhaps the most striking passage in Shelley's review is that in which he rises, with all the ardour of one who knows the sanctity of love, to utter his reprobation and horror of the merchandise of sensual pleasures.

That he felt bitterly, during these days of heart-wasting anxieties about money, how his higher self was depressed and almost borne under by the throng of meaner cares, cannot be doubted. "You know," he wrote to Godwin in 1816, "my habitual, my constitutional inability to deal with monied men ;" not that he was unable to comprehend their views, but that his staying power was exhausted before theirs, and at last, after strenuous resistance, he fell a prey into their hands. The days of sorest trial, including those of severance from Mary, lay between October 23 and November 9. On the evening before the earlier of these dates—a Saturday evening—just when the table-cloth had been removed after the six-o'clock dinner, the servant of the lodgings—lodgings now in St. Pancras—entered with a letter, which had been delivered by a little boy, who said that it had been given to him by a lady waiting in the opposite field. The letter was from Fanny Godwin and warned Shelley, it would seem, of some design against his personal liberty, in which directly or indirectly the Hookham brothers were believed to be concerned.* A little later Godwin declared to Fanny that if she should see her sister Mary he would never speak to her again, and Mrs. Godwin refused to allow her—a young woman of twenty—to come down to dinner because she had received a lock of Mary's hair ; but Fanny, while

---

* The debt seems to have been one of Harriet's, for which, of course, Shelley was responsible, and perhaps Hookham had informed the creditor—Chartres—of Shelley's address.

T

obedient and anxious to please those who stood to her in the place of parents, was attached to Mary, her nearest in kinship—her mother's child—and for Shelley her regard was true and deep. She had not dared to run counter to Godwin's instructions by entering the St. Pancras lodgings; but she could not leave Mary and Shelley in ignorance of impending danger. Starting up, Shelley and Clara ran to the field opposite their place of abode. There stood Fanny. Clara caught her, on which, screaming, she shook herself free and escaped. "Shelley and I," wrote Clara in her journal, "hasten to Skinner Street. We watch through the window. We see Papa, Mamma, and Charles. Step into Wallis's and write Charles a little note: take it into the shop myself; I request a moment's interview. Charles, after much deliberation, grants it. He comes out. I ask him everything about the Hookhams. He denies knowing anything in such a voice that I thought him sincere." Next day, Sunday, was one of careless freedom for debtors at large. Shelley was determined first to understand, and then, if possible, anticipate and avert the coming danger. Clara's journal relates the events of the day, and shows how useful she could be as an intermediary between Mary and the Godwin household, and again between Shelley and Harriet. When night came, Shelley and Mary were for the first time parted, he having taken refuge against approaching evil with his friend Peacock in Southampton Buildings, Chancery Lane.

In good time Shelley quitted his St. Pancras lodgings, for next day and again on Wednesday "suspicious men' knocked, and inquired for him. "A visit from Shelley's old friends," writes Mary (journal, October 26); "they go away much disappointed and very angry." To raise sufficient money to meet the most pressing debts was Shelley's endeavour morning after morning, and meanwhile for instant necessities five pounds were procured by pawning or selling his beloved microscope. At the London Coffee House in St. Paul's Churchyard, in Holborn, at Southampton or Bartlett's Buildings, in Kentish Town Fields, meetings with Mary were contrived, from which she would return strengthened at heart by the comfort of loving words, but sometimes, after pacings to and fro, while business engagements still detained Shelley, with faint and weary limbs, "tired," she says, "to death." Frequent letters were despatched to make appointments for meeting, or, when an interview was difficult and dangerous, to fill with fond assurances the vacancy of absence. By Wednesday, November 9, all danger of arrest was over; the lodgings at Church Terrace, St. Pancras, were given up, and others more suitable were taken in Nelson Square, where once again Shelley and Mary were together.

CHAPTER XII.

RESIDENCE IN LONDON AND AT BISHOPSGATE (JANUARY, 1815, TO MAY, 1816).

THE opening month of the year 1815 placed Shelley in a new position, and one from which he could withstand the onsets of adversity with a better chance of success. On January 6 his grandfather, Sir Bysshe, upwards of eighty-three years of age, died ; Shelley's father succeeded to the baronetcy, and he himself became the immediate heir to a great property. Tidings of the old man's death first reached his grandson through the public papers. Accompanied by Clara—travel being now undesirable for Mary—he journeyed into Sussex ; and having left his companion at Slinfold, a few miles distant from Horsham, he presented himself at the doors of his former home. By his father's orders he was refused admittance. To hear the long-inwoven clauses of the will read aloud amid the mourning relatives was a privilege denied to an erring grandson ; but who could forbid him to sit outside by the door, filling his inward ear with the melody of " Comus," read from Mary's pocket copy of Milton ? Was ever so ridiculous and provoking a son and heir born to a worthy country squire ? " While I am at breakfast," wrote Mary (January 13) in her journal, " Shelley and Clara arrive. The will has been opened, and Shelley is referred to

Whitton [Sir Timothy's solicitor]. His father would not allow him to enter Field Place; he sits before the door and reads 'Comus.' Dr. Blocksome comes out; tells him that his father is very angry with him. Sees my name in Milton. Shelley Sidney comes out; says that it is a most extraordinary will. Shelley returns to Slinfold. Shelley and Clara set out and reach Kingston that night. Shelley goes to Whitton, who tells him that he is to have the income of £100,000 after his father's death if he will entail the estate."

Sir Bysshe's possessions, in real and personal property, which at one time were supposed by his grandson to amount to £240,000, probably did not fall short of £200,000. One portion, valued at £80,000, consisted of certain entailed estates, but without Shelley's concurrence the entail could not be prolonged beyond himself. The other portion consisted of landed property, unentailed, and of personal property amounting, it is said, to £120,000. It was Sir Bysshe's desire that this accumulation of his long life should be kept together by his descendants, and should pass from eldest son to eldest son through future generations. But with his grandson lay the power to determine whether this desire should or should not be realized. Should he survive his father, Shelley, on executing certain legal forms, would obtain absolute possession of the fee-simple of the settled estates; and with this in prospect he might now, if he pleased, encumber them, or part with his future interest in them, or leave them by will to a stranger. To avert such a catastrophe, Sir Bysshe in his will offered his grandson a valuable consideration. If he would concur in prolonging the entail, and further, would agree to entail the unsettled estates, he should, after his father's death, not only enjoy their rentals, but also the income to be derived from the great personal property, half of which was to be invested in land by trustees appointed in the interest of Sir Bysshe's descendants, and to be settled by them in like manner with the entailed estates. In other words, if Shelley would resign his claim to the fee-simple of the settled estates, and would accept a life-interest in them ; if, also, he would concur in entailing the unsettled estates ; then, upon the death of his father, all should be his, and should pass, undiminished, from his hands to those of his son. But if Shelley should refuse to accept these conditions, the reversion of the settled estates—for of this it was impossible to deprive him—should alone be his. His power of choice between these two courses was limited to one year after his grandfather's decease.

Shelley's negotiations with his father, having for their basis his grandfather's will, extended over nearly eighteen months. Still, as in 1811, he objected, on the ground of moral principles, to the entailing of a great property, but those principles must be " rightly limited and understood." In dealing with his father, with his legal advisers, and with Godwin, who through his own necessitous position was interested in Shelley's chances of being able to afford him relief, he spoke and wrote like a clear-sighted man of business, and rarely, if at all, assigned philosophic-romantic reasons as those which determined his action. To possess immense wealth at a remote period, and to leave that wealth to his children, was no part of Shelley's ambition. It seemed to him more in accordance with his true interests, and with the interest of all persons for whose well-being he ought to provide, that he should possess at once and for the rest of his life an ample competency, which would permit him to pursue his true vocation undisturbed by anxieties about money. Let his brother John be the county magnate, and for his own part let him be free to go where he might please, to think, to read, to write, master of sufficient wealth, but not loaded with riches. To secure such an ample competency, why should he not sell the reversion of the settled estates to his father? Fortunately, Sir Timothy was quite willing that his eldest son should disinherit himself; the personal property, forfeited by Percy Bysshe, would greatly augment the importance of the second son, John, in whom the hopes of the family must now be centred. On discovering that it was his father's desire to buy the reversion of the settled estates, Shelley was less eager to come forward, prudently opining that a more favourable bargain might be made if he showed no excessive alacrity in parting with what his father desired to obtain. In the early months of 1815, while the result of these negotiations was still pending, Shelley suffered some lack of the means of living; debts, including those of Godwin, for which he had made himself responsible, still hung heavily around him, amounting to no less than £5000; and in April he wrote urgently to a money-lender, requesting him to procure immediately the sum of five hundred pounds. He still had occasion to seek such advances of money, on his own account or on that of Godwin; but now his position was a much stronger one than it had been before his grandfather's death, inasmuch as he could offer ample security for a loan.

While the question as to the sale of the principal reversions remained doubtful, it was ascertained that his son's interest in one small portion of the estates, valued at £18,000, might at once be purchased by Sir Timothy. This was done, what was considered as an equivalent of £11,000 being allowed; and in June, 1815, Shelley by the agreement became entitled to a yearly income of one thousand pounds, during the joint lives of his father and himself, secured as a rent-charge out of certain estates, while, in addition, a considerable sum of money was advanced by Sir Timothy towards the payment of his son's debts. On passing from poverty to comparative wealth, and thus becoming owner of a thousand pounds a year, Shelley at once decided to appropriate a just proportion of that sum to the uses of Harriet Shelley. He sent her forthwith two hundred pounds to pay her debts, and he wrote immediately to his father, requesting him to give directions to the bankers, through whom he was to receive the annuity, to pay to Harriet, or to her order, the annual sum of two hundred pounds, in quarterly payments of fifty pounds. Mr. Westbrook continued to his daughter the annuity of two hundred pounds, which he allowed before she and her husband had parted ; she was, therefore, now adequately provided for, being in receipt of four hundred pounds a year.

Thus Shelley's calamitous position of the winter of 1814 was altered to one of comparative comfort and repose. But if it went well with him as regards his worldly goods, he was not free from other causes of discomfort, anxiety, and grief. The excitement and exhausting misery of the early summer of 1814, the keen joy mingled with suffering of its later months, the wretched cares, annoyances, and privations of the winter, perhaps also his persistence in the vegetarian diet, told with injurious effect upon his health. In the following spring " an eminent physician," we are informed by Mrs. Shelley, " pronounced that he was dying rapidly of a consumption ; abscesses were formed on his lungs, and he suffered acute spasms." " Suddenly," she adds, " a complete change took place, and though through life he was a martyr to pain and debility, every symptom of pulmonary disease vanished." It has been said that he made acquaintance with disease at this time, or a little earlier, not only in his own person, but as a student of medicine in the wards of a hospital. Possibly Shelley's dream of pursuing the profession of a physician, which had floated before him in 1811, returned during the period of worldly distress in the winter of 1814–15; but that he walked the wards of a hospital may well be doubted. The statement is Medwin's, and not a single entry in the journal lends support to the assertion of that untrustworthy witness. Once, for an instant, Shelley acknowledged the attraction of another profession than that of medicine. It may have been in the early summer of 1815, or perhaps later, when Shelley resided at Marlow, that of a sudden he conceived with characteristic vividness the purity and tranquillity and moral beauty of the life of the village pastor, and to conceive such a life was to wish for a moment that it were his own. "I well remember the occasion," writes Peacock. "We were walking in the early summer through a village where there was a good vicarage house with a nice garden, and the front wall of the vicarage was covered with corchorus in full flower. . . . He stood some time admiring the vicarage wall. The extreme quietness of the scene, the pleasant pathway through the village churchyard, and the brightness of the summer morning, apparently concurred to produce the impression under which he suddenly said to me, 'I feel strongly inclined to enter the Church. . . . Of the moral doctrines of Christianity I am a more decided disciple than many of its more ostentatious professors. And consider for a moment how much good a good clergyman may do. . . . It is an admirable institution that admits the possibility of diffusing such men over the surface of the land.'"

Besides his broken health, other troubles darkened the opening year for Shelley and Mary. On February 22, or a few days earlier, a seven-months' child—a girl—was born. Mary's suffering was well and quickly over; but the little one was not expected to live. To the glad

surprise of Shelley and of Mary, on whom the new joy of
motherhood was strong, the child seemed to gain in
animation, and the first fears passed away. Shelley himself
during these days was ailing seriously ; but the little girl
would surely thrive. On Monday, March 6, Mary woke
and found her baby dead. The entries in the journal are
brief, but poignant with the pathos of a mother's first days
of desolation.

[*Shelley the diarist: entry undated in consequence of
pages torn from journal, but immediately precedes February
23 ; therefore, perhaps, relating events of February 22.*]
" Maie perfectly well and at ease. The child is not quite
seven months ; the child not expected to live. Shelley
sits up with Maie ; much agitated and exhausted. Hogg
sleeps here.

" *Wednesday, March* 1 [*Mary writes*].—Nurse the baby
read ' Corinne ' and work. Shelley and Clara out all
morning. In the evening Peacock comes. Talk about
types, editions, and Greek letters all the evening. Hogg
comes. They go away at half-past eleven. Bonaparte
invades France.

" *Thursday, March* 2.—A bustle of moving [to new
lodgings]. Read ' Corinne.' I and my baby go about
three. . . .

" *Monday, March* 6.—Find my baby dead. Send for
Hogg. Talk. A miserable day. . . .

" *Wednesday, March* 8.—Finish ' Rinaldini.' Talk with
Shelley. In very bad spirits, but get better ; sleep a little
in the day. . . .

" *Thursday, March* 9.—Read and talk. Still think about
my little baby—'tis hard indeed for a mother to lose a
child.

" *Monday, March* 13.—Shelley and Clara go to town
Stay at home : net and think of my little dead baby

This is foolish, I suppose; yet whenever I am left alone to my own thoughts, and do not read to divert them, they always come back to the same point—that I was a mother, and am so no longer. Fanny comes, wet through; she dines and stays the evening; talk about many things; she goes at half-past nine. Cut out my new gown.

"*Sunday, March* 19.—Dream that my little baby came to life again; that it had only been cold, and that we rubbed it before the fire, and it lived. Awake and find no baby. I think about the little thing all day. Not in good spirits. Shelley is very unwell.

"*Monday, March* 20.—Dream again about my baby."

Fanny Godwin, as the journal shows by several entries referring to her, had either received permission, or had asserted the right, to be now and again with Mary during her days of weakness and sorrow. But Godwin and his wife still held aloof. On a day late in March, Mary, with Shelley by her side, passed Godwin and Charles Clairmont in the street; in the afternoon Charles called at the lodgings; "he tells us," writes Mary, "that Papa saw us, and that he remarked that Shelley was so beautiful, it was a pity he was so wicked." As to Mrs. Godwin, she was capable of an act of capricious kindness, and on the birth of the babe could send, by Charles's hands, a gift of linen; yet she could not look patiently on the face of Mary, the author of her woes. When she went out from the house in Skinner Street in a temper with her husband, and would not return for the night, to parade up and down before Shelley's window was an odd mode of manifesting her wounded feelings. "*April* 10.—Shelley reads Gibbon. . . Mrs. Godwin after dinner parades before the windows. Talk in the evening with Hogg about mountains and lakes and London. *April* 11.— . . . Receive letters from Skinner Street to say that Mamma had gone away in the pet and had staid out all night." Affairs in Skinner Street were, indeed, in a lamentable condition, and possibly Mrs. Godwin's "pet" may have had its sufficient reason. In spite of her honourable exertions to keep the wolf from the door, his hateful pawing and snuffing were always painfully near. There was talk of Charles Clairmont's going to America—a proposal which seemed to Mary, when she heard of it, "a rather wild project in the Clairmont style." As to Clara, her mother and Godwin hoped that she might be placed in some suitable situation— perhaps with Godwin's acquaintance, Mrs. Knapp. Some such plan had been discussed in October, and Clara had not taken to it kindly. To Mary her presence had grown most irksome, and it would have been an infinite relief were Clara suitably provided for in some other home than hers. Though never dreaming that Shelley's love could be transferred to another, Mary had a jealousy, natural and not dishonourable, which made her unwilling to share with another the higher companionship of his mind. In Shelley's walks and talks Clara equally with herself was by his side ; in his Italian studies, Clara went forward with him day by day; "Shelley and Clara read 'Pastor Fido,'" "Shelley and Clara begin 'Orlando Furioso'"—these and such-like are Mary's entries in the journal. "Very unwell," Mary writes in the journal (March 11, 1815). "Hogg goes to town. Talk about Clara's going away ; nothing settled. I fear it is hopeless. She will not go to Skinner Street ; then our house is the only remaining place, I plainly see. What is to be done ?"

At length, towards mid-May, it was decided that Clara should be sent, on the excuse of needing country air, to Lynmouth—a spot known to Shelley and to Godwin ; known also to Mrs. Godwin, who had once visited her sister there, and made the acquaintance on that occasion of Mrs. Bicknall, the widow of a retired Indian officer who resided in a charming cottage on the Devon coast. Thither, in May, Clara was removed—a consummation devoutly wished at least by Mary, who chronicles the event of Clara's departure with touches of unusual asperity.

"*Friday, May* 12.—Not very well. After breakfast read Spenser. Shelley goes out with his friend [Clara]; he returns first. Construe Ovid (90 lines); read Spenser. . . . Read over the Ovid to Jefferson [Hogg] and construe about ten lines more. Read Spenser (canto 10 of 4th book). Shelley and the lady walk out. After tea, talk; write Greek characters. Shelley and his friend have a last conversation.

"*Saturday, May* 13.—Clara goes; Shelley walks with er. Charles Clairmont comes to breakfast; talk. Shelley goes out with him. Read Spenser all day (finish canto 8, book 5); Jefferson does not come till five. Get very anxious about Shelley; go out to meet him; return; it rains. Shelley returns at half-past six; the business is finished. After dinner Shelley is very tired, and goes to sleep. Read Ovid (60 lines). Charles Clairmont comes to tea. Talk of pictures."

"I begin a new journal with our regeneration," Mary wrote on Clara's departure, in May, 1815. Unhappily, the journal from that date onwards for more than twelve months has been lost. Clara's journal, for a still longer period, if she continued to keep this daily register of her doings, is also lost. Our materials for the story of Shelley's life from June, 1815, to July of the following year are scanty. Happily, the finer motions of his spirit during the autumnal days of 1815 are reflected for us in the magic mirror of the "Alastor."

Relieved from poverty and the oppression of debt,

Shelley longed to escape from London, and settle alone
with Mary, in some beautiful solitude—far from the averted
faces of former friends—in Wales, or perhaps in Devon.
Part of the summer passed in a tour along the south coast
of Devon, and in search for a suitable residence. But even
amid the loveliness of southern bay and ferny coombe,
Shelley's heart reverted fondly to Nantgwillt and to
Tremadoc. In July Shelley was alone, house-hunting,
and Mary was now at Clifton. August 4, Shelley's birthday, was drawing near, and Mary's heart was filled with
longing for his presence on that day. Could Clara in her
Lynmouth cottage have heard that Shelley was in South
Devon? and if so, might she not have taken it into her
head to start off and join him? Such a possibility was
not to be contemplated with patience. And was it not
right that Shelley should be with "the own Maie" to
receive his birthday present from her hands? With little
tender words, that were caresses, and pet names, Mary
wrote to Shelley, entreating that their severance should be
at an end. Of these little playful names one, which could
serve as noun or adjective, we cannot explain. Why Mary
was "Pecksie" must remain a Shelleyan mystery; nor can
we throw light on the incident of the Dormouse and the
brooch.* If Mary was "Pecksie," Shelley became for her
the "Elfin Knight," under which name the author of the
"Hymn to Intellectual Beauty" was afterwards veiled in
the announcement of that poem in Leigh Hunt's *Examiner.*
The two love-names appear in playful conjunction on a
blank space at the end of the first volume of the manuscript journal, where Mary had noted for her private use
the items of some simple recipe, and Shelley, not without
a smile at his own former interest in romantic horrors, adds

* Possibly "Pecksie" has some connection with the Pecksy of Mrs
Trimmer's "History of the Robins."

a ghastly parody of Mary's prescription, drawn from the pharmacopœia of the land of ghouls :—"[In Mary's hand-writing.] A tablespoonful of the spirit of aniseed, with a small quantity of spermaceti.

"[In Shelley's.] 9 drops of human blood, 7 grains of gunpowder, ½ oz. of putrified brain, 13 mashed grave-worms—the Pecksie's doom salve. The Maie and her Elfin Knight."

The Maie's letter from Clifton to her vanished Knight of Elfland ran as follows :—

Mary to Shelley.

Clifton, July 27, 1815.

My beloved Shelley,

What I am now going to say is not a freak from a fit of low spirits, but it is what I earnestly entreat you to attend to and comply with.

We ought not to be absent any longer ; indeed, we ought not. I am not happy at it. When I retire to my room, no sweet love ; after dinner, no Shelley ; though I have heaps of things *very particular* to say ; in fine, either you must come back, or I must come to you directly. You will say, shall we neglect taking a house—a dear home ? No, my love, I would not for worlds give up that ; but I know what *seeking* for a house is, and, trust me, it is a very, *very* long job, too long for one love to undertake in the absence of the other. Dearest, I know how it will be ; we shall both of us be put off, day after day, with the hopes of the success of the next day's search, for I am frightened to think how long. Do you not see it in this light, my own love ? We have been now a long time separated, and a house is not yet in sight ; and even if you should fix on one, which I do not hope for in less than a week, then the settling, etc. Indeed, my love, I cannot bear to remain so long without you ; so, if you will not give me leave, expect me without it some day ; and indeed, it is very likely that you may, for I am quite sick of passing day after day in this hopeless way.

Pray, is Clara with you ? for I have inquired several times, and no letters ; but, seriously, it would not in the least surprise me (if you have written to her from London, and let her know that you are without me) that she should have taken some such freak.

The Dormouse has hid the brooch ; and, pray, why am I for ever and ever to be denied the sight of my case ? Have you got it in your own possession ? or where is it ? It would give me very great pleasure if you would send it me. I hope you have not already appropriated it, for if you have I shall think it un-Pecksie of you, as Maie was to give it you with her own hands on your birthday ; but it is of little consequence, for I have no hope of seeing you on that day ; but I am mistaken, for I have hope and certainty, for if you are not here on or before the 3rd of August, set off on the 4th, in early coach, so as to be with you on the evening of that dear day at least.

To-morrow is the 28th of July.* Dearest, ought we not to have been together on that day ? Indeed we ought, my love, and I shall shed some tears to think we are not. Do not be angry, dear love ; your Pecksie is a good girl, and is quite well now again, except a headache, when she waits so anxiously for her love's letters.

Dearest, best Shelley, pray come to me ; pray, pray, do not stay away from me ! This is delightful weather, and, you better, we might have a delightful excursion to Tintern Abbey. My dear, dear love, I most earnestly and with tearful eyes beg that may come to you, if you do not like to leave the searches after house.

It is a long time to wait, even for an answer. To-morrow may bring you news, but I have no hope, for you only set off to look after one in the afternoon, and what can be done at that hour of the day ?

It is almost certain that Mary's wish had its fulfilment and that she and Shelley met at Clifton before August. In that month a resting-place at length was found by them, but it was neither in Merionethshire nor Devon. On the borders of Windsor Park, at Bishopsgate, the eastern entrance of the park, in a furnished house, Shelley and

---

* The anniversary of their flight to Dover.

Mary were once more together, and alone. To one who had been an Eton boy, and at a later time a resident at Bracknell, the ground was doubtless familiar. Its umbrageous solitudes were dear to him for meditation and repose ; and at no great distance was the river, to which during his entire life in England—at Eton, at Oxford, at Marlow—his flights reverted and clung like the rapid wheelings of a swallow. Nor were he and Mary quite without companionship, for Peacock, then residing at Marlow, would often walk over, and become for a while their guest. The August days that year were golden, a favourable season for pasture-land and corn-crop ; and when a shower had fallen, clear breezy hours bore away the moisture, and the sky again was blue. The river-navigation of the Reuss and Rhine, just twelve months since, had delighted Shelley, and the memory of it now quickened in his imagination, making him long for a new experience of like enjoyment. Since his return from the Continent he had read aloud to Mary his favourite "Thalaba," and in fancy had been companion of the young Arabian wanderer in his voyage. Why should not some days of this delightful season be spent in rowing towards the source of the Thames ? Peacock would take an oar ; so, in his turn, would Charles Clairmont ; Mary should sit at the wherry's end, presiding over her chief boatman's toil. The project happily conceived was executed as happily. The excursion occupied about ten days, terminating only because the boat had reached shallows near the river-head, where, says Peacock, "the cattle stood entirely across the stream, with the water scarcely covering their hoofs." Shelley's fancy had now taken wing, and it would have pleased him to explore, by river and canal and lake, wild Wales and northern England, and the regions of Forth and Tweed. Perhaps it was fortunate that money barred the way, or

U

the force which, that autumn, created "Alastor" might have been transmuted into the tugging of an oar.

Peacock's testimony and that of Charles Clairmont tell of the surprising improvement effected in Shelley's health by the few days of life upon the water. Part of this change Peacock was inclined to ascribe less to his open-air existence than to the fact that Shelley on this occasion fell from his height of vegetarianism and tasted flesh again. "He had been living chiefly on tea and bread and butter, drinking occasionally a sort of spurious lemonade, made of some powder in a box, which, as he was reading at the time the 'Tale of a Tub,' he called the *powder of pimper-limpimp*." Peacock's prescription of peppered mutton-chops wrought kindly on him, bringing back the wholesome heat to his blood. "He lived in my way," writes his amateur physician, "for the rest of our expedition, rowed vigorously, was cheerful, merry, overflowing with animal spirits, and had certainly one week of thorough enjoyment of his life."

With calm and health and freedom from disintegrating cares, Shelley's higher and truer self expanded. The poet within him wakened from the oppression and the trance, and his stature was that of manhood. The voice in which his spirit uttered itself was no longer a boyish treble or the broken voice of a youth; it had the fulness and purity of early adult years, with some of the violin's lyric intensity. The happiness and calm had, however, followed hard upon a season of pain, and disappointment, and melancholy foreboding. Already at twenty-three Shelley was disillusioned of some eager and exorbitant hopes; the first great experiment of his heart had proved a failure; his boyish ardour for the enfranchisement of a people had been without result; his literary efforts had met with little sympathy or recognition; and, during the early months of the year, he had felt how frail was his hold on life, and had almost confronted that mystery which lies behind the veil of mortal existence. Therefore if now he sang, there must needs be something of pain and melancholy wisdom mingled with the rapture of his song. In the midst of his vigorous rowing-enjoyment and the bounding animal spirits, of which Peacock tells us, he had mused on death, while the stars came out above the graves of Lechlade Churchyard. And later, as he wandered alone in the glades of Windsor Great Park, now when in still autumnal mornings the foliage was brightening to decay, or when the autumnal winds drove to east or west the leaves of chestnut and elm and oak, his thoughts had in them some of the breadth and solemnity of the season of the year. "Alastor" is an imaginative rendering of the mood which came upon him on his return to Bishopsgate, an interpretation of his past experiences and of the lore that he had gathered from life, and a record, marvellously exalted and enhanced, of all the impressions derived from external nature during the past year—from snowy mountain and valley of Switzerland, from the arrowy Reuss and rock-guarded passes of the Rhine, from the gentler loveliness of our English river, and the woodland glories of Windsor. In its inmost sense the poem is a pleading on behalf of human love. This, which had now been found by Shelley, he might have sought for ever and in vain, and then his fate would have been that of the solitary dreamer in "Alastor;" but when he returned from lonely musings under the Windsor oaks to his home, it was to find a place of rest in Mary's heart. Three years after "Alastor" was conceived, Shelley, when in Italy, wrote of his wife as the "dear friend with whom added years of intercourse only add to my apprehension of its value, and who would have had more right than any other one to complain that she has not been able to extinguish in me the very power of delineating sadness." In 1815 her nearness quickened his conception of the pain of one who, having long neglected or scorned the natural sympathies of the heart, is suddenly overmastered by a tyrannous need of love, and at the same time is disqualified for ever finding satisfaction for his ideal aspiration and desire. Shelley in " Alastor " would rebuke the seeker for beauty and seeker for truth, however high-minded, who attempts to exist without human sympathy, and he would rebuke the ever-unsatisfied idealist in his own heart. Yet, at the same time, he would exhibit the advantage possessed by such an one over the worldling, blind and torpid ; for the very fact that he is punished by an avenging fate, and thirsts for love, becomes his purification. Better this, Shelley would say, than to fatten in a loveless lethargy, " deluded by no generous error, instigated by no sacred thirst of doubtful knowledge, duped by no illustrious superstition, loving nothing on the earth and cherishing no hopes beyond." Such are, indeed, already morally dead. "They are neither friends, nor lovers, nor fathers nor citizens of the world, nor benefactors of their country Among those who attempt to exist without human sym pathy, the pure and tender-hearted perish through the intensity and passion of their search after its communities when the vacancy of their spirit suddenly makes itself felt All else, selfish, blind, and torpid, are those unforeseeing multitudes, who constitute, together with their own, th lasting misery and loneliness of the world." * " Alastor has been described as hectic and unhealthy in sentiment in truth, it was the product of calm and happy hour and the mood which it expresses is one of sanity. It influencings upon us are like those of the autumnal win

* Preface to " Alastor."

not joyous but pure and spiritual, enlarging the horizons and revealing to us the boundaries of hope and joy.

"I have been engaged lately," wrote Shelley to Hogg, "in the commencement of several literary plans, which, if my present temper of mind endures, I shall probably complete in the winter. I have consequently deserted Cicero, or proceed but slowly with his philosophic dialogues. I have read the Oration for the poet Archias, and am only disappointed with its brevity.

"I have been induced by one of the subjects which I am now pursuing to consult Bayle. I think he betrays great obliquity of understanding and coarseness of feeling. I have also read the four first books of Lucan's 'Pharsalia,' a poem, as it appears to me, of wonderful genius, and transcending Virgil. Mary has finished the fifth book of the 'Æneid,' and her progress in Latin is such as to satisfy my best expectations.

"The east wind—the wind of autumn—is abroad, and even now the leaves of the forest are shattered at every gust. When may we expect you? September is almost passed, and October, the month of your promised return, is at hand, when we shall be happy to welcome you again to our fireside.

"No events, as you know, disturb our tranquillity."

Among the literary plans to which Shelley in this letter alludes, were a series of speculations on metaphysics, of which some fragments were written and remain to us, and a little treatise—also represented by a few fragments—on the elementary principles of morals. These, with the reflections "On Love," embodying some of the same thought and sentiment which found expression in "Alastor," and the reflections, still more remarkable, "On Life," show how far Shelley had moved from the position which he once occupied as a disciple of the materialistic philosophers of the French Illumination.* But of more worth than any philosophical reasonings of Shelley, is the poet's religious awe with which he contemplates the mysteries of human life and death, renewing for us the sense of that unrealized world in which we move. True and vivid is also his apprehension of the community and harmony which subsist between mind and the spiritual Presence in nature. It is as a poet, no less than as a moralist, that Shelley, writing of ethics, urges that man is "not a moral, and an intellectual, but also, and pre-eminently, an imaginative being." And it is as a poet that he conceives and images forth the difficulty which attends the analysis of our own mind. "Thought can with difficulty visit the intricate and winding chambers which it inhabits. It is like a river whose rapid and perpetual stream flows outwards; like one in dread who speeds through the recesses of some haunted pile, and dares not look behind." If such writing as this adds little to our knowledge, is does what is more important, awakening us to feel anew the wonder and the freshness of the universe.

The months at Bishopsgate went by calmly and quietly. During the winter Peacock often came from Marlow, and Hogg often walked down from London. These were Shelley's only visitors. "One or two persons called on him," writes Peacock, "but they were not to his mind, and were not encouraged to reappear." The only exception was the Quaker, Dr. Pope, of Staines. This worthy old gentleman "liked to discuss theology with Shelley. Shelley at first avoided the discussion, saying his opinion

* It may be, however, that the fragments on Life and on Love are of late date. That "On Life" I should be inclined to assign to the year 1819. A copy of it in Shelley's handwriting occupies part of the note-book—evidently an Italian note-book—which contains his "Philosophical View of Reform." Mr. Rossetti assigns it to the year 1815.

would not be to the doctor's taste ; but the doctor answered, 'I like to hear thee talk, friend Shelley ; I see thou art very deep.'" Perhaps it was to confute the friendly doctor that Shelley plunged into the "History of Arianism." For the rest, his studies were exclusively, or almost exclusively, Greek—Theocritus, Moschus, Homer, the "Prometheus" of Æschylus, Lucian, Herodotus, Thucydides. The winter, as Hogg expressed it, was a mere Atticism.

The opening months of 1816 were not uneventful. On January 24 Mary gave birth to a boy—beloved of his parents, and a centre of hope and joy during a few years—to whom the name of William, that of Mary's father, was given. In March the little volume containing "Alastor" was published, and evidence that a great poet had arisen in England (evidence slow indeed to produce its true effect) was before the world. To Southey, his former friend and kind entertainer at Keswick, Shelley was moved to send a copy of the slender octavo which contained his first published verse since their meeting. "Regarding you," he wrote, "with admiration as a poet and with respect as a man, I send you, as an intimation of those sentiments, my first serious attempt to interest the best feelings of the human heart, believing that you have so much general charity as to forget, like me, how widely in moral and political opinions we disagree, and to attribute that difference to better motives than the multitude are disposed to allege as the cause of dissent from their institutions."

While Shelley was thus occupied with study and authorship and domestic joys, the negotiations with his father for the sale of his reversion and a division of the family property dragged on their weary length. These proceedings were probably watched by Shelley with less anxiety than that which Godwin felt in their issue, for the sum of one thousand pounds which he had received from Shelley in April of the preceding year was soon devoured by the pack of hungry creditors, and they were again in full pursuit. Still Godwin, an indignant moralist, refused to see Shelley's face or to take his hand, and still he petitioned for Shelley's money. While the settlement with his father was pending, to obtain money on *post-obits* or by the sale of reversions was impossible ; it must, therefore, be raised by loans, with greater difficulty and on harder terms. To Shelley, who had taken Mary Godwin to himself, for better for worse, till death should part him and her; to whom, as he afterwards wrote, " it was matter of the deepest grief " that he was by the law rendered incapable " of exhibiting to the world, according to those formalities which the world requires," that his preference for Mary "arose from no light or frivolous attachment ; " who was now living regularly and quietly in his country home ;—to Shelley it seemed strange that Godwin, whose earlier views on marriage had helped to determine his own, should treat him as if he were a common seducer ; and it strained his feeling of respect for his former guide and master to perceive that, while Godwin refused to enter into any relations with him of kindness or of common benevolence, he was ready enough to enter into relations tending to his own personal advantage at Shelley's risk and loss Kindness without approbation, Godwin replied, would not be accepted by Shelley, and torture could not wring from him approbation of the act which had separated them. Therefore their communications must be of a merely business nature. " I return your cheque," Godwin wrote, preserving a point of honour with something like the pedantry of virtue, " because no consideration can induce me to utter a cheque drawn by you and containing my name. To what purpose make a disclosure of this kind to your banker ? I hope you will send a duplicate of it by the post which will reach me on Saturday morning. You may make it payable to Joseph Hume or James Martin, or any other name in the whole directory. I should prefer its being payable to Mr. Hume." We can hardly wonder that Shelley, who was composed of human, not angelic, elements, and had the passions of a man, should once or twice have allowed his indignation to have its way. " I knew," Godwin wrote to his wife three years later, " that Shelley's temper was occasionally fiery, resentful, and indignant." This is true ; yet his desire to benefit Godwin was constant, and was shown by the sacrifice, not alone of his money, but of time and repose of mind ; and if, now and again, wrathful words broke forth, he quickly recovered his natural gentleness of temper, and sought by expressions of regret and goodwill to undo the ill—if ill it was—which he had wrought.

During the early months of 1816 frequent letters were exchanged between Godwin and Shelley. The strict limits imposed on the communications, and the constraint under which Shelley wrote, deprive his letters of a great part of the interest which they would otherwise have possessed. Yet they are valuable as exhibiting his business faculty and his mastery of practical details ; they contain passages of importance, revealing how keenly he suffered from the alienation, or contempt and hatred of his fellows, among whom were some former friends or acquaintances. They exhibit in part the motives which induced him to seek a home on the Continent, and they render sufficiently clear the progress of the weary negotiations with his father, which were finally brought to a fruitless close by the advice of high legal authorities, confirmed by the decision of the Court of Chancery.

Before February, 1816, had passed, Shelley had thoughts of bidding farewell to England, and settling in Italy. The prospect of his departure from England struck alarm into Godwin ; though he could not take Shelley's hand in friendship, it was desirable that hands which held the vile trash of gold should not be wholly out of reach. Shelley hastened to set his mind at rest, and at the same time took occasion to explain some of the motives which induced him to seek residence in a foreign land :—

[February 21, 1816.]—I shall certainly not leave this country or even remove to a greater distance from the neighbourhood of London, until the unfavourable aspect assumed by my affairs shall appear to be unalterable, or until all has been done by me which it is possible for me to do for the relief of yours. This was my intention from the moment that I first received an intimation of the change. I wrote to you for the purpose of giving you an opportunity of making my assistance as available to you as possible before I departed.

When I wrote to you from London I certainly was more firmly persuaded than now of the inefficacy of any further attempt for the settlement of my affairs. You have suggested a view of the question that makes me pause. At all events I shall remain here, or in this neighbourhood, for the present, and hold myself in readiness to do my utmost towards advancing you the money.

You are perhaps aware that one of the chief motives which strongly urges me either to desert my native country, dear to me from many considerations, or resort to its most distant and solitary regions, is the perpetual experience of neglect or enmity from almost every one but those who are supported by my resource I shall cling, perhaps, during the infancy of my children to all the prepossessions attached to the country of my birth, hiding myself and Mary from that contempt which we so unjustly endure. think, therefore, at present only of settling in Cumberland Scotland. In the event the evils which will flow to my children from our desolate and solitary situation here point out an exile the only resource to them against that injustice which we can easily despise.

" I am too generally hated not to feel that the smallest

kindness from an old acquaintance is valuable." These words, which closed a letter of February 26, were an indirect appeal to Godwin's good feeling, and his response (March 5) would seem to have been that the very fact of his receiving from Shelley pecuniary obligations now forbade any show of friendliness, lest it should seem that he were bribed into acquiescence with wrong-doing. Shelley's reply overflows with bitterness and indignation.

[March 6, 1816.]—The first part of your letter alludes to a subject in which my feelings are most deeply interested, and on which I could wish to receive an entire explanation. I confess that I do not understand how the pecuniary engagements subsisting between us in any degree impose restrictions on your conduct towards me. They did not, at least to your knowledge or with your consent, exist at the period of my return from France, and yet your conduct towards me and your daughter was then precisely such as it is at present. Perhaps I ought to except the tone which you assumed in conversation with Turner respecting me, which, for anything that I learn from you, I know not how favourably he may not have perverted. In my judgment neither I, nor your daughter, nor her offspring, ought to receive the treatment which we encounter on every side. It has perpetually appeared to me to have been your especial duty to see that, so far as mankind value your good opinion, we were dealt justly by, and that a young family, innocent and benevolent and united, should not be confounded with prostitutes and seducers. My astonishment, and I will confess when I have been treated with most harshness and cruelty by you, my indignation has been extreme, that, knowing as you do my nature, any considerations should have prevailed on you to have been thus harsh and cruel. I lamented also over my ruined hopes, of all that your genius once taught me to expect from your virtue, when I found that for yourself, your family, and your creditors, you would submit to that communication with me which you once rejected and abhorred, and which no pity for my poverty or sufferings, assumed willingly for you, could avail to extort. Do not talk of *forgiveness* again to me, for my

blood boils in my veins, and my gall rises against all that bears
the human form, when I think of what I, their benefactor and
ardent lover, have endured of enmity and contempt from you and
from all mankind.

To which outbreak Godwin replied immediately with
the equanimity which he cultivated and in which he had a
pride. " I am sorry to say," he wrote, "that your letter
this moment received is written in a style the very opposite
of conciliation, so that if I were to answer it in the same
style we should be involved in a controversy of inex
tinguishable bitterness. As long as understanding and
sentiment shall exist in this frame, I shall never cease from
my disapprobation of that act of yours which I regard as
the great calamity of my life. But the deed being past and
incapable of being recalled, it may become a reasonabl
man to consider how far he can mitigate that anguish
which he has felt towards the actor in the affair unde
which he suffers. The sense of the first paragraph of my
letter is to be found in every book of sound morality and
the principles of moral conduct that ever was written.
On the following day Shelley replied :—

The hopes which I had conceived of receiving from you th
treatment and consideration which I esteem to be justly due to m
were destroyed by your letter dated the 5th. The feelings occa
sioned by this discovery were so bitter and so excruciating that
am resolved for the future to stifle all those expectations which
my sanguine temper too readily erects on the slightest relaxatio
of the contempt and the neglect in the midst of which I live.
must appear the reverse of what I really am, haughty and hard,
I am not to see myself and all that I love trampled upon and ou
raged. Pardon me, I do intreat you, if, pursued by the convictio
that where my true character is most entirely known, I there me
with the most systematic injustice, I have expressed myse
with violence. Overlook a fault caused by your own equivoca

politeness, and I will offend no more.   We will confine our communications to business. . . .

I plainly see how necessary immediate advances are to your concerns, and will take care that I shall fail in nothing which I can do to procure them.

I shall remain in town at least another week, that I may give every possible attention to this subject.   My own concerns are decided, I fear, already.

Shelley's mind was now set upon a residence abroad, but he waited for the final decision of the Court of Chancery on the question in doubt between himself and his father, and bargained meanwhile with attorneys and money-lenders—Hayward, Bryant, Dawe—on Godwin's behalf, not without a sense that such bargaining was a task for which he was ill qualified by his character and temper of mind.

Shelley repeatedly called at the house in Skinner Street; we may surmise that Godwin was absent, or that his absence was professed as an excuse for not admitting Shelley.   Our authentic information is, however, limited to what we learn from the brief entry in Godwin's diary: " P. B. S. calls three times ; C[harles] C[lairmont] twice ; Jane [Clairmont] sleeps."   Early in April Godwin started for Scotland, where he desired to confer with Constable on the subject of his novel " Mandeville," on which he was now engaged, and the correspondence with Shelley ceased for a time.   Before it was resumed a decision had been given in the Court of Chancery against the projected purchase of the reversion by his father, and Shelley, who would seem to have waited for this decision before leaving the neighbourhood of London, was now on his way to the Continent.

CHAPTER XIII.

IN SWITZERLAND WITH BYRON (MAY TO SEPTEMBER, 1816).

THE motives which determined Shelley to withdraw from his native country are apparent, at least in part, to one who has read the letters addressed to Godwin. It is evident that, on receiving the first intimation that the agreement with his father for the sale of the reversion could not legally be completed, he perceived that he was far from wealthy, and that he deemed it expedient to contract his expenses. On the Continent he could live more economically than at home. It is also evident that, suffering acutely (more, perhaps, on Mary's account than his own) from the social odium and stigma consequent upon his unwedded union with one whom he regarded as, in the truest sense, his wife, he now proposed to make the experiment of a residence among strangers. In the early summer of 1816, says Peacock, " the spirit of restlessness again came over Shelley, and resulted in a second visit to the Continent." And to the spirit of restlessness, driving him forth in search of a repose never quite attained, something may have been due. But Peacock, it would seem, was not aware that Shelley's resolve to leave England, or at least to withdraw to some remote district, was of no sudden or hasty formation, and that he had delayed to

arry that resolve into act because the negotiation with his
father was awaiting an issue—an issue which, if favourable,
might at once alter Shelley's position and way of life in
important respects. The issue, as it proved, was not
favourable to Shelley; some few hundred pounds would
e allowed to him by his father to cancel obligations
incurred during the progress of the affair and in expecta
on of the result which both father and son desired. For
the rest his wealth was in a distant future ; but a moderate
sufficiency was his, and on this he could live respectably
in Italy or Switzerland.

A strange incident is said to have occurred on the eve
of Shelley's departure for the Continent. Here Medwin
is our informant, and the story related to him by Shelley
was received by him in all good faith, was apparently
credited by Byron, and was to some extent confirmed by
the testimony of Miss Clairmont. The night before Shelley
set forth for Dover he received a visit in London, says
Medwin, from a married lady, "young, handsome, and of
noble connections," whose name, known to Medwin, was
withheld by him from publication, but " whose disappearance," he observes, " from the world of fashion, in which
he moved, may furnish to those curious in such inquiries
clue to her identity." She had long known Shelley, she
declared, as the creator of " Queen Mab ; " she had entered
enthusiastically into his ideas and aspirations ; she had
dreamed of him by night and by day ; and now, after vain
struggles with herself, she had come to renounce her name,
er fame, her family and friends, to lay her fortunes at his
feet and follow him throughout the world. It was Shelley's
task, according to the reporter of the strange story, to
explain to this rash admirer that another already possessed
his heart, and to do this in words which should carry in
them as little pain as might be to a woman's pride and

love and shame. We hear once more of this lady, when she reappears, veiled and nameless as now, during Shelley's days at Naples, where she was seen by Miss Clairmont— if we may credit Miss Clairmont's statement—and where, to close the romantic tale, she died.

In the opening days of May, 1816, Shelley, accompanied by Mary and Clara Clairmont, started for Paris *en route* to Geneva. Of Miss Clairmont's history, during the interval between the summer of 1815, when she resided at Lynmouth, and her departure with Shelley and Mary for the Continent, few traces can be recovered. That she again became an inmate of Shelley's home seems probable, for in Godwin's diary we find an entry of New Year's Day, 1816: "Write to P. B. S. inviting Jane" (Godwin and her mother had not adopted the romantic name Clara or Claire, which Jane preferred). In compliance with that invitation Clara came and slept for three nights in Skinner Street; and from later entries in the same diary it is certain that now and again during the early months of the year she visited London, and dined or slept at home. It was the time when Byron's brief union with his wife, its brighter hours gone by, was darkening to its close. A little after the second statement made by Lady Byron to Dr. Lushington had determined her adviser to pronounce reconciliation with her husband impossible, Clara Clairmont was tasting an intoxicating excitement, which was to fill all her future life with wormwood and gall—a bitterness growing ever more bitter to the last days of her existence. She called on Byron, we are told, knowing him to be of influence at Drury Lane, and hoping by his assistance to secure a theatrical engagement. Clara Clairmont was unhappy and unknown; of little experience—a girl in her eighteenth year. Byron, already the most famous poet of England, was a man of twenty-eight, who had learnt the havoc wrought by intemperate passion, and was skilled in the dangers which beset a woman's heart. But Clara had a beauty and brilliance of her own ; and why should a man of genius set bounds to his triumphs ? To Clara the rapture was a blinding one—to know herself beloved of the most extraordinary genius, the highest singer, the most romantic and most famous person of the time ; one whom the world had misunderstood, who had wrongs and griefs and a lacerated heart, to which she might bring healing. What was the marriage-tie to one who had of late been a student in the school of " Political Justice " and " Queen Mab " ? It is not strange that a girl of excitable temperament, unbalanced judgment, and intellect imbued with the social doctrines of revolutionary thinkers, should have been lightly whirled out of her regular orbit by such a force as that of Byron.

That her own friends and kinsfolk would view with disapproval her connection with Byron was at once perceived by Clara ; and she eagerly desired to keep the great event of her life a secret. A letter in her handwriting, written, one would surmise from certain expressions in it, just before Byron's departure from England, warns her lover that Mary was profoundly ignorant of the nature of their intimacy ; she did not so much as know that Byron was acquainted with Miss Clairmont's name. On April 25 of that year, Byron, for the last time in his life, gazed at the cliffs of England, as he sailed away from Dover towards Ostend. In his coach, unwieldy through its luxury, attended by three men-servants and his young companion and physician Polidori, he travelled through Flanders and by the Rhine towards Geneva. For English poetry the journey was made memorable by its splendid, imaginative record in the third canto of " Childe Harold.' Towards Geneva also, by the Paris route and with greater

X

celerity, were advancing Shelley and Mary, with their little
blue-eyed boy. Clara Clairmont accompanied them, and
took credit to herself for having determined Shelley to
travel abroad, now that business did not keep him in
England. The company of her fellow-travellers was indeed
irksome to her, but it was inevitable. If Byron should
communicate with her through the Geneva *poste restante* he
must address his letters to her under a feigned name. That
Shelley had decided to leave England, independently of
Clara's solicitations, we know for certain ; it is not improbable, however, that her desire to visit Geneva may
have hastened his departure, and may have helped to
determine his destination.

On May 8, Shelley, Mary, and Clara were in Paris for
the second time, more desolate than on the former occasion
without a friend in the wide city, and vexatiously delayed
by the necessity of obtaining signatures to passports. From
Paris, as far as Troyes, their road was that which they had
traversed two years since on foot and mule-back. Thence
onwards through Dijon and Dôle they advanced toward
the Jura range, arriving, by the light of a stormy moon, on
the fourth night after leaving Paris, at the little mountain
village of Champagnolle. Next day, winding in chill air
among ravines overhung by pine-forests, or climbing amid
the snows which still gathered in the tardy spring, they
passed the village of Les Rousses, and, with the aid of
a team of four horses and ten men to support the carriage
pushed on through pelting snowflakes to the neighbourhood of Geneva. Huge pines, rising in clumps from the
white wilderness, looked weird in the twilight, and the
wide silence of the desert was broken only by the call
and clamour of their labouring mountaineers.

With the new morning the world was changed for them
From the windows of their hotel—Dejean's Hôtel of

l'Angleterre—at Sécheron, a small suburb of Geneva, on the northern side of the lake, they looked out upon the blue waters sparkling in the sunshine. All was warmth and animation and the beauty of cultured landscape, save in the distance the black mountain ridges and the remoter gleaming of Mont Blanc. A glow of pleasure ran along their veins, and animated their thoughts and words. " We have not yet found out any agreeable walks," wrote Mary on May 17 ; "but you know our attachment to water-excursions. We have hired a boat, and every evening at about six o'clock we sail on the lake, which is delightful, whether we glide over a glassy surface or are speeded along by a strong wind. The waves of this lake never afflict me with that sickness that deprives me of all enjoyment in a sea-voyage ; on the contrary, the tossing of our boat raises my spirits and inspires me with unusual hilarity. Twilight here is of short duration, but we at present enjoy the benefit of an increasing moon, and seldom return until ten o'clock, when, as we approach the shore, we are saluted by the delightful scent of flowers and new-mown grass, and the chirp of the grasshoppers, and the song of the evening birds."

On Saturday, May 25, about ten days after Shelley's arrival, there was bustle at Dejean's, and Clara's heart must have moved quick, for Byron had entered the hotel. Byron's writings were well known to Shelley, but he had not as yet made the personal acquaintance of his great contemporary. To Byron he had sent, long since, a copy of "Queen Mab," with a letter setting forth in detail the accusations brought against himself, and adding that, if Byron discredited these accusations, it would make him happy to be honoured with his lordship's acquaintance. The poem reached Byron, and its opening lines won his admiration ; the singular letter miscarried. At the

Sécheron hotel they were naturally and inevitably drawn
together. Both were poets ; both were children of the
Revolution—the one, representing its temper of indignant
revolt ; the other, its doctrinal evangel and its wild-eyed
hopes—both had warred against the laws of society, and
were rebels under the ban. The mass and momentum of
Byron's genius in its impact with the mind of Shelley had
an effect like that of a planet sheering its way through the
luminous mist of a comet in flight. At times an over-
powering sense of his own slightness and impotence
subdued Shelley ; and having a gift for admiration, he
effaced himself in homage to the power exerted by Byron
with so much ease and with so vast an effect. Yet from
the first he was sensible of the coarser elements in Byron's
composition. "Lord Byron," he wrote from Geneva, "is
an exceedingly interesting person ; and as such, is it not
to be regretted that he is a slave to the vilest and most
vulgar prejudices, and as mad as the winds ? "

To be near water was with Shelley to long for a boat
and a boat, keeled and clinker-built, was found, which
became the joint property of himself and Byron. Evening
after evening of late May and early June, they embarked
with Mary and Clara in their company, and Polidori, the
young Anglo-Italian, with his handsome southern outline
of face and his melancholy air ; and before they would
again touch shore the dew was falling and the moon had
come forth in the heavens. One evening, while the
rowers struggled against tide and wind, Byron, animated
by the contest of man with nature, mingled his voice with
that of the wild north-east. " ' I will sing you an Albanian
song,' he cried ; ' now, be sentimental and give me all your
attention.' It was a strange, wild howl that he gave forth,
but such as, he declared, was an exact imitation of the
savage Albanian mode—laughing the while," writes Mr

Shelley, " at our disappointment, who had expected a wild Eastern melody." Perhaps it was after this evening that Byron was re-named, by Shelley and his companions, the " Albaneser," or oftener in a more familiar form as Albè.

Finding, probably, the cost of living at a hotel excessive, and looking forward to a residence of some months in the neighbourhood of Geneva, Shelley, with Mary and Clara and little William, moved by the end of May from Sécheron to a cottage, known as Campagne Chapuis or Campagne Mont Alègre, about two miles from the city, near Coligny, on the opposite side of the lake. The cottage, separated from the water's edge only by a small garden overgrown by trees, stood some five or eight minutes' walk below the Villa Diodati, where Milton, returning from Italy in 1639, had visited his friend Dr. John Diodati, the Genevan professor of theology. A vineyard lay between the villa and Shelley's cottage, with a narrow winding lane leading from the upper house to the terrace and little harbour where lay the boat at her moorings. " The spot," writes Medwin, who visited it in 1818, "was one of the most sequestered on the lake, and almost hidden by a grove of umbrageous forest trees, as is a bird's nest among leaves." From this southern shore of the lake Mont Blanc and his snowy *aiguilles* were invisible ; but Jura, northwards, made amends, behind whose range the sun sank, while darkness winged onward along the valley, from the Alps still glowing and roseate in the sunset glamour. Haunted and hunted by the British tourist and gossip-monger, Byron took refuge on June 10 at the Villa Diodati ; but still the pursuers strove to win some wretched consolation by way-laying him in his evening drives, or directing the telescope upon his balcony, which overlooked the lake, or upon the hillside, with its vineyard, where he lurked obscure.

When the evenings were fine, the boat was never allowed

to rock idly in its bay. Before Byron's migration from Sécheron, he would cross the lake to visit his friends at Mont Alègre, and as he returned over the darkened waters, says Mrs. Shelley, "the wind from far across bore us his voice," singing a Tyrolean song of liberty by Moore. On his arrival at Diodati, Shelley was his constant companion upon the water. To feel the lapping of the waves about him, and to gaze into the sky above—to live between two wonderful worlds, the waters beneath, the heavens over-head—was for Shelley an emancipation from all cramping anxieties and memories of pain. He was in the habit, said Maurice, the boatman, " of lying down at the bottom of the vessel, and gazing at heaven, where he would never enter." As June went by, the voyagers conceived the happy project of circumnavigating the lake, and on the afternoon of the 23rd, in windless weather, their boat drew off from the little port of Mont Alègre, bound on this ambitious voyage. Luckily Polidori, having sprained his ankle, was left behind, though he grumbled at the wrong that was done him. Byron's young physician was not pre-eminent for good temper or good sense ; in his vanity he would be a tragic poet, and earned his patron's sarcasms or ironical applause by his attempt. "After all," said Polidori to Byron, "what is there you can do that I cannot ? " "Three things," replied Byron. "I can swim across that river, I can snuff out that candle with a pistol shot at the distance of twenty paces, and I have written a poem of which fourteen thousand copies were sold in one day." Towards Shelley the doctor's feeling was a con-stantly self-vexing jealousy, and on one occasion, suffering from the cruel wrong of having been loser in a sailing-match, he went so far as to send Shelley a challenge, which was received with a fit of becoming laughter. "Recollect," said Byron, "that though Shelley has some scruples about duelling, *I* have none ; and shall be, at all times, ready to take his place." Polidori, who afterwards put an end to his life, on such occasions would retire in mortification to his room, there to pestle his poisons, pursuing " conclusions infinite of easy ways to die."

Coasting the southern margin of the lake, the voyagers reached at sunset the little village of Nernier, and gazed forth from the shore upon " purple and misty waters broken by the craggy islets." Next day, as their boat advanced eastwards, the snowy summits of the mountains of Savoy, with pine forest, and groves of walnut and oak and lawny fields, ennobled the prospect. The weather was changeful, with fits of wilfulness and fine caprice—now with thunder-showers and baffling breezes, now with a warm southern gust, the summer clouds upon the peaks and deep chasms of blue between. At midday, on June 25, blown by a rising gale, they reached enchanted ground, where Rousseau was the magician, and Julie and Saint-Preux spirits which his art evoked. Having dined at Meillerie, and tasted its honey, " the very essence of the mountain flowers and as fragrant," they re-embarked, and scudded in a south-easterly direction under a single sail, amid breaking waves and a chaos of whirling foam. " One of our boatmen," writes Shelley, " who was a dreadfully stupid fellow, persisted in holding the sail at a time when the boat was on the point of being driven under water by the hurricane. On discovering his error, he let it entirely go, and the boat for a moment refused to obey the helm ; in addition, the rudder was so broken as to render the management of it very difficult ; one wave fell in and then another. My companion [Byron], an excellent swimmer, took off his coat ; I did the same, and we sat with our arms crossed, every instant expecting to be swamped. The sail was, however, again held, the boat obeyed the helm, and, still in imminent peril from the immensity of the waves, we arrived in a few minutes at a sheltered port, in the village of St. Gingoux. I felt in this near prospect of death a mixture of sensations, among which terror entered, though but subordinately. My feelings would have been less painful had I been alone; but I knew that my companion would have attempted to save me, and I was overcome with humiliation when I thought that his life might have been risked to preserve mine."

With early morning of June 26, while his companion still lay drowsing, Shelley was up and abroad among slant meadows and caverned rocks, " to hunt the waterfalls." " I gathered in these meadows," he writes, " a nosegay of such flowers as I never saw in England, and which I thought more beautiful for that rarity." A few hours later they were inspecting the dungeons of Chillon, a most terrible monument—as they appeared to Shelley—of that cold and inhuman tyranny which man delights to exercise over man. Thence, through a heavy swell, they advanced to Clarens—a visit commemorated in stanzas of " Childe Harold," which condense into a few ardent verses the very spirit of Rousseau. " I read 'Julie' all day," says Shelley, " an overflowing, as it now seems, surrounded by the scenes which it has so wonderfully peopled, of sublimest genius and more than human sensibility." From Clarens to Vevai, beautiful in its simplicity, from Vevai to Ouchy, completed the tour of the most interesting portion of the lake. During two days at Ouchy the rain fell; but the travellers found opportunity to visit Lausanne and see the house where Gibbon, in view of Mont Blanc, brought his great history to a close. " My companion gathered some acacia leaves to preserve in remembrance of him. I refrained from doing so, fearing to outrage the greater and more sacred name of Rousseau." The heart-beats of

ulie seemed of more import at this moment to Shelley
han the giant death-throes of the Roman empire. "On
Saturday, the 30th of June," so closes Shelley's record of
he lake-voyage, "we quitted Ouchy, and after two days of
pleasant sailing arrived on Sunday evening at Montalegre."

On resuming residence at Mont Alègre and Diodati,
Shelley and Byron resumed the ways of life which had
been interrupted by their excursion round the lake. To
read, to write, to go abroad in the boat together or alone,
to meet at Diodati in the evening for talk prolonged far
into the night—such was the constantly repeated round.
While Shelley and Byron maintained the nightly debate,
Mary, with her clear hazel eyes and great placid brow,
would look on and listen, penetrated to the heart by their
words and the sound of the alternate voices. Afterwards,
when Shelley's voice was for ever silent, the voice of Byron
would fill her with melancholy by the demand which it
seemed to make for that other which her heart must listen
for henceforth in vain. "I do not think that any person's
voice," she wrote in her journal for October 19, 1822, "has
the same power of awakening melancholy in me as Albè's.
I have been accustomed, when hearing it, to listen and
speak little ; another's voice, not mine, ever replied—a
voice whose strings are broken. When Albè ceases to
speak, I expect to hear *that other* voice, and when I hear
another instead it jars strangely with every association.
I have seen so little of Albè since our residence in Switzerland, and, having seen him there every day, his voice—a
peculiar one—is engraved on my memory with other
sounds and objects from which it can never disunite
self. . . . Since my incapacity and timidity always prevented my mingling in the nightly conversations of Diodati,
they were, as it were, entirely *tête-à-tête* between my Shelley
and Albè ; and thus, as I have said, when Albè speaks and

Shelley does not answer, it is as thunder without rain—th
form of the sun without heat or light—as any familia
object might be, shorn of its best attributes; and I liste
with an unspeakable melancholy that yet is not all pain."

Yet, amid the delights of lake and mountain, and th
strenuous pleasure of intercourse with such a mind as tha
of Byron, Shelley thought lovingly of England, its greye
skies, its fields, its green lanes, its hills and streams, an
the peace of a settled home.   He was, indeed, out of sym
pathy with many English institutions, but he did not scor
or spurn his native land; rather his heart reverted toward
it like the heart of a child towards a mother.   He wrot
accordingly (July 17) to Peacock—his tenancy of the hous
at Bishopsgate ceasing on August 3—to look out for
home for him and Mary and little William and the kitte
now *en pension*.   " I wish you to get an unfurnished hous
with as good a garden as may be, near Windsor Fores
and take a lease of it for fourteen or twenty-one years.
wish the situation to resemble as nearly as possible that c
Bishopsgate, and should think that Sunning Hill, or Wink
field Plain, or the neighbourhood of Virginia Water, woul
afford some possibilities. . . . My present intention is t
return to England, and to make that most excellent
nations my perpetual resting-place.   I think it is extreme
probable that we shall return next spring—perhaps befor
perhaps after, but certainly we shall return."   It is remar
able with what a warm glow of domestic feeling Shelle
one of those

> " Wanderers o'er Eternity
> Whose bark drives on and on, and anchor'd ne'er shall be,"

anticipates the fireside joys.   Not Southey himself coul
have sung a more devout hymn to the household god
" The shrines of the Penates are good wood fires, or windo

frames intertwined with creeping plants ; their hymns are the purring of kittens, the hissing of kettles ; the long talks over the past and dead ; the laugh of children ; the warm wind of summer filling the quiet house, and the pelting storm of winter struggling in vain for entrance." Beautiful surroundings Shelley desired as an added charm to a fixed abode. Windsor Forest pleased him much " because of the sylvan nature of the place and the beasts with which it was filled ; " but he was not insensible to the beauties of the Thames, and if Peacock dwelt at Marlow, it would be a pleasure to reside near his friend. " Recollect, however," he added, in conclusion, " we are now choosing a fixed, settled, eternal home, and as such its internal qualities will affect us more constantly than those which consist in the surrounding scenery, which, whatever it may be at first, will shortly be no more than the colours with which our own habits shall invest it."

The spirit of motion was now in Shelley's veins ; and before July had closed, he and Mary and Clara were off and away from the lake-side dwelling, on the road to Chamouni. The impressions which this excursion left with him were widely different from those produced by his sail along the shores of Lake Leman—all was more savage, solitary, and colossal. The Arve, untamable, swollen by rains and raving among its boulders, the eternal forests, the waterfalls dashing from rock to rock, or assuming shapes like an exhalation, and overhung by a multitude of sun-bows, the wild ravines, the pinnacles of snow intolerably bright, which shot into the bright blue sky, the smoke and smothered thunder of the avalanche, the dizzying wonder of the sea of ice—these raised Shelley's spirit to rarer heights of wonder and of joy than it had touched among the flowery meadows of St. Gingoux or in the love-laden atmosphere of Clarens. A morning was spent in a visit to the source of the Arveiron ; on the next, in spite of rain, the tourists pushed on towards Montanvert, but were at length compelled to return, wet through, with their object unattained. The mule on which Shelley rode falling in a *mauvais pas*, he narrowly escaped being precipitated down the mountain ; in his descent on foot he tripped, and, falling upon his knee, fainted, and was for a time incapable of continuing his course.

Not to be defeated, they renewed the attempt to view the Mer de Glace from Montanvert on the following day (July 25), and this time their effort was rewarded with success. For some distance Shelley walked upon the ice, wondering at the horror and beauty and mystery of its blue-green chasms ; then the three travellers dined on the grass, in the clear, cold air. Before they left Montanvert, the Travellers' Album had received in unusual form, but one not to be mistaken, the sign-manual of P. B. Shelley. His predecessor had exhaled his orthodox sentiment in some devout platitude. The golden opportunity of demonstrating that his heterodoxy stood unsubdued in presence of Mont Blanc was too tempting to be lost by Shelley, and taking the pen, he subscribed his name to Greek words as incorrect in form as in sentiment—

Εἰμι φιλάνθρωπος δημωκράτικος τ' ἄθεος τε.

A third comer, it is said, added the word μωρός, and Byron, —so declares Lord Broughton—on visiting Montanvert, defaced Shelley's *atheist* and his successor's *fool*.

Deeper feelings than he would expose in a Travellers' Album Shelley put on record in his poem " Mont Blanc,' the inspiration of which came to him as he lingered on the bridge of Arve on his way through the Valley of Chamouni —in this, and in the noble " Hymn to Intellectual Beauty,' which was also an overflow of thought and emotion in presence of the landscape of Switzerland. Vast and wonderful as the material universe is, so Shelley writes in his verse, it borrows its greatness and glory from what is spiritual ; it is but like a river flowing through a world of Thought, the hues and forms of which it mirrors. Nor is it merely in and through humanity that this spiritual Power lives and moves and has its being. A Presence, or its radiant yet awful shadow, haunts and startles and waylays us in all that is beautiful, sublime, or heroic in the world without us or in the world within ; to this we dedicate our powers in all high moments of joy or aspiration ; and when the ecstasy has sunk and the joy has faded, still in a calmer, purer temper, it may become the habit of our soul to follow upon the track of this ideal Loveliness, until in a measure we partake of its image. Such is the idea of his poem.

Bringing with them some specimens of minerals and dried flowers, the travellers, daunted by a renewed fall of rain, turned their faces from Chamouni on the fourth day after their arrival. To Mary there was compensation for loss of the Col de Balme, with its view of Mont Blanc, eminent above his giant wardens of the plain, in the growing nearness to her small blue-eyed boy. She writes thus in her journal of the second day of the return journey : "*Saturday, July* 27.—It is a most beautiful day, without a cloud. We set off at twelve. The day is hot, yet there is a fine breeze. We pass by the Great Waterfall, which presents an aspect of singular beauty. The wind carries it away from the rock, and on towards the north, and the fine spray into which it is entirely dissolved passes before the mountain like a mist. The other cascade has very little water, and is consequently not so beautiful as before. The evening of the day is calm and beautiful. Evening is the only time that I enjoy travelling. The horses went

fast and the plain opened before us. We saw Jura and the
Lake like old friends. I longed to see my pretty babe.
At nine, after much inquiring and stupidity, we find the
road and alight at Diodati. We converse with Lord Byron
till twelve, and then go down to Chapuis, kiss our babe,
and go to bed."

For some time past Mary's thoughts had been much
occupied with an imaginative invention of her own. During
a few days of ungenial weather, which confined them to
the house, some volumes of ghost stories, "Fantasma-
goriana, ou Recueil d'histoires d'apparitions, de spectres,
revenans, etc."—a collection translated into French from
the German—fell into their hands, and its perusal probably
excited and overstrained Shelley's imagination. On the
night of June 18, over a blazing wood fire, there was
ghostly talk at Diodati, and when midnight was past, and
the tales of spectres had been told, Byron lifted the theme
of their talk—the supernatural and its manifestations—to
the higher region of poetry. Coleridge's "Christabel" had
just been published by Murray, to whom Byron had
introduced its author. A copy of the poem had not yet
reached Geneva, but its verses lived in the memory of
Byron, who had read it in manuscript, and perhaps had
heard it recited by Coleridge himself. He now repeated
the lines descriptive of the mysterious horror of the witch's
bosom. "When silence ensued," wrote Polidori in his
diary, "Shelley, suddenly shrieking and putting his hands
to his head, ran out of the room with a candle." "Threw
water on his face," the physician continues, "and gave him
ether. He was looking at Mrs. Shelley, and suddenly
thought of a woman he had heard of, who had eyes instead
of nipples ; which, taking hold of his mind, horrified him."
When the horror passed away and calm was restored,
"We will each write a ghost story," said Byron, and, with

an agreement to carry his proposal into effect, they parted for the night. A story, founded on the experiences of his early life, was begun by Shelley and was soon abandoned. Morning after morning he inquired of Mary, " Have you thought of a story ? " and morning after morning came the disappointing answer, " No." One night she sat listening to a conversation between the two poets at Diodati ; what was the nature—they questioned—of the principle of life ? would it ever be discovered, and the power of communicating life be acquired ?—" perhaps a corpse would be reanimated ; galvanism had given token of such things." That night Mary lay sleepless, while moonlight struggled through the closed shutters of her bedroom, and she seemed to be aware of the lake and high white Alps beyond. But nearer than Alps or lake was the persecuting phantom of a pale student of the unhallowed arts engaged in creating a man-monster, at last endowed with life, and the shame and terror of the artist who had brought him into being. Such was the origin of the tale of " Frankenstein," so much of the scenery of which is that of Geneva, its lake, the high banks of Belrive, Sécheron, the mountains of Jura, and the Alps of Savoy.

Before Shelley left Geneva for England he had the pleasure of making the acquaintance of Byron's guest, Matthew Gregory Lewis, long known to him through his " Tales of Wonder," " The Monk," and other writings in prose and verse. The inventor of spectral horrors, which had held his readers in a trance of awed illusion, was himself curiously incredulous of the mysteries of the spirit-world. He was no better than a kindly English gentleman, with the narrow-mindedness of his class—a " jewel of a man had he been better set," as Byron found him, but decidedly " a bore." " We talk of ghosts," Shelley notes in the journal on August 18, four days after Lewis's arrival

at Diodati; "neither Lord Byron nor Monk G. Lewis seem
to believe in them; and they both agree, in the very face
of reason, that none could believe in ghosts without also
believing in God." Lewis now had thoughts for the living
whose interests concerned him more deeply than the affairs
of the dead. He had just returned from his West Indian
property, and was much moved by the thought of the
uncertain tenure, at a master's will or caprice, of their
rights and comforts by his negroes. Shelley, who in 181.
had read with horror of the cruelties of the slave-traffic
doubtless entered with sympathetic zeal into Lewis's views
and on August 20 was signed a remarkable codicil to
Lewis's will, requiring the heir of his Jamaica estates to
pass three months once at least in every three years upon
the property, and forbidding the sale of any negro, or the
diminution of any of the comforts or indulgences which
their kindly master had himself allowed to his slaves
The codicil, which is written with a vehement ardour of
humanity, unlike the colourless manner of a legal instru
ment, was witnessed by Byron, Percy Bysshe Shelley, and
John Polidori.

A few days later, on August 28, for the last time they
were floating upon the sapphire waters of the lake, and
next morning at nine they had started on their journey
to England. As far as Dijon, the route by which they
had come in May was followed; thence by Rouvray and
Auxerre they proceeded to Fontainebleau and Versailles
'Could a Grecian architect," Shelley writes, "have com
manded all the labour and money which are expended on
Versailles, he would have produced a fabric which the
whole world has never equalled." As it was, in the
arrangement of the costly materials Shelley perceived
"something effeminate and royal." The librarian displayed
for the inspection of visitors a book containing coloured

illustrations of a tournament of the court of Louis XIV.; to Shelley it seemed that "the present desolation of France, the fury of the injured people, and all the horrors to which they abandoned themselves, stung by their long sufferings, flowed, naturally enough, from expenditures so immense as must have been demanded by the magnificence of this tournament." "The vacant rooms of this palace," he adds, "imaged well the hollow show of monarchy." The Imperial House in the fifth canto of "The Revolt of Islam"—a "gorgeous grave," its storied walls answering vacantly to the footfalls of Laon, while the twilight gathers "like a charnel's mist within the radiant dome"—may be a reminiscence of the solitude and desolation of Versailles.

CHAPTER XIV.

AUTUMN AND WINTER IN BATH (SEPTEMBER TO DECEMBER, 1816).

HAVING travelled to Havre, Shelley and his party sailed for Portsmouth in a baffling wind on September 7, and after a voyage of twenty-seven hours reached England. When free to proceed, a day having been lost by detention at the Custom House, Shelley and Mary parted—he to transact business in London and seek a house in the country with Peacock's aid, she to remain in Bath with little William and Clara, and the Swiss nurse, Elise. At what precise date Shelley and Mary became aware of the fact that Clara in reckless passion had given herself to Byron, we cannot tell. Medwin, speaking of the residence at Geneva, states that he had reason to believe that the intrigue was carried on with the greatest secrecy, and that "neither the Shelleys nor Polidori were for a long time privy to it." In fact it may have been for Byron, during his sojourn at Diodati, a thing of the past, though he did not yet openly break with the woman who was to be mother of his child. The occasional references to Clara in Mary's journal rather favour Medwin's statement. But the anticipated birth of Byron's child could hardly have been unknown to Mary and Shelley when they landed in England. Clara was most anxious to conceal what had taken place from Godwin and her mother, and Shelley and

Mary had no desire to betray her secret. It would seem to have been arranged that she was to remain in Bath under the name of Mrs. Clairmont, and that Mary was to be her companion there until Shelley should have found a suitable house. The moral indignation which Byron's act might justly arouse seems to have been felt by neither Shelley nor Mary. Shelley's conception of the social and moral obligations between man and woman in organized societies was radically unsound; all offences against order were in his eyes sanctified by love, if love were deep and true, and Byron had not yet given evidence that he could be false and cruel to Clara.

From Marlow, where Shelley was the guest of Peacock, he conveyed Peacock's invitation to Mary to join them there. It was little more than a twelvemonth since they had voyaged together up the Thames, and now they were once again close to its loveliest reaches, in the delightful autumn days. With Rousseau and Richardson for indoor recreation, and outdoor walks to the Fisherman's Cliff and Medmenham Abbey, nestling beneath its woody uplands, the time from September 20 to September 24 went sunnily by, and no ill news from Bath came to disturb the pleasure of the autumnal calm.

On September 25 they were back at 5, Abbey Church-yard, Bath, with Clara and their eight-months-old boy. The hope which Shelley entertained of receiving a considerable sum of money from his father, in part to clear off debts contracted on the faith of a successful issue to their negotiations of the spring, had been dashed, and to his grief he found himself unable to pay Godwin the three hundred pounds which he had promised. To Godwin, who had given an exacting creditor a bill on demand for that sum, the disappointment was cruel. His novel of " Mande-ville " was progressing well ; but everything depended on his tranquillity of mind. "I have already written more than half a volume," he told Shelley in August. "I am satisfied with my plan; I think it will be better than 'St. Leon,' and will take place next after 'Caleb Williams.' I am in good tone, and anxious to proceed. The tone, however, I must confess, is kept up with considerable effort, and is only preserved by a faith that relates to you, and a confident hope that the relief so long expected from your quarter will at length be fully realized. If I am disappointed in this, if my affairs in the mean time go to a wreck that can no longer be resisted, then the novel will never be finished." Such an appeal as this was peculiarly moving to Shelley, who prized inordinately Godwin's imaginative work; but to fulfil his engagements was not in his power. Such money as he had, however, he sent without delay.

Great and sudden calamities, pain, and sorrow, were to bring Godwin and Shelley once more together before the year had closed, and anxieties connected with money were for a time to seem trivial in comparison with griefs more cruel and overwhelming. During the spring and summer Fanny Godwin had suffered from deep dejection of spirits. In July she wrote to Mary of "the dreadful state of mind" under which she generally laboured, and of which she endeavoured in vain to rid herself; "my mind," she added "always keeps my body in a fever; but never mind me. "My Aunt Everina," she wrote, "will be in London next week, when my future fate will be decided. I shall the give you a full and clear account of what my unhappy lif is to be spent in." How Fanny's fate was decided we do not know; but we know that Everina Wollstonecraft ha withdrawn her confidence and affection from Fanny i the spring, and that, although friendly relations had bee restored, she was capable of a harsh decision. Wit

Godwin's affairs so painfully entangled, with Mary and Clara in great measure lost to her, and the house in Skinner Street saddened, with Mrs. Godwin's violence and suspicion of temper, with the sense of her own uselessness and dependence—she, a burden to every one—it needed but a slight cause to transform Fanny's wretched dejection to despair. Mary Wollstonecraft, her mother, who had written to Imlay so gladly, so exquisitely, about Fanny's baby ways, in her own anguish of spirit had sought for peace in the waters below Putney Bridge, and had barely been rescued from untimely death. Godwin, whose cool temper preserved him from any temptation to self-destruction, had argued in "Political Justice" that suicide is not necessarily criminal—"the difficulty is to decide in any instance whether the recourse to a voluntary death can overbalance the usefulness I may exert in twenty or thirty years of additional life." As to Fanny, she might well conclude that the death of a feeble and unhappy being was a thing to be desired, and that it was no ill deed to remove from the world one who, she believed, had been nothing but a cause of pain and injury to those connected with her. It was a theory satisfactory to Mrs. Godwin, and one which Godwin adopted, that the unhappy girl perished because she was consumed by a hopeless passion for Shelley. Miss Clairmont, at least in later years, when she thought more piously of her mother than in the days when she fled from home and refused to return under her mother's guardianship, accepted this explanation of the cause of Fanny's death. But assuredly Fanny would not have made Godwin and his wife her confidants in such a case. And Clara Clairmont had been absent from home not only since July, 1814, setting aside a few short visits, but for the two years immediately preceding that date, a fact which may account for her having less affection for Fanny, as she confessed after Fanny's death, than might have been expected. Were even slender evidence discoverable which should confirm the opinion of Godwin, we might contentedly accept that opinion as true. But no vestige of evidence lends it confirmation. On the other hand, it is clear that for a considerable time before her death Fanny's depression of spirits, caused by a number of circumstances, was extreme, and from her dying declaration, made in writing, it appears that she looked upon herself as worse than useless, as a source of unhappiness to those most closely connected with her; they might grieve for her loss during a few days, but her departure from life—so she had come to believe—would soon bring them relief and positive benefit. The tone of her letters lends no colour to the notion that she was pining through love for Shelley or for any one; there is in them an affectionate frankness when Shelley is mentioned, and she can even take him to task, in a sisterly manner, for a supposed lack of just and open dealing with Godwin in his financial embarrassments. Gentle, fair-minded, and considerate towards every one except herself, Fanny desired that even Mrs. Godwin, who had made home unhappy for her, should suffer no injustice in the thoughts of others; it is touching to observe, in her letter to Mary, written a few days before her death, how sincere is her solicitude that Mrs. Godwin, though to herself far from amiable, should be valued for the good qualities which she undoubtedly possessed. Fanny withdrew from life as one defeated, for whom the struggle had been too hard, and who lacked the toughness of fibre which can endure a long-continued strain; she withdrew from life because, in her weakness and her melancholy, she looked upon herself as a sad encumbrance to the world; she withdrew, not in violence or passion, but stealing away with hopeless eye and rapid step to darkness and oblivion.

Everina Wollstonecraft, I am assured by a lady who still remembers her, was an overbearing, disagreeable, ill-tempered woman, very sarcastic and very clever—a great contrast to her sister, Mrs. Bishop, who had beautiful brown eyes, most winning gentle manners, and whose whole bearing gave the idea of a perfectly lady-like and refined person. On questioning my informant as to the cause of Fanny's suicide, the answer came without doubt or hesitation, " Because Everina would not have Fanny with her. It was just like Everina ; she was a hard woman." From Godwin's letter, written to Mary after her sister's death, we learn that it had been in contemplation that Fanny should go to her aunts in Ireland ; but that she was not on her way to Ireland when she died ; rather that she had left home seeking a place wherein to die, and had written from Bristol announcing, though in veiled words, her fatal resolution. A harsh missive from Everina Wollstonecraft might well have sufficed, with one in Fanny's mood of deep dejection, to reduce her to despair. To her sister Mary the cause of Fanny's death seemed evident— that she was without a home in which it was possible for her to be happy or at rest ; had she but lived a few weeks longer, thought Mary, had she but lived until her sister was Shelley's wedded wife, then Fanny's death would never have taken place, for a fit home and happy resting-place would have been open to her. As it was, she seems to have been a cause of disturbance to Mrs. Godwin in the Skinner Street house; Aunt Everina in Dublin " would not have her ; " and she did not possess, as she tells Mary, a *sou* of her own.

Mirth and anguish are in odd juxtaposition in Mary's journal for the opening days of October. On the 6th Shelley makes a playful entry: " On this day Mary put her head through the door, and said, 'Come and look ;

here's a cat eating roses ; she'll turn into a woman ; when beasts eat these roses they turn into men and women.' " Three days later came a very alarming letter from Fanny, who suddenly had left Godwin's home, and having passed through Bath without calling on her sister, now wrote from Bristol. "Shelley goes immediately to Bristol," the journal records. "We sit up for him till two in the morning, when he returns, but brings no particular news." On that night Fanny, having arrived at the Mackworth Arms Inn, Swansea, by the Cambrian coach from Bristol, retired to rest, telling the chambermaid that she was exceedingly fatigued, and would herself take care of the candle. When she did not appear next morning they forced her chamber door, and found her lying dead ; her long brown hair about her face ; a bottle of laudanum upon the table, and a note which ran thus : "I have long determined that the best thing I could do was to put an end to the existence of a being whose birth was unfortunate, and whose life has only been a series of pain to those persons who have hurt their health in endeavouring to promote her welfare. Perhaps to hear of my death will give you pain, but you will soon have the blessing of forgetting that such a creature ever existed as . . ." She had with her the little Genevan watch, a gift of travel from Mary and Shelley ; and in her purse were a few shillings. She had stated to a fellow-passenger on the coach that she was on her way to Ireland, but the sum of money in her possession would not nearly have sufficed for such a journey. In 1814 she had visited Wales, and possibly may have known Swansea, where now she chose to set up her everlasting rest. On Thursday, October 10, Godwin, informed from Bristol of her resolve, set out from London in pursuit, and on the same morning Shelley again visited Bristol and obtained more certain traces. Godwin's stay at the scene of the disaster was as rief as possible; on his return journey he slept at Bath, ut did not visit his daughter. Next day, October 12, ₊helley brought the lamentable tidings to Mary. "He eturns," the journal tells us, "with the worst account. A ₁iserable day. Two letters from Papa. Buy mourning nd work in the evening."

The shock of excitement and grief caused by so terrible ₁ event was for a time disastrous to Shelley's health. He ₊mained at Bath with shattered nerves, writing a little, ₀rrecting proofs of Byron's new canto of "Childe Harold" he manuscript of which he had brought from Switzer- ₁nd), and gleaning what pleasure was possible at such a ₁me from Montaigne, Plutarch, Cervantes, and Milton. ₁ary, with characteristic firmness of will, set herself steadily ₊ work; pushed forward with "Frankenstein;" studied atin; read Locke with Shelley; dipped into chemistry; ₊ok lessons in drawing. Clara, anxieties of her own being ₁dded to the recent misery, passed wretched hours brood- g over all that could afflict her, and often wishing herself possession of that everlasting repose to which Fanny ₁d attained.

In this season of sorrow one happiness came unex- ₊ctedly to Shelley—the gain of a friend who had himself ₁own care and sorrow, but whose bright temper, buoyant ₁cy, and generous heart leaped resurgent from the ₊okes of fortune. On December 1, 1816, arrived at Bath ₁etter from Leigh Hunt, and on the same day appeared the *Examiner*, Leigh Hunt's journal, an article entitled ₍oung Poets," noticing three writers who, according to ₊ critic's judgment, promised to bring a considerable ₁dition of strength to the new school of English poetry. ₁e, John Hamilton Reynolds, had published a slender ₁ume or two of verse. Another had not yet published ything except in a newspaper; "but a set of his

manuscripts was handed us the other day," said the re
viewer, whose signature—a hand pointing—identifies hin
with Leigh Hunt, " and fairly surprised us with the truth
of their ambition and ardent grappling with nature." Thi
second writer was John Keats. The work of the thir
was little known to the critic, for he had mislaid the one c
two specimens he had had before him ; " but we sha
procure what he has published," the article went on, " an
if the rest answer to what we have seen, we shall have n
hesitation in announcing him for a very striking an
original thinker. His name is Percy Bysshe Shelley, an
he is the author of a poetical work entitled ' Alastor ; c
The Spirit of Solitude.' " " A very striking and origin:
thinker "—no characterization of his powers could hav
been more gratifying to Shelley. Leigh Hunt had bee
long known to him, as the most prominent champion
liberal ideas among journalists, and as one who ha
suffered for the cause. From Oxford Shelley had a
dressed a letter to the *Examiner*, proposing an Associatic
of the friends of liberty for mutual encouragement an
defence, but the letter had not been inserted by the edito
Later Shelley had called on Hunt to seek advice about
poem which he desired to publish, but the slight acquain
ance had not ripened into intimacy. Shelley was then "
youth not come to his full growth ; very gentlemanl
gazing earnestly at every object that interested him, an
quoting the Greek dramatists." Yet again at a later dat
when the editor of the *Examiner* was undergoing impriso
ment for his libel on the Prince Regent, Shelley wrote
him, making a " princely offer," of which, however, at th
time Hunt did not stand in need. Thus communicatio
favourable to the growth of friendship had already tak
place between Shelley and Hunt, but neither as yet cou
be said to possess a real, personal knowledge of the oth

Now, when Shelley most needed a sympathizing friend, such a friend he was to have. Early in December he left Bath to visit Peacock at Marlow and inquire for a house, and from Marlow he turned townwards, to be the guest of Hunt in the old-world suburb of Hampstead.

The visit to Leigh Hunt was brief, but delightful. "Letter from Shelley," Mary writes in her journal (December 13) ; "he is pleased with Hunt." On the day after his return to Bath—December 15—came a note from Hookham, which brought appalling tidings. For a short time past Shelley had lost sight of Harriet. In March of the present year, while the arguments with respect to the sale of the reversion to Sir Timothy were proceeding, her infant son, Charles Bysshe, had been produced on Shelley's behalf in the Court of Chancery. "Whitton," * Shelley writes, in a letter to Godwin of March 9, "said that the production of the infant had already procrastinated the proceedings, much to the displeasure of Sir Timothy." It is probable that Shelley was not present on that occasion, for in the later Chancery action he declared that he had never seen his son ; but it seems likely that he would have communicated with Harriet on the subject. Unhappily the journal for the early months of 1816 has been lost, and no positive evidence is procurable. In June Harriet was in communication with Peacock, and through him with Sir Timothy Shelley's solicitor. She had received, on March 1, her half-yearly instalment of one hundred pounds, paid in advance, and she was assured that future instalments would be as punctually paid in September and March of each year. She applied to Sir Timothy for an additional sum, and it was pointed out to her by Whitton, communicating through Peacock, that in addition to the two hundred a year allowed to her by her husband, she

* Sir Timothy Shelley's solicitor.

had also two hundred a year allowed by Mr. Westbrook.
Whitton further expressed his opinion that it was in her
power to purchase an annuity of £200 or £400, with a
portion of her reversionary interest; but he forbore
advising such a step. "He cannot do anything in the
matter himself," Peacock wrote to Harriet on June 24,
"further than this, that he will state the case for the
opinion of an insurance office as the equivalent value of an
annuity and a portion of your reversion, and he will send
me the result." In September Shelley returned to England,
and in the midmost days of that month he was Peacock's
guest at Marlow. At what precise date Harriet disappeared from the cognizance of Shelley we cannot say.
But we know that in November he was seeking for her
and seeking in vain. That she lived with or under the
protection of her father until a short time before her death
was affirmed on oath by her sister. Immediately before
her death she resided in a house in Queen Street,
Brompton, at no great distance from Hyde Park and the
Serpentine river. To this house she did not return on the
night of November 9. A month later, on December 10—
a day on which Shelley's visit to Leigh Hunt had just
begun—her body was found in the Serpentine river. She
had been far advanced in pregnancy; on her finger was a
valuable ring.*

Harriet Shelley's life, apart from that of Shelley, forms
no portion of the story told in this volume. There is no
doubt that she wandered from the ways of upright living

---

* The entries in Godwin's journal are as follows: "November 9, H. S.
dies." "December 10, H. S. found; disappeared three weeks." The entry
of November 9 was probably inserted after the facts had been more exactly
ascertained than they were when Godwin wrote on December 10. It should
be noted, however, that in the Westbrooks' Chancery declarations Harriet is
said to have died in December. Those who wish to look further into the
matter may see the *Times* for December 12, 1816.

how far she wandered we need not inquire.   If she sinned, she also sorrowed ; we would think of her, not as a desperate fugitive from life, but as the fair, bright, innocent, kind-hearted Harriet of her early wedded days.   That no act of Shelley's during the two years which immediately preceded her death tended to cause the rash act which brought her life to its close, seems certain.   He had written to her kindly, undertaking to watch over her interests ; he had seen that she was safe in the protection of her nearest relatives ; at her urgent entreaty, much against his own desire, he had left his children in her care ; he had, according to his means, guarded her against want or poverty ; when for a time she disappeared from his ken, he had instituted inquiries to discover her whereabouts. By his teaching, indeed, he had led her to think lightly of the established rule and order of society ; but this he had done conscientiously, believing that the revolutionary creed which he had accepted from Godwin's writings was favourable to virtue.   He had been the cause to her of suffering which she was unable to endure.   His example had not been an example of the patience, endurance, and self-denial which, when old ties are broken, should be practised before the formation of new ties.   Had such self-denying fortitude been his, not only would his life have been saved from much misrepresentation and some pain, not only would he have left a nobler precedent for other lives entangled in like difficulties with his own, but a strenuous virtue might have passed from his life into his art, which would have strengthened its nerve and fibre, and enriched and sobered its enthusiasm.   At twenty-two neither was his judgment mature nor his moral temper fully formed.

According to the story which reached Shelley, and which he accepted as true—a story which we have no means of verifying or disproving—Harriet, through her sister's influence, had been driven from her father's house, and being subsequently deserted by one on whom she had a claim for kindness and consideration, she sought in death a speedy and desperate issue from her perplexities and griefs. Frequently, from the days of early girlhood, she had spoken of suicide with a composure which led those acquainted with her to assume that no serious meaning underlay her words. To live for her children was indeed a duty with Harriet after the parting between her and her husband had taken place ; but how if she were conscious that she had disqualified herself for rendering to her children a mother's highest services? * Nothing would then remain to bind her to the wretchedness of an unhappy life, in a world where all seemed to have abandoned her. Yet Shelley at this moment, or but a few days later, was seeking her in vain through the vast labyrinth of London.

It was three days after Harriet Shelley's body had been found that Hookham wrote, informing Shelley of the event.

T. Hookham to Shelley.

My dear Sir,

It is nearly a month since I had the pleasure of receiving a letter from you, and you have no doubt felt surprised that I did not reply to it sooner. It was my intention to do so ; but, on inquiry, I found the utmost difficulty in obtaining the information you desire relative to Mrs. Shelley and your children.

While I was yet endeavouring to discover Mrs. Shelley's address, information was brought me that she was dead—that she had destroyed herself. You will believe that I did not credit the report. I called at the house of a friend of Mr. Westbrook ; my

---

* As a fact, the infant children had been sent away to Warwick, to the care of a schoolmaster named Kendall.

oubt led to conviction. I was informed that she was taken
rom the Serpentine river on Tuesday last, apparently in an
dvanced state of pregnancy.* Little or no information was laid
efore the jury which sat on the body. She was called Harriet
mith, and the verdict was *found drowned*.

Your children are well, and are both, I believe, in London.

This shocking communication must stand single and alone in
ne letter which I now address to you : I have no inclination to
ll it with subjects comparatively trifling : you will judge of my
eelings and excuse the brevity of this communication.

Yours very truly,
T. HOOKHAM, JUN.

Old Bond Street, December 13, 1816.

On the afternoon of the day on which this letter
eached him at Bath—a Sunday—Shelley hastened to
London to claim his children, and on the following day
is letter, making Mary a sharer in his sufferings, his fears,
nd hopes, was on its way.

Shelley to Mary.

London, December 15, 1816.

I have spent a day, my beloved, of somewhat agonizing
ensations, such as the contemplation of vice and folly and hard-
eartedness, exceeding all conception, must produce. Leigh
Iunt has been with me all day, and his delicate and tender
ttentions to me, his kind speeches of you, have sustained me
gainst the weight of the horror of this event.

The children I have not got. I have seen Longdill, who
ecommends proceeding with the utmost caution and resoluteness;
e seems interested. I told him I was under contract of marriage
) you, and he said that, in such an event, all pretence to detain
e children would cease. Hunt said very delicately that this
ould be soothing intelligence to you. Yes, my only hope, my
arling love, this will be one among the innumerable benefits
hich you will have bestowed upon me, and which will still be

* As shown at the inquest. See *The Times*, Dec. 12, 1816.

inferior in value to the greatest of benefits—yourself. It
through you that I can entertain without despair the recollectic
of the horrors of unutterable villany that led to this dark, dreadf
death. I am to hear to-morrow from Desse [Mr. Westbrook
attorney] whether or no I am to engage in a contest for th
children. At least it is consoling to know that its termination
your nominal union with me—that after having blessed me wit
a life, a world of real happiness—a mere form appertaining
you will not be barren of good. . . .

Everything tends to prove, however, that beyond the shock
so hideous a catastrophe having fallen on a human being once
nearly connected with me, there would in any case have bee
little to regret. Hookham, Longdill, every one, does me fu
justice; bears testimony to the upright spirit and liberality of n
conduct to her. There is but one voice in condemnation of th
detestable Westbrooks. If they should dare to bring it befo
Chancery, a scene of such fearful horror would be unfolded
would cover them with scorn and shame.

How is Claire? I do not tell her, but I may tell you, hc
deeply I am interested in her safety. I need not recommen
her to your care. Give her any kind message from me, and cal
her spirits as well as you can. I do not ask you to calm your ow

I am well in health, though somewhat faint and agitated; b
the affectionate attentions shown me by Hunt have been su
tainers and restoratives more than I can tell. Do you, deare
and best, seek happiness—where it ought to reside—in your ov
pure and perfect bosom; in the thoughts of how dear and hc
good you are to me; how wise and how extensively benefic
you are perhaps now destined to become.

Remember my poor babes, Ianthe and Charles. How tend
and dear a mother they will find in you—darling William, to
My eyes overflow with tears. To-morrow I will write again.

Your own affectionate

SHELLEY.

The death of Harriet Shelley, following hard up
that of Fanny Godwin, shook Shelley to the centre; b
of the two calamitous events, the death of Fanny broug

with it, as Shelley declared, far the crueller anguish. How
he should have survived shock following on shock was a
thing, as he himself wrote, not to be understood. Two
duties, however, were clear : he must place Mary, with as
little delay as possible, in her right position as his wife ;
and he must obtain possession of his children, Ianthe and
Charles. For himself, nothing would be changed by the
ecclesiastical ceremony of marriage ; but Mary desired it,
especially because her new position would restore her to
her father, who naturally was importunate on the subject.
Leaving Claire, with Elise and little William, in Bath,
Shelley and Mary came to town. On December 27,
Godwin saw his future son-in-law at Skinner Street, and
next day called with him at Doctors' Commons, and
proceeded thence to visit his daughter. On the morning
of December 30, at St. Mildred's Church, in the city, in
the presence of Godwin and his wife, the marriage was
celebrated. "Call at Mildred w[ith] P. B. S., M. W. G.,
and M. J.," writes Godwin in his diary, with curious
secretiveness ; "they dine and sup. . . . See No. xviii.
infra pag. ult." And turning to the blank page at the
end of the eighteenth fasciculus of his journal (that which
chronicles events of the year 1814), we find, safe for
reference, but removed from its correct chronological place,
the record of the ceremony of the morning, with its date
truly and faithfully given. During these days Mary
neglected her journal, and the incidents of this eventful
fortnight are recorded in a few lines : " I have omitted
writing my journal for some time. Shelley goes to London
and returns ; I go with him ; spend the time between
Leigh Hunt's and Godwin's. A marriage takes place on
the 30th December, 1816. Draw ; read Lord Chesterfield
and Locke."

On the afternoon of his marriage-day, Shelley wrote

to Claire Clairmont in Bath, a letter to which it was
intended that Mary should add her part. He smiles at
the magic ceremony which had been undergone; but the
smile appears upon a dark background of melancholy
pain.

. . . The ceremony, so magical in its effects, was undergone
this morning at St. Mildred's Church, in the City. Mrs. G. and
G. were both present, and appeared to feel no little satisfaction
Indeed Godwin throughout has shown the most polished and
cautious attentions to me and Mary. He seems to think no
kindness too great in compensation for what has past. I confess
I am not entirely deceived by this, though I cannot make my
vanity wholly insensible to certain attentions paid in a manner
studiously flattering. Mrs. G. presents herself to me in her real
attributes of affectation, prejudice, and heartless pride. Towards
her, I confess, I never feel an emotion of anything but antipathy
Her sweet daughter is very dear to me.

We left the Hunts yesterday morning and spent the evening
at Skinner Street, not unpleasantly. We had a bed in the
neighbourhood, and breakfasted with them before the marriage
Very few inquiries have been made of you, and those not of a
nature to show that their suspicions have been alarmed.*
Indeed, all is safe there. . . .

I will not tell you how dreadfully melancholy Skinner Street
appears with all its associations. The most horrid thought is
how people can be merry there! But I am resolved to overcome
such sensations—if I do not destroy them I may be myself
destroyed.

Thus closed the year 1816—a year eventful in Shelley'
life. The negotiation with Sir Timothy and its collapse
the publication of "Alastor;" the visit to Switzerland
the acquaintance with Byron; the death of Harriet; the
death, if possible more lamentable, of Fanny Godwin; the
issue of Byron's intrigue with Claire Clairmont, which

---

* *I.e.* as to Miss Clairmont's connection with Byron.

threw her upon Shelley for human sympathy, and in great measure for material support; the friendship of Leigh Hunt; the marriage which brought the year to a close;— these filled the twelve months with incident and passions, and helped to mature the character of Shelley by experiences of pain and joy.

CHAPTER XV.

IN CHANCERY.

Two duties had been clear to Shelley.   One of these was
now fulfilled by the performance in St. Mildred's. Church,
on the morning of December 30, of the ceremony "so
magical in its effects."   The other—to obtain possession
of his children—was of more difficult accomplishment.
Miss Westbrook and her father were determined to dispute
the claim of Shelley to hold and rear and educate his son
and daughter.   When, together with Leigh Hunt, he
demanded and re-demanded his children, the demand
was refused, and no information would be vouchsafed as
to their whereabouts.   As a fact, when Harriet died, her
daughter, aged three, and her infant boy of two years old
were away in Warwick, under the care of the Rev. John
Kendall, master of the Earl of Leicester's Hospital, and
vicar of Budbrooke.

The Chancery proceedings, although the main question
was decided in March, 1817, did not come to a close until
midsummer of the following year, when Shelley and his
wife had been for some months residents in Italy; but it
will be convenient to follow the course of these affairs
from first to last, at a single view.   On January 8, 1817, the
infants Eliza Ianthe Shelley and Charles Bysshe Shelley,
their maternal grandfather and next friend John Westbrook acting on their behalf, filed their Bill of Complaint

to Lord Eldon as High Chancellor of Great Britain. Their father, they declare, deserted his wife three years since, to cohabit unlawfully with Mary Godwin, daughter of the author of "Political Justice," ever since which desertion they have remained in the custody and under the protection of Mr. Westbrook and his daughter Elizabeth. The father, who now claims possession of them, "avows himself to be an Atheist," and "has written and published a certain work called 'Queen Mab,' with notes, and other works," wherein he has "blasphemously derided the truth of the Christian revelation and denied the existence of God as the Creator of the universe." Having recited the provisions made with reference to the money placed on their behalf by Mr. Westbrook in the hands of trustees, the infant orators pray that their persons and fortunes may not be placed in the custody of their father, but under the protection of the Court of Chancery, in whose power it lies to appoint, after due inquiry, proper persons to act as their guardians, and to issue directions for their maintenance and education. For their immediate relief they further pray that their father may be restrained by the injunction of the Court from taking possession of their persons.

On January 18, Shelley filed his answer to this Bill of Complaint. The alleged desertion of his first wife is clearly and positively denied. "This Defendant saith that the said Complainants are the only issue of the said marriage, and that after the birth of the said Complainant Eliza Ianthe Shelley, this Defendant and his said late wife agreed, in consequence of certain differences between them, to live separate and apart from each other, but this Defendant denies that he deserted his said wife, otherwise than by separating from her as aforesaid." What follows is of importance :—

" And this Defendant says that at the urgent entreaty
of his said late wife he permitted his said children to
reside with her under her management and protection,
after her separation from this Defendant, although this
Defendant saith he was very anxious, from his affection
for his said children, to have had them with him under his
own care and management during his said wife's life, but
that he forbore so to do in compliance with the wishes of
his wife and on account of their tender age, intending
nevertheless to have them under his own care, and to
provide for their education himself, as soon as they should
be of a proper age, or in case of the death of his said wife,
and never having in any manner abandoned or deserted
them, or had any intention of so doing."

For the Westbrooks the most distinguished leader of
the Chancery bar, Sir Samuel Romilly, a man as eminent
by his character as by his talents, was engaged. Shelley
was not so fortunate. His chief counsel, Mr. Wetherell, who a
little later became conspicuous by his volunteered defence of
Thistlewood, Watson, and others, charged with high treason,
was a speaker of more volubility than argumentative power.

Mr. Wetherell's brief, prepared by Longdill, is still in
existence, and some of the " Observations " on the Bill of
Complaint indicate the line of argument which it was
intended to take. " Little," it is admitted, " can be said
in defence of ' Queen Mab.' It was, however, written and
printed by Mr. Shelley when he was only nineteen, and as
to the publication of it, it was merely distributed to some
few of his personal friends ; not twenty ever got abroad.
The copy referred to by Miss Westbrooke appears to be
one which Mr. Shelley confidentially gave to his late wife.
Mr. Shelley has not been able to get a copy of his 'Letter
to Lord Ellenborough.' A very few copies of that were
printed, and none ever publicly circulated.

"Notwithstanding Mr. Shelley's violent philippics against the 'despotism of marriage' as a contract 'against delicacy and reason,' and as a system 'hostile to human happiness,' and notwithstanding his anticipated delights of the free enjoyment of 'choice and change,' which woul result from the 'abolition of marriage' (see page 147 *e seq.* of 'Queen Mab'), Mr. Shelley marries twice before he is twenty-five! He is no sooner liberated from the despotic chains, which he speaks of with so much horror and contempt, than he forges a new set, and becomes again a willing victim of this horrid despotism! It is hoped that a consideration of this marked difference between his speculative opinions and his actions will induce the Lord Chancellor not to think very seriously of this boyish and silly, but certainly unjustifiable, publication of 'Queen Mab.' . . .

"Part of the prayer of the petition is that Mr. and Miss Westbrooke should be appointed guardians. That part of the prayer, it is presumed, cannot, in the present state of the affair, be granted, but it is thought right to say that Mr. Westbrooke formerly kept a coffee-house, and is certainly in no respect qualified to be the guardian of Mr. Shelley's children. To Miss Westbrooke there are more decided objections : she is illiterate and vulgar, and what is perhaps a still greater objection, it was by her advice, and with her active concurrence, and it may be said by her *management*, that Mr. Shelley, when of the age of nineteen, ran away with Miss Harriet Westbrooke, then of the age of seventeen, and married her in Scotland. Miss Westbrooke, the proposed guardian, was then nearly thirty, and if she had acted as she ought to have done as the guardian and friend of her younger sister, all this misery and disgrace to both families would have been avoided."

On Friday, January 24, 1817, the case was heard before Lord Eldon. Before a more cautious, deliberate, and painstaking judge the case of Shelley's children could not have come. In the first hearing of the case stress was laid by Sir Samuel Romilly upon Shelley's religious or irreligious opinions, as set forth in "Queen Mab," on which it was afterwards found expedient to insist less strongly. The defence lay chiefly with Mr. Montagu, and was made in a most impressive and spirited manner. "Queen Mab," he contended, had never been published; it was one of those works of the brain that a man creates for his own amusement, without intending to send them out to the world. A man for his amusement might write many things which he intended that his children should never see. Why, then, should the outcome of his mind, although in caricature, bereave him of his paternal rights? Moved by such considerations as these, his lordship, he had no doubt, would dismiss the petition with costs. Lord Eldon's Chancery rule of *festina lente* was not violated on the present occasion. He would take home the petition and affidavits, he said, and give his decision on a future day. Further hearings of the case should be held, not in the public court, but in the Lord Chancellor's private room.

Although the Lord Chancellor would pronounce no decision, the result of the day's proceedings was held to be unfavourable to Shelley. While he in London watched the progress of the affair, Mary waited anxiously at Bath for tidings. "My William's birthday," she writes in her journal on January 24 (the day on which the case was heard). "How many chances have occurred during this little year! May the ensuing one be more peaceful, and my William's star be a fortunate one to rule the decision of this day! Alas! I fear it will be put off, and the influence of the star pass away. Read the 'Arcadia' and 'Amadis;' walk with my sweet babe." And on the following day: "Saturday, January 25.—An unhappy day. I receive bad news, and determine to go up to London"— a determination carried into effect without delay.

As the case proceeded, the stress of the argument shifted from a consideration of Shelley's theological or anti-theological creed to that of his avowed opinions respecting the institution of marriage, and his conduct taken in connection with those opinions. It was probably soon after the first day of hearing that Shelley himself drew up a statement to be laid before the Court—a statement which received the advantage of Godwin's criticism. A rough draft of a fragment of this document in Shelley's handwriting still exists, with many erasures and alterations, and with comments curt, decisive, and by no means flattering in the writing of Godwin. "I understand," wrote Shelley, "the opinions which I hold on religious matters to be abandoned as a ground of depriving me of the guardianship of my children; the allegations from which this unfitness is argued to proceed are reduced to a simple statement of my holding doctrines inimical to the institution of marriage as established in this country, and my having contravened in practice, as well as speculation, that institution. If I have attacked religion, it is agreed that I am punishable, but not by the loss of my children; if I have imagined a system of social life inconsistent with the constitution of England, I am punishable, but not by the loss of my children.

"I understand that I am to be declared incapable of the most sacred of human duties and the most inestimable of human rights, because I have reasoned against the institution of marriage in its present state; because I have in my own person violated that institution, and because I have justified that violation by my reasoning. The argument of my adversaries, then, as it presents itself to the Lord

Chancellor's mind, reduces itself, I imagine, to this plain consideration — not whether I shall teach my children religious infidelity, not whether I shall teach them political heterodoxy, but whether I shall educate them in immodest and loose sentiments of sexual connexion. I feel that on this particular point I ought to be heard in explanation.

"The institutions and opinions of all ages and countries have admitted in various degrees the principle of divorce. They have admitted that the sexual connexion once having taken place may be dissolved by some cause, which, according to their respective maxims, are to be considered destructive of the design of its institution—adultery, incompatibility of temper, difference of religion, madness, have all been established by different codes as conditions under which the parties to this union might be free to amend their choice. [Milton's name is here written, and a pen drawn through it.] Selden, perhaps the most learned man and the greatest lawyer this country has produced, and other illustrious writers have already vindicated these doctrines with impunity. My reasonings, I solemnly affirm amount to as much and no more than I here state. I consider the institution of marriage, as it exists precisely in the laws and opinions of this country, a mischievous and tyrannical institution, and shall express publicly the reasonings on which that persuasion is founded. If I am judged to be an improper guardian for my children on this account, no men of a liberal and inquiring spirit will remain in the community, who, if they are not more free from human feelings or more fortunate in their development and growth than most men can sincerely state their own to be, must not for some protest against the opinions of the multitude, equivalent to my tenets, live in the daily terror lest a court of justice should be converted into an instrument of private vengeance, and its edicts be directed, under some remote allegement of public good, against the most deep and sacred interests of his heart.

"I am aware of the nature of the institution of marriage in this country, and that the opinions exist which give its vitality to that institution. [Godwin comments, 'This is sadly expressed. It is about as significant as if you said, "I am aware the sun rises every Monday."'] So far as my own practice has been concerned, I have done my utmost in my peculiar situation to accommodate myself to the feelings of the community, as expressed in these opinions and laws. It was matter of the deepest grief to me, to instance my particular case, that, at the commencement of my union with the present Mrs. Shelley, I was legally married to a woman of whom delicacy forbids me to say more than that we were disunited by incurable dissensions, and rendered incapable, by that marriage contracted at eighteen years of age [from the word 'and' to 'age' has a pen-stroke drawn through it], of exhibiting to the world, according to those formalities which the world requires, that my motives of preference towards my present wife arose from no light or frivolous attachment, but such as in their sense of the word, as well as in mine, I wish to express by the word wife [from 'but such' to 'word wife' is struck out]; and that these feelings were sincere, and that I gave weight to public opinion, there can be no better proof than that immediately on the death of my late wife, I married the lady whose previous connexion with me, alleged to be the consequence, not of the common affections of human nature, but of my peculiar tenets, is now to be made the ground of depriving me of my children [from 'alleged to end of sentence is struck out, and the following inserted and again struck out: 'I protest against my previous connexion with her being interpreted into a consequence of my peculiar tenets.']

"My notions of the education of my children, with respect——" [*Fragment ends.*]

It is noticeable that while Shelley's counsel argued that the views set forth in the notes to "Queen Mab" were or might have been no more than the idle speculations of a boy, Shelley himself, with greater candour, admits that his opinions on marriage, as at present instituted, differ from those accepted in English society, adding, however, that he had in his practice accommodated himself to the feelings of the community.

On March 27 Lord Eldon gave his judgment. He would not pronounce that the father should be deprived of his children, and that they should be handed over to the Westbrooks. It might be that Shelley would name fit and proper persons by whom the children should be educated. All that the Chancellor at present could see his way to decide was that the children must not be placed in the exclusive care of their father, and that until a proper plan for their maintenance and education should be proposed and should be approved by the Court, Shelley must be restrained from taking possession of their persons. It was not because Shelley held atheistical opinions that the Chancellor so decided ; it was not because he held opinions opposed to the institution of marriage. Nor was it Shelley's conduct in leaving his wife, and during her life entering into an irregular union with Mary Godwin, on which Lord Eldon based his judgment. It was neither opinions nor conduct taken alone that determined the Chancellor to place the children under the protection of the Court. It was these two taken together—opinions leading to conduct : opinions avowed, or at least not disavowed, leading directly to conduct which the law of the land pronounced to be immoral.

Lord Eldon's judgment was accompanied by an

injunction restraining Shelley from intermeddling with the children until the further order of the Court. Meanwhile Mr. Alexander, one of the Masters in Chancery, was to inquire as to a proper plan for the children's maintenance and education, and as to the selection of proper persons in whose care they should be placed during their minority.

The main battle was fought, and Shelley had suffered a defeat; but it still remained to be determined whether the nominees of the Westbrooks should be entrusted with the education of little Ianthe and Charles, or whether the persons proposed on Shelley's behalf might not be preferred. Mr. Westbrook and his daughter did not themselves desire to undertake the arduous duty of rearing and educating a boy of two years old and a girl of three. The children being in the hands of the Rev. John Kendall, a schoolmaster of Warwick, in his hands the Westbrooks were content to leave them. On Shelley's part it was proposed (June 21) that the children should be entrusted to the care of Mr. and Mrs. Longdill (in the present case Longdill had acted as Shelley's solicitor) ; whatever sum was needful for their maintenance and education, over and above the eighty pounds a year provided by Mr. Westbrook, Shelley undertook to supply.

When, on August 1, Mr. Alexander gave in his report to the Lord Chancellor, it seemed as if Shelley were about to suffer a second and final defeat, for the report expressed an opinion in favour of the Westbrooks' proposal. No objection against Mr. Longdill was raised, except that his position as Shelley's solicitor disqualified him for the duty of loyally carrying out the directions of the Court. Mr. Kendall was to Shelley a complete stranger ; the effect of placing the children with him *in loco parentis* would be to dissolve all ties between them and their father. He had proposed no plan for their education, as intended by the order of the Court. It seemed to Shelley that although his right to the personal care of his children and to the direction of their education had been suspended, he had not lost the right of nominating or appointing the person to whom they should be entrusted, provided that person were free from all reasonable objections. These considerations having been set forth in a petition from Shelley, the Chancellor perceived their justice, and ordered, on November 10, that the matter should be referred back to the Master to receive further proposals as to a proper person under whose care the infants should remain during their minority, or until further order of the Court.

Other proposals, accordingly, were made on Shelley's part, and on the part of the Westbrooks. The Rev. Jacob Cheesborough, of Ulcomb, in Kent, who also held a vicarage in Cheshire, now displaces the Warwick schoolmaster ; and instead of Longdill, Dr. and Mrs. Hume, persons of unexceptionable orthodoxy, were proposed by Shelley. Dr. Hume resided at Brent End Lodge, Hanwell, and was physician to his Majesty's forces, and to his Royal Highness the Duke of Cambridge. He would place the boy, when seven years of age, at a good private school, whence he should pass to a public school and one of the universities. In the choice of a school Dr. Hume would prefer one under the superintendence of an orthodox clergyman of the Church of England. The girl should be educated at home by Mrs. Hume, with the assistance, when needful, of suitable masters. To such a proposal Mr. Alexander could offer no objection. On April 28, 1818, when Shelley and Mary were in Milan, the Master reported in favour of Dr. and Mrs. Hume ; and in spite of a petition from the Westbrooks, praying that Mr. Alexander should review his report, that report was confirmed by the Chancellor on

July 25. As to the interference with Shelley's parental authority, the Court acted with as much consideration for his feelings as was consistent with a determination to allow him no opportunity of inculcating on the children his peculiar opinions. He might visit them once in each month, the interview to take place in the presence of Dr. and Mrs. Hume, or, if more convenient to him, since he might desire to travel abroad, his visits might be when he pleased, provided that their number did not exceed twelve in a year. Should he desire further intercourse with his children, it was open to him to apply to the Court. As to the Westbrooks, the number of their visits to the children was also limited to twelve, but the presence of Dr. and Mrs. Hume was not required on those occasions. Finally, as to Sir Timothy Shelley and his family, perfect freedom of intercourse with either or both of the children was granted.

From Lord Eldon's point of view the decision was not unjust. Shelley had put forth extravagant opinions on the subject of marriage ; he had not disavowed them ; his conduct seemed to have proceeded from them ; and he might be expected to inculcate on his children those opinions, leading, in great relations of life, to conduct which the law pronounced immoral. It was not to be expected that the Chancellor should discover, by inspiration or some intuition of genius, all that was gentle, beautiful, and elevated in Shelley's character or Shelley's creed ; or that he should be able to estimate, as we are able, all the gains to be derived by little Charles and Ianthe from the communities of such a father's love. Nor could he be aware how in Mary Shelley they would have found a mother tender, wise, and faithful. Lord Eldon acted sternly indeed, but, according to the evidence laid before him, not unjustly, the justice being such as may be expected from

a tribunal incapable of dealing with the finer issues o
human life.*

* *Shelley's will.* Shelley's will was executed on February 18, 1817. Byro
and Peacock were appointed executors. A sum of £6000 was assigned as
provision for his son Charles Bysshe; a like sum as that for his daughte
Ianthe; a like sum as that for his son William; these sums being bequeathe
in trust to Byron and Peacock for the children's benefit. The sum of £600
was bequeathed to Miss Clairmont; a second sum of £6000 was bequeathe
to the executors in trust, to be invested in the purchase of an annuity for th
term of Miss Clairmont's life, and the life of such other person as she ma
name. (Allegra was perhaps meant.) The sum of £2000 was bequeathed t
Hogg, and £2000 to Byron; £500 to Peacock; the executors, besides, to inves
£2000 in purchase of an annuity, payable quarterly, for the term of Peacock
life, and the life of such other person as he may name. To his wife Shelle
bequeathed all his "manors, messuages, lands, tenements, hereditaments, an
real estate, both freehold and copyhold, whether in possession, reversio
remainder, or expectancy," and also all his "monies, stocks, funds, an
securities for money, mortgages in fee, and for years, and the lands, tenement
and hereditaments therein comprised for all his interest and estate therein,
and all his goods, chattels, and personal estates whatsoever. It has been sai
that the second sum of £6000 was left to Miss Clairmont by an error in drav
ing up the document; but this statement seems to be unproved. I have
thank Mr. Forman for allowing me to examine his copy of the will.

CHAPTER XVI.

SHELLEY AT MARLOW.

WHILE the Westbrooks were at work preparing their case for hearing in the Court of Chancery, in the early days of January, 1817, Shelley left his wife with Claire at Bath, and was in consultation with his legal advisers in London. During his absence, on January 12, was born the daughter of Byron and Claire Clairmont—an infant of unusual beauty, with eyes of deep blue, baby-mouth exquisitely shaped, and form of perfect symmetry. Until some one with a better right to bestow a Christian designation should rename the babe, they would call her by a name that resembled Albè's, and at the same time expressed the brightness of her opening beauty and sensibility—Alba, or the Dawn. The good news of Claire's safety and that of her child was needed to cast a gleam on tne gloom that encompassed Shelley. The last autumn had left dread memories to haunt his spirit. To the circumstances of Harriet's death, so full of appalling horror, he dared hardly, ne says, advert in thought. "For a time," says Leigh Hunt, that event "tore his being to pieces." And this had followed hard upon the death of Fanny Godwin, which affected him, he declares, far more deeply. Now his children, more than ever dear, were to be objects of contention, perhaps to be won after long struggle, perhaps to be wholly lost to him. And might it not happen that he should himself be imprisoned as a revolutionist and an atheist? Might not his fortune, as author of "Queen Mab," be to stand, as Eaton had stood, from day to day in the pillory? Such were Shelley's apprehensions in January, and though he understood that he might purchase victory by recantation, he would choose any penalty rather than such a triumph. These, indeed, were overheated apprehensions; yet they were natural to a time of terror and reaction. A little later Cobbett fled for safety to America. Nor could Shelley know that there lived in Englishmen the spirit which, before the year was out, rose against the prosecution of Hone for blasphemous libel, and procured the acquittal of Watson, Thistlewood, and Hooper from the charge of treason.

Moved by the thought of Shelley's solitude, and by the ill news of the first morning's proceedings in Chancery, Mary, not without a pang in parting from little William ("I wish Blue Eyes was with me," she exclaims in the diary), started for town on January 26. The days which followed, though full of anxiety, were cheered by the pleasures of social intercourse with Godwin, Hunt, and Hunt's circle of literary acquaintances.

That was a memorable evening (February 5) when the three "Young Poets" of his *Examiner* article of two months since—Reynolds, Keats, and Shelley—supped together at Hampstead with their generous critic. Keats, we are told by Leigh Hunt, "did not take to Shelley as kindly as Shelley did to him. . . . Keats, being a little too sensitive on the score of his origin, felt inclined to see in every man of birth a sort of natural enemy." The enthusiasm for abstract ideas by which Shelley was affected was unknown to Keats, who, with power of broad thinking and feeling as yet undeveloped, could lose himself in rich sensation and brooding pleasures in a way never experienced by Shelley. To Keats there appeared to be a thinness in Shelley's poetical work ; why could he not pause in his too rapid race, and amass around him the materials of substantial delight? Nor did Hazlitt, whose acquaintance Shelley also made at one of Hunt's supper-parties, feel much drawn towards the eager boyish disputant with whom he discussed the subjects of monarchy and republicanism until three in the morning. Himself oppressed by the passion of ideas, and mingling with these ideas his passionate prejudices, Hazlitt at thirty-eight, a pale anatomy of a man, worn and wan with study, craved in youth more of health and calm and sober certainty of happiness than Shelley, ailing in body and dejected in spirits, seemed to possess. His eye was too preternaturally bright ; his voice, in moments of excitement, too keenly vibrating ; his cheek lacked the hue of health ; his figure drooped or bent forward too much, "like a plant that has been deprived of its vital air." These physical characteristics, thought Hazlitt, were the symbols of an unwholesome craving after unnatural excitement, a morbid tendency towards interdicted topics, an unwise quest after the hidden secrets of human destiny. He did not know how Shelley, a little more than a year since, had been the robust and joyous oarsman on the Thames ; how he had of late endured blow upon blow of almost shattering force ; how his health and spirits had suffered ; how even now his dearest hopes as a father seemed to him to be desperately at stake. One true friend beside Leigh Hunt these days brought to Shelley—a friend whose sound head, generous heart, and manly hand were henceforth, according to his ability, at Shelley's service. The enthusiastic recognition of his genius by one twelve years his senior, and well skilled in forms and fashions of literature, was but one of many good offices rendered to Shelley by Horace Smith. With the ardour of a poet and the zeal of a political reformer, there mingled in Horace Smith some of the solid judgment and prudence of a city man of business.

As a companion in his country rambles in the neighbourhood of Hampstead, Shelley had often by his side his friend's eldest child, little Thornton Hunt. He delighted in the broken ground and fresh air of Hampstead, especially when the north-west wind blew a gale of intoxicating health and freedom. "I went with him rather than with my father," writes Thornton Hunt, "because he walked faster, and talked with me while he walked, instead of being lost in his own thoughts and conversing only at intervals. A love of wandering seemed to possess him in the most literal sense ; his rambles appeared to be without design, or any limit but my fatigue ; and when I was 'done up' he carried me home in his arms, on his shoulder, or pickback." In Shelley's delight at this time in the companionship of a child there was, perhaps, some of that feeling which he afterwards described in the words—

> " The devotion to something afar
> From the sphere of our sorrow."

He was himself suffering in body and in mind. Sudden seizures of agonizing pain left him at times shaken in nerve and exhausted ; and his thoughts turned ever anxiously to anticipate the issue of the Chancery struggle. But in the mirth and gladness of children he found a consolation for his private pain. "I can remember one day at Hampstead," writes his former playfellow ; "it was soon after breakfast, and Shelley sat reading, when he suddenly threw up his book and hands, and fell back, the chair sliding sharply from under him, and he poured forth shrieks, loud and continuous, stamping his feet madly on the ground.

My father rushed to him, and while the women looked out
for the usual remedies of cold water and hand-rubbing,
applied a strong pressure to his side [the seat of Shelley's
pain], kneading it with his hands ; and the patient seemed
to be gradually relieved by that process.   This happened
about the time when he was most anxious for the result of
the trial which was to deprive him of his children.   In the
intervals he sought relief in reading, in conversation—
which especially turned upon classic literature—in freedom
of thought and action, and in play with the children of the
house."   To play at "frightful creatures," with rampant
paws and terrifying gestures,' was a favourite diversion of
Shelley's, when, to make his aspect more dreadful, he would
screw his long and curling hair in front, until the little
ones, snatching a fearful joy, grew alarmed at the realistic
monster, and begged him "not to do the horn."   Sometimes he would tease little Thornton with provoking
banter, while the small boy sat with an arm around him ;
and once in revenge the boy, looking up in Shelley's face,
cried out that he hoped his persecutor would be beaten in
the Chancery suit, and have his children taken from him.
"I was sitting on his knee," Thornton Hunt relates, "and
as I spoke, he let himself fall listlessly back in the chair,
without attempting to conceal the shock I had given him.
But presently he folded his arms round me and kissed me ;
and I perfectly understood that he saw how sorry I was,
and was as anxious as I was to be friends again."   In the
background of Shelley's mirth with his pretty comrades lay
melancholy thoughts.   Once, while watching his paper
boats speed across the pond in the Vale of Health, or
caught and swamped by its tiny billows, "How much,"
said Shelley, smiling, "I should like that we could get into
one of these boats and be shipwrecked—it would be a
death more to be desired than any other."

But, in the midst of his anxiety and suffering, the old love of freakish jest would sometimes break forth. " Does Shelley go on telling strange stories of the deaths of kings?" asked Keats of Leigh Hunt, in a letter written in May, 1817. Shelley was fond, Hunt tells us, of quoting a passage from " Richard the Second," in which the king gives fantastic expression to his misery.

"He was once going to town with me in the Hampstead stage, when our only companion was an old lady, who sat silent and still, after the English fashion. . . . Shelley, who had been moved into the ebullition by something objectionable which he thought he saw in the face of our companion, startled her into a look of the most ludicrous astonishment by suddenly calling to mind, and, in his enthusiastic tone of voice, addressing me by name with the first two lines. 'Hunt,' he exclaimed—

'" For God's sake! let us sit upon the ground,
And tell sad stories of the death of kings."'

The old lady looked on the coach-floor, as if expecting to see us take our seats accordingly."

Shelley's sympathetic delight in the innocent joy of children and all happy creatures went hand in hand with a passion of charity for those who were sufferers, brethren of his own in sorrow, sickness, need. Returning from the opera one fierce winter night, when snow lay white upon heath and hill, Leigh Hunt heard, near his own door, strange and alarming shrieks, mingled with the voice of a man. It was Shelley, who was bearing down the Vale a woman whom he had found near the top of the hill in fits. She had been attending her son, who accompanied her, on a criminal charge made against him, and excitement and fatigue had overpowered her in the bleak and windy night Seeking shelter for her, Shelley had knocked at door after

door, and had found none. It was impossible to admit a
stranger—perhaps an impostor. "At last," Leigh Hunt
writes, "my friend sees a carriage driving up to a house at
a little distance. The knock is given; the warm door flies
open; servants and lights pour forth. Now, thought he, is
the time. He puts on his best address . . . and plants
himself in the way of an elderly person, who is stepping
out of the carriage with his family. He tells his story.
They only press on the faster. 'Will you go and see her?'
'No, sir; there's no necessity for that sort of thing, depend
on it. Impostors swarm everywhere; the thing cannot be
done. Sir, your conduct is extraordinary.' 'Sir,' cried
Shelley, assuming a very different manner, and forcing the
astonished householder to stop out of his astonishment, 'I
am sorry to say that *your* conduct is *not* extraordinary;
and if my own seems to amaze you, I will tell you something which may amaze you a little more, and I hope will
frighten you. It is such men as you who madden the
spirits and the patience of the poor and wretched; and if
ever a convulsion comes in this country (which is very
probable), recollect what I tell you. You will have your
house, that you refuse to put this miserable woman into,
burnt over your head.' 'God bless me, sir! Dear me, sir!'
exclaimed the poor frightened man, and fluttered into his
mansion." Sheltered and warmed and fed by Hunt and
Shelley, and cared for by a doctor whom they procured,
the woman recovered. "The next day," says Hunt, "my
friend sent mother and son comfortably home to Hendon,
where they were known, and whence they returned him
thanks full of gratitude."

Shelley's concern for his fellows was not confined to
individual and private cases of want and suffering.
England, in 1817, was full of misery and feverish agitation.
Loyal and patriotic writers like Southey pleaded that

England, having achieved her great deliverance, and the deliverance of Europe from the tyranny of Napoleon, needed before all else to maintain her strength by internal union, by the suppression of factious disturbance, and by a wise but gradual reform. Men of a different temper declaimed against the war of European liberation as a profligate and purposeless attack upon the French people, and urged that England, now at last awakened to her internal misery and servitude, should on the instant reform root and branch. The editor of the *Examiner* was a conspicuous opponent of the government of the Regent, Sidmouth, and Castlereagh ; and Shelley applauded his friend for the part he took in public affairs. But, with all Shelley's ardent hopes and visions, there was in him a certain moderation of temper and opinion which preserved him from the extreme views of the Hampden Clubs and of Major Cartwright. As to universal suffrage, it was at present rather to be dreaded than desired. " I confess," Shelley wrote, " I consider its adoption, in the present unprepared state of public knowledge and feeling, a measure fraught with peril. I think that none but those who register their names as paying a certain small sum in *direct taxes* ought, at present, to send members to Parliament." An extension of the franchise, within due limits and annual parliaments, might reasonably be demanded at once by the voice of the nation. But how to make that voice audible ? How, save by a plebiscite, the votes of the people for or against reform to be collected by a system of visitation from door to door throughout the length and breadth of Great Britain and Ireland. To defray the expenses which must attend such a method of obtaining a plebiscite on the question of reform, Shelley was himself prepared to lay down one hundred pounds, the tenth part of his annual income. His convictions and

ractical suggestions, together with this offer of aid to carry
hem into effect, were set forth in the pamphlet, "A Pro-
osal for putting Reform to the Vote throughout the
Kingdom," issued in March, 1817, by the brothers James
nd Charles Ollier, young publishers to whom Shelley had
robably been introduced by their common friend, Leigh
Hunt.

Shelley did not place his name on the title-page of his
amphlet; its author was "the Hermit of Marlow." A few
days before its appearance he, with his household, had
migrated to that pleasant little town by the Thames side,
well known to him already by his visits to Peacock. In
he river flowing between rich meadows, whose grass and
flowers dip to the water, or mirroring cliff and wooded
lope, the beech-groves of Bisham, the ozier aits of Cookham,
Shelley was to find inexhaustible delight. The town of
Great Marlow had an air of old-world peace about it.
Shelley's house—Albion House—which had been taken
ome time since on a lease of twenty-one years, stood in
West Street—half a country road—at some distance from
he river. It had some feeble pretensions to an ornamental
front, with a gabled roof broken by dormer windows, which
suggested the once vaguely complimentary term "Gothic;"
at least it was spacious, including among its rooms one
large enough for a village ball-room, which Shelley fitted
up as a library; but it had no view Thamesward, and was
damp and cold. To make amends for the lack of view in
front was a considerable garden to the rear, including a
shady orchard plot, a kitchen garden, evergreen shrubs,
and a mound surrounded by cypresses and yews, with a
cedar tree among them; still further was the prospect of
open meadows, leading towards undulating wooded slopes.

Here Shelley hoped that he had found a lifelong resting-
place, or, if not this, that at least it should be his home

while Sir Timothy Shelley held the family estates. Her
in his study, were the books in which he took deligh
while the youthful Apollo and Venus, in casts of ampl
size, made the room, as it were, a temple of beauty an
radiant force. Here, with her husband, her books, an
her blue-eyed boy, Mary was happy ; no longer, as la
year, for ever haunted by the thought of the certainty
death, and now saddened only by the sense of the flight
time, and the irreparable loss of these serenest hour
And here was Claire, with little Alba, whose baby-fa
seemed daily to grow more bright in its glad intelligenc
Claire, who at Bath had been " Mrs. Clairmont," no
resumed her maiden style ; and Alba passed for the chil
of a friend in London, sent into the country for her healt
The Swiss nurse, Elise, attended to the children ; a coc
was duly instructed in the master's vegetarian rule ; an
Harry, the man-servant, did indoor and outdoor jobs, an
kept the garden from running to wildness. Mary studie
sketched, and had the happiness to see the manuscript
" Frankenstein " growing towards completion. Claire als
dreamed of authorship and wrote ; but her especial delig
was in the piano, procured for her by Mary and Shelle
to which she sang in a voice compared by her form
music-master, Corri, to "a string of pearls."

New friends, except a few among humble folk u
known to fame, Shelley did not seek or find. But
Peacock he saw something ; and he rejoiced to be able
invite Godwin and the Hunts, and afterwards Hogg, an
Mary's old friend of Dundee, William Baxter, and Hora
Smith, to his house at Marlow. " I am not wretc
enough," he said to Peacock, " to tolerate an acquain
ance ; " but in truth he was not wretch enough to liv
without true friends. To escape from one alien to h
mind or mood, Shelley would resort to comical devices,

did not choose rather to avoid the calamity by pre-
cipitate flight; yet the Marlow house was never for any
long period untenanted by one or more of his little band
linked companions. Hunt was to come as soon as
possible after they had settled in their new abode. "You
shall never be serious when you wish to be merry," wrote
Mary, "and have as many nuts to crack as there are words
in the Petitions to Parliament for Reform—a tremendous
promise." And to Godwin, whom he had failed to see in
a recent visit to town, Shelley wrote, expecting that the
pleasure of a meeting was but for a short time deferred.

On April 2 Godwin became the guest of his son-in-law
at Marlow. In company with Peacock they visited Bisham
Wood, and went by water to Medmenham Abbey. But
the early April days were drearily cold, and Godwin chose
to return soon to his familiar quarters in Skinner Street,
where all seemed to him rich in such comfort and quiet as
a student loves. If only he were free from the weight of
debts which still hung upon him! Five hundred pounds
owing, in spite of his constant struggle—a struggle sometimes almost "beyond human strength." "Once every
three months," he wrote to Shelley, "I throw myself pros-
trate beneath the feet of Taylor, of Norwich, and my other
discounting friends, protesting that this is absolutely for
the last time. Shall this ever have an end? Shall I ever
be my own man again?" While Godwin thus pleaded
for help in his distress, Peacock also must be placed above
want—an annuity of one hundred pounds was conferred on
him by Shelley; the Hunts were never far from pecuniary
straits; and Charles Clairmont, away among the Pyrenees,
had been charmed by Miss Jeanne Morel, and he and she
would be exquisitely happy in being devoted to each other,
if only Shelley gave consent. She had the advantage of
him in age by about five years, was not ugly, though no

one would dare to say she was handsome, and had pass
her life among the delicious solitudes near Bagnères;
annual sufficiency to support a little *ménage* would
desirable. It can scarcely be wondered at that there w
moments when Shelley resembled, as Godwin declared
him, a blood-horse, starting away in furious mood, a
losing a thousand steps ere he drew in. The gadflies w
so many, so incessant, and so keen.

On the evening of his father-in-law's departure arri
the Hunts — Mrs. Hunt ailing, and requiring care a
attendance from Mary. Still, notwithstanding interruptic
walks by the river-side, boating excursions, and classi
studies, "Frankenstein" drew towards completion.
May 14 the last page was corrected, and the preface
written. Her task at last achieved, Mary decided to pl
her manuscript in the hands of Murray, the publisher, a
proposed to her father that she should occupy a room
his house while she stayed in town.

The hot June of 1817 was favourable to Shelley's hea
and spirits. He was often on the water in his boat, wh
was made for both oars and sail, or he would join H
Hunt's wife and sister-in-law, and the children, in tl
woodland rambles. Thornton Hunt, calling back to m
his appearance at this time, remembered his sunken cl
and rounded shoulders, more apparent from an habi
eagerness of mood, which, thrusting forward his face, m
him stoop; yet he seemed to abound in vitality, phys
as well as intellectual. "In his countenance there was
instead of weariness; melancholy more often yielded
alternations of bright thoughts; and paleness had gi
way to a certain freshness of colour, with something
roses in the cheeks." Though after violent exercise
panted, and sometimes suffered from acute pain in
side, he could undergo, without injury, long and ste

l. He often walked with Peacock to London, over fields, ...es, woods, and heath, a distance of more than thirty ...les; with rope on shoulder he could tow the boat a ...nsiderable distance; and though he often chose to steer, ...would, if necessary, take an oar, and "could stick to his ...t," says Thornton Hunt, "for any time, against any ...ce of current or of wind, not only without complaining, ...t without being compelled to give in until the set task ...s accomplished, though it should involve some miles of ...rd pulling." It was, indeed, a point of honour with ...elley to prove that some grit lay under his outward ...pearance of weakness and excitable nerves; for he was ...apostle of the vegetarian faith, and a water-drinker, and ...st not discredit the doctrine which he preached and ...ctised. His habit was to rise early, and to walk or ...d before breakfast; during the forenoon he studied ...d wrote; then he would go forth again, book in hand, ...netimes with uncovered head under the glowing summer ..., strolling or striding along, sometimes stopping to pluck ...lower; or he would row up or down the river to some ...ourite spot, and there let the boat drift while, as often ...Lake Leman, he lay in the bottom gazing upward; or, ...ving the boat, he would strike alone into the woodlands, ...d be invisible for many hours. He had christened his ...ndering pinnace "The Vaga;" "bond," added a witty ...ghbour in letters on the stern. "I have often met him," ...tes a correspondent of Lady Shelley's, "going or coming ...m his island retreat near Medmenham Abbey. . . . He ...s the most interesting figure I ever saw; his eyes like ...leer's, bright but rather wild; his white throat unfettered; ...slender, but to me almost faultless, shape; his brown ...g coat with curling lambs' wool collar and cuffs—in fact ...whole appearance—are as fresh in my recollection as ...occurrence of yesterday. . . . On his return his steps

were often hurried, and sometimes he was rather fantast
ally arrayed ; . . . on his head would be a wreath of wh
in Marlow we call 'old man's beard' and wild flow
intermixed ; at these times he seemed quite absorbed, a
he dashed along regardless of all he met or passed." .
uncanny hours of night he would wander alone in Bish;
Wood, to the astonishment of sensible neighbours.   Shell
had not lost his love of mirth, and explained that he h
been engaged in necromantic efforts to raise the de\
verifying his awful statement by a recital of the opprobric
names used in the evocation.

Shelley's love of solitude and study did not, howev
seclude him from active sympathy with his poorer neig
bours.   The distress consequent upon the cessation of t
war, the bad harvest of 1816, and the oppressive taxati
was keenly felt at Marlow.   When our purse runs low
first curtail our luxuries, and the Marlow lace-makers co\
now find no market for their wares.   He went, sa
Peacock, continually among the poor, and to the extent
his ability relieved the most pressing cases of distre
His beneficence was not that of a Lord Bountiful, w
bestowed gifts of condescension while remaining on l
heights, and regarding the sea of human suffering belo
he went from cottage to cottage, and in the winter of 18
suffered from a severe attack of ophthalmia caught duri
his brotherly ministrations.   Aiding Godwin to the utm
of his power, and bestowing liberal gifts on Peacock, his o
resources were at times slender enough ; yet each we
whatever happened, he contrived to put by a certain s\
for the poor.   On Saturday evening came his pension
for their allowance, widows and children being preferred
other claimants.   If Shelley and his wife were absent fr
Marlow, the bag of coins was left in Mrs. Madocks's han
to be dispensed at the close of the week by her.   "Ev

oot," writes Mrs. Madocks, "is sacred that he visited ; he
as a gentleman that seldom took money about with him,
id we received numerous little billets, written sometimes
i the leaf of a book, to pay the bearer the sum he specified,
>metimes as much as half a crown ; and one day he came
>me without shoes, saying that he had no paper, so he
ive the poor man his shoes." When winter came he felt
e shiverings of the poor, and ordered for his friends and
eighbours in need a supply of blankets of the kind sup-
ied to the officers of the British army while serving in
e Peninsula, with sheets to add cleanliness to warmth ; in
e centre was stamped in large letters the name "Shelley,"
prevent their becoming the prey of the pawnbroker.

During the summer and autumn of 1817 Shelley read
ss, perhaps, than in some earlier years, for his days were
ent rather in creating than acquiring ; yet he read much,
id with his characteristic intensity and swiftness.

But the months at Marlow were chiefly memorable for
ger and aspiring song. It was in his first resentment
ainst Lord Eldon on his passing the decree, says Mrs.
ielley, that the father, cruelly robbed, as he conceived,
his offspring, uttered his curse on tyranny and fraud,
incarnated in the person of the Chancellor, in stanzas
mulous with indignation, love, and anguish. "No
rds," she adds, "can express the anguish he felt when
s elder children were torn from him." And Leigh
unt's testimony is to the same effect. After the
iancellor's adverse decision Shelley "never dared to
ist himself," says Hunt, "with mentioning their names
my hearing, though I had stood at his side throughout
e business." While the question was still pending, some
rds of the Chancellor led Shelley to imagine that he
ght even be deprived of his little William. "He did
t hesitate to resolve," writes Mrs. Shelley, "if such were

menaced, to abandon country, fortune, everything, and t
escape with his child." Mary looked forward to the birth c
an infant in the autumn, and it was probably before th
baby Clara, born on September 2, was in her arms, tha
Shelley addressed the stanzas to his boy, in which h
imagines him safe, with father and mother and a ne
playmate, in some free land beyond the waves.

> " We soon shall dwell by the azure sea
>   Of serene and golden Italy,
>   Or Greece, the mother of the free.
>   And I will teach thine infant tongue
>   To call upon those heroes old
>   In their own language, and will mould
>   Thy growing spirit in the flame
>   Of Grecian lore ; that by such name
>   A patriot's birthright thou may'st claim.

But the birthright claimed by Shelley's beloved child wa
only a handful of Italian earth amid the majesty of Rom
"I envy death the body," Shelley afterwards wrote, "fa
less than the oppressors the minds of those whom the
have torn from me."

Poetical designs of wide scope and lofty purpose occupie
Shelley's imagination as he floated in his boat under th
beech-groves of Bisham, or, pencil in hand and manuscri
book on knee, sat on a prominence among the woods whi
looked towards the tranquil river. For a time, perhap
he wavered between the attractions of a theme chose
from the history of the individual soul and one which shou
present an epoch in the life of humanity, and include, und
imaginative forms, something like an ideal philosophy
history. In the individual life the supreme event is t
quest for love and for one who shall be love's avatar c
earth ; and the supreme tragedy in the life of the individu
soul is to accept a false or earthly love in place of what

highest, divinest, and most human. For there are two goddesses Aphrodite, as Pausanias maintained in Plato's "Banquet," and two Loves, a heavenly and an earthly; and that a seeker for the highest beauty and the highest love should err or be deceived, and fix his affections on the lower—this is the most piteous of all failures in life. Such a tragedy of the individual soul Shelley designed to exhibit in his poem of "Prince Athanase." The poem stands in conception midway between "Alastor" and "Epipsychidion," and as in this latter piece there may be found something like a veiled record of the history of Shelley's heart, so, doubtless, it would have been with "Prince Athanase." He, too, had cherished one whom in the Lynmouth days he had taken for his Uranian love; and she had, as he conceived, mocked his hopes and deserted him. And now, when pain haunted him, and life seemed insecure and death never far away, another had appeared, whom, in "Prince Athanase," he idealizes as the Uranian lady who comes and touches with her lips the dying youth.

A second Marlow fragment, but one which was afterwards carried to completion, is the English portion of 'Rosalind and Helen." It can hardly be doubted that while the general frame and setting of the poem is of Italian origin, much of the story of Helen, and part, perhaps, of that of Rosalind, was written under the impulses of feeling which produced the greater poem of "Laon and Cythna." Shelley's ardour on behalf of the poem paled and grew faint, probably because its theme was handled in more heroic fashion in his ideal epic of revolution. It can hardly be doubted that the incidents and feelings portrayed were to some extent suggested to Shelley by Mary's relations with the friend of her girlhood, in the old Dundee days— Isabel Baxter. Since Mary's flight from her father's house in July, 1814, Isabel had fallen away from friendship. Now she was herself a wife, and rumours, probably false rumours reached Mary that Isabel was not a happy wife. A visit of Isabel's father, William Baxter, to Marlow, in September tended to draw the alienated friends once more together and when it was proposed that Isabel Booth should be Mary's companion on the journey to Italy, she would gladly have acceded to the proposal. But David Booth her husband, no ordinary man, had heard scandalous and lying tales of Shelley's life; his strong moral sense was shocked by the thought of danger to his wife's character or fame, and sternly yet tenderly he forbade a renewal of the intimacy. So by the Lake of Como there was no meeting, like that represented in the poem, of the sundered friends.

In her letter of September 26, Mary speaks of Shelley's poem (the name "Laon and Cythna" had not yet been given to it) as finished; it was, in fact, finished three or four days before that date. The poem had been the work of little more than six months, devoted to his task, as Shelley says, "with unremitting ardour and enthusiasm." We note in Mary's journal for mid and later April the entries—"Shelley reads Spenser aloud," "Shelley reads Spenser in the evening," "Shelley reads 'History of the French Revolution,'" "Shelley reads 'History of the French Revolution' and Spenser aloud in the evening." These entries take us back a little more than six months from the date at which "Laon and Cythna" is said by Mary to have been complete. "Laon and Cythna," written in the Spenserian stanza, is an epic of Revolution and Counter-revolution. We cannot doubt that in April, when beginning his poem, Shelley, as he read Spenser aloud, was accustoming his ear to the measure which he had chosen while in the "History of the French Revolution" he obtained materials for his narrative, studying the life of a people during such a crisis in its history as that which he was about to exhibit in an idealized outline. Behind both form and material, behind Spenser and his study of the facts of the great upheaval in France, lay certain abstractions—Shelley's guiding principles in ethics and politics. These he had acquired from Godwin; and among the books read in 1817 was one which indeed was never absent for any long period from his hands—"Political Justice."

"Shelley told me," says Medwin, "that he and Keats had mutually agreed, in the same given time (six months each) to write a long poem, and that the 'Endymion' and 'Revolt of Islam' were the fruits of this rivalry." There is no improbability in some such resolve having been uttered by the two young poets, each having a brain which teemed with ideas and imagery. We know that on February 4, 1818, Shelley, Keats, and Hunt, in generous rivalry, wrote each a sonnet on a common theme, the river Nile. But assuredly the spirit of emulation was not that which sustained either Keats or Shelley in their wide-orbed poetic flights of the preceding year. All of Keats's native enthusiasm for beauty in its quintessential forms poured itself into his "Endymion." It was the firstfruits of that vow or prayer which he had uttered—

> "O for ten years, that I may overwhelm
> Myself in poesy; so I may do the deed
> That my own soul has to itself decreed!"

Hanging over his own joy more broodingly than did Shelley, Keats lived longer with his cherished imaginings; it was mid-winter or the edge of spring before his happy task was at an end. Other motives than those which were purely poetical urged on Shelley; he had a prophetic message to deliver, and he feared that death might come

swiftly and put its dust upon his lips. Deeply moved by
the misery of England in 1817, the feverish hopes and fear
of the people, the prevailing distress, the triumph of re
action in home and foreign politics, the suspension of th
Habeas Corpus, the trials for treason, the trials for blas
phemous libel, the buttressing of the Bourbon dynasty i
France by foreign bayonets, the panic of vindictive loyalty
Shelley could not at this moment sequester himself, as di
Keats, from the public interests of his time. When h
mused alone in his boat under the woods of Bisham, c
on some islet of the Thames with the swan for sole com
panion, it was in the spirit of a prophet who has withdraw
into the desert to see more clearly, as from a distance, th
present or the future life of his people and of mankinc
Shelley saw, or thought he saw, as the great fact of hi
age that vast movement towards a reconstruction of societ
in which the French revolution had been a startling incider
—an incident fruitful of much evil and much good. H
saw the terror, the despair, the apathy, the recoil, conse
quent on the violence and excesses in France; and seein
these, and gazing into the past and the future, he did no
despair—he hoped. It was his desire to rekindle in me
the aspiration towards a happier condition of moral ar
political society, and at the same time to warn men of th
dangers which arise in a movement of revolution from the
own egoisms and greeds and grosser passions; it was h
desire, therefore, to present the true ideal of revolution—
national movement based on moral principle, inspired l
a passion of justice and a passion of charity, unstained l
blood, unclouded by turbulence, and using material for
only as the tranquil putting forth in act of spiritual powe

Unhappily, with all that was admirable in the Revol
tion—its enthusiasm of humanity, its ideal of justice,
recognition of a moral element in politics, its sentiment

the brotherhood of man—there are united in Shelley's poem
all its shallow sophisms,—its disregard of tradition and
inheritance, its total misconception of history, its grotesque
notion that governments and religions have been the
artificial manufacture of knaves, its intoxication with abstract
ideas, its false contrast of a benevolent Nature with society
regarded as selfish, its too-liberal faith in the innate virtue
of all men—save only of kings and priests. The history
of the Christian centuries was for Shelley the history of a
giant imposture, however much he might venerate the
character of the founder of Christianity. In ancient
Greece he recognized "the mother of the free;" forgetful
of the fact that the Greek republics were a congeries of
slave states, in which the taste and intellect of a close
aristocracy were sustained by the toil and anguish of its
myriad victims. Shelley's illusions are such as now could
deceive no thinking mind; his generous ardours, the
quivering music of his verse, the quick and flame-like
beauty of his imagery, bear still their living gifts to the
spirits of men.

During the summer and autumn days the house at
Marlow was a hive of workers. "Frankenstein" being now
in the hands of the publishers, Mary occupied herself in
August and October, before and not long after the birth
of her little girl (September 2), in transcribing, with emen-
dations and additions, the journal of her tour with Shelley
to the Continent in 1814, together with the letters from
Geneva of 1816. The "Six Weeks' Tour," accepted by
Hookham, was published by him in December. Claire, too,
had written a book, of what description we know not; but
Shelley's efforts to procure a publisher for it proved un-
successful. In her journal Mary notes, on November 3, that
she has been engaged in writing from Shelley's dictation
"the translation of Spinoza"—a translation, doubtless, of a

part of the "Tractatus Theologico-politicus," of which a fragment in Shelley's handwriting was afterwards obtained from Mr. Madocks, of Marlow, by Middleton, and was printed by him as an original composition of the poet's, belonging, as he conjectured, to the period of "Zastrozzi" and "St. Irvyne." This treatise of Spinoza had a peculiar attraction for Shelley. From Tanyrallt, in 1813, he had written to Hookman, begging the bookseller to send him a copy of the "Tractatus." At Marlow he was engaged on the translation, which was taken up again in March and April, 1820, at Pisa. Not many months before his death (November, 1821) Shelley proposed to his friend Edward Williams to assist him in rendering the work into English. Byron would put his name upon the title-page, and would furnish as preface a life of the Jewish philosopher. Shelley and Williams achieved a portion of their task ; but the strange introduction—a life of the tranquil geometer of the Infinite by the passionate child of the romantic movement—was probably never begun. Spinoza's treatise, we can believe, interested Shelley chiefly because it helped to distinguish what is of abiding and universal importance in the Bible—a book precious to Shelley—from what is temporary and accidental.

The excitement and prolonged strain of poetical creation, hardly felt during the summer days, told injuriously on Shelley's health as the vivifying heat withdrew, and the autumn chills began to touch the flowers and the woodlands. "Shelley writes his poem ; his health declines," Mary notes in her journal, when briefly chronicling the events between September 2, the date of Clara's birth, and September 19 "Much of what the volume [of 'Laon and Cythna'] contains," Shelley wrote to Godwin, "was written with the same feeling, as real, though not so prophetic, as the communications of a dying man." On September 23, accompanied

by Claire, he went to town, taking with him his poem,
now happily complete, to consult Mr. William Lawrence,
a distinguished pupil of Abernethy.

The physician's opinion, that rest and change of air
were needful to restore Shelley's health, was communicated
without delay to Mary, and to her was left the decision
whether they should move to some English watering-place
or journey to Italy. For his own part, Shelley was inclined
towards spending the winter in Pisa. The warmer climate,
he was assured, would act as a certain remedy for his
ailments. It was, moreover, much to be desired that little
Alba should be placed under her father's care. If Byron
was ever to take an interest in his child, he ought to know
her bright infancy and pretty baby ways. She and Shelley's
little William were indeed fast friends, and talked to each
other in the gladdest babblement of babyhood; but William
had now a sister of his own to be his future companion. The
presence of Alba in Shelley's house was embarrassing, and
Claire's peculiar interest in her had given rise to monstrous
and revolting speculations. If Claire was the mother of
his "Miss Auburn" (such was the feigned name of the yet
unnamed Allegra), who was her father? In July Shelley had
proposed to Byron that the little one should be placed
under the care of two respectable young ladies in Marlow,
who would undertake the charge of her, as a provisional
measure until she could be entrusted to her father's hands.
Now the prospect of a journey to Italy suggested an easy
mode of conveying the child safe to Venice, where Byron
was at present residing.

On the morning of November 6, 1817, the Regent's
only child, the Princess Charlotte, died in childbirth. Her
youth and beauty, the innocence and sweetness of her life
and character, the fairness of this one blossom sprung from
an ill stock, had won upon the heart of the English people,

and the event was felt as if it were a national calamity.
As Shelley conceived it, there was indeed cause for mourning in the untimely death of one who had so lately been
full of life and joy and hope ; yet there were causes for
bitterer grief in England little attended to or felt.　Once
more, therefore, the " Hermit of Marlow " would lift up his
voice in prophetic utterance.　On the morning after the
death of the Princess, three men, convicted of having taken
part in what was styled "the Derbyshire insurrection," were
led forth to be executed.　To Shelley it seemed that the
discontent which led these half-educated or wholly un-
educated men to the violence which he deplored, had been
caused by a real grievance under which all Englishmen
suffered.　The creation of a vast national debt had produced a second aristocracy beside the aristocracy of birth—
an aristocracy of moneyed worldliness, subsisting on the
taxes of the nation, and lacking the chivalric virtues of the
elder aristocracy.　"It was a moot question," writes Leigh
Hunt, "when he entered your room, whether Shelley would
begin with some half-pleasant, half-pensive joke, or quote
something Greek, or ask some question about public affairs.
He once came upon me at Hampstead, when I had not
seen him for some time ; and after grasping my hands
with both his, in his usual fervent manner, he sat down
and looked at me very earnestly, with a deep though not
melancholy interest in his face.　We were sitting with our
knees to the fire, to which we had been getting nearer and
nearer, in the comfort of finding ourselves together.　The
pleasure of seeing him was my only feeling at the moment ;
and the air of domesticity about us was so complete, that
I thought he was going to speak on some family matter,
either his or my own, when he asked me, at the close of
an intensity of pause, what was 'the amount of the national
debt.'"　Shelley's question should hardly have surprised

is friend, for the amount of the national debt served with
Shelley as a measure of the people's sufferings, and it
weighed at times like a nightmare upon his heart. Were
he people duly represented in Parliament, they could
indeed state their case, and endeavour to abate their
grievance; but when the cry for Parliamentary Reform
was met by suspensions of the Habeas Corpus and prosecutions of the press, what could be expected but such rash
and futile manifestations of popular passion as that which
resulted in the hideous executions at Derby?

In the *Examiner* for Sunday, November 9, Shelley
read the report, with all its harrowing details, of the work
in the north. Two evenings later Godwin and Charles
Ollier took tea with the Shelleys at Mabledon Place, and
there was talk with Ollier of a pamphlet to be written by
Shelley on the grief of the Royal House as viewed in
connection with the deeper cause for national mourning in
the wrongs of a much-afflicted people. When the visitors
had said good night, Shelley hastened to set down in writing
the thoughts and feelings which laboured within him for
utterance. "Shelley begins a pamphlet," Mary records in
her journal of the 11th; and on the 12th, "Shelley finishes
his pamphlet."

"An Address to the People on the Death of the
Princess Charlotte" was perhaps never published, in the
full sense of the word. It is stated that not more
than twenty copies were printed; and we can well believe
that in 1817 Ollier was little inclined to take his chance of
government prosecution. The English people were overwhelmed with sorrow because a young and beautiful woman
had perished with her newborn child. Yes: to her mourning was due. But there was another fairer, nobler, more
queenly, for whose death no tears were shed—the virgin
Liberty, not taken from us by the will of God, but foully

murdered by man. And yet, even in her ruin, all hope was
not extinct. " Let us follow the corpse of British Liberty
slowly and reverentially to its tomb ; and if some gloriou
Phantom should appear, and make its throne of broken
swords and sceptres and royal crowns trampled in the dust
let us say that the Spirit of Liberty has arisen from its
grave, and left all that was gross and mortal there, and
kneel down and worship it as our Queen." The same
contrast between the lighter affliction of England in its loss
of a Princess and the more grievous calamity of a nation's
wrongs had struck Leigh Hunt, and formed the subject of
the leading article of the number of the *Examiner* which
appeared at the beginning of the week after that in which
Shelley's pamphlet had been written.

During these days Mr. M'Millan's printers were making
progress with the sheets of " Laon and Cythna," and by
November 21 the poem was almost ready for publication
The seven hundred and fifty copies which made up the
edition were printed at Shelley's expense, the publishers
Sherwood, Neely, and Jones, and Messrs. Ollier, undertaking
to sell it on the author's account. In October he had
attempted in vain to find a purchaser of the copyright.

Poetry—poetry, above all, such as " Laon and Cythna,"
remote from common sympathies, exalted, copious—is
seldom regarded by the discreet publisher with enthusiasm
and Shelley might have deemed himself not unfortunate
if he had had no other cause for complaint than that
a man of business declined to invest his capital in the
Golden City revolutionized by Laon and Cythna. But an
unusual trouble was in store for him and his work. Having
woven his web of glittering abstractions around himself
Shelley was insensible to the shock which his glorifying of
forbidden love must give to the moral sense of society
Never, perhaps, having lived in the intimacy of one who

truly drew spiritual life from the faith of Theism or of
Christianity, Shelley could not feel how words, which to
him seemed but a protest against prejudice and superstition,
would carry pain and sudden shock to hearts that were
tender, innocent, and full of devout reverence.   It was a
blindness of the soul to feel no moral sympathy with those
whose intellectual convictions he opposed.   But men of the
world, living far less of the life ideal than Shelley, could
perceive what was invisible to him.   The printer, Mr.
Buchanan M'Millan, not improbably called the attention
of the Olliers to certain passages—few in number but formidable in substance—which could not fail to arouse public
indignation, which might even draw down a prosecution
for blasphemy.   Not a moment was to be lost.   Some few
copies had been issued, and already voices of protest were
raised.   Ollier did not hesitate, and announced his not
unreasonable decision that either the offending passages
must be removed, or he must decline to appear as publisher
of the volume.   To Shelley, who during six months had
wrought upon his poem with an intensity of ardour, who
had poured into its verse all his faiths and hopes and
charities, who had felt towards this impassioned song as a
prophet might feel towards the last burden of his lips which
should soon be silent in death, the unexpected decision of
the principal publisher seemed a cruel and intolerable
injustice.   In the first moments of his disappointment he
wrote to Ollier, with urgency, yet with a certain moderation
of temper, beseeching him to reconsider his resolve.

Ollier's reply was in some degree reassuring ; perhaps
he pointed out that by a few altered lines and a few
cancelled pages all obstacles in the way of publication
could be removed.   With his habitual good feeling and
courtesy Shelley wrote again (December 13), inviting his
publisher to confer with him at his house at Marlow.

The invitation was instantly accepted, and Shelley without delay went to work on the alterations of his poem. For a long time, says Peacock, Shelley refused to alter a line. It was not so ; Shelley immediately complied with his publisher's request. "The whole of the alterations," writes Peacock, "were actually made in successive sittings, of what I may call a literary committee. He contested the proposed alterations step by step ; in the end sometimes adopting, more frequently modifying, never originating, and always insisting that his poem was spoiled." What at least is certain is, that no petulant or impatient word of Shelley's remains on record. When in a short time the needful changes were effected, the offending leaves cancelled, and proofs of the substituted leaves revised, and "Laon and Cythna" had become "The Revolt of Islam," its author, who was zealous in calling in the copies previously issued, transferred his affections to the revised poem, and interested himself in its publication and due advertisement as eagerly as if it had been the first-begotten offspring of his brain.

A few evenings before this trouble came upon Shelley, he had received Godwin's long-expected novel, "Mande-ville," and while Mary hurried through its pages, he wrote, acknowledging the arrival of the volumes, and breaking the news to Godwin, in whose money troubles he still took an active interest, that a journey to Italy was now in prospect.

A week later the novel had been read—read in a breathless excitement of delight—and in Shelley's letter to Godwin appears already in its first form a portion of that criticism on the novel which occupied some columns of the last number of the *Examiner* for the year 1817. Having prepared Godwin to contemplate the proposed journey of his daughter and son-in-law to Italy, Shelley now enters more fully into the motives of his journey to the South.

Shelley to Godwin.

. . . My health has been materially worse; my feelings at intervals are of a deadly and torpid kind, or awakened to a state of such unnatural and keen excitement that, only to instance the organ of sight, I find the very blades of grass and the boughs of distant trees present themselves to me with microscopical distinctness. Towards evening I sink into a state of lethargy and inanimation, and often remain for hours on the sofa, between sleep and waking, a prey to the most painful irritability of thought; such, with little intermission, is my condition. The hours devoted to study are selected with vigilant caution from among these periods of endurance. It is not for this that I think of travelling to Italy, even if I knew that Italy would relieve me. But I have experienced a decisive pulmonary attack; and although at present it has passed away without any very considerable vestige of its existence, yet this symptom sufficiently shows the true nature of my disease to be consumption. It is to my advantage that this malady is in its nature slow, and, if one is sufficiently alive to its advances, is susceptible of cure from a warm climate. In the event of its assuming any decided shape, it would be my *duty* to go to Italy without delay; and it is only when that measure becomes an indispensable duty that, contrary to Mary's feelings and to mine as they regard you, I shall go to Italy. I need not remind you, besides the mere pain endured by the survivors, of the train of evil consequences which my death would cause to ensue. I am thus circumstantial and explicit, because you seem to have misunderstood me. It is not health but life that I should seek in Italy; and that not for my own sake—I feel that I am capable of trampling on all such weakness—but for the sake of those to whom my life may be a source of happiness, utility, security, and honour, and to some of whom my death might be all that is the reverse.

I ought to say I cannot persevere in the meat diet. What you say of Malthus fills me, as far as my intellect is concerned, with life and strength. I believe that I have a most anxious desire that the time should quickly come that, even so far as you are personally concerned, you should be tranquil and independent. But when I consider the intellectual lustre with which you clothe this world, and how much the next generation of mankind may be benefited by that light flowing forth without the intervention of one shadow, I am elevated above all thoughts which tend to you or myself as an individual, and become by sympathy part of those distant and innumerable minds to whom your writings must be present.

I meant to have written to you about "Mandeville" solely, but I was so irritable and weak that I could not write, although I had much to say. I have read "Mandeville," but I must read it again soon, for the interest is of that irresistible and overwhelming kind that the mind in its influence is like a cloud borne on by an impetuous wind, like one breathlessly carried forward who has no time to pause or observe the causes of his career.

The last month at Marlow—January, 1818—was troubled for Shelley by serious indisposition, and when his illness passed away, this was followed by a renewal of the attack of ophthalmia from which he had suffered somewhat earlier. Yet he busied himself with a translation of the Hymns of Homer, to which at a later date he returned ; he was eager to examine Chapman's rendering of the same pieces ; and in the publication of his "Revolt of Islam," now after such unforeseen delays accomplished, he took no slight interest. "Don't relax in the advertising," he wrote to Ollier on January 22. "I suppose at present that it scarcely sells at all. If you see any review or notices of it in any periodical paper, pray send it to me ; it is part of my reward—the amusement of hearing the abuse of the bigots." Abundant reward of this kind was in store for Shelley during future days.

The journal for some of the days of February and March tells of the farewell to Marlow—Mary on the 10th of the former month following Shelley, who had left

or London on the 7th, and Claire, who had taken Willy
and Allegra to town two days later. It tells also of
the pleasantly filled weeks that went by in the interval
before the departure for the Continent. Although at
Marlow Shelley had suffered much ill health, caused in
part, as he believed, by the cold and damp of his house,
he could not quit without some regret a place surrounded
with beauty, and now associated for him with the delight
of imaginative creation. "My thoughts for ever cling to
Windsor Forest and the copses of Marlow," he wrote six
months later from the Baths of Lucca, "like the clouds
that hang upon the woods of the mountains, low trailing,
and though they pass away, leave their best dew where
they themselves have faded." But these days in London
were not consumed in regretful retrospection. Encouraged
by the publication of his remarks on "Mandeville" in the
Examiner, Shelley now wrote a review—enthusiastic and
eloquent—of his friend Peacock's new poem "Rhododaphne."
Himself about to visit classic ground, the verses of Peacock
seemed to lead him on, like "a voice heard from some
Pythian cavern in the solitudes where Delphi stood." "We
are transported," he writes, "to the banks of Peneus, and
linger under the crags of Tempe, and see the water-lilies
floating on the stream. We are with Plato by old Ilissus,
under the sacred Plane-tree among the sweet scent of
flowering sallows; and above there is the nightingale of
Sophocles in the ivy of the pine, who is watching the
sunset so that it may dare to sing." The transcript of this
review, in Mary's handwriting, Shelley gave or sent to
Leigh Hunt, probably for insertion in the *Examiner*, where,
however, it did not find a place. In Hunt's society, and
that of Horace Smith, Keats, Novello; in visits to the
Italian Opera, where Mdlle. Milanie led the ballet; in
visits to Covent Garden, where Miss O'Neill played the

part of Bianca in Milman's "Fazio," the evenings wer
brightly past. "We look up to your box," wrote Hur
more than a year later, recalling these evenings, "almo:
hoping to see a thin, patrician-looking cosmopolite yearnin
out upon us, and a sedate-faced young lady bending in
similar direction, with her great tablet of a forehead, an
her white shoulders unconscious of a crimson gown." Da
after day Hogg and Peacock came to dine at the lodging
No. 119, Great Russell Street. To fill the vacant hou
there were sundry preparations for departure. It wa
doubtless Mary Shelley's wish that her children, before th
flight for foreign lands, should receive their names in th
orderly English fashion, and be able, in case of need t
refer to the registry of their baptism. Accordingly, c
March 9, at the parish church of St. Giles-in-the-Field
William Shelley and Clara Everina Shelley were dul
christened. On the same occasion little Alba received h
baptismal names of Clara Allegra. In the register o
baptisms her parents are named: "Right Hon. Georg
Gordon Lord Byron, the reputed father, by Clara Mar
Jane Clairmont."

CHAPTER XVII.

EARLY DAYS IN ITALY.

ON the evening of March 10, while Hunt and his wife were at the lodgings in Great Russell Street, Shelley fell into one of his deep slumbers. It was decided that he should not be aroused. Defrauded of Hunt's farewell grasp of the hand and of Marianne's kiss, Shelley awoke to find his friends departed. Early next day the travellers were on the road to Dover.

On Wednesday, March 11, 1818, and on the morning of the following day, Shelley looked for the last time on English fields and English skies.

His health and spirits, which in London had been feeble and depressed, improved as he and his companions journeyed towards the spring, which was hastening to meet them from the south. "Though our weather was at first abominable," he wrote to Hunt from Lyons (March 22), "we have now warm sunny days, and soft winds, and a sky of deep azure, the most serene I ever saw." Light in its plenitude, heat as of the solstice, the affluence of nature were never in excess for Shelley's enjoyment or his health.

The road of forty miles from Susa to Turin, through a fertile plain, amid cornfield and vine row and mulberry grove, was traversed on the last day of March, and before darkness fell upon that evening they had driven through

2 C

the long avenue of elms which runs from Rivoli to the south-east, and had entered the little capital of Piedmont.

It was Shelley's purpose to spend the summer months on the shores of the Lake of Como, thus renewing under altered circumstances some of the delights which had been his two years since at the Maison Chapuis, beside the bright waters of Geneva. A few days, therefore, at Milan sufficed for the first inspection of its objects of beauty and historical interest. The morning of his waking among the pealing bells of the city of St. Ambrose was that of Sunday, and the travellers, refreshed and alert for sight-seeing, wandered at will through its streets, and visited the amazing cathedral. "The effect of it," Shelley wrote a fortnight later, when he had seen the Duomo under various aspects, "piercing the solid blue with those groups of dazzling spires, relieved by the serene light of this Italian heaven, or by moonlight when the stars seem gathered among those clustered shapes, is beyond anything I had imagined architecture capable of producing." Even its Catholic interior did not now move him to such intellectual hostility and defiance as in earlier days he had expressed upon sight of our nobler minster at York. From Dante he was learning —learning perhaps unconsciously—some of the finer humanities of Catholicism ; and with the "Purgatorio" or "Paradiso" in his hand, he would come alone, a docile rebel, to sit in the fragrant gloom of an aisle behind the altar.

On April 9, Shelley and Mary set forth to seek a summer residence by the Lake of Como, leaving Claire and Elise with the little ones at Milan. In the express purpose of his visit, Shelley was not successful ; the house for which he was negotiating never became his ; but he had not lost these days, for he brought back the happiest memories of his excursion. To him, whose chief pleasure in life, he declared, was the contemplation of nature, there came a sense of heavy loss when it was ascertained that they must forego "the divine solitude" of Como.

April 27 was Claire Clairmont's twentieth birthday—a sorrowful birthday, for on the morrow she must part from the child, a most lovely and engaging creature, in whom her heart was centred. From Lyons Shelley had written to Byron, who had refused to correspond with Claire, informing him that Allegra had come thus far upon the way. Again from Milan he had written, inviting Byron to visit him when he could, and take the child into his own charge; but Byron's heart had hardened against the woman whom he had wronged, and it may be that he dreaded and hated the scenes which might be expected when the mother should part from her beloved one. "Letter from Albè," Claire enters in her journal (April 21); "nothing but discomfort." On the next day she took courage and explained to Byron by letter the motives and feelings which induced her, so much against the promptings of her heart, to comply with his desire to have possession of his daughter. At this point Shelley might well have withdrawn from an affair which, strictly, was none of his. But Byron's written words had seemed to make it clear that in his view the approaching farewell between Claire and her child must be absolute and final; and against a decision so unjust and cruel Shelley felt bound to plead. His letter had not been long despatched before he encountered at the Milan post-office a Venetian, whose tidings of Byron's way of life, enlivened perhaps with tales of Marianna Segati, were far from reassuring. "Shelley," writes Claire in her journal (April 24), "has a curious *encontre* at the post-office with a Venetian, and hears no agreeable news of Albè." But the decision had been made, and no doubts or apprehensions ought to stand in the way of Allegra's brilliant future as daughter of an English nobleman—the most illustrious poet of Europe. Accordingly, on April 28, Elise, in whom Mary had the utmost confidence as an affectionate and faithful nurse, started with the little one for Venice, where, it was hoped, she might remain in Byron's employ, and take the place of a mother to the child. On that cruel day Claire's unhappiness was bitter and profound. "Before we parted at Geneva," she afterwards wrote in a note-book, "he [Byron] talked over with me our situation ; he proposed to place the child when born in Mrs. Leigh's care. To this I objected, on the ground that a child always wanted a parent's care at least till seven years old ; rather than that, I would keep the child with me, though of course for the child there were great objections to that. He yielded, and said it was best it should live with him ; he promised, faithfully promised, never to give it until seven years of age into a stranger's care ; I was to be called the child's aunt, and in that character I could see it and watch over it without injury to any one's reputation. Believing in these promises, in the spring of 1818 I sent my little darling. She was the only thing I had to love, the only object in the world I could call my very own ; and I had never parted with her from her birth, not for an hour even. . . . I will say nothing as to what the parting cost me ; but I felt that I ought not for the sake of gratifying my own affections deprive her of a brilliant position in life." It would appear that at the last moment Shelley warned Claire of the risk she ran of losing the child for ever. "Remember, Claire," he wrote to her when, not many days before Allegra's death, the mother was eager to obtain possession of her darling, "when you rejected my earnest advice, and checked me with that contempt which I have not merited from you at Milan, and how vain is now your regret!

This is the second of my sibylline volumes ; if you wait
for the third, it may be sold at a still higher price." But
Claire was resolute ; it was for Allegra's welfare that the
father should know and love his child.

The journey from Milan to Pisa was accomplished in
the early days of May. Two nights at the Tre Donzelle,
with a visit to the cathedral and the Leaning Tower,
satisfied the travellers' curiosity as regards Pisa. A letter
from Elise, assuring them of Allegra's safe arrival at
Venice, was received, and left them free to depart. Pisa,
indeed, had attractions not possessed by bustling Leghorn,
city of warehousemen, and Jews, and galley-slaves, and
vagabonds, and beggars ; but at Leghorn resided Mr. and
Mrs. Gisborne, to whom they bore a letter of introduction
from Godwin ; and Mary could not but take a peculiar
interest in forming the acquaintance of a lady who was an
old and valued friend of her father.*

When the wanderers reached Leghorn, a week of May
had gone by. Soon the oppressive heats of summer would
drive them from the streets and quays in search of some
leafy coolness. Meanwhile the days were pleasantly passed
in walks and talks with their new friends, in Italian lessons,
and in multifarious reading for study or recreation.

While Shelley and Mary steadily progressed together
from canto to canto of Ariosto, he also read with eager
delight the Greek tragedians, the " Hippolytus " of Euripides
being succeeded by the " Philoctetes," the " Electra," and
the " Ajax " of Sophocles. Was he thus disciplining his
imagination for dramatic writing ?—for to Shelley it seemed
that the dramatic art was never understood or practised,
according to the true philosophy of it, as at Athens
Except the sight of the sea, there was little in Leghorr

* Mrs. Gisborne, born in the year 1770, was the daughter of an English
merchant at Constantinople, named James.

outside their apartment to interest Shelley. Maria Gisborne
was to him "the sole attraction in this most unattractive
of cities." At a later date, he wrote of Mr. Gisborne to
Peacock, in anticipation perhaps of a severe sentence from
the author of so many sparkling witticisms, as though he
would find Gisborne a proser, and a sieve through which
much learning had passed ; but, in truth, Shelley's letters
addressed to Gisborne prove that he was a man who could
follow with intelligent sympathy his friend's highest studies
in literature. To Peacock he appeared agreeable and well-
informed. And if the vastitude of Mr. Gisborne's nose
was, as Shelley says, Slawkenbergian, the extent of his
library might be considered a redeeming feature of the
man. "Mrs. Gisborne," Shelley wrote to Peacock in 1819,
" is a sufficiently amiable and very accomplished woman ; she
is δημοκρατικη and αθεη—how far she may be φιλανθρωπη
I don't know, for she is the antipodes of enthusiasm. Her
husband, a man with little thin lips, receding forehead, and
a prodigious nose, is an excessive bore. His nose is something quite Slawkenbergian—it weighs on the imagination
to look at it. It is that sort of nose which transforms all
the *g*'s its wearer utters into *k*'s. It is a nose once seen
never to be forgotten, and which requires the utmost stretch
of Christian charity to forgive. I, you know, have a little
turn-up nose ; Hogg has a large hook one ; but add them
both together, square them, cube them, you will have but
a faint idea of the nose to which I refer." If Mr. Gisborne
was himself dull, it is at least evident that his nose could
be a cause of wit in other men.

Towards the close of May, Shelley, unaccompanied by
Mary or Claire, visited the Baths of Lucca. It would seem
that he went thither to seek a house for the summer months,
and if so he was successful in his quest. "Travel to Bagni
di Lucca," Mary enters in her journal (June 11, 1818),

"and settle ourselves a little in our house." The season for the Baths had not yet quite come, and the heat was hardly so great as to make late sunrises and early sunsets in the leafiest of Tuscan valleys a necessity. But the inland quiet and refreshment tasted exquisite to senses somewhat fatigued by the bustle of an Italian Wapping and the dull pomps of Corpus Christi processions.

It was an uneventful life under green chestnut boughs, and within hearing of the Lima dashing upon its rocks. "We lead here," wrote Mary to Mrs. Gisborne (June 15), "a very quiet, pleasant life, reading our canto of Ariosto, and walking in the evening among these delightful woods." The Casino, resort, especially on Sunday evenings, of those who loved to dance, was not yet open, or at least was not frequented. But with the early days of July visitors crowded to the Baths, among whom the British sight-seer made himself conspicuous—not to Mrs. Shelley's delectation. "We see none but English," she wrote (July 2), "we hear nothing but English spoken. The walks are filled with English nursery-maids—a kind of animal I by no means like—and dashing staring Englishwomen, who surprise the Italians (who always are carried about in sedan chairs) by riding on horseback." If her countrywomen did not please Mary, to Shelley the women of Italy did not appear more attractive. When, on Sunday evenings of July, the Casino filled, he would look on charmed by the grace of the dances —"so exquisitely beautiful," he says, "that it would be a little dangerous to the newly unfrozen senses and imaginations of us migrators from the neighbourhood of the pole ;" dances in which Mary and Claire did not join—whether they refrained from philosophy or Protestantism Shelley could not tell. But his delight in the motions of the dances—of the waltz especially—did not beguile him into admiration of the dancers. "The modern Italians," he writes to Godwin (July 25), "are a miserable people, without sensibility, or imagination, or understanding. Their outside is polished, and an intercourse with them seems to proceed with much facility, though it ends in nothing and produces nothing. The women are particularly empty, and, though possessed of the same kind of superficial grace, are devoid of any cultivation and refinement." Dearer to Shelley than the faces and fashions of the Casino were the changeful aspects of sky and air, of gathering or disparting clouds, and of the great star that rose luminous in the south-east when the sun had sunk. "I take great delight in watching the changes of the atmosphere here, and the growth of the thunder-showers with which the noon is often overshadowed, and which break and fade away towards evening into flocks of delicate clouds. Our fire-flies are fading away fast; but there is the planet Jupiter, who rises majestically over the rift in the forest-covered mountains to the south, and the pale summer lightning which is spread out every night, at intervals, over the sky. No doubt Providence has contrived these things that, when the fire-flies go out, the low-flying owl may see her way home." While he gazed eastward upon Jupiter, Shelley remembered the Venus of last summer, when, in place of the Lima or the Serchio, the Thames flowed near —a planet more aerially radiant, with a softer yet more piercing splendour than belonged to this Italian Jupiter, possessed in virtue, perhaps, of its nature, at once female and divine. "I have forgotten," adds Shelley, "to ask the ladies if Jupiter produces on them the same effect."

As the heat increased, Mary and Claire, like other English ladies, rode—with Shelley for escort—either before breakfast, or after dinner when the evening began to grow cool, returning home by the light of the stars. About midday, or in the early afternoon, it was Shelley's custom

seek refreshment in a bathing-place hidden deep in the
oodlands, where the torrent paused, after it had flung itself
ito a rocky basin. "My custom is to undress and sit on
ie rocks, reading Herodotus, until the perspiration has
absided, and then to leap from the edge of the rock into
iis fountain—a practice in the hot weather excessively
efreshing. The torrent is composed, as it were, of a
accession of pools and waterfalls, up which I sometimes
muse myself by climbing when I bathe, and receiving
ie spray over all my body, whilst I clamber up the moist
ags with difficulty." On the last day of June, Shelley
id Mary rode to the Prato Fiorito, a meadow on the top
: one of the neighbouring Apennines, thick-strewn with
lossoming jonquils, whose excess of sweetness, it is said,
most caused Shelley to faint. If it be true, as Medwin
eclares, that Shelley described to him the faintness which
eized him in midst of the piercing sweetness of the odorous
.eadow, we have evidently a reminiscence of this day
nong the Apennines in certain lines of "Epipsychidion"—

> " From the moss violets and jonquils peep,
>   And dart their arrowy odour through the brain
>   Till you might faint with that delicious pain."

 sense of decaying sweetness must have hung over the
eauty of the Prato Fiorito at the close of June.

Shelley's box of books reached him while he was a
sitor at the Baths. With his wonted ardour, while standing
oof from the motley company of the Italian watering-
ace, he sought delight and instruction in "the choice
ciety of all ages." The "Persæ" of Æschylus, the
Clouds," the "Plutus," and the "Lysistrata" of Aristo-
ianes, Theocritus, Xenophon's "Memorabilia," Herodotus,
ucian, Virgil's "Georgics," Horace, are names which
ppear in Mary's journal as forming part of Shelley's studies

at this period. Of English authors he read chiefly amon
the Elizabethans, and from day to day Mary listened t
the poetry of Spenser, and chosen plays of Beaumont an
Fletcher or Shakespeare interpreted by the voice of Shelle
Nor was history quite neglected. Gibbon, as so ofte
before, was still in Shelley's hands. Godwin, led on perhap
from his novel of "Mandeville" to thoughts of a seriou
historical study of the period which had interested h
imagination, had suggested that his daughter should unde
take a series of "Lives of the Commonwealth's Men"-
Vane, Bradshaw, Milton, Ludlow, Sidney, and others. Tl
needful books were not to be obtained among the ile
groves or chestnut woods of the Baths of Lucca ; but Shell
read aloud to his wife from Hume's "History of England
and it may have been these readings which long afterwar
led him to contemplate and in some small part achieve a
historical drama on the subject of Charles I. "I a
exceedingly delighted," he wrote to Godwin (July 2
"with the plan you propose of a book illustrating tl
character of our calumniated Republicans. It is precise
the subject for Mary ; and I imagine that, but for the fe
of being excited to refer to books not within her reac
she would attempt to begin it here, and order the wor
you notice. I am unfortunately little skilled in Engli
history, and the interest which it excites in me is so feeb
that I find it a duty to attain merely to that general kno
ledge of it which is indispensable." It was not possib
for Mary, under existing circumstances, to accomplish t
work suggested for her by Godwin ; but Shelley imagin
that the invention and constructive power displayed
"Frankenstein" gave evidence of dramatic talent of
mean order ; and for the writer of a dramatic work a gre
historical library is not indispensable. Accordingly,
now urged Mary to undertake a tragedy of Charles I., a

by-and-by his own imagination went to work on her behalf. "Remember, remember 'Charles the First,' and 'Mirra,'" he wrote to her from Padua in September. "I have been already imagining how you will conduct such scenes. The second volume of 'St. Leon' begins with this proud and true sentiment, 'There is nothing that the human mind can conceive which it may not execute.' Shakespeare was only a human being." The pleading was more that of a lover than a logician ; and that inexorable logician, Time, came to demonstrate the difference between aspiration and achievement.

Shelley's own creative power slumbered. He had come to Italy for health, and had been warned by the physicians in the preceding autumn against the excitement of composition. He still suffered from languor and depression of spirits, which the bright Italian air had not wholly borne away. The suffering in his side was acute and of frequent recurrence.

The weeks at the Baths of Lucca, however, were not quite unproductive. Finding himself totally incapable of original composition, Shelley, on the morning of July 9, set himself to render into English the most admirable in form of all the Platonic dialogues. "I am employed just now," he wrote next day to Mr. and Mrs. Gisborne, "having little better to do, in translating into my faint and inefficient periods the divine eloquence of Plato's 'Symposium ;' only as an exercise, or, perhaps, to give Mary some idea of the manners and feelings of the Athenians—so different in many subjects from that of any other community that ever existed." Nine or ten mornings completed his work, and in her journal for July 17 Mary notes, "Shelley finishes the translation of the 'Symposium' and reads Herodotus ; walks out in the evening to his bath." From the "Symposium" he proceeded, while Mary was engaged in transcribing

his manuscript, to the "Phædrus," but without attempt
ing to render it from the original. His task of a translatc
had excited him to an effort towards independent authorshi
It had been felt by Mrs. Shelley that Plato's conceptio
of love and friendship "in many particulars shocks ou
present manners." To anticipate and obviate such a shoc
Shelley undertook to write "A Discourse on the Manne
of the Ancients relative to the Subject of Love."
fragment of this discourse, on a subject to be handle
with delicate caution, was in fact written, and remains, b
it is no more than the introduction leading up to the speci
study. The translation of the "Banquet," not always exa
in scholarship, has much of the vivid life, the grace of mov
ment, and the luminous beauty of Plato.

At this moment it seemed to Shelley that in the Per
clean age humanity had attained a complete development
and an energy of noble life never since approached. Y
the mediæval Italian poets had done much to inform an
temper Shelley's mind, and had presented to him a sic
of historical Christianity which he had not hitherto appr
hended. He could now recognize the fact that at least
the abolition of slavery and the elevation of woman th
Christian world had gained upon the social and moral stat
of earlier ages. Through Dante and Petrarch the spiritu
power of Catholicism and chivalry reached him, an
becoming sensible of this, he could not value so highly
in former days the services of those who had assailed wi
criticism or ridicule that outward garb, emblazoned wi
quaint emblems and devices, arrayed in which the augu
spirit of the new religion had moved among men. Alor
of the greater Italian poets, Ariosto, whose "Orlanc
Furioso" he read daily with Mary, pleased him but litt
Entertaining and graceful he found Ariosto, entertainir
and graceful, and *sometimes* a poet. But where, he as

s the gentle seriousness, the delicate sensibility, the calm
and sustained energy, without which true greatness cannot
be? In assigning to Ariosto a different and a lower rank
from that of his great predecessors, Shelley found support
in Leigh Hunt's bright letter to Mary. "Petrarch, Boccaccio, and Dante," writes Hunt, "are the morning, noon,
and night of the great Italian day; or rather Dante,
Petrarch, and Boccaccio are the night, morning, and noon.
'And the evening and the morning were the first day.'"

Before leaving London, Shelley had placed a portion
of his "Rosalind and Helen," begun at Marlow, in the
hands of Ollier, requesting him to send the printed sheets
to Peacock for revision. To please Mary, who had liked
the poem—her "pretty eclogue"—now in the August days
at the Baths of Lucca he took up his unfinished tale in
verse, and quickly carried it to the close. It did not interest
the writer profoundly; and sentiment, not quite robust and
masculine, saps in upon the passion of the theme, and
enfeebles it. Shelley was content if the poem were fitted
to "awaken a certain ideal melancholy favourable to the reception of more important impressions." "I have finished,"
he wrote to Peacock (August 16), "by taking advantage
of a few days of inspiration—which the *Camœnœ* have been
lately very backward in conceding—the little poem I began
sending to the press in London. Ollier will send you the
proofs. Its structure is slight and aery; its subject ideal.
The metre corresponds with the spirit of the poem, and
varies with the flow of the feeling." "Rosalind and Helen"
was published by Ollier, together with the "Lines written
among the Euganean Hills," the "Hymn to Intellectual
Beauty," and the sonnet "Ozymandias," forming but a
slender volume, in the spring of 1819.

While wandering from Milan to Pisa, from Pisa to
Leghorn, from Leghorn to Lucca, Claire Clairmont thought

longingly of Venice and her beloved Allegra. How did
it fare with the little one, away from her mother's arms
under the protection of so strange a father? Allegra was
no longer under the same roof with Byron and his motley
crew of followers. Mrs. Hoppner, wife of the English
Consul-General at Venice, had proposed to Byron to take
charge of her, and Byron had given his consent. Letters
received from the nurse Elise, on August 14 and 16, seem
to have decided Claire to set forth immediately for Venice
with Shelley as companion of her travel, whose part it should
be to see Byron and entreat on her behalf for the comfort
of at least some brief intercourse with her child. On the
day after the reception of Elise's second letter, Shelley
and Claire started on their journey, and on August 19 were
jolting along in a one-horse cabriolet, over a rough road
towards Florence. The heat was considerable, but for
Shelley's enjoyment not excessive, and the rickety vehicle
seemed to have shaken the pain away from his side—a
most delightful respite. The country, as they drove, was
beautiful with its glories of early autumn—now low-lying
lands, where the bunches of purpling grapes hung heavy
among vine-festoons ; now castled crag, or olive copses, amid
which some ruined tower could be half discerned ; and
again, as Florence drew near, the villa-dotted plain, bounded
by blue and misty mountains.

"Claire's plans with regard to Albè," Shelley had written
to Mary from Florence, "have undergone a good deal of
modification, and her present impression is that I should
call on Albè whilst she remains either at Fusina or Padua
so as not to irritate him by entering the same city, but
not to conceal—and there I think she is right—her having
departed from Lucca. The worst of this plan is, that it
will not succeed, and that she will never be quite satisfied
that all has been done. But we shall see." On reaching

dua, however, Claire could not bear to be left behind,
ll of eager and irrepressible anxiety, in a strange city.
Claire changed her plan of remaining at Padua," Shelley
rote on arriving at Venice, "partly from the badness of
e beds, and partly from the strangeness and solitude of
e place. At present, I believe that I shall call on the
lbaneser with a letter from her, and without any direct
terference on my own part. He will not be up yet, and
e interval she proposes to employ in a visit to Mrs.
oppner. All this casts, as you see, 'ominous conjecture
the whole success.'" From Padua, on the afternoon of
turday, August 22, the travellers proceeded by water to
enice ; a boat was always more delightful in Shelley's eyes
an a carriage ; and a gondola, seen for the first time,
emed to him the most beautiful and convenient boat in
e world. The weather had grown extremely, even pain-
ly cold, and we hear no raptures uttered by Shelley in
esence of the banks of the Brenta, Palladian villas, gay
rdens, and views of the Rhætian Alps. The cold August
ilight fell upon him and his companion, housed in their
ack-garmented gondola, listening to the plash of the
ters, or the talk of their boatman, who, by curious chance,
s one of Byron's gondolieri, and entertained them with
edifying tales of the *giovanotto Inglese*. A famous man
was, who lived so luxuriously, spent great sums of money,
ned a *nome stravagante*, and had lately received "two
his daughters over from England," of whom one, said
e narrator, with, perhaps, an incredulous smile, "looked
arly as old as himself." The approach to Venice was
no golden sunset, such as voyagers love to describe, with
e lagune showing its "leagues of rippling lustre," and the
chanted city rising like a gorgeous exhalation from the
som of ocean. "We passed the laguna," Shelley wrote
xt morning to his wife, "in the middle of the night, in

a most violent storm of wind, rain, and lightning. It wa
very curious to observe the elements above in a state (
such tremendous convulsion, and the surface of the wate
almost calm ; for these lagunas, though five miles broad
a space enough in a storm to sink any gondola, are s
shallow that the boatmen drive the boat along with
pole. The sea-water, furiously agitated by the wind, shon
with sparkles like stars. Venice, now hidden and no
disclosed by the driving rain, shone dimly with its light
We were all this while safe and comfortable, except tha
Claire was now and then a little frightened in our cabin
It was midnight when they reached their hotel.

On Sunday morning, again at late night, or rather towar(
the dawn of the following day, and " by scraps and patche
interrupted every minute," on Monday, Shelley continue
to write to his wife a detailed account of his doings
Venice. From that portion of the letter—unhappily b
a fragment—dated " Sunday night, five o'clock in the mor
ing," so many passages of interest have been hither
omitted in the printed collections, that it is right to r
produce it here as little imperfectly as may be.

" Well, I will try to relate everything in its order. Aft
breakfast we took a gondola, and went to the Hoppner
Claire went in first, and I, who had no idea of calling, sa
in the gondola. Soon a servant came down, and request
me to go upstairs. I found Mr. Hoppner and Clai
and soon after Mrs. Hoppner, a most agreeable and amial
lady, who instantly paid Claire the kindest attentio
They received me with great politeness, and expressed t
greatest interest in the event of our journey. Soon aft
—for Mrs. Hoppner sent for them instantly—came Eli
and little Ba, so grown you would hardly know her ; s
is pale, and has lost a good deal of her liveliness, but
as beautiful as ever, though more mild. The account whi

they gave of Albè unfortunately corresponds too justly with most of what we have heard, though doubtless with some exaggeration. We discussed a long time the mode in which I had better proceed with him, and at length determined that Claire's being there should be concealed, as Mr. Hoppner says that he often expresses his extreme horror of her arrival, and the necessity which it would impose on him of instantly quitting Venice. The Hoppners enter into all this as if it were their own dearest concern. At three o'clock I called on Albè; he was delighted to see me, and our first conversation of course consisted in the object of my visit. The success of this is yet doubtful, though certainly the spirit in which he receives the request, and the anxiety he shows to satisfy us and Claire, is very unexpected. He says he does not like her [Allegra] going away to Florence for so long a time, because the Venetians will think that he has grown tired of her and dismissed her; and he has already the reputation of caprice. Then he said, 'Why, Claire will be as unwilling to part with her again as she is to be absent from her now, and there will be a second renewal of affliction and a second parting. But, if you like, she shall go to Claire to Padua for a week' (when he said this he supposed that you and the family were there); 'and in fact,' said he, 'after all, I have no right over the child. If Claire likes to take it, let her take it. I do not say what most people would in that situation, that I will refuse to provide for it, or abandon it, if she does this; but she must surely be aware herself how very imprudent such a measure would be.' Well, dear Mary, this talk went off, for I did not see in that moment how I could urge it further; and I thought that at least many points were gained in the willingness and good humour of our discussion. So he took me in his gondola—much against my will, for I wanted to return to Claire at Mrs.

2 D

Hoppner's, who was anxiously waiting for me—across the laguna, to a long sandy island which defends Venice from the Adriatic. When we disembarked, we found his horses waiting for us, and we rode along the sands of the sea, talking. Our conversation consisted in histories of his wounded feelings, and questions as to my affairs, and great professions of friendship and regard for me. He said that, if he had been in England at the time of the Chancery affair, he would have moved heaven and earth to have prevented such a decision. We talked of literary matters; his fourth canto [of ' Childe Harold '], which he says is very good, and indeed repeated some stanzas of great energy to me; and ' Foliage,'* which he quizzes immoderately. When we returned to his palace, which † . . . [The Hoppners are the] most amiable people I ever knew. Do you know that they have put off a journey of pleasure solely that they might devote themselves to this affair, and all with so much ease, delicacy, tenderness! They are much attached to each other, and have a nice little boy, seven months old. Mr. Hoppner paints beautifully; and this excursion, which he has just put off, was an expedition to the Julian Alps, in the neighbourhood, for the sake of sketching, to procure winter employment. He has only a fortnight's leisure, and he has sacrificed two days to strangers whom he never saw before. Mrs. Hoppner has hazel eyes and sweet looks—rather Maryish."

Led to believe that Mrs. Shelley, with her children and Claire, were now at Padua, Byron in a friendly mood proposed that Shelley and his household should occupy for a time the villa at Este, which he had himself taken for two years as a place of *villeggiatura*. It was beautifully situated among the Euganean Hills, close to the old castle of the Este family, and within a few miles of Arqua, where Petrarch

* Leigh Hunt's volume of verse.   † The letter is here torn.

dwelt and died.* Here Claire might welcome Allegra and for a time enjoy companionship with her child. Such a proposal Shelley, well pleased to have attained the object of his journey, could not but accept. He wrote without delay to Mary, begging her to come instantly to Este, and adding minute and exact instructions for her guidance on the journey. "I have been obliged," he says, "to decide on all these things without you. I have done for the best ; and, my own beloved Mary, you must soon come and scold me if I have done wrong, and kiss me if I have done right, for I am sure I do not know which, and it is only the event that will show. We shall at least be saved the trouble of introduction, and have formed acquaintance with a lady [Mrs. Hoppner] who is so good, so beautiful, so angelically mild, that, were she as wise too, she would be quite a Mary ; but she is not very accomplished. Her eyes are like a reflection of yours ; her manners are like yours when you know and like a person. . . . If you knew all that I had to do ! Dearest love, be well, be happy ; come to me and confide in your own constant and affectionate P. B. S. Kiss the blue-eyed darlings for me, and do not let William forget me. Ca cannot recollect me."

Mrs. Shelley, in her loneliness at the Baths, had invited Mr. and Mrs. Gisborne to be her guests, and on August 25 they had arrived. But, on receiving Shelley's letter and consulting with her friends, she decided, in accordance with her instructions, to set forth immediately for Este. Her birthday, August 30, was a day of bustle and packing ; next morning she was off, with Paolo acting as her courier and attendant. Shelley waited anxiously at Este, and wondered when the hours passed and no Mary appeared. Mary's journey had, indeed, been neither rapid nor

* The house had been transferred from Mr. Hoppner. See Byron's letter to Rogers, dated "Venice, March 3, 1818."

agreeable. At Florence she was detained an entire day, while waiting for a signature to her passport. Little Clara, in whose baby-face Mary discerned a remarkable likeness to Shelley, suffered from an attack of dysentery, caused by heat, fatigue, and the troubles of teething, and when they reached Este she was dangerously ill. The physician at Este was a stupid fellow; the Paduan physician, a man in great practice, was not one in whom Shelley placed entire confidence. The days went on, and the child, although the dysentery had been in part subdued, was still in a frightful state of weakness and fever. Miss Clairmont was far from well, and on September 22 Shelley accompanied her to Padua to call upon the *medico;* but the *medico* was not to be seen. Claire waited at Padua in order to visit her physician next morning, after which she returned to Mary. Shelley, in accordance with his wife's wishes, but sooner than she had expected, proceeded to Venice ("Am I not like a wild swan to be gone so suddenly?" he asks), there intending to make arrangements for receiving Mary and little Ca. "My poor little Clara," he wrote, "how is she to-day? Indeed I am somewhat uneasy about her, and, though I feel secure that there is no danger, it would be very comfortable to have some reasonable person's advice about her." Shelley's trust that the danger was past changed two days after to the sad assurance that all suffering for her, and all anxieties of hope and fear for her parents, were at an end. On September 24 Mary, with Claire and the one-year-old baby, drove to Padua, where they were met by Shelley. Claire returned to Este to watch over William and Allegra. Shelley, with his wife and child, hastened forward towards Venice. At Fusina a halt was necessary; there stood the great dogana, "like a prison on the edge of the Adriatic, filled with German faces and guarded by Austrian arms." In their trouble and hurry the travellers had neglected to bring their passport with them. The soldiers on duty attempted to prevent their crossing the laguna ; "but," writes Mary, "they could not resist Shelley's impetuosity at such a moment." It was a time of miserable anxiety for father and mother in the gondola, while every minute the babe grew more alarmingly ill. The inn was at length reached, but within an hour or two the child lay dead in its mother's arms.

The early days of October were spent somewhat sadly at the villa among the hills. "We have all had bad spirits enough," Shelley wrote to Peacock (October 8), "and I, in addition, bad health. I *intend* to be better soon : there is no malady, bodily or mental, which does not either kill or is killed." If delightful surroundings could make life pleasant, the autumn days might have been a season of content for the occupants of I Cappuccini. The house was cheerful, with a vine-trellised walk leading from the hall-door to the summer-house at the end of the garden, which Shelley made his study. A slight ravine, with a road in its depth, divided the garden from the hill, on which stood the ruins of the ancient castle of Este, of which the dark and echoing wall harboured in its crevices owls and bats until twilight and moonrise called them into activity. "We looked from the garden," writes Mrs. Shelley, "over the wide plain of Lombardy, bounded to the west by the far Apennines, while to the east the horizon was lost in misty distance. After the picturesque but limited view of mountain, ravine, and chestnut wood at the Baths of Lucca, there was something infinitely gratifying to the eye in the wide range of prospect commanded by our new abode." This delight in wide prospect finds vivid and exquisite expression in a poem of Shelley's written in the main at Este, retouched and completed at Naples, which tells of a sudden access of unlooked-for joy among the hills—joy ringed around at morning and evening with a leaden band of pain too heavy to be removed. The "Lines written among the Euganean Hills" have in them the purified gladness in sorrow of an autumnal day upon the heights— a day measured from sunrise to the hour of the climbing crescent moon, with her one ministering star.

The memories of his recent visit to Venice dwelt with Shelley, and were food for his imagination. Ailing in body and depressed in spirits, he was driven to poetry as to a world in which life, finer and more intense, was still possible for him ; and Venice and Byron became for his imagination vivid centres around which that higher life might gather. His first impressions of Byron were favourable, for Byron had presented his friendliest and most cheerful aspect to Shelley. "I saw Lord Byron," he wrote to Peacock (October 8), "and really hardly knew him again ; he is changed into the liveliest and happiest-looking man I ever met. He read me the first canto of his ' Don Juan ' —a thing in the style of Beppo, but infinitely better, and dedicated to Southey, in ten or a dozen stanzas, more like a mixture of wormwood and verdigris than satire." And of Venice, "Venice is a wonderfully fine city. The approach to it over the laguna, with its domes and turrets glittering in a long line over the blue waves, is one of the finest architectural delusions in the world. It seems to have— and literally it has—its foundations in the sea. The silent streets are paved with water, and you hear nothing but the dashing of the oars and the occasional cries of the gondolieri. I heard nothing of Tasso. The gondolas themselves are things of a most romantic and picturesque appearance ; I can only compare them to moths of which a coffin might have been the chrysalis." A mournful image, but which might well have suited the boat that bore the baby Clara to her grave.

On October 12, Shelley, with his wife and little William, now attended by the nurse Elise, was again in Venice. Mrs. Shelley spent much of her time with the Hoppners. Shelley passed several evenings with Byron at his palazzo on the Grand Canal. It is probable that during these days Shelley saw more of the life led by Byron at this period, and of the ruin which it was working in his character, than had been visible to him during the first dim days of sorrow after Clara's death. As Shelley conceived, the spirit of Byron's poetry was being degraded and dragged into the mire by his habits of coarse self-indulgence, and the cynicism and apathy in which they resulted. The pseudo-sublime in "Childe Harold's" melancholy was, in fact, an expression of the dull distaste for life which succeeded to vulgar orgies of sensuality. "I remonstrated with him in vain," Shelley wrote to Peacock a few weeks later, "on the tone of mind from which such a view of things alone arises. . . . The fact is that, first, the Italian women with whom he associates are perhaps the most contemptible of all who exist under the moon—the most ignorant, the most disgusting, the most bigoted ; countesses smell so strongly of garlic that an ordinary Englishman cannot approach them. Well, L. B. is familiar with the lowest sort of these women, the people his gondolieri pick up in the streets. He associates with wretches who seem almost to have lost the gait and physiognomy of man, and who do not scruple to avow practices which are not only not named, but I believe seldom ever conceived, in England. He says he disapproves, but he endures. He is heartily and deeply discontented with himself ; and contemplating in the distorted mirror of his own thoughts the nature and the destiny of man, what can he behold but objects of contempt and despair? But that he is a great poet, I think the address to ocean proves. And he has a certain degree of candour while you talk to him, but unfortunately it does not outlast your departure. No, I do not doubt, and for his sake I ought not to hope, that his present career must end soon in some violent circumstance." And to the care of such a father the little Allegra must be confided!

Such was the real Byron as he showed himself at this time to Shelley—a "tempest-cleaving swan," paddling in the foulest mire. In "Julian and Maddalo," written in the summer-house at Este, perhaps in the interval between Shelley's first visit to Venice and the death of Clara, a portrait of Byron is given without those baser lines and darker colours which were perceived only during the later days of their intercourse in the autumn of 1818. The poem is no less interesting for the sake of its idealized portrait of Shelley himself—"an Englishman of good family"—so Julian is described in the preface—"passionately attached to those philosophical notions which assert the power of man over his own mind, and the immense improvements of which, by the extinction of certain moral superstitions, human society may be susceptible. Without concealing the evil in the world, he is for ever speculating how good may be made superior. He is a complete infidel, and a scoffer at all things reputed holy. . . . Julian, in spite of his heterodox opinions, is conjectured by his friends to possess some good qualities." The ride with Byron on the Lido, the sunset seen from the water's edge or the gondola's covert, with Venice appearing like a city of enchantment, its temples and palaces piled to heaven, the picture of Allegra's beautiful childhood—

> " A lovelier toy sweet Nature never made ;
> A serious, subtle, wild, yet gentle being ;
> Graceful without design, and unforeseeing "—

the approach through the fast-falling rain and high-wrought seas to the dreary island of the bell and tower,—these

re probably recasts made by the imagination from material
upplied by the remembrance of Shelley's earliest days at
Venice.   Never before had he written with such an union
f freedom, strength, and grace as the earlier pages of this
poem show.   The excess of unbalanced sensibility, not
usually a characteristic of the greatest poets, and too often
a source of weakness in Shelley's writings, is here in large
measure checked and controlled by the variety of the material
handled, and by the vigour of his adult genius.   Two of
the three principal portraits are drawn from life, and are
drawn with the greater strength because the originals were
immediately present to his mind ; the third—a fainter
and feebler sketch—that of the wronged and distracted lover,
is also, says Shelley, "in some degree a painting from
nature, but with respect to time and place ideal."   It has
been suggested, and probably on good grounds, that Shelley
here idealizes his past self, and presents in a kind of magic
mirror his own unhappy relations with his first wife.

Admirable, at least in part, as "Julian and Maddalo" is
in conception and execution, a fortunate product of some
autumn days among the hills, it seemed to Shelley but a
slight achievement, such as might be suitable for insertion
in Leigh Hunt's *Examiner.*   Another and a more arduous
enterprise in poetry engaged his highest thoughts.   During
his early wanderings in Italy, Shelley meditated three subjects
as the groundwork for lyrical dramas.   One was the madness
of Tasso, to the treatment of which theme he had intended
to devote the summer of 1818, and, indeed, the following
year.   If properly treated, it would be found, he believed,
admirably dramatic and poetical.   "But you will say," he
had written from Milan to Peacock, "I have no dramatic
talent ; very true, in a certain sense ; but I have taken the
resolution to see what kind of a tragedy a person without
dramatic talent could write."   The design was never executed,

and the only fragments of the tragedy of Tasso which w
possess are a short scene and an unfinished song. It ma
be, however, that some of Shelley's studies for the madne
of Tasso overflowed into the mournful soliloquies of th
distraught lover and lunatic in " Julian and Maddalo."
second theme, more suitable for lyrical drama, was foun
in the Book of Job—itself, as Shelley conceived it,
dramatic poem of "irresistible grandeur" in its plan, an
unequalled sublimity in its imagery. This design Shelle
never abandoned in idea; no trace, however, of an in
dependent drama, suggested by the most majestic of th
Hebrew writings, remains among his papers. In 182
when engaged upon his lyrical drama of "Hellas," Shelle
reverted in thought to his project of three years earlie
and wrote those noble fragments of a prologue to "Hellas
deciphered by the piety of Mr. Garnett, in which the sce
is the roofless senate-house of God whose floor is Chao
and the speakers are the angelic herald of Eternity, th
Christ, and Satan standing, as does the Adversary in th
Book of Job, among the sons of God. It was a bold desig
to ally the genius of Hebraism with that of Hellenis
and to present Christ as pleading "by Plato's sacred ligh
on behalf of revolutionary Greece.

The third of Shelley's great enterprises of the ear
months in Italy was his "Prometheus Unbound." "Th
Greek tragedians," writes Mrs. Shelley, "were now his mo
familiar companions in his wanderings, and the sublim
majesty of Æschylus filled him with wonder and delight
The "Prometheus Vinctus" of Æschylus was connecte
with a lost play of its author, "Prometheus Unbound
in which a chorus of Titans condole with the hero, wh
was delivered by Heracles and reconciled with Zeus. Th
such a play had existed, Shelley vaguely remembere
and no more. During all his wanderings from Milan

Como, and thence to Pisa, Leghorn, the Baths of Lucca,
Venice, he meditated the subject of his drama.   Immediately
on arriving at the villa at Este, although ailing in health
and full of anxiety for his child, he set himself to his great
task.   The martyrdom of a heroic lover and saviour of
mankind was a theme around which Shelley's highest and
purest feelings and imaginings must gather ; and for him
such a martyrdom must needs be the pledge of the final
victory of joy and wisdom and love.

When, after a visit of twelve days, Shelley, on October 24,
left Venice for Este, his spirit, in anticipation of wintry
days, was already turning towards the south.   At the Baths
of Lucca, when little Clara as well as William was to be
thought of, high debate had been held as to whether the
land or sea journey to Naples would be the safer and the
more agreeable.   Now November was not far off, and
the time for their departure had almost arrived.   Allegra
must be redelivered to her father, and, with the purpose of
escorting her to Venice, Shelley had returned to the country
villa.   Very bitter for Claire Clairmont's spirits must have
been the parting from her beloved child.   On October 29,
Shelley, with Allegra, was again in Venice.   Next morning
farewells were said, and after a few days of rest at Este
and preparation for renewed wayfaring, the travellers, who
had decided in favour of the land journey to the south,
were (November 5) on the road to Rovigo.

CHAPTER XVIII.

ROME AND SOUTHERN ITALY (NOVEMBER, 1818, TO JUNE, 1819).

UNDER grey clouds, along roads so bad that oxen we
sometimes needed to assist the horses, the carriage, wi
its six occupants—Shelley, Mary, Claire, Elise, with litt
William, the maid Milly, and Paolo as driver—struggl
slowly towards Ferrara. The cloudy skies, the redden
leaves that hung from the vines, the piled stalks of Indi
corn round the threshing-floors, the vast heaps of man
coloured pumpkins—winter food for the hogs—stored
the farmyards, told of the late season of the year.   In t
level lands through which they passed nothing seemed
Shelley so beautiful as the "milk-white oxen" which he h
described in his "Lines written among the Euganean Hill
and which were to be seen at labour or in repose in love
teams or troops.   The November evening which broug
the travellers to Ferrara was followed by a night of r
and thunder ; but the weather next day permitted them
drive through the desolate and grass-grown streets to vi
the cathedral, the public library, and the Hospital of !
Ann.   The manuscripts and relics of Ariosto and Tasso
particular deeply interested Shelley.   There were Ariost
bronze inkstand, with its Cupid commanding silence, a
his walnut armchair, in which Shelley would imagine

aw the poet seated; there were his satires in his own
handwriting; and there the "Gerusalemme Liberata," copied
and re-copied and interlined by its author. With emotion
which left no room for historical scepticism, Shelley viewed
the narrow dungeon of Tasso—hero of the intended lyrical
drama—and to Peacock was despatched, as a memorial of
the visit, "a piece of the wood of the very door, which for
seven years and three months divided this glorious being
from the light and air, which had nourished in him those
influences which he has communicated, through his poetry,
to thousands."   On November 8, amid falling rain, through
dull and marshy lands, the carriage rolled towards Bologna.
In 1818, the fame of the Bolognese school of painting stood
higher than it does to-day, and Shelley devoted himself very
zealously during two visits to the Academy of Fine Arts
to mastering at least the subjects and motives of the chief
pictures—for he did not aspire to connoisseurship or the
criticism of *technique*—until some of that fatigue and bewilderment came down upon him, which must oppress any
but the most stalwart sight-seer among Italian galleries
and cathedrals.

At Spoleto—most romantic of cities—the aqueduct
spanning the vale, in view of the ramparted citadel, was
duly visited. "I never saw," said Shelley, "a more impressive picture, in which the shapes of nature are of the
grandest order, and over which the creations of man,
sublime from their antiquity and greatness, seem to pre-
dominate." But upon this journey marvel succeeded marvel,
scarcely leaving breathing-time to the spectator. In a
letter to Peacock, Shelley has attempted the impossible
in his effort to depict in words the wonder and beauty
and terror of the falls of the Velino at Terni.

"We travel all day the Campagna di Roma," writes
Mary in her diary,—"a perfect solitude, yet picturesque,

and relieved by shady dells. We see an immense hawk sailing in the air for prey. Enter Rome. A rainy evening. Doganas and cheating innkeepers. We at length get settled in a comfortable hotel."

It was late November; but November in Rome is not like the month of mists in London. Day followed day of clear and sunny weather, and with unbounded ardour Shelley gave himself up to the spectacle and the influencings of the majestic city. More impressive than any other object within the circuit of its vast and antique walls was the crumbling yet majestic Coliseum. Here Mary sketched, while little William sported beside her; and perhaps it was here that Shelley, on her second day of sketching (November 25), began that fragment of a tale which takes its name from the sublime ruin. The fragment of narrative is of interest, not only as conveying, in language of vivid yet elaborated beauty, Shelley's impression of the vast relic of ancient Rome, but because it is inspired by his religious feeling, and contains the first outline of an idealized and transmuted portrait of himself.

One other spot in Rome, in after-days to be for ever associated with his poetry and with his life and death, was viewed by Shelley with deep and solemn interest. In his days of boyhood the mystery and fascinating horror of death had at times overpowered his spirit; now he could feel its beauty and serious peace. "The English burying-place," he writes, "is a green slope near the walls, under the pyramidal tomb of Cestius, and is, I think, the most beautiful and solemn cemetery I ever beheld. To see the sun shining on its bright grass, fresh, when we first visited it, with the autumnal dews, and hear the whispering of the wind among the leaves of the trees which have overgrown the tomb of Cestius, and the soil which is stirring in the sun-warm earth, and to mark the tombs, mostly of women

.nd young people, who were buried there, one might, if one
vere to die, desire the sleep they seem to sleep.   Such is
he human mind, and so it peoples with its wishes vacancy
nd oblivion."

On November 27, one day in advance of the others, in
rder to secure lodgings before the arrival of Mrs. Shelley,
Villiam, and Claire, Shelley set forth for Naples.   Of the
ountry and its inhabitants he noticed little, except that
he wild beauty of the one and the barbarous ferocity of
he others increased as they drove to the south.

A lodging was found which faced the royal gardens, and
he blue waters of the bay, for ever changing, yet for ever
he same ; and on the evening of December 1, Mary, very
-eary after a long day's journey, was welcomed to her new
bode.   The climate was delicious, like that of an English
pring, though lacking its spirit of hope and arrowy summons
f delight.   With windows open, and without a fire, they
ould sit indoors and read, or could saunter outside among
tatues and myrtle and orange groves in the gardens, or
ide abroad to visit the sights of the city, or, if they should
lease, enjoy from a boat the glories of the bay.   In Madame
e Staël's "Corinne" Shelley found a romantic handbook
) Naples and its environs ; through Livy he kept himself in
lose relation with the history of antiquity ; his guide and
1aster in the study of ancient art was Winckelmann.

At Pompeii, Shelley found himself face to face with the
st life of ancient Greece.   It was a warm and radiant day ;
nd here was a whole city which in its days of joy and
eauty had not shut men out from the light of nature, but
ad brought humanity into the perpetual presence of what
 most glorious and most free in the visible world.   The
oble prospect around was admitted, and, "unlike the in-
abitants of the Cimmerian ravines of modern cities, the
1cient Pompeians could contemplate the clouds and the

lamps of heaven; could see the moon rise high behin
Vesuvius, and the sun set in a sea, tremulous with an atmo
sphere of golden vapour, between Inarime and Misenum.
But of all things the tombs placed along the consular roa
were to Shelley the most impressive. "The wild wood
surround them on either side; and along the broad stone
of the paved road which divides them, you hear the lat
leaves of autumn shiver and rustle in the stream of th
inconstant wind, as it were, like the steps of ghosts.
Even in presence of death, the inspirations of externa
nature had been felt, and these kept men sweet-tempere
and sane.

Shelley had come to Naples without introductions t
either English or Italians; and the common Neapolitar
seemed to him so sullen and stupid, that it was impossibl
to hold agreeable intercourse with them. He suffere
greatly in health, and the English physician, who treate
him for disease of the liver, applying caustic to his sid
caused him much discomfort and afforded him no relie
"We lived in utter solitude," says Mrs. Shelley, "and suc
is not often the nurse of cheerfulness." The excitemen
of his delight in excursions hither and thither was followe
by a corresponding reaction of spirits. The statues of th
museum afforded him infinite pleasure, but the bodil
fatigue of standing for hours in the galleries exhausted hir
"I have," he says, "depression enough of spirits and n
good health, though I believe the warm air of Naples do
me good." The thought of his children, alienated fro
their father by a decree of the Court of Chancery, wa
often in his mind. "We have reports here of a change
the English ministry," he wrote to Peacock (January 2
1819); "to what does it amount? For, besides my nation
interest in it, I am on the watch to vindicate my mo
sacred rights, invaded by the chancery court." Domes

affairs had not gone quite smoothly for Mrs. Shelley since they left Este. Paolo Foggi, the Italian servant, who, it was supposed at first, would cheat his master within reasonable limits, had proved himself to be an unqualified rascal. His robberies had far exceeded the bounds ; and worse, he had corrupted and betrayed the Swiss nurse, Elise. At first, while it seemed that he was making honourable advances to her, Mrs. Shelley had opposed their union. Now she insisted that at least the ceremony of marriage should be celebrated. At the church of the British envoy Elise was "made an honest woman," and she and her husband (who cherished a bitter feeling of revenge against Shelley) took their departure for Rome.

Some events which occurred at Naples in December, 1818, exposed Shelley's reputation to the risk of malignant slander, and this fact Paolo in after-days knew how to turn to account. "The rascal Paolo," wrote Shelley, in the summer of 1820, to Mr. and Mrs. Gisborne, "has been taking advantage of my situation at Naples in December, 1818, to attempt to extort money by threatening to charge me with the most horrible crimes." The threatening letters were placed by Shelley in the hands of a lawyer, and Paolo for a time was crushed. We cannot doubt that the dangerous rascal's lying story was akin to that which he repeated afterwards to the Hoppners—that Miss Clairmont had given birth to a child, of which Shelley was the father, and that Shelley, whether with or without Claire's consent, had sent it to a foundling hospital.

It had been Shelley's plan to return in the spring to Rome, where he had hoped to spend three months in the study of its treasures of antiquity and art. Illness confined him much to the house during February, but on the 23rd of that month he was well enough to start, with Mary and Claire, on a long-contemplated expedition to Pæstum.

2 E

Unluckily the weather, which had been of cloudless serenit
broke, and rain fell in torrents as they drove towards Nocei
and La Cava ; but as they approached Salerno the declinin
sun shot forth, amid tempestuous mists, a beam of splendou
Not more than two hours could be allowed for contempla
tion of the temples, and those hours went swiftly by. "C
course we could only bring away," says Shelley, "as in
perfect a conception of these sublime monuments as is th
shadow of some half-remembered dream."

Four days later, on the afternoon of February 28, 181
they looked for the last time on bay and mountain as the
drove towards Capua on the way to Rome.

Having obtained lodgings in the Palazzo Verospi c
the Corso, Shelley, Mary, and Claire set themselves vigo
ously to the study of the city—the Rome of dead centurie
and the Rome of the living to-day. With that zeal for sel
improvement which had been a part of their nature sin
girlhood, Mary and Claire sought training each for h
special faculty or aptitude. Mary had her drawing-maste
Claire her lessons in singing. Nor was Shelley idle. F
read Lucretius, Euripides, Plutarch, Winckelmann ; und
the quickening influence of a radiant spring he wrote wi
ardour ; he visited the museums, the galleries, the churche
the monuments of ancient Rome. "You know not," I
wrote to Peacock, "how delicate the imagination becom
by dieting with antiquity day after day." His health i
proved, although towards the close of April he was for
time seriously ailing, and it was feared that the Roman a
was sapping his strength. His spirits were "not the mc
brilliant in the world," but that, he says, "we attribute
our solitary situation, and though happy, how should I
lively?" The society of English residents and tourists w
distasteful to him ; but the Romans pleased him much—
least for a time—and especially the Roman women, wh

in their lack of culture and innocent *naïveté*, seemed to him like uncorrupted children, or a kind of gentle savages.

Modern Italy, viewed as a whole, appeared to Shelley to have sunk to a state of spiritual impotence and moral degradation. In the square of St. Peter's he saw the herd of fettered criminals at work, while near them sat or sauntered groups of soldiers armed with loaded muskets. The clank of the chains was heard above the musical dashing of the fountains, while overhead shone the infinite azure of an April sky, and around rose the magnificence of Roman architecture. Such a contrast of human wretchedness with human grandeur, and again with the inviolable freedom of nature, caused in Shelley "a conflict of sensations allied to madness." It is the emblem of Italy, he writes—"moral degradation contrasted with the glory of nature and the arts." The first impression made upon him by St. Peter's was one of disappointment. Externally it seemed inferior in beauty to St. Paul's ; internally, he says, "it exhibits littleness on a large scale." Nor did this impression pass away, although Shelley could feel that the vast design, conceived by the brain and achieved by the hand of man, is an astonishing monument of human energy and daring. The genius of Michael Angelo disconcerted and almost repelled him. Insensible to the profoundly Christian spirit of an art which recognizes man as the lord and conqueror of nature, and as the humble yet aspiring servant of the invisible God, Shelley saw in Michael Angelo's work, as painter, sculptor, and architect, only the attempt of a barbarian to be classical. Where in Michael Angelo was there to be discerned any sense of beauty or of moral dignity? where any perception of the creative power of mind? His "Moses" was only less monstrous and detestable than the Moses of the Old Testament ; his "Day of Judgment" was a kind of "Titus Andronicus" in painting. Of his tenderness, his ardour of love, his passion of inspiration, Shelley could perceive nothing.

It was in solitude, among the flowery ruins of ancient Rome, that his highest mountings of the mind, his finest trances of thought, came to Shelley. The first act of his "Prometheus Unbound" had been achieved for the most part in the summer-house of his garden at Este. From Naples, on January 26, he had written to Peacock, informing him that the act was now complete. The second and third acts were wrought out amid surroundings fitted to sustain his imagination in its highest endeavours. The days were bright and beautiful, and in the mountainous ruins of the Baths of Caracalla he lived in communion at once with nature and with the energies of human genius. There morning after morning, he devoted himself to his great poem ; there, in the springtime, he was with Asia in the springtime, deep in a vale of the Indian Caucasus ; there he pursued, with the sister-spirits of Love and Faith, that forest-path which leads to the realm of Demogorgon ; and there the vision passed before him of the ultimate ruin of tyranny and the redemption of the better genius of mankind. Shelley has himself described the majestic and beautiful desolation in the midst of which he wrote— a passage well known and which hardly permits itself to be abridged. "I think I told you," he wrote to Peacock (March, 20, 1819), "of the Coliseum and its impression on me, on my first visit to this city. The next most considerable relic of antiquity, considered as a ruin, is the Thermæ of Caracalla. These consist of six enormous chambers above two hundred feet in height, and each inclosing a vast space like that of a field. There are, in addition, a number of towers and labyrinthine recesses, hidden and woven over by the wild growth of weeds and ivy. Never was a desolation more sublime and lovely. The perpendicular wall of ruin is cloven into steep ravines filled up with flowering shrubs, whose thick twisted roots are knotted in the rifts of the stones.   At every step the aërial pinnacles of shattered stone group into new combinations of effect, and tower above the lofty yet level walls, as the distant mountains change their aspect to one travelling rapidly along the plain. . . . These walls surround green and level spaces of lawn, on which some elms have grown, and which are interspersed towards their skirts by masses of the fallen ruin overtwined with the broad leaves of the creeping weeds. The blue sky canopies it, and is as the everlasting roof of these enormous halls."

Critics endeavouring to find what is of most value in Shelley's highest poem, have analyzed the ideas which lie behind its marvellous imagery.   It is not here that we shall discover what is of chief worth in "Prometheus Unbound." Shelley's ideas are abstractions made from a one-sided and imperfect view of facts.   No dream or prophecy of the future of the human race can be of authentic value which ignores the true conditions of human existence.   Humanity is no chained Titan of indomitable virtue.   It is a weak and trembling thing, which yet, through error and weakness, traversed or overcome, may at last grow strong.   To represent evil as external—the tyranny of a malignant God or Fortune, or as an intellectual error—is to falsify the true conception of human progress.   The progress which indeed concerns us is that which consists in working out the beast, and gradually growing to the fulness of the stature of the perfect man.   But Shelley, now as always, wrote as the disciple of William Godwin.   All the glittering fallacies of Political Justice"—now sufficiently tarnished—together with all its encouraging and stimulating truths, may be found in the *caput mortuum* left when the critic has reduced the poetry of the "Prometheus" to a series of doctrinaire statements. But fortitude, justice, love, beauty, hope, un-quenched desire—these indeed lead men on towards the highest ends of their existence, and these are animating moral powers of Shelley's radiant song. And the life and joy of Earth, in her moments of rapture, have passed into his verse, so that its music sounds like the voice of the quickening April winds. He himself has spoken more truly and happily of the poem than any of his critics. "The blue sky of Rome," he writes, "and the effect of the vigorous awakening of spring in that divinest climate, and the new life with which it drenches the spirits even to intoxication, were the inspiration of this drama." These, passing from the senses to the poet's spirit in sense.

By April 6, the third act of "Prometheus Unbound," which concludes the poem as at first designed, was nearly finished. The intense intellectual strain, the solitude of Rome, the absence of friends, left Shelley's heart at times weak, and he thought longingly of England. But health, competence, tranquillity were attainable in Italy, and of these England would deprive him. And at best his friends were few; they might, he supposed, be counted on one hand. "I am regarded by all who know or hear of me," he writes, with an excess of despondent feeling, "except, I think, on the whole five individuals, as a rare prodigy of crime and pollution, whose look even might infect. This is a large computation, and I don't think I could mention more than three. Such is the spirit of the English abroad as well as at home." And yet he felt at times a craving for the grey skies and pleasant English firesides. "I shall return," he said to Peacock, "some fine morning out of pure weakness of heart." Not now, however, nor for some time to come. He and Mary had planned to start for Naples towards the end of May, and seek a seaside house for the summer months at Castellamare, where Mr. and

Mrs. Gisborne might become their guests. The physicians promised much good to Shelley's health from a Neapolitan summer. "What shall I say to entice you?" Shelley wrote to his friends at Leghorn. "We shall have a piano and some books, and—little else, beside ourselves. But what will be most inviting to you, you will give much, though you may receive but little, pleasure." Shelley's ill-health seemed to make it advisable that they should quit Rome earlier than had been intended, and May 7 was now fixed for their departure. A fortnight before that date, when driving in the Borghese Gardens, Mary and Claire believed that they recognized a former guest of Godwin's—Miss Curran, daughter of the Irish Master of the Rolls. Next day they left a card at Miss Curran's, and on Tuesday, April 27, had the pleasure of receiving at their lodgings their old acquaintance. Miss Curran had some skill in painting; Mary Shelley was a beginner in the art. Morning after morning the two friends spent together happily employed. Shelley's feebleness and feverish depression had passed away. When the day for leaving Rome arrived, Miss Curran was at work on two portraits—one of Claire, who had given a couple of sittings, and one of Shelley, begun upon that morning (May 7). It was decided to postpone the journey to Naples, and again on the next day Shelley gave Miss Curran a sitting. This portrait, begun when Shelley was but lately recovered from a feverish illness, the hasty work of an imperfectly trained amateur, is that by which the face of Shelley is most widely known. The portrait was at first condemned by Mary Shelley. Miss Curran believed that it would never be inquired for by the friends for whom it had been painted, and when about to leave Italy, she was on the point of burning it, with artistic lumber that would have impeded her travel. Happily, just as the fire was scorching it, the picture was saved—saved to become, in

spite of its defects, a precious possession to those who most
hold Shelley's memory dear. Other portraits followed on
Miss Curran's easel—one of little William, painted on
May 14 and 15, and one of Mary, begun on May 28.
These were considered to be more successful likenesses
than that of Shelley.

Happy it was for Mary that she had found a friend just
at this moment. Expecting the birth of a babe in the
autumn, she was ill fitted to endure strain and shock, and
a wave of calamity was now about to break and overwhelm
her. The design of spending the summer at Castellamare
was abandoned towards the close of May. Little William,
his father's blue-eyed darling, had been unwell, and it was
feared that the heat of the southern climate might increase
his disorder. The surgeon whose attendance Mary would
need in the autumn was following the Princess Pauline
Borghese to the Baths of Lucca, and would be either at
Pisa or Florence at the time when Mrs. Shelley would
require his services. It was decided, therefore, to travel
northwards ; to pass the hotter months at the Baths of
Lucca, or the Baths of Pisa, and to settle for the winter
in the city of Pisa, a place strongly recommended as likely
to benefit Shelley's health. Sunday, June 6, was fixed as
the day of departure from Rome. "We should like of all
things to have a house near you by the seaside at Livorno,"
Mary wrote to Mrs. Gisborne, "but the heat would frighten
me for William, who is so very delicate that we must take
the greatest possible care of him this summer." On the
evening of Wednesday, June 2, William, who had been
gaining in strength, was seized with an alarming gastric
attack. Mr. Bell, an excellent English physician, called
three times to see him ; Claire sat night-long by his bed.
When the evening of the next day came, he seemed better.
Miss Curran called, and kindly wrote to Mrs. Gisborne

for Mary, who was very unwell, informing her that the journey to Lucca was for the present postponed. On Friday, Mary's journal stops abruptly, as that of Claire's had stopped on the previous day. The hours passed miserably, with fluctuations of hope and fear—fear ever growing the stronger. On Saturday, Mary contrived to write a few lines to her friend at Leghorn. "William," she says, "is in the greatest danger. We do not quite despair, yet we have the least possible reason to hope. Yesterday, he was in the convulsions of death, and he was saved from them; yet we dare not, must not, hope. I will write as soon as any change takes place. The misery of these hours is beyond calculation. The hopes of my life are bound up in him. Ever yours affectionately, M. W. S. I am well, and so is Shelley, although he is more exhausted by watching than I am. William is in a high fever." At noon, on Monday, June 7—the day following that which had been fixed for their departure from Rome—William Shelley died. His father had watched during sixty hours of agony without closing his eyes; yet on Tuesday he roused himself to write a mournful note to Peacock. "Yesterday, after an illness of only a few days, my little William died. There was no hope from the moment of the attack. You will be kind enough to tell all my friends, so that I need not write to them. It is a great exertion to me to write this, and it seems to me as if, hunted by calamity as I have been, that I should never recover any cheerfulness again. If the things Mary desired to be sent to Naples have not been shipped, send them to Livorno. We leave this city for Livorno to-morrow morning, where we have written to take lodgings for a month. I will then write again." In the English burial-ground, near the Porta San Paolo, which on his first visit to Rome had so soothingly impressed Shelley with a sense of its lovely and solemn seclusion, the body of his beloved son was laid. "This spot," he wrote, "is the repository of a sacred loss, of which the yearnings of a parent's heart are now prophetic; he is rendered immortal by love, as his memory is by death.' The father, who, when he feared that the Court of Chancery might deprive him of William, had sung to him of the life they should lead

> "By the azure sea
> Of serene and golden Italy,"

now attempted to sing a requiem for his dead child.

> "Where art thou, my gentle child?
> Let me think thy spirit feeds,
> With its life intense and mild,
> The love of living leaves and weeds,
> Among these tombs and ruins wild;—
> Let me think that, through low seeds
> Of the sweet flowers and sunny grass,
> Into their hues and scents may pass
> A portion——"

At which point the fragment closes, as if the writer's heart had drawn down his imagination into the dark and silent chamber of grief.

CHAPTER XIX.

VILLA VALSOVANO, LEGHORN : FLORENCE (JUNE, 1819,
TO JANUARY, 1820).

THE gap in Mary Shelley's journal, which occurs upon the
death of her beloved child, is partly filled by a short entry
in the journal of Miss Clairmont, summing up the incidents
of the month of sorrow.

Claire Clairmont's Journal (June, 1819).

"Monday, June 7, at noonday. Thursday, June 10, set
out from Rome for Livorno. We visit the waterfall of
Terni once again. We see also the Lake of Thrasimene,
now called the Lake of Perugia. Arrive at Livorno—
'Aquila Nera'—Thursday, 17th. Stay there a week ; see
the Gisbornes. Remove to Viletta Valsovano, near Monte
Nero. Read Cobbett's 'Journal in America,' Birkbeck's
'Notes on the Illinois,' 'Nightmare Abbey,' and the 'Heart
of Midlothian' by Walter Scott."

It was good for Mary now that she should not live
quite alone, nor yet amid the uncongenial gaieties of a
summer watering-place. Leghorn or its neighbourhood
would suit her well, where Mrs. Gisborne's society might
help to hold in check the desolating inroads of grief and
pain, and where some quiet dwelling-place might be found

outside the bustle of the town. The thought of proceeding
to the Baths of Lucca, or to Florence, was accordingly
abandoned, and the Villa Valsovano, an airy little country
house, at a short distance from Leghorn—about halfway
between the city and Monte Nero—was taken for three
months. The house stood at the end of a green lane, and
was surrounded by a tiny estate, worked as a market-garden.
The summer was one of unusual heat, diversified by thunder-
storms of majestic terror. There was refreshment for the
senses in the vine-festoons alternating with rows of cabbages,
in the olive, fig, and peach trees, in the myrtle hedges, with
their faint sweet perfume, in green grassy walks leading
through the vines, and in the creak of the water-wheel as
the process of irrigation went on. The peasants, bare-
breasted, brown-legged, at work in the heat, sang cheerfully,
if not very melodiously, to the cicala's noisy accompaniment.
At night, the myrtle hedges were alive with the pale-green
meteors of the fire-flies.

But pleasant surroundings will not stay the cruel aching
of a heart. Mary Shelley had endured the loss of her little
Clara, and had bravely struggled to be calm ; her affections
had twined themselves closer and with tenderer vehemence
around her surviving child ; and now William's body lay
among the roots and dews of the Roman cemetery. It was
impossible for her to keep her spirits from sinking into the
depths, impossible not to feel that the waves and billows
had gone over her. William's grave—on this Mary's gaze
seems perpetually to be anchored. "Let us hear, also,"
she wrote to Miss Curran (June 27), "anything you may
have done about the tomb, near which I shall lie one day,
and care not, for my own sake, how soon. I shall never
recover that blow ; I feel it more now than at Rome ; the
thought never leaves me for a single moment ; everything
on earth has lost its interest to me. You see I told you

that I could only write to you on one subject; how can
I, since, do all I can (and I endeavour very sincerely), I
can think of no other? so I will leave off." And to Mrs.
Hunt, on August 28: "I never am in good spirits—often
in very bad; and Hunt's portrait has already seen me shed
so many tears, that, if it had his heart as well as his eyes,
he would weep too in pity. But no more of this, or a tear
will come now, and there is no use for that."

"Our house," Shelley wrote to Peacock, "is a melancholy one, and only cheered by letters from England."
Naturally his thoughts reverted to the happier days at Marlow and in London, where Mary and he had been cheered
and sustained amid their anxieties by the love of friends.
"I most devoutly wish," he says, "I were living near
London. . . . My inclinations point to Hampstead; but I do
not know whether I should not make up my mind to something more completely suburban. What are mountains,
trees, heaths, or even the glorious and ever-beautiful sky,
with such sunsets as I have seen at Hampstead, to friends?
Social enjoyment, in some form or other, is the Alpha and
the Omega of existence. All that I see in Italy—and from
my tower window I now see the magnificent peaks of the
Apennine half enclosing the plain—is nothing; it dwindles
into smoke in the mind, when I think of some familiar
forms of scenes, little perhaps in themselves, over which
old remembrances have thrown a delightful colour." At an
early age grey hairs appeared among the brown on Shelley's
head, and in such words as these there is already a touch
of the autumnal feeling.

Shelley's "tower" was the terrace roofed and glazed at
the top of the house. Here he studied, meditated, gazed
forth over the wide prospect towards the hills or seawards,
watched the storms as they drove across the landscape, as
the lurid clouds dipped to the waves, or were chased and

scattered by the tempest ; or if the sun glared and glowed, Shelley basked in the excessive heat, with health and spirits reviving under its influence. "My employments," he tells Peacock, "are these : I awaken usually at seven ; read half an hour ; then get up ; breakfast ; after breakfast ascend *my tower*, and read or write until two. Then we dine. After dinner I read Dante with Mary, gossip a little, eat grapes and figs, sometimes walk, though seldom, and at half-past five pay a visit to Mrs. Gisborne, who reads Spanish with me until near seven. We then come for Mary and stroll about till supper-time." The most important addition made in the autumn of 1819 to the objects of Shelley's literary homage or enthusiasm was Calderon, to the study of whom he was led on by Mrs. Gisborne. The poetry in its foreign garb again and again solicited him to clothe it in English speech, and not many months before his death, he rendered, with that fidelity in freedom at which he aimed in his work as translator, some admirable scenes from the " Magico Prodigioso." But translation from such a poet as Calderon could ill content Shelley ; it seemed that at best he was throwing over the "perfect and glowing forms" of the original the "grey veil" of his own words. "I am bathing myself," he wrote to Mr. Gisborne in November, 1820, "in the light and odour of the flowery and starry *Autos ;* " and it is somewhat remarkable to find his imaginative delight so little troubled by the religious ardours of the great Catholic poet.

With high creative minds one effort seems sometimes to leave behind a force and impetus which must expend themselves in a second. We might imagine that when Shelley had completed the second and third acts of " Prometheus Unbound " he would have paused, or for a while have slept upon the wing. But it was not so. From one creative mood he passed immediately into another. And,

as if his imagination found sufficient relief through a change
in the direction of its activity, he turned from the visions
of the " Prometheus," impersonating his own apprehensions
of the beautiful and the just, to a dramatic study of human
character and passion in tragic circumstances. While at
Leghorn, in May of the preceding year, he had read a
manuscript narrative of the appalling story of the wrongs
and the vengeance of Beatrice Cenci ; Mrs. Shelley had
copied the manuscript (May 25, 1818) before she proceeded
to the Baths of Lucca. On his arrival at Rome, he found
that the story of the Cenci was universally known, and
could not be mentioned in Italian society without awakening
"a deep and breathless interest." This profound national
interest in the tale of horror first suggested to Shelley the
conception of its fitness for dramatic treatment. On
April 22, he and Mary visited the Colonna Palace, and
gazed at the alleged portrait of Beatrice attributed to
Guido, in which simplicity and dignity are united with the
pathos of an inexpressible sorrow. The union of gentleness
with heroic strength and energy in woman had for Shelley's
imagination a peculiar attraction ; the tyranny of evil power
and the warfare in the world between hatred and love
aroused his highest spiritual ardour. It was, as De Quincey
has said, the strife between darkness and light in the story
of the Cenci which fascinated Shelley ; its horror was to be
ennobled or counterpoised by its piteousness and beauty.
The drama, as he conceived it, is not so much a tragedy
of unnatural lust as of monstrous and unnatural hate. A
deed which should bring two human creatures into union
most sacred and equal, becomes by a hideous inversion the
crowning feat of tyrannous malignity, the ground of deepest
loathing and deadliest alienation. That Shelley should
have had power to disengage his mind from the visions
and abstractions which possessed him while writing the

"Prometheus Unbound," and should have handled a story of actual human passion with so much imaginative vigour give us some measure of the strength of his maturing genius. The year 1819 was his *Annus mirabilis*, and in one year to have created such poems as the " Prometheus " and the " Cenci " is an achievement without parallel in English poetry since Shakespeare lived and wrote.

In the death of his son, Shelley's work upon the story of the Cenci had a mournful interruption ; but when away from the scene of his anguish and cruel death-bed watching he sought a refuge in art from the pain of recollection, and in his sunny "tower" of the Villa Valsovano made swift progress with his tragedy. In no other instance did he take counsel with any one as to the conduct or evolution of any one of his greater poems ; but in the case of the "Cenci," perhaps because he had at first urged the subject on Mary as one fitted for a tragedy, perhaps because he desired to employ every means to lift her out of despondency, from day to day he talked over the arrangement of the scenes with his wife. The drama, in spite of its painful subject pleased her better than did some of his poems which were freer in fantasy and more remote from human interest The excitement of composition told injuriously on Shelley' health, keeping up the pain in his side, he says, as stick do a fire. Within three months the whole had been accom plished. On Sunday, August 8, he brought the first rough draft to an end (and the last lines uttered by Beatrice were regarded by their author with peculiar affection) ; during some later days of the same month he was engaged in copying and correcting the poem. At Leghorn was a printing office—that of Masi—from which several English books had been issued on terms more reasonable than those of London houses. Here two hundred and fifty copies of the "Cenci" were struck off in small quarto, and were conveyed to England to be sold by the Ollier brothers. The tragedy was dedicated in words of affectionate esteem to Leigh Hunt. "I have written something," he tells Hunt (September 3), "and finished it, different from anything else, and a new attempt for me ; and I mean to dedicate it to you. I should not have done so without your approbation, but I asked your picture last night and it smiled assent."

But it was not Shelley's intention that his tragedy, although printed, should be immediately published. Written with a special view to dramatic effect, and therefore eschewing "what is commonly called 'mere poetry,'" the "Cenci," Shelley hoped, might be set forth on the English stage as an acting drama. Accordingly, when despatching the printed copies to Ollier in October, he directed his publisher to keep the box unopened, or, if by necessity it were opened, to abstain from examining the contents. Hunt would inform Ollier in a general way respecting the nature of the new volume, and in the course of the winter directions would be sent for its publication. Meanwhile Peacock was to procure, if possible, the presentation of the play at Covent Garden. "The principal character, Beatrice," wrote Shelley, "is precisely fitted for Miss O'Neill, and it might even seem written for her (God forbid that I should ever see her play it—it would tear my nerves to pieces), and in all respects it is fitted only for Covent Garden. The chief male character, I confess, I should be very unwilling that any one but Kean should play—that is impossible, and I must be contented with an inferior actor." The author's name was to be kept a profound secret ; this Shelley held to be essential to the success of his attempt, for his public enemies, he believed, were many, and there was one private enemy whose malice, as he supposed, would spare no exertion to procure him an injury—"his sister-in-law alone,"

2 F

writes Mary Shelley to Miss Curran, "would hire enough people to damn it." The "Cenci" was not presented at Covent Garden ; its subject, as Shelley surmised might be the case, inevitably excluded it from the English public stage ; nor had the writer, unversed in the secrets of theatrical effect, known how to fit an acting play for the boards.

The "Cenci" was not ranked among his highest works by its author. To "Prometheus Unbound" he assigned —and justly—a far higher place. The manuscript of the "Prometheus Unbound" was now on its way to England (September 12), in the hands of Mr. Gisborne, who had undertaken the journey home in the hope of obtaining some suitable employment for his step-son, Henry Reveley. "Julian and Maddalo" had been sent in mid-August to Hunt, with a view to its publication, but a publication without the writer's name. Some months since had appeared the little volume containing "Rosalind and Helen," the "Lines written in the Euganean Hills," and the "Hymn to Intellectual Beauty." It was a gratification to Shelley to hear that his "eclogue" was a favourite with Charles Lamb, whose "Rosamund Gray" had given him a high sense of the writer's familiarity with the deepest and sweetest parts of our human nature. In the *Examiner* Leigh Hunt also had warmly commended the "Rosalind and Helen." "Your kind expressions about my 'eclogue,'" said Shelley, in acknowledgment of this review, "gave me great pleasure ; indeed, my great stimulus in writing is to have the approbation of those who feel kindly toward me. The rest is mere duty."

"We shall quit Leghorn in about a fortnight," Mary wrote to Miss Curran on September 18 ; "but as yet we do not know where to go." A few days later, Shelley having Charles Clairmont as his companion, set off for

Florence, and there engaged lodgings for six months. Travel was now a difficulty with Mary, but it was decided that she should journey by slow stages in the carriage; and on the morning after her husband's return—the last day of the month—much regretted by Mrs. Gisborne and by Oscar, the demonstrative dog, Shelley, Mary, and Claire bade farewell to the Villa Valsovano, and were on the road to Pisa. On October 2, they had taken possession of their apartment in Florence.

Florence, beautiful in situation, beautiful in its public buildings, rich in its galleries of art, and rich in the memories of a noble past, could not fail to prove a fortunate environment for Shelley's spirit. But the months of late autumn and early winter made clear that it was ill fitted to promote his physical comfort. The keen, dry, piercing winds that sweep from the Apennines, says Medwin, acted injuriously upon his sensitive nerves; and if his chief ailment, as has been alleged, was of a nephritic nature, the water of Florence, impregnated with lime, would tend to increase his suffering. His general health, indeed, seemed to improve, but the pain in his side, from which he had already endured much, now became aggravated and constant. Yet, in spite of physical discomfort, Shelley had many delightful hours. "I like the Cascine very much," he wrote to Mrs. Gisborne, "where I often walk alone, watching the leaves and the rising and falling of the Arno." The prospect from the Boboli Gardens even in winter filled him with delight—Florence below, a smokeless city; the valleys beyond, gently unfolding themselves from the Apennines; the remote summits clad with snow; nearer, the villa-dotted hills; and Arno in the midst full with the winter rains.

But for Shelley the special joy of residence in Florence lay in his visits to its collections of works of art, and above all in contemplating its examples of ancient sculpture. The ideality of the art of sculpture—each object presenting beauty or passion in an immortal abstraction from all that is temporary and accidental—appealed in a peculiar degree to Shelley's imagination. During his visits to the galleries, he added to that series of "Notes on Sculpture" which he had begun at Rome. These are not the comments of one skilled in the *technique* of the art, nor of one who, like Lessing, had thought out for himself its fundamental laws. They are the criticisms of a poet, who endeavours to penetrate to the centre of emotional life in each marble form, to catch the spirit which flows through the limbs and animates the countenance. To drink in the spirit of their forms—this was what Shelley desired as he stood long at gaze before the monuments of ancient art. In the fragment "On the Medusa of Leonardo da Vinci," we have an example of his power to translate the impressions derived from pictorial art into poetry.

Before leaving Leghorn, Shelley had grieved over Mary's continued depression of spirits. On November 12, when, after only two hours' suffering, she lay at ease with a little new-born boy by her side, her husband had the happiness of observing a new light of content in her eyes. "It seems a wonder," he wrote next day to Leigh Hunt, "that she stays in bed. The babe is also quite well, and has begun to suck. You may imagine that this is a great relief and a great comfort to me, amongst all my misfortunes, past, present, and to come. . . . Poor Mary begins (for the first time) to look a little consoled. For we have spent, as you may imagine, a miserable five months." The babe, who thus was the bringer of joy to his parents, was small, healthy, and pretty, not unlike their lost William. Three weeks after his birth, Mary Shelley wrote, "The little boy is nearly three times as big as when he was born; he thrives well and cries little, and is now taking a right-down earnest sleep, with all his heart in his shut eyes." On January 25, 1820, he was baptized by Mr. Harding, an English clergyman, and received his father's name, Percy, to which was added Florence, the name of his place of birth. Comforting his mother's heart after her affliction of 1819, he continued to fulfil the promise of his birth, and remained her centre of joy and comfort through all losses and trials to the close of her life.

While thus in Shelley's domestic life a new happiness began to dawn, he was deeply moved with grief and in-dignation by tidings of public affairs in England. On August 16 the great Reform meeting held in St. Peter's Field, Manchester, had been dispersed by yeomanry and hussars ; in the attempt to arrest the popular leaders some sabre-wounds had been dealt by the cavalry, and, beside a special constable and one of the yeomanry killed by a brickbat, four persons had died from injuries received on that unfortunate day. Radical journalists had dignified the affair with the title of the "Manchester Massacre ;" the sacred rights of the people, they declared, had been violated ; a new series of dragonnades had commenced. While at Leghorn, Shelley had heard the news of "Peterloo," and feared that this might be for England the beginning of evils like those of the French Revolution. His chief desire was that the liberal movement in English politics should be kept within constitutional lines, and should be unstained by blood-shedding or violence. It was the hardships and sufferings of the industrious poor that especially claimed his sympathy, and he thought of publishing for them a series of popular songs which should inspire them with heart and hope, and perhaps awaken and direct the imagi-nation of the reformers. The "Songs and Poems for the Men of England," written in 1819, remained unpublished until several years after Shelley's death, when the first great battle for reform had been fought and won.

In more direct connection with the Manchester "massacre" was written the admirable "Mask of Anarchy." Shelley hoped that Leigh Hunt might see fit to give it a place in the *Examiner.* "I did not insert it," Hunt wrote, "because I thought that the public at large had not become sufficiently discerning to do justice to the sincerity and kindheartedness of the spirit that walked in this flaming robe of verse." The poem is interesting as an occasional piece mediating between Shelley's visions of the future, such as those embodied in the "Prometheus Unbound" and his political pamphlets. The ideals of man's better life, which at times appear so vague and unreal in the imagery of the "Prometheus," are here conceived with all the definiteness and limitations imposed by reality. To attain the happier life in the future, Shelley exhorts his countrymen to ways of peace. If violence be displayed against them, let their bearing be resolute and calm—the bearing, if need be, of the martyrs of public order ; and let the laws of England be the arbiters of their contention :—

> "The old laws of England—they
> Whose reverend heads with age are grey,
> Children of a wiser day ;
> And whose solemn voice must be
> Thine own echo—Liberty."

These are words which accord little with the conception of Shelley as a rash, revolutionary propagandist ; but they are in strict agreement with his prose utterances on political subjects, with the boyish pamphlets addressed to the Irish people, and with the maturer "Proposal for putting Reform to the Vote."

It was, as Shelley believed, in a peculiar degree a poet's duty to sustain the hopes and aspirations of men in their

movement of advance, and at the same time to endeavour
to hold their passions in check by presenting high ideals,
and showing that the better life of society is not to be won
out of the air by sudden and desperate snatching.   And
that a poet should use his powers to damp man's ardour
for what is best, and to maintain in permanence the evil
status quo—this seemed to Shelley to be the capital crime
of high treason against the spirit of truth and justice.
Wordsworth had been a master with Shelley's imagination
in youth ; but even when " Alastor " was published, Shelley
believed that Wordsworth was a deserter from the cause
of liberty to which his early writings had been dedicated.
The support which the elder poet had recently given at the
parliamentary election to the representatives of the house
of Lowthèr, in opposition to Brougham, made him conspicuous among men of letters as an antagonist of the
Liberal party.   In 1819 was published " Peter Bell," a poem
written twenty years earlier, and containing some of Wordsworth's most characteristic and admirable writing.   In a
flippant notice by Leigh Hunt it was described as a " didactic horror of Mr. Wordsworth's, founded on the bewitch-
ing principles of fear, bigotry, and diseased impulse."
Hunt's friend, J. Hamilton Reynolds, had made its appearance the occasion of a parody chiefly directed against Wordsworth's alleged puerility of style and inordinate self-esteem.
What struck Shelley as most lamentable was Wordsworth's
defection, as he imagined, from those faiths and hopes and
charities which sustain a poet's genius in its onward flight ;
and he believed that, as it were by way of judicial punishment for this defection, a cloud of dulness had settled down
upon the poet's heart and brain.   Thus Wordsworth's career,
as conceived by Shelley, became a type and representative
of the self-betrayal of genius to the stupefying influences
of the world—custom, convention, tyranny, hypocrisy ; his

sensibility, at first strong though circumscribed, Shelley maintained, had gradually hardened ; his understanding, at one time penetrating, if not wide-ranging, had been stricken with panic and perverted. With such views Shelley wrote rapidly in the latter days of October his fantastic satire—half-jest, but whole-earnest—" Peter Bell the Third ; " and on November 2 Mary's transcript of the poem was posted to Hunt, with a request that he should desire Ollier to print and publish it immediately. The author's name was for the present to be concealed ; Tom Brown the younger, that is, Tom Moore, as author of the " Fudge Family," received the honour of a dedication signed by " Miching Mallecho." Nothing written by Shelley in 1819 could fail to possess considerable interest, and in its central idea, apart from the application of that idea to Wordsworth, " Peter Bell the Third" expresses an important truth. Yet Shelley said well in this satire—

> " It is a dangerous invasion
> When poets criticize ; their station
> Is to delight ; "

and we cannot regret that a piece of criticism, more than half unjust in its reference to Wordsworth, remained un-printed until that great poet had won the mastery over the spirits of a generation of Englishmen which was his due.

"I have deserted the odorous gardens of literature," Shelley wrote to Mr. and Mrs. Gisborne on November 6, " to journey across the great sandy desert of politics ; not, as you may imagine, without the hope of finding some enchanted paradise. In all probability, I shall be overwhelmed by one of the tempestuous columns which are for ever traversing, with the speed of a storm and the confusion of a chaos, that pathless wilderness. You meanwhile will be lamenting in some happy oasis that I do not return." " I consider

petry very subordinate to moral and political science," he
ad written to Peacock in the opening of the year, "and,
' I were well, certainly I would aspire to the latter, for I
an conceive a great work, embodying the discoveries of
ll ages, and harmonizing the contending creeds by which
nankind have been ruled." Shelley did not dare to attempt
uch a work as this ; but he designed to produce a treatise
ccasional, and at the same time philosophical, which might
erve the cause of liberal reform by appealing from the
assions to the reason of men. In December, this intended
olume had been begun, and by May, 1820, it was in great
art achieved. "Do you know any bookseller," Shelley
sks Hunt (May 26, 1820), "who would publish for me an
ctavo volume, entitled 'A Philosophical View of Reform'?
t is boldly but temperately written, and I think readable.
t is intended for a kind of standard book for the philo-
ophical reformers politically considered, like Jeremy Ben-
ham's something, and perhaps more systematic. I would
end it sheet by sheet. Will you ask and think for me?"
The "Philosophical View of Reform" was never published,
ut happily the treatise, occupying some two hundred pages
f a small note-book, has been preserved in Shelley's manu-
cript. It is a first draft, with many cancelled sentences
nd interlineations, and unhappily it remains unfinished ; yet
t sets forth the writer's opinions on political subjects with
ufficient fulness, and makes us acquainted with the side
f his mind presented to actual politics as no published
vriting of Shelley's has done.

Abolition of the National Debt ; disbanding of standing
rmies ; cessation of tithes (due regard, however, being had
o vested interests) ; the attainment of absolute freedom
or opinions and their public expression ; the rendering of
ustice cheap, speedy, and secure ;—these were the chief
nds, as Shelley conceived, which should be aimed at by

a reformed Parliament. Such were the immediate object
towards which the nation should aspire. But Shelley gaze
forward to the remotest future, and imagined a time whe
equality in possessions might be realized as "the last resu
of the utmost refinements of civilization." We deriv
courage, tranquillity, and grandeur of soul, he says, fror
contemplating ideals at present wholly unattainable, an
thus we quicken our hearts with "delusions which are n
delusions." From such dreams and visions we return t
the actual ; and "it becomes us with patience and resolutio
to apply ourselves to accommodating theories to immediat
practice.

"These are not times in which one has much spirit fc
writing poetry, although there is a keen air in them tha
sharpens the wits of men, and makes them imagine vividl
even in the midst of despondence"—so wrote Shelley fror
Florence to his cousin, Thomas Medwin. But in truth
was not possible to silence within him the spirit of song
In hours when he did not feel himself capable of pur
creative work, he translated, into admirably lithe and grace
ful English verse, Euripides' satyric drama "The Cyclops.
No rendering from Greek literature can possibly be mor
animated or more strong in its lightness. Now also it wa
in the mid-winter of 1819, and here in Florence, that th
fourth act of "Prometheus Unbound"—a sublime after
thought—came into existence.

Several weeks earlier, on a day when the tempestuou
west wind was collecting the vapours which pour down th
autumnal rains, Shelley conceived and in great part wrot
in a wood that skirted the Arno, that ode in which ther
is a union of lyrical breadth with lyrical intensity unsur
passed in English song—the "Ode to the West Wind." A
sunset on that day the expected tempest came, attende
by the magnificent thunder and lightning peculiar to th

Cisalpine regions. The poem is the clarion-cry of hope in the presence of tumultuous ruin and inevitable decay.

> "Spring come to you, at the farthest
> In the very end of harvest,"

was the marriage blessing of Ceres to Prospero's pair of happy lovers. But Shelley dares to welcome autumnal sadness and wintry bareness, finding in the wild wind which sweeps the forest leaves away an exultant harbinger of the awakening year. Harmonizing under a common idea the forces of external nature and the passion of the writer's individual heart, the stanzas, with all the penetrating power of a lyric, have something almost of epic largeness and grandeur.

In the ode Shelley makes confession of his hours of weakness and pain. "I fall upon the thorns of life! I bleed!" With one who acknowledged that love and fame (fame, which is but love disguised) are the poet's food, the indifference or hostility with which his writings had been received would assuredly have depressed his poetic powers, were not his native strength and instinctive promptings as a poet of a rare and enduring quality, and did he not receive from a little circle of friends the love and esteem which the world refused. While at Leghorn, he had heard of an article in the *Quarterly Review* for April which noticed in no fair or courteous spirit "The Revolt of Islam," and made that poem the occasion of a personal attack on its author's character and conduct.

Leigh Hunt sprang forward to the defence of his friend, and in three successive numbers of the *Examiner* for September and October replied to the criticisms and calumnies of the anonymous reviewer. He had resided for nearly three months in the same house with Mr. Shelley, and how was this "shamefully dissolute" poet living all that time? "As much like Plato himself as any of his theories resemble Plato—or rather still more like a Pythagorean. . . . We never met, in short, with a being who came nearer, perhaps so near, to that height of humanity mentioned in the conclusion of an essay of Lord Bacon's, where he speaks of excess of Charity, and of its not being in the power of 'man or angel to come in danger by it.'" Shelley was touched by Hunt's generous words. The *Quarterly* article, written in fact by his former schoolfellow, J. T. Coleridge, he ascribed with a confident and ready injustice to Southey, who from time to time obtained the credit of more than one cruel piece of criticism in Gifford's review, with which he had been wholly unconcerned.

His health suffering from the severe climate, Shelley had decided to leave Florence in February, 1820. The thought of visiting England alone, or of migrating to Rome, was abandoned, and Pisa was chosen as a suitable place of residence for the spring. The milder climate and the singularly pure water from the reservoirs of Pisa, it was believed, would be of service to Shelley's health; and when he needed medical advice, he had the opportunity at Pisa of consulting one of the most eminent physicians in Europe, Vaccà Berlinghieri, who had studied in England under Bell and Hunter, and acquired fame by the invention of various useful instruments, and by a series of remarkable publications on surgery. The weather in November and December had been unusually harsh at Florence, on which Shelley "Calderonized," calling it "an epic of rain, with an episode of frost, and a few similes concerning fine weather." In January, the episode of frost was cruelly lengthened out, causing with Shelley extreme nervous irritability. During these days, when indoor warmth was more agreeable than the frore air without, Shelley read much from the Bible, and with Mary set himself to translate from that great religious thinker, who had already at Marlow drawn him into discipleship—Spinoza.

On Sunday, January 16, the cold suddenly disappeared ; a great thaw took place. Lovely days, almost spring-like, followed ; and it was decided on a sudden to depart by the Arno for Pisa. "We embark," Shelley wrote to Mr. Gisborne, "and I promise myself the delight of the sky, the water, and the mountains. I must suffer at any rate, but I expect to suffer less in a boat than in a carriage." The treacherous skies, however, did not keep their pledge ; the morning of January 26 proved bleak and windy ; and at Empoli the voyagers were glad to exchange their boat for a carriage in which they jolted the rest of the way to Pisa. "Set off at eight," Claire records in her journal. "Mr. and Mrs. Meadows and Zoide walk with us to the side of the Arno, where we begin our navigation. The weather was at first very severe, a keen wind blowing all the time. The banks of the Arno are very beautiful, somewhat like those of the Rhine, but of a much softer character. We see hills the whole length of our course, now hanging over the river, and now receding in long green valleys to meet others. We arrived at Empoli about two, having done thirty miles in five hours. There we landed and took a carriage for Pisa, which city we reached about six at night. We lodge at the Tre Donzelle." *

* During the autumn and winter months of 1819–20 Shelley was much interested in the attempt of Mrs. Reveley's son Henry to construct a steamer which should ply between Leghorn, Genoa, and Marseilles, and aided Reveley with contributions of money towards his experiment.

CHAPTER XX.

PISA: LEGHORN: THE BATHS OF ST. GIULIANO (JANUARY TO OCTOBER, 1820).

PISA in 1820 was a tranquil, a beautiful, and stately city "It looks," wrote Leigh Hunt, "like the residence of an university: many parts of it seem made up of colleges and we feel as if we ought to 'walk gowned.'" But the days of its greatness were in the past; the number of its inhabitants, said to have been formerly one hundred and twenty thousand, had dwindled to about eighteen thousand in the remoter streets, where the hands of the red-liveried convicts were not at work, the grass had leave to sprout and spread. "A look out upon the Lung' Arno at noonday is curious," wrote Hunt. "A blue sky is overhead, dazzling stone underneath, the yellow Arno gliding along, generally with nothing upon it, sometimes a lazy sail; the houses on the opposite side sleeping with their green blinds down and nobody passing but a few labourers, carmen, or country women in their veils and handkerchiefs, hastening with bare feet, but never too fast to forget a certain air of strut and stateliness." Yet, in its comparative desolation, Pisa retained its grace, and amid all its sobriety there was a certain cheerfulness. The clear atmosphere, the evening sea-breeze, the bright houses beside the bright river, the forest to the west, the gleaming waters at no great distance n summer-time the waving breadths of corn bordered by ledgerow trees, the vine-festoons, the peasant busy in his field, the hills hoary with olive, the solemn Apennines, the clear Carrara peaks, gave its peculiar charm to the Tuscan city. On the whole, the choice of Pisa, with its mild climate and pure water, and quietude and beauty, as a place of residence for Shelley was not unwise, and was justified by the event.

Nor were Shelley and Mary quite without acquaintances at Pisa. At Casa Silva, in the Via Mala Gonella, lived Mr. and Mrs. Mason, with their daughters Nerina and the pretty Lauretta. Mrs. Mason, as Lady Mountcashell now called herself, had been the favourite pupil of Mary Wollstonecraft more than thirty years since, when Mary had occupied the situation of governess in the family of Lord Kingston. In 1791, her "dear Margaret" had been married to Stephen, the second Earl Mountcashell. When Godwin visited Ireland in 1800, the countess was warmly hospitable towards the illustrious husband of her former teacher, and delighted to act as his guide through the beautiful scenery of the county Wicklow. In political principles there was much in common between the author of "Political Justice" and his kind entertainer; but the year 1800 – that of the Union—gave a fatal blow to Lady Mountcashell's patriotic enthusiasm. "Since my country sank never to rise again," she wrote to Mrs. Shelley in 1819, "I have been a cool politician; but I cannot forget how I once felt, and can still sympathize with those capable of similar feelings." Miss Clairmont's description of Lady Mountcashell in Italy, now an elderly lady, is far more pleasing than that of Godwin of an earlier date. "She was very tall," writes Claire, "of a lofty and calm presence. Her features were regular and delicate; her large blue eyes singularly well set; her complexion of a clear pale, but yet full of life,

and giving an idea of health. Her countenance beamec
mildly, with the expression of a refined, cultivated, anc
highly cheerful mind. In all my intercourse with her
never saw the smallest symptom of the melancholy anc
discontent which was so striking both in Byron and Shelley
She was ever all hopefulness and serenity and benevolence
her countenance was perfectly irradiated by these senti
ments, and at the same time [by sentiments] of purity anc
unconscious sweetness and beauty." The Earl Mountcashel
was still living; her severance from him had taken plac
long since; and for many years she had resided in Italy
as the wife of Mr. George William Tighe, son of Edwarc
Tighe, M.P., of Rossana, County Wicklow, and cousin tc
the celebrated authoress of "Psyche." Setting aside th
one fact—and that, indeed, a cardinal fact—that thei
union was a violation of law and duty, the manner of "Mi
and Mrs. Mason's" life appears to have been faultless i
its regularity and propriety; and in spite of their breach o
the bond of wedlock, both were looked up to as person
deserving a respect almost amounting to veneration. Mi
Tighe lived much in his library, and, being a lover c
solitude, seldom appeared in Mrs. Mason's drawing-roon
Those who met him were impressed by his high-brec
courtesy and fine old-fashioned notions of the honour tha
becomes a gentleman. He was, says Claire, "a mos
accurate and penetrating judge of human nature; he hac
lived with the hermit and the sage in their refined solitude
he had lived in the world, and had learned that the mai
bred in the world and living for it has seldom any heart o
conscience." During the early days at Pisa, both befor
and after lodgings had been found at Casa Frasi on th
Lung' Arno, much time was spent by Shelley, Mary, anc
Claire at the hospitable house of Mr. and Mrs. Mason.

These early days at Pisa glided by quietly, almos

without events. Shelley continued his readings from the Bible—Isaiah, Jeremiah, Ezekiel—readings that did not go ill with his study of Plato, Æschylus, Virgil, Shakespeare, or the translation of Spinoza, which Mary wrote from his dictation. At the same time, husband and wife—the pair of wedded students—set themselves to advance in mathematics, but they do not appear ever to have proceeded far. Claire, for her part, was engaged with her lessons in singing and dancing, and she found no little pleasure in the society of Mrs. Mason. But, excepting their friends at Casa Silva, few acquaintances were seen. "I ought to tell you," Shelley wrote to Medwin (April 16), "that we do not enter into society. The few people we see are those who suit us, and I believe nobody but us. I find saloons and compliments too great bores; though I am of an extremely social disposition." He would gladly have received his cousin as a visitor, but felt bound to warn Medwin that the *ménage* at his Pisan lodgings was "too philosophic to abound in much external luxury," and that he himself was a wretched invalid. With Professor Vaccà, who at least relieved Shelley from the torment of useless drugs, a Liberal in politics and in his philosophical opinions, he had some pleasant social intercourse. His purse at this time was far from overflowing. "I am printing some things," he wrote to Medwin, "which I am vain enough to wish you to see. Not that they will sell; they are the reverse, in this respect, of the razors of Peter Pindar. A man like me can, in fact, only be a poet by dint of stinting himself of meat and drink to pay his printer's bills; that is, he can only print poems on this condition."

"I am on the whole greatly benefited by my residence in Italy," Shelley wrote to Peacock in May, "and but for certain moral causes should probably have been enabled to re-establish my system completely." These moral causes which hindered Shelley's recovery were various. It was no slight source of uneasiness and regret that Godwin, whom he had tried so zealously to serve, and towards whom Mary felt such affectionate reverence, should have come to regard him with distrust and even hostility, and that he himself should be compelled to speak of Godwin as his "bitterest enemy." "Added years," said Shelley, "only add to my admiration of his intellectual powers, and even the moral resources of his character." But Godwin had suffered the inevitable disintegration of spirit which results from the worship of exalted ideals on the one hand, and on the other the neglect of one commonplace virtue. He was a votary of reason, justice, and benevolence; but at the expense of every friend and every amiable stranger from whom he could beg or borrow the means of his support. Perpetually harassed by debts, he caught at the nearest means of deliverance, however inconsistent with personal dignity or independence, and found compensation for any loss of self-respect in contemplating himself as the exalted, intellectual benefactor of his race.

"I have given you," Shelley wrote to Godwin on August 7, "the amount of a considerable fortune, and have destituted myself, for the purpose of realizing it, of nearly four times the amount. Except for the *good will* which this transaction seems to have produced between you and me, this money, for any advantage that it ever conferred on you, might as well have been thrown into the sea."

While a painful correspondence on money matters with Godwin was disturbing the household peace of Shelley and Mary, the rascal Paolo, who had been dismissed at Naples for robbery of his master and shameful conduct towards Elise, made his attempt to extract money from Shelley by threatening to charge him with most grievous crimes. Early in June Paolo's machinations became known. Shelley instantly visited Leghorn, and put the matter into the hands of the attorney, Del Rosso. "That same Paolo," wrote Mary to Mrs. Gisborne on June 18, "is a most superlative‧ rascal. I hope we have done with him; but I know not, since as yet we are obliged to guess as to his accomplices‧ . . . Tell my father I have not heard from him a long, long time, and am dreadfully anxious. The path of our life is a very thorny one, as you well know, nor is my anxiety concerning him the least of my troubles. . . . Shelley, of course, is not well; his troubles have given him a bilious attack." They played at consulting Virgil to obtain an oracle as to Mr. Gisborne's future. "For us," Mary goes on, "so darkling is our destiny, neither Virgil nor Homer would unfold the recesses of time, but spoke mysteriously of woes." Paolo's infamous accusations were in some way connected with an infant child at Naples who had somehow come under Shelley's guardianship. To add to his distress, he learnt in June that the little girl had sickened, and in a few days came tidings of her death.

Perhaps it is to this time that we should refer the tale related by Medwin of a dastardly assault made upon Shelley at the post-office of Pisa by an English officer in the Portuguese service—an assault ascribed by Medwin to the prejudice and passion excited against Shelley by the article reviewing his "Revolt of Islam" in the *Quarterly Review*. He stood asking for his letters when a stranger in a military cloak, on hearing him pronounce his name, exclaimed, "What, are you that damned atheist Shelley?" and "without more preamble, being a tall, powerful man, struck him such a blow that it felled him to the ground and stunned him." Mr. Tighe, adds Medwin, tracked the aggressor to the Tre Donzelle, but he had fled to Genoa, whither Mr. Tighe and Shelley followed, but without being able to overtake him or learn his route from that city.

Partly in order to be near Del Rosso, the attorne
employed against Paolo, Shelley, with Mary, Claire, an
little Percy—"the merriest babe in the world"—migrate
in the middle of June from Pisa to Leghorn. The Gisborne
house, Casa Ricci, being now unoccupied, was at the
service. Here they proposed to remain a month or two
and then seek some shelter, chiefly for the child's sake
from the summer heats. The experience of the past ha
thrown a shadow of uncertainty over all their plans fo
the future. "Our little Percy," his mother wrote to Mis
Curran, "is a thriving, forward child; but after what ha
happened, I own it appears to me a fading cloud, all thes
hopes that we so earnestly dwell on."

The first days at Casa Ricci were not joyous day
Beside the anxiety on Godwin's behalf, and the annoyanc
caused by Paolo's villainy, a fresh coil of mischief wa
tangling itself around their hearts. Since Claire had parte
from her little Allegra at Este, in October, 1818, she ha
not seen her child, and had received but scant tidings from
Venice—tidings which seemed even scantier than the
actually were. In January, 1819, Mary had heard from
Mrs. Hoppner that the little one had been entrusted b
her, with Byron's consent, to a maid of her choice, an
that she suffered constantly from the cold. She regrette
that Miss Clairmont should insist on the child's remainin
at Venice, in an unwholesome climate, for the ill effects c
which she received no compensating advantages from
father whose life was now "une débauche affreuse." Byro
she added, would certainly never restore the child to he
mother; nothing good was to be hoped for on behalf of th
dear little one, unless Providence should provide for th
innocent in ways which man could not foresee. Fou
months later, Claire was informed of Mrs. Vavassour
proposal to adopt and provide for Allegra—a proposal t

which, involving as it did the entire surrender of his paternal authority, Byron refused to accede. Then followed a blank of dreary silence. "The most pressing entreaties on my part, as well as Claire's," wrote Mary Shelley on September 18, "cannot draw a single line from Venice It is now six months since we have heard, even in an indirect manner, from there. God knows what has happened, or what has not! I suppose Shelley must go to see what has become of the little thing; yet how or when I know not, for he has never recovered from his fatigue at Rome." At length, by November, their anxieties were relieved, and Mary could report to Miss Curran that all was going on well at Venice (November 18). "Letter from Madame Hoppner," Claire enters in her journal seven weeks later. "The Hero is gone to Ravenna." At Ravenna, in the palace of Count Guiccioli, under the authority of Byron's mistress, Allegra's lot might indeed be hard. Claire longed passionately once more to embrace her child. "I beg from you," she wrote to Byron, "the indulgence of a visit from my child, because that I am weaker every day and more miserable. I have already proved in ten thousand ways that I have so loved her as to have commanded, nay, to have destroyed, such of my feelings as would have been injurious to her welfare. You answer my request by menacing, if I do not continue to suffer in silence, that you will inflict the greatest of all evils on my child—you threaten to put her in a convent where she will be equally divided from us both. . . . This calls to my remembrance the story in the Bible, where Solomon judges between the two women ; the false parent was willing the child should be divided, but the feelings of the real one made her consent to any deprivation rather than her child should be destroyed : so I am willing to undergo any affliction rather than her whole life should be spoilt by a convent education."

Claire's impulse was to start immediately for Ravenna, and endeavour to come to an understanding with Byron. Shelley was prepared to act as her escort. But, on second thoughts, it was held that Claire's presence in Ravenna could not serve her cause; rather, it would tend to exasperate Byron against her. In May, Shelley addressed a letter to Byron, expressing regret that his lordship should have written to Claire with so little tenderness or sympathy; admitting that in her letters, which Shelley did not see, she may have said vexatious things; and pleading that she should be forgiven for her very weakness' sake. Five months later he wrote again. "I have no conception," he says, "of what Claire's letters to you contain, and but an imperfect one on the subject of her correspondence with you at all. One or two of her letters, but not lately, I have indeed seen; but as I thought them extremely childish and absurd, and requested her not to send them, and she afterwards told me that she had written and sent others in place of them, I cannot tell if those which I saw on that occasion were sent to you or not. I wonder, however, at your being provoked at what Claire writes; though that she should write what is provoking is very probable. You are conscious of performing your duty to Allegra, and your refusal to allow her to visit Claire at this distance you conceive to be part of that duty. That Claire should have wished to see her is natural. That her disappointment should vex her, and her vexation make her write absurdly, is all in the usual order of things. But, poor thing, she is very unhappy and in bad health, and she ought to be treated with as much indulgence as possible. The weak and the foolish are in this respect the kings—they can do no wrong." Shelley declined to be "the instrument of the communication of Claire's sentiments or wishes" to Byron; "of course I should be always happy," he adds, "to convey yours to her."

Mary's state of nervous agitation, caused by anxiety about her father, Claire's eager hunger for a sight of Allegra, did not predispose them to quietude or harmony in their mutual relations. Misunderstandings between them grew frequent, with little, perhaps, that deserved blame on either side. "A better day than most days," Mary records in her journal (June 8), "and good reason for it, though Shelley is not well. Claire away at Pugnano." And Claire, in her journal for July 4, with her way of bitter jesting, breaks into a rhyme—

> "Heigh-ho! the Claire and the Ma
> Find something to fight about every day."

Among the "moral causes" disturbing Shelley's health, these unhappy incidents occurring between Mary and Claire must also be reckoned.

Yet life at Casa Ricci had its pleasures. Here it was, near bustling Leghorn, that Shelley and Mary, wandering on a beautiful summer evening "among the lanes whose myrtle-hedges were the bowers of fire-flies," heard the carolling of the skylark which inspired that spirit-winged song known to all lovers of English poetry—a song vibrating still with such a keen and pure intensity. And here Shelley wrote the most delightful of all poetical epistles— his letter to Maria Gisborne. In Henry Reveley's workshop, which he had taken for his study, surrounded by

> "Forms of unimaginable wood,
> To puzzle Tubal Cain and all his brood;
> Great screws, and cones, and wheels, and grooved blocks,"

he sailed his paper boat, not now on lake or river, but in Henry's mysterious bowl of quicksilver; or sat "like some weird Archimage"—

> "Plotting dark spells and devilish enginery,—
> The self-impelling steam-wheels of the mind."

Readers of this admirable poem will be inclined to ascribe to some passing fit of depression Shelley's complaint to Medwin (July 20) that his passion for nature was suffering a decay: "I see the mountains, the sky, and the trees from my windows, and recollect, as an old man does the mistress of his youth, the raptures of a more familiar intercourse, but without his regrets, for their forms are yet living in my mind."

"It is not our custom, when we can help it," Shelley once wrote with reference to himself and Mary, "to divide our pleasures." In the summer of 1820 many of their happiest hours were possessions held in common by both Having on June 26 finished reading Virgil together, on the next day but one they began Lucretius. In the evenings Shelley read aloud from the Greek romances—among which the pastoral of Longus especially pleased him—or from Forteguerra's bright poem of chivalry, mirth, and satire, "Ricciardetto." Although unable as yet to be her husband's companion in his study of Greek literature, Mary was determined to follow him, even at a distance. "I want Jones's 'Greek Grammar' very much for Mary, who is deep in Greek," Shelley wrote to Peacock; and the entry "Read Greek," repeated day after day in her journal, shows how resolutely Shelley's pupil went to work. He had himself entered with spirit on a delightful task as a translator— that of rendering into *ottava rima* the Homeric hymn, which tells the rogueries of the divine Autolycus in his precocious infancy—the "Hymn to Mercury." On July 14, Shelley brought his translation to an end. It has been noticed that the playful form of speech common to the "Hymn to Mercury" and the "Witch of Atlas" is not found elsewhere in Shelley's poetry. Are we to attribute it to his recent readings of "Ricciardetto"?

On June 24 and 25, Mary busied herself with the

Quarterly Review. Possibly it was this which, recalling the late scandalous attack on his private life, led Shelley, on June 26, to address a letter to Southey, begging for an assurance that he—Shelley's former friendly entertainer at Keswick—was not the author of that unjust and rancorous article on "The Revolt of Islam."

To this communication Southey replied with a resolute desire to press home on Shelley what he regarded as truth, and with a sense that, as in former days he showed his good-will by friendly offices of various kinds, so now it was his part, as the elder man, faithfully to instruct, to warn, and to rebuke.

Shelley's reply is important as an earnest pleading against judgment pronounced upon him by one whom he could not suspect of ill-will, and whom it was not in his power to despise.

Shelley to Southey.

Pisa, August 17, 1820.

Dear Sir,

Allow me to acknowledge the sincere pleasure which I received from the first paragraph of your letter. The disavowal it contained was just such as I firmly anticipated. . . .

I confess your recommendation to adopt the system of ideas you call Christianity has little weight with me, whether you mean the popular superstition in all its articles, or some other more refined theory with respect to those events and opinions which put an end to the graceful religion of the Greeks. To judge of the doctrines by their effects, one would think that this religion were called the religion of Christ and Charity *ut lucus a non lucendo*, when I consider the manner in which they seem to have transformed the disposition and understanding of you and men of the most amiable manners and the highest accomplishments, so that even when recommending Christianity you cannot forbear breathing out defiance, against the express words of Christ. What would you have me think? You accuse me, on what evidence I cannot guess, of *guilt*—a bold word, sir, this, and one which would have required me to write to you in another tone had you addressed it to any one except myself. Instead, therefore, of refraining from "judging that you be not judged," you not only judge but condemn, and that to a punishment which its victim must be either among the meanest or the loftiest not to regard as bitterer than death. But you are such a pure one as Jesus Christ found not in all Judea to throw the first stone against the woman taken in adultery !

With what care do the most tyrannical Courts of Judicature weigh evidence, and surround the accused with protecting forms ; with what reluctance do they pronounce their cruel and presumptuous decisions compared with you ! You select a single passage out of a life otherwise not only spotless, but spent in an impassioned pursuit of virtue, which looks like a blot, merely because I regulated my domestic arrangements without deferring to the notions of the vulgar, although I might have done so quite as conveniently had I descended to their base thoughts—this you call *guilt*. I might answer you in another manner, but I take God to witness, if such a Being is now regarding both you and me, and I pledge myself if we meet, as perhaps you expect, before Him after death, to repeat the same in His presence—that you accuse me wrongfully. I am innocent of ill, either done or intended ; the consequences you allude to flowed in no respect from me. If you were my friend I could tell you a history that would make you open your eyes ; but I shall certainly never make the public my familiar confidant.

You say you judge of opinions by the fruits ; so do I, but by their remote and permanent fruits—such fruits of rash judgment as Christianity seems to have produced in you. The immediate fruits of all new opinions are indeed calamity to the promulgators and professors ; but we see the end of nothing, and it is in acting well, in contempt of present advantage, that virtue consists.

I need not to be instructed that the opinion of the ruling party, to which you have attached yourself, always exacts, contumeliously receives, and never reciprocates toleration. But "there is a tide in the affairs of men"—it is rising while we speak. . . .

I cannot hope that you will be candid enough to feel, or, if you feel, to own that you have done ill in accusing, even in your mind, an innocent and a persecuted man, whose only real offence is the holding opinions something similar to those which you once held respecting the existing state of society. Without this, further correspondence, the object for which I renewed it being once obtained, must, from the differences in our judgment, be irksome and tedious. I hope some day to meet you in London, and ten minutes' conversation is worth ten folios of writing. Meanwhile assure yourself that among all your good wishers you have none who wish you better than, dear sir,

Your very faithful and obedient servant,

P. B. SHELLEY.

P.S.—I ought not to omit that I have had sickness enough, and that at this moment I have so severe a pain in my side that I can hardly write. All this is of no account in the favour of what you or any one else calls Christianity; surely it would be better to wish me health and healthful sensations.*

One other letter followed, in which Southey took upon himself to review Shelley's conduct, and again exhorted, admonished, and advised. In the Scriptures and the Book of Common Prayer might be found the antidote to all the evil of his heart. To this letter Shelley did not reply; it was Southey's express wish that the correspondence should cease, and where was the good of prolonging a painful discussion which could lead to no satisfactory issue?

With the first days of August the heat at Leghorn grew intense. It was now far advanced in the season for the Baths of Pisa, but the more fashionable Baths of Lucca had drawn away many of its former visitors, and when Shelley, late in July, had gone to seek a house, he had not found it difficult to obtain an excellent one—Casa Prinni—which he hired for three months at about thirteen sequins a month. The village and baths of San Giuliano di Pisa, about four miles distant from Pisa, lie at the foot

* Southey had written that Shelley might live to bless God for a visitation of sickness

of the ridge of mountains to the north of the city. With their sloping olive-grounds, and marble quarries, and shadowy dells, the hills are a delightful change from the monotonous landscape of the plain of which they form the boundary. The warm baths are tranquillizing in their effect, and served to soothe Shelley's nervous irritability It was probably no cause of regret to him that the large ball-room and card-rooms were less lively and crowded than those of the neighbouring Baths of Lucca.

On August 5, at five o'clock in the morning, Shelley and his party arrived at their new abode. The weather was now delightful ; the heavens deep and radiant ; and all the surroundings promised pleasure or undisturbed repose. The 12th of August was one of the hottest days of the month, and on that day, while Mary and Claire visited Lucca, viewed the churches, and drove around the ramparts, Shelley climbed in solitude to the Monte San Pellegrino, a mountain on the summit of which is a chapel, the resort of pilgrims at certain seasons of the year. Next morning—the morning of Sunday—he descended to the Baths. "The excursion," writes Mrs. Shelley, "delighted him while it lasted, though he exerted himself too much, and the effect was considerable lassitude and weakness on his return. During the expedition he conceived the idea, and wrote in the three days immediately succeeding to his return, the 'Witch of Atlas.'" It was a surprise to him when Mary expressed herself as but half pleased with his fantastic creation. She had perceived that he suffered in his imaginative isolation ; suffered through lack of the sympathy of the lovers of literature in his own country. His depression of spirit would be blown away like a cloud, Mary believed, by one strong breath of popular applause ; and, with restored strength of heart, all his faculties would organize themselves for yet higher achievement. It was not because she was "critic-bitten" that she was inclined to discourage the treatment by Shelley of themes which to most readers must appear vaporous, unaccountable, "hollow like a breathing shell;" but because she saw that a long and great career for his genius was all but impossible unless a bond of sympathy were established between the singer and his audience. Shelley took her kindly chiding in good part, and apologized for his erratic poem with charming good temper. We may rejoice at the fault-finding which drew forth so graceful a rejoinder as the introductory stanzas to Mary.

In 1820, the spirit of freedom, like fire trodden under-foot but not extinguished, burst into a flame in the South of Europe. Shelley was an eagerly interested observer of public events. In March came tidings to Pisa of the successful insurrection in Spain. "I suppose," wrote Mary to Mrs. Gisborne (March 26), "that you have heard the news—that the beloved Ferdinand has proclaimed the Constitution of 1812, and called the Cortes. The Inquisition is abolished, the dungeons opened, and the patriots pouring out. This is good. I should like to be in Madrid now." At Naples, the Carbonari had been watching their opportunity, and it was not long in arising. On July 2, the troops mutinied, and the king found himself deserted; the people from all the provinces joined the revolt. Without striking a blow, Ferdinand yielded to the insurgents, and proclaimed the Spanish Constitution of 1812. A bloody insurrection immediately followed in Sicily; here the troops were on the side of the viceroy and his junta; but on October 5 Palermo capitulated to the forces despatched in aid of the insurgents by the revolutionary government at Naples.

The sword which Shelley could fitliest wield was that of keen-edged song. In the spring of the year, moved by the uprising of the Spaniards, he had written his "Ode to Liberty," in which the grave Muse of History is summoned to utter oracles of hope for the cause of freedom. In August, between the 17th and 25th of the month, was written the "Ode to Naples." Recollections of Shelley's visit to Pompeii and Baiæ mingle in it with his aspiring thoughts and visions of the future ; we listen to the stir and flitting of autumnal leaves in the desolate streets like the light footfalls of spirits ; we hear the deep muttering of the mountain ; in such sounds we become aware of prophesyings around us which grow articulate and must be uttered.

Affairs in England contrasted strangely, as it seemed to Shelley, with those of Italy and Spain. Under the rule of George IV. and Castlereagh no event took place in any way likely to inspire an ode to Liberty. Instead of being caught by any sacred fire, England in 1820 was attacked by the sham ardours of a vulgar enthusiasm. Queen Caroline, saint and martyr, had returned home, and her progress from Dover to London, and through the streets of the metropolis, was "one continued triumph." Lord Castlereagh had read the king's message to the House of Lords, commending an inquiry into the queen's conduct, and had offered the green bag full of poisonous venom for their inspection. The hopes of the nation seemed to hang on the result of the inquiry and the second reading of the bill of pains and penalties. To Shelley this particular instance of heroine-worship seemed a conspicuous example of "the generous gullibility of the English nation." Not that he wished her Sacred Majesty any harm ; but why should a vulgar woman, whose habits and manners any one would shun in private life, be "turned into a heroine because she is a queen, or, as a collateral reason, because her husband is a king" ?

On August 24, Mrs. Mason came from Pisa to the Baths to spend the day with her friends. It was a fair-day at St. Giuliano, and the square beneath Shelley's window was full of movement and noise. While Shelley read aloud the "Ode to Liberty," he was riotously accompanied, says Mrs. Shelley, by the grunting of a number of pigs brought for sale to the fair. "He compared it to the 'chorus of frogs' in the satiric drama of Aristophanes ; and it being an hour of merriment, and one ludicrous association suggesting another, he imagined a political-satirical drama on the circumstances of the day, to which the pigs would serve as chorus—and 'Swellfoot' was begun." "Swellfoot the Tyrant," which dramatizes in satirical fashion the affair of Queen Caroline, is not one of Shelley's happier inspirations. Allied with beauty, his elvish *espièglerie* might have some of the grace of a will-o'-the-wisp in its antics ; so we see it in certain stanzas of the "Witch of Atlas." The theme of "Swellfoot" is ugly, and its author lacked that robust humour which can discover sources of mirth or satire in the gross stuff of life. "Œdipus Tyrannus, or Swellfoot the Tyrant," was published in London in 1820. When only seven copies of the pamphlet had been sold, the bookseller was induced to suppress the publication, thus averting a prosecution about to be instituted by some loyal inhabitants of the ward of Cheap, in accordance with resolutions of the wardmote.

In the autumn of 1820 a change took place in Shelley's household, which on the whole tended to its quietness and comfort. At length Claire, under Mrs. Mason's advice, had taken a decisive step ; had freed herself from the pain of her position in a household where her presence was felt at times by one at least of its members to be an inconvenience, and had accepted an engagement as governess in the family of Professor Bojti at Florence. To Shelley

it was a grief to part from one who had been a close companion during many years, but he was convinced that the
step now taken was for the good of Claire. On October 20
he accompanied her to Florence, and saw her next day to
her new quarters at Casa Bojti, opposite the Pitti Palace.
She was far from strong in health; far from happy in her
circumstances and her temper; separated from her child,
poor, and engaged in an employment which might be
laborious and irksome; alone, among strange faces. Shelley
could not but feel very tenderly towards the exile from his
home, and he was aware that Mary, though the reverse
of ill-disposed towards Claire, could but partially enter
into his desire to watch over the unfriended girl with a
zeal of fond protectiveness. When he wrote to Claire he
longed to cheer her drooping spirit with cordial words
which should make her feel in her solitude how true and
deep was the love of at least one faithful friend. Such
words might have seemed to Mary needless, or excessive in
their effusion, and therefore they should be seen by Claire
alone. The first two or three letters of Shelley to Claire,
written when the sense of her desolate position was keen
with him, contain utterances which, if we did not know
how ardently Shelley gave himself away in friendship,
might be regarded as the speech of a lover. The tone
afterwards grew more calm and measured; during considerable intervals the correspondence was left altogether to
Mary. But though Shelley clearly perceived Claire's errors
of judgment and infirmities of temper, she never ceased
to be cherished by him—cherished even for her weakness'
sake. Perhaps it would have been braver and better if he
had trusted more to Mary's generosity of feeling; but a
man's generosity of feeling and a woman's cannot always
be made to work together. We can well believe that
Claire had presented to Mary a very different side of

herself from that which she presented to Shelley ; it would, accordingly, be impossible that Mary should feel towards her as Shelley felt.   Letters of pleasant gossip came to Claire from Mary ; there was at present no breach between them, but also assuredly no ardour of affection.   More could not have been expected from Mary Shelley; and in such cases it is a man's wisdom to have a loyal regard even for what may seem the infirmities of heart of one who has given her entire self to him.

When Shelley returned from Florence to the Baths (October 22) he was not alone.   His cousin and former schoolfellow at Syon House Academy, Thomas Medwin, captain in the 24th Light Dragoons, recently returned from Bombay, was with him.   Medwin had a *dilettante* love of letters, and lately, while staying near Geneva, he had received an invitation to visit his old companion in Italy, "the Paradise of exiles."   At Pisa, in the Tre Donzelle, they met for the first time since 1813.   "It was nearly seven years since we had parted," writes Medwin, "but I should immediately have recognized him in a crowd.   His figure was emaciated, and somewhat bent, owing to near-sightedness and his being forced to lean over his books with his eyes almost touching them ; his hair, still profuse and curling naturally, was partially interspersed with grey ; but his appearance was youthful, and his countenance, whether grave or animated, strikingly intellectual.   There was also a freshness and purity in his complexion that he never lost."   The season for the Baths ended in September, and now it was late October.   In the deserted watering-place the presence of an old friend brought some brightness, and it was not yet discovered that the inanity of Medwin's mind and character could prove weighty in the oppression of its boredom.   During Shelley's brief absence Mary had studied in Villani's chronicle and Sismondi's history for the novel

2 H

—"Valperga, or the Life and Adventures of Castruccio, Prince of Lucca"—on which she was now engaged; but she had also observed with unusual attention the signs and portents of the weather. "Rainy day and rainy morning," she writes in her journal on the day of Shelley's return; "as bad weather as is possible in Italy. A little patience and we shall have St. Martin's summer. At sunset the arch of clear sky appears where it sets, becoming larger and larger, until, at seven o'clock, the dark clouds are alone over Monte Nero; Venus shines bright in the clear azure; and the trunks of the trees are tinged with the silvery light of the rising moon." Next day and next the rain descended; and when the downpour ceased, the waters rose in flood. The garden behind the Casa Prinni was on the banks of the canal which branches from the Serchio to the Arno; the rising waters overflowed the garden and burst open the doors of the house. "It was a picturesque sight at night," says Mrs. Shelley, "to see the peasants driving the cattle from the plains below to the hills above the baths. A fire was kept up to guide them across the ford; and the forms of the men and the animals showed in dark relief against the red glare of the flame, which was reflected again in the waters that filled the square." Having escaped in a boat, says Medwin, from the upper windows of their flooded house, Shelley, his wife and son, on October 29, found a resting-place in Pisa. "We have now removed," he wrote to Claire on that day, "to a lodging on the Lung' Arno, which is sufficiently commodious and for which we pay thirteen sequins a month. It is next door to that marble palace, and is called Palazzo Galetti, consisting of an excellent mezzanino, and of two rooms on the fourth story, all to the south, and with two fireplaces. The rooms above, one of which is Medwin's room, and the other my study (congratulate me on my

seclusion), are delightfully pleasant, and to-day I shall
be employed in arranging my books and gathering my
papers about me. Mary has a very good room below,
and there is plenty of space for the babe. I expect the
water of Pisa to relieve me, if indeed the disease be what
is conjectured."

This return to Pisa in the autumn of 1820 marks the
opening of a new period in Shelley's life

CHAPTER XXI.

SPRINGTIME AT PISA (JANUARY TO MAY, 1821).

HITHERTO Shelley's life in Italy had passed in almost complete seclusion. At Leghorn, Mr. and Mrs. Gisborne; at Rome, Miss Curran; at Pisa, Mr. and Mrs. Mason, had been his only intimate associates. Now a company began to gather around him, and his life quickened with social interests. "Shelley never liked society in numbers," Mary wrote; "it harassed and wearied him; but neither did he like loneliness, and usually when alone sheltered himsel against memory or reflection in a book. But with one or two whom he loved, he gave way to wild or joyous spirits or in more serious conversation expounded his opinions with vivacity and eloquence. If an argument arose, no man ever argued better. He was clear, logical, and earnest in supporting his own views; attentive, patient, and impartia while listening to those on the adverse side." Mary Shelley for her own part, enjoyed the society of cultivated persons and found in it the stimulant needed to oppose her droop ing spirits. During the short remainder of his life Shelley was seldom quite solitary or unfriended, and Mary found in Pisa, among many acquaintances less agreeable, th exhilarating companionship of persons eminent for bright ness of intellect or grace of manner.

Claire's trial-month as governess to Professor Bojti's children passed unhappily. On November 21, she was again in Pisa for a period of refreshment and repose. The house on the Lung' Arno in the winter days was not altogether cheerful, for Medwin fell seriously ill. "Shelley," he writes, "tended me like a brother. He applied my leeches, administered my medicines, and during six weeks that I was confined to my room was assiduous and unintermitting in his affectionate care of me." Yet in the days between Claire's arrival and the close of the year new and memorable acquaintances were made by Shelley and Mary.

Pacchiani, Emilia Viviani, Mavrocordato, the Princess Argiropoli, the *improvvisatore* Sgricci, Taaffe—to the solitary dwellers at the Casa Galetti, acquaintances seemed not to rain but to pour

It was "il Professore" who brought about the introductions. Francesco Pacchiani, known in Pisa as "il diavolo Pacchiani," a man of forty-eight years old, distinguished as a chemist, was, or had lately been, a professor of physics at the University. Although still received in good society, Pacchiani had fallen in fortune and in repute. He was in orders, but his religion was that of "Epicurus owne sone." "Pacchiani is no great favourite of ours," Mary writes. "He disgusted Shelley by telling a dirty story." The professor, by whom Shelley was introduced to Emilia Viviani, is pictured by Medwin as "somewhat above the common height, with a figure bony and angular, and covered with no more superfluous flesh than a prize-fighter. His face was dark as that of a Moor, his features marked and regular, his eyes black and gloomy." Pacchiani's learning was considerable; his conversation sparkling and full of repartee. Shelley at first, says Medwin, "listened with rapt attention to his eloquence, which he compared to that of Coleridge." But if "il diavolo" was ever welcome at Casa Galetti, it can have been only for a very brief period. Even the devil, however, writes Mary, has his use, for it vas Pacchiani who led to her acquaintance with Prince Mavrocordato.

Alexander Mavrocordato, soon to become distinguished as the foremost statesman of the Greek Revolution, was two years older than Shelley. His father, for a time hospodar of Wallachia, had retired into private life, prizing his library and his literary pursuits above the cares of office. Mavrocordato had an eager desire for study, an indefatigable power of toil. His heart was with his own country, and he endeavoured to employ his enforced leisure in qualifying himself in every possible way to serve his country. The attraction between him and Shelley was mutual and strong ; nor was Mary less favourably impressed by the learned and ardent Greek. Soon Shelley was instructing the prince in Milton's "Paradise Lost ;" or listened to his reading aloud of the "Agamemnon" with an accent and pronunciation which, Mavrocordato contended, were essential to the beauty of the verse, and which Shelley's ear could not endure ; or he and his turbaned friend faced each other in mimic war at the chess-board ; or Mary, who had earnestly studied Greek for some months past, became the prince's pupil in the "Antigone," and in turn his instructor in English. "Prince Mauro is a man much to my taste," Mary tells Claire (January 21, 1821) ; "gentlemanly, gay, learned, and full of talent and enthusiasm for Greece. He gave me a Greek lesson, and stayed until eight o'clock." "Do you not envy my luck," she wrote to Mrs. Gisborne (February, 1821), "that, having begun Greek, an amiable, young, agreeable, and learned Greek prince comes every morning to give me a lesson of an hour and a half ?" And later, "I have finished the two 'Œdipi' with my Greek, and am now half-way through the 'Antigone.' He is also my pupil in English, though not very regular. He is exceedingly clever, as you will judge when I tell you that he has learned English only four months; he can read any prose, poetry with very little help, and writes it very tolerably, and indeed he could do all this two months ago."

If the Greek prince was the chief heroic or romantic figure in Shelley's Pisan circle, its comic or burlesque element was supplied by the Irishman, Count Taaffe. The butt afterwards of Lord Byron's wit, Taaffe looked upon himself as poet laureate of Pisa, and as a learned critic of Italian literature. But Taaffe, in spite of his verse, which, Byron supposed, might be "very good Irish," seemed "really a good fellow;" and his notes on the "Divine Comedy" were not unworthy of publication. In June, 1821, Shelley wrote to Ollier, sending a specimen of Taaffe's translation and commentary, which had been printed at Pisa from the types of Didot, and begging that he would arrange with the author for its publication in England. It was Murray, not Ollier, who put his name on the title-page of the first volume of Taaffe's "Comment on the Divine Comedy." The public did not encourage the annotator to produce a second volume.

Among those who professed the art of improvisation, a fashion at this date, as at earlier times, in Italy, by far the most distinguished and celebrated was Sgricci. "There is a great deal of knack in these gentry," said Byron; "their poetry is more mechanical than you suppose." Yet he acknowledged the genius of the young improvisatore from Arezzo. Shelley's admiration for Sgricci was yielded with more generosity—perhaps with less discretion; and the wonder and delight of Mary were, for a time at least, unqualified by any critical scepticism. A performance at Lucca on January 12, from which Shelley was detained by the discomfort of a swelled face, appeared to Mary "a miracle." The improvisatore's tragic theme on that occasion was the story of Inez de Castro. A *tête-à-tête* of two hours with the inspired poet confirmed Mary's favourable opinion. "I was extremely pleased with him," she writes; "he talked with delight of the inspiration he had experienced the night before, which bore him out of himself and filled him, as they describe the Pythoness to have been filled, with divine and tumultuous emotions." It has been conjectured by Mr. Garnett that Shelley's blank-verse poem "Orpheus" is the outcome of an attempt at improvisation suggested to him by the performances of Sgricci.

Pacchiani, the devil of Pisa, must be forgiven his many sins by all who love English poetry, since to him we indirectly owe the "Epipsychidion." Il Professore, we are informed by Medwin, was friend and confessor to the noble family of Viviani, one of the most ancient houses of Pisa; friend and confessor and tutor, for he had instructed Count Viviani's two daughters in languages and polite literature. The count had given his grown-up girls a stepmother not much older than either of them. Emilia and her sister were beautiful, and their mother, whose manners and morals were those of her countrywomen and her time, feared that they might become dangerous rivals in the eyes of her attendant *cavaliere*. Through her influence they were sent from home, and were placed each in a separate convent under pretence of completing their education. Teresa Emilia, the elder, had now been confined for two years in the Convent of St. Anna. Her father desired to see her married, but sought a husband for her who would take her off his hands without a dowry. Pacchiani spoke enthusiastically of the beauty and accomplishments of the lovely girl. "Poverina, she pines like a bird in a cage—ardently longs to escape from her prison-house. She was made for ove. A miserable place is that Convent of St. Anna ; and f you had seen, as I have done, the poor pensionnaires shut up in that narrow suffocating street in the summer, and in the winter, as now, shivering with cold, being allowed nothing to warm them but a few ashes, which they carry about in an earthen vase, you would pity them." It is not surprising that Shelley's fancy was fired at thought of the beautiful victim of oppression.

The earliest mention of the contessina in the journals of 1820 occurs in that of Claire. "*November* 29.—Go with Mary to a funzione in the Church of San Niccolo. Pacchiani, Fudge [Claire's jesting name for a certain Fuggi], and Campbells. Then with Pacchiani to the Convent of St. Anna. The beautiful Teresa Viviani." Next day she again visted Emilia, and on December 1 Mary accompanied her to the convent. From that date visits and letters became frequent. On what day of December Shelley, in company with Medwin and Pacchiani, first saw the captive girl in the convent *parloir*, we cannot precisely say. The Convent of St. Anna, a ruinous building, was situated in an unfrequented street in the suburbs. "After passing through a gloomy portal that led to a quadrangle, the area of which was crowded with crosses, memorials of old monastic times," writes Medwin, "we were soon in the presence of Emilia. . . . Emilia was indeed lovely and interesting. Her profuse black hair, tied in the most simple knot, after the manner of a Greek Muse in the Florence Gallery, displayed to its full height her brow, fair as that of the marble of which I speak. She was also of about the same height as the antique. Her features possessed a rare faultlessness, and almost Grecian contour, the nose and forehead making a straight line. . . . Her eyes had the sleepy voluptuousness, if not the colour, of Beatrice Cenci's. They had, indeed, no definite colour, changing with the changing feeling, to dark or light, as the soul animated them. Her cheek was pale, too, as marble, owing to her confinement and want of air, or perhaps to 'thought.'" With a prettily pathetic address of Emilia to a caged lark in the convent parlour, Medwin's account of the interview ends.

Of a sudden three persons had fallen in love with Emilia —Mary, Claire, and Shelley. In Mary's regard there was indeed a moderating good sense which to Emilia at times appeared to have a touch of coldness in it. Yet Mary's visits to the convent were frequent, and grew more frequent as the weeks went by ; nor were they discontinued even when she removed in May from Pisa to the Baths of St. Giuliano. At Christmas, Mary's gift of a chain, and her invitation to the forlorn girl to come and stay with her, gave no slight pleasure to Emilia.

Claire's zeal on behalf of her new friend took the form suitable to one who had no richer gift to bestow, of an attempt to instruct Emilia in the English language ; and soon the contessina and "her little Chiara" were closeted together over dictionary and grammar. Shelley and Mary sent her books—"Corinne," "La Nouvelle Héloïse"—and birds to beguile the captive hours ; with letters, invitations and costlier tokens of their regard. What higher or more chivalrous enterprise for Shelley could there be than to effect the enfranchisement of a being so persecuted, so innocent, so beautiful, so spiritual, so exalted ? Not many days had passed before Mrs. Shelley was the "most dear sister," the "adored Mary," of Emilia's ardent and effusive letters—letters still extant, written in very choice Italian ; while the "sensibile Percy" became her "caro fratello," and even, we are told, in a refined and transcendental sense, her "adorato sposo." Transplanted from the language of the south into the hardier air of our northern speech,

Emilia's flowers of sentiment droop and lose their colour ;
and even in their native dialect, after sixty years, the
ardent words of a lovely girl are not quite so quick and
spirit-stirring as when, fresh from the fancy or the heart,
they lived and lightened on the page.

Shelley, in the winter days of 1820–21, did not find the
letters too frequent or too long. An inexhaustible fund of
the power of idealizing lay within him. Womanhood—above
all, womanhood chained and panting for liberty—appealed
with peculiar force to the idealizing chivalry of his imagination. Mary, after years of closest union, had become
a good portion of his own life ; she was Mary Shelley,
daughter of William Godwin, known in all her strong
points and weak points of character ; a very definite, concrete being. Emilia, scarcely known to him at all, whose
life was not intertwined with his own life—Emilia, beautiful,
spiritual, sorrowing, became for him a type and symbol of
what Goethe names "the eternal feminine," a type and
symbol of all that is most radiant and divine in nature,
all that is most remote and unattainable, yet ever to be
pursued—the ideal of beauty, truth, and love. She was at
once a living and breathing woman, young, lovely, ardent,
afflicted, and the avatar of the Ideal. Such illusions may
be of service in keeping alive within us the aspiraton for
the highest things, but assuredly they have a dangerous
tendency to draw away from ordinary events and from
real persons some of those founts of feeling which are
needed to keep fresh and bright the common ways and
days of our life.

"Call on Emilia Viviani," Mary writes in her journal of
January 31. "Shelley reads the 'Vita Nuova' aloud to
me in the evening." "*February* 2.—Read Greek. Write.
Emilia Viviani walks out with Shelley in the evening."
Probably during these days Shelley was engaged on that

wonderful poem, the "Epipsychidion," which he himself
compares, with respect to its translation of the actual into
the ideal, to the "Vita Nuova" of Dante. In the note
prefixed to the poem, the supposed writer is said to have
died at Florence as he was preparing for a voyage to one
of the wildest of the Sporades, where it was his hope to
realize a scheme of life hardly suited perhaps for this low
earth. Shelley desired to detach the passion and imagery
of the poem from his veritable historical self; and this
perhaps all the more because it is indeed a fragment of
a confession, and an ideal history of his own feelings. Its
higher and more abiding meanings, he felt, would live
and act more purely and freely if they gained a certain
generalization or abstraction, and were not complicated
with personal and temporary details; yet at the same time,
like the "Vita Nuova" or Shakespeare's "Sonnets," his
"Epipsychidion" was to possess the fascination of an
enigma whose beauty subdues and stimulates and again
subdues all mere curiosity. On February 16, the "Ode to
Naples," a sonnet, and the "Epipsychidion" were sent to
the publisher, Ollier. "The longer poem," wrote Shelley,
"I desire should not be considered as my own; indeed,
in a certain sense, it is a production of a portion of me
already dead; and in this sense the advertisement is no
fiction. It is to be published simply for the esoteric few;
and I make its author a secret, to avoid the malignity of
those who turn sweet food into poison, transforming all
they touch into the corruption of their own natures. My
wish with respect to it is, that it should be printed immediately in the simplest form, and merely one hundred
copies; those who are capable of judging and feeling
rightly with respect to a composition of so abstruse a
nature certainly do not arrive at that number—among those
at least who would ever be excited to read an obscure and

anonymous production ; and it would give me no pleasure
that the vulgar should read it." "The 'Epipsychidion,'"
he wrote to Mr. Gisborne, "is a mystery ; as to real flesh
and blood, you know that I do not deal in those articles ;
you might as well go to a gin-shop for a leg of mutton,
as expect anything human or earthly from me. I desired
Ollier not to circulate this piece except to the συνετοί, and
even they, it seems, are inclined to approximate me to the
circle of a servant-girl and her sweetheart. But I intend
to write a symposium of my own to set all this right."
Yet the "Epipsychidion" had as the starting-point of its
advance into the ideal Emilia Viviani, a mortal maiden—
"the only Italian," said Shelley to Peacock, "for whom
I ever felt any interest."   And when Emilia, like Elizabeth
Hitchener in the days of boyhood, proved no other than
an ordinary human creature, Shelley felt a certain humiliation in remembering how his heart had been the dupe of
his imagination.   "The 'Epipsychidion,'" he wrote in June,
1822, "I cannot look at ; the person whom it celebrates
was a cloud instead of a Juno ; and poor Ixion starts from
the centaur that was the offspring of his own embrace. If
you are curious, however, to hear what I am and have
been, it will tell you something thereof. It is an idealized
history of my life and feelings. I think one is always in
love with something or other ; the error—and I confess it
is not easy for spirits cased in flesh and blood to avoid it
—consists in seeking in a mortal image the likeness of
what is, perhaps, eternal."   With a like sense of Shelley's
unwisdom, but with less indulgence towards the error of
the idealist, Mary wrote to Mrs. Gisborne (March 7, 1822),
"Emilia has married Biondi ; we hear that she leads him
and his mother (to use a vulgarism) a devil of a life. The
conclusion of our friendship (*à la Italiana*) puts me in mind
of a nursery rhyme which runs thus :—

'As I was going down Cranbourne Lane,
    Cranbourne Lane was dirty,
And there I met a pretty maid
    Who dropt to me a curtsey.

'I gave her cakes, I gave her wine,
    I gave her sugar-candy;
But oh! the little naughty girl,
    She asked me for some brandy.'

Now turn 'Cranbourne Lane' into Pisan acquaintances,
which, I am sure, are dirty enough, and 'brandy' into that
wherewithal to buy brandy (and that no small sum *però*),
and you have the whole story of Shelley's Italian Platonics."
It was natural that Mary should think with impatience of
Shelley's expense of spirit with so little profit, as he himself
admits, to his life as a man, however it may have been
with his art as a poet. As for the hapless Emilia, she was
seen by Medwin some years after her ill-starred wedding;
as she lay on her couch and extended a thin hand, she was
so changed that the visitor could hardly find a trace of her
former beauty. Not long after this interview, poisoned by
the malaria of the Maremma, and broken in heart and
hope, Emilia died.

Shelley's interest in Emilia was not such as to seclude
him from all other interests. "A Defence of Poetry,"
suggested by Peacock's essay entitled "The Four Ages of
Poetry," was written in February and March, 1821, and
was despatched to England for insertion in *Ollier's Literary
Miscellany* by the 21st of the latter month; but it remained
unprinted until many years after Shelley's death. This,
the most admirable of his prose writings, is conceived in
another and a higher strain than that of Peacock's clever
budget of paradoxes. Here Shelley does not write as a
humble disciple of William Godwin, but straight from his
own spirit. Poetry, as Shelley maintained, is the order

and beauty of the universe expressing themselves through the mind of man, and gaining from man's mind a higher and intenser life. Nor did he regard the times on which he had fallen as evil times—an age of brass ; rather, he recognized in the great outburst of poetry which filled the spacious days of the opening of this century a prophecy of the awakening of a great people. "In spite of the low-thoughted envy which would undervalue contemporary merit," he wrote, "our own will be a memorable age in intellectual achievements, and we live among such philosophers and poets as surpass beyond comparison any who have appeared since the last national struggle for civil and religious liberty." "A Defence of Poetry," if completed, would have consisted of three parts, of which we possess only the first, that which treats of poetry in its elements and principles, and surveys the history of the past. The second part of the essay would have had for its object an application to contemporary poetry of the principles laid down in the first part, and would have included "a defence of the attempt to idealize the modern forms of manners and opinions, and compel them into a subordination to the imagination and creative faculty." Apart from its general interest, "A Defence of Poetry" possesses much autobiographical importance as an undesigned exposition of the processes of the mind of Shelley as a creator and an artist.

Claire Clairmont had returned to Florence before the close of the year ; but new acquaintances, soon to become friends, had arrived. At the Maison aux Grenades, on the shores of the Lake of Geneva, there resided with Medwin, in the summer of 1820, George Jervoice, of the Madras Artillery, and Edward Elliker Williams, a lieutenant on half-pay, late of the 8th Dragoons. Williams and his wife had moved from Geneva to Châlons-sur-Saône, and, influenced by Medwin's persuasions, thence by Marseille and Leghorn to Pisa. It was January 13, 1821, when they landed at Leghorn, and many days did not pass before they were introduced by Medwin to Shelley and Mary Edward Williams was younger than Shelley by a year or two. At a very early age he had entered the navy, but soon changed his mode of life. "I liked the sea," he said "but detested the tyranny practised on board men-of-war I left the navy, went into the dragoons, and was sent to India. My mother was a widow; a man married her for her money. Her money he would have, and he defrauded me of a large portion of my inheritance. I sold my commission, marred my prospects of rising by marrying, and drifted here." Williams, although possessed of no scholastic erudition, had, like Medwin, an interest in literature, and he even aspired to write a play; but he had none of Medwin's literary vanity, and was, in freshness and brightness and simplicity of nature, all that Medwin was not. No man ever existed, says Mary Shelley, more gentle, generous, and fearless. Jane Williams had a grace and insinuating sweetness of manner which won by degrees upon all who became acquainted with her. The prospect of meeting Shelley had been for Williams one of the chief attractions of Pisa, and it was soon found that the gain was not to be all on one side.

While Shelley's social life was thus enlarging and enriching itself, if he looked abroad on the state of Italy there was much to excite his fears for that patriotic movement which a few months since had, as Shelley imagined such a glorious birth.

Clasping, through a noble error, as he says, "the shadow of Freedom," Italy found only disillusion, apathy, and for a time despair. But the struggle on behalf of liberty is not of one generation; the battle-plain is wide, and a various points of the strife the fortunes of the day are various. The ardour of spirit which leads to temporary misfortune here may elsewhere be the pledge of victory. Italy might not overthrow the Austrians in 1821, yet, were not the spirit abroad which brought defeat upon her hopes, Greece might never have found deliverance from the Turk. Sunday, April 1, was a memorable day at Casa Aulla. "Read Greek," Mary records in her journal. "Alex. Mavrocordato calls with news about Greece. He is as gay as a caged eagle just free. Call on Emilia Viviani. Walk with Williams. He spends the evening with us." And next day, "*Monday, April 2.*—Read Greek. Alex. Mavrocordato calls with the Proclamation of Ipsilanti. Write to him. Ride with Shelley into the Cascine. A divine day, with a north-west wind. The theatre in the evening." Mary Shelley's letter of April 2 to Mavrocordato, bright with ardent aspirations for the Greek cause, released the prince, her tutor, during the remainder of his residence in Pisa from the self-imposed task of a daily lesson in Greek. "Très chère et généreuse amie," he wrote in reply, "si une seule goutte de sang ne coulait pas dans mes veines, votre chère lettre de hier aurait été assez suffisante pour réveiller dans mon âme l'amour de la liberté." Yes, he would accept her offer of freedom during the hours of tuition ; but his only happy hours henceforth in Pisa would be those spent at Casa Aulla. On the banks of Achelous, as on those of the Arno, he would ever be Mary Shelley's very grateful, very faithful, very devoted friend and admirer.

"My health is very fluctuating and uncertain," Shelley wrote on April 2, "and a change of season brings a change rather than a relief of ills." These sad words receive confirmation from Medwin's account of Shelley's state of " prostration, physical and psychical," in the winter of 1820–21. It was cruel, says Medwin, to witness his condition ; yet he was "never querulous or out of temper, never by an irritable word hurt the feelings of those about him." He walked too little, Medwin thought, and read too much; never was his book forgotten, but he lacked that sign of an orderly mind—a regard for dinner, the central fact or axis of the diurnal round. "Mary," he would ask in bewilderment, "have I dined?" Tea, however, was a liquor that he loved. "There!" he would exclaim on emptying a cup, "you see I am no *a-théist.*" It would be an error to suppose that he was always dejected. "At times," says Medwin, "he was as sportive as his child, with whom he would play by the hour on the floor, and his wit flowed in a continuous stream." Yet his physical anguish was occasionally intense; during the paroxysms of his malady "he would roll on the floor in agony." At Shelley's request, Medwin tried the effect of what at that time was termed "animal magnetism," and threw him with ease into the mesmeric trance. After Medwin's departure from Pisa, Jane Williams became the operator. "How may your malady be cured?" the sleeper was asked. The enigmatical answer came, "What would cure me, that would kill me."

Never before, since he was a schoolboy, had Shelley lived so long on the shore of lake or river without becoming the possessor of a boat. There were no pleasure-boats on the Arno, and the shallowness of its waters, says Mrs. Shelley, except in winter-time, when the stream is too turbid and impetuous for boating, rendered it difficult to get any skiff light enough to float. But a boat Shelley must have, a boat of some sort, and one which should suit a buyer with but little money to spend on his recreation. For a few pauls Henry Reveley obtained at Leghorn a flat-bottomed boat about ten feet long; at Shelley's request a keel was contrived, and a small mast and sail were added. It held three persons, and Shelley in his frail shallop, to the horror of Italian onlookers, delighted to navigate the Arno, alone or with a friend. On obtaining possession of his new toy, Shelley, who was at Leghorn with Williams, resolved to start on a trial-trip that same evening (April 16), and voyage by moonlight along the canal to Pisa. Mrs. Gisborne insisted that Henry, who was skilful with his hands and an excellent swimmer, should be of the crew. Under a huge sail, and with a stiff breeze blowing, the craft made rapid way. When about half-way to Pisa, Williams, standing up of a sudden, laid hold of the top of the mast to steady himself. In a moment the boat was overset.

"That canal," writes Henry Reveley, "is broad and deep ; so finding no bottom, I sent Williams on shore, as he could swim a little, and then caught hold of Shelley, and told him to be calm and quiet, and I would take him on shore. His answer, characteristic of his undaunted courage, was, ' All right ; never more comfortable in my life , do what you will with me.' But as soon as I set him down on shore, he fell flat down on his face in a faint. I left him to the care of Williams, who was already on shore, and plunged into the water to secure the wreck, and hauled the boat on shore. By that time Shelley was recovered, and we started off across country towards a ' casale,' which I perceived in the distance by moonlight. . . . The women were knocked up, and set to blow up the fire on their enormous hearths, which they did with a will. They lent us dry warm clothes, and brought out plenty of good though homely food. Poor Shelley was in ecstasies of delight after his ducking. Williams and I did not care for it. After breakfast, Shelley and Williams walked off to Pisa, and I took the boat back to Leghorn and repaired her."

"Our ducking last night," Shelley wrote from Pisa to Henry Reveley, "has added fire instead of quenching the

nautical ardour which produced it ; and I consider it a good
omen in any enterprise that it begins in evil, as being more
probable that it will end in good." From a letter to Claire,
written about a fortnight after the adventure, it appears
that he waited with longing for the arrival of the boat from
Leghorn, which happy event took place on the day after
that on which he wrote. Mary was his companion upon
the river on May 3 ; and on the 4th, in a sea of glassy
calm, Shelley and Reveley voyaged from the mouth of
the Arno round the coast to Leghorn.

"Claire has passed the Carnival at Florence," Shelley
wrote to Peacock, "and has been preternaturally gay." Her
journal shows how bright and full of varied interests was
the time. But the Carnival had only just gone by when
a blow struck her under which she staggered and reeled.
"Rainy day," she writes in the journal on March 15.
"Letters from Emilia, Shelley, and Mary, with enclosures
from Ravenna. The child in the convent of Bagnacavallo.
Spend a miserable day." Allegra being now four years
old, and quite beyond the control of servants, so Byron
told Mr. Hoppner, he had no resource but to place her for
a time in the convent at Bagnacavallo, twelve miles distant
from Ravenna, his present place of abode. At Bagnacavallo
the air was good, and she would have "her learning
advanced" and "her morals and religion inculcated." He
did not purpose to give an English education to a natural
child ; with a fair foreign education, and five or six thousand
pounds, she might marry respectably. He desired that
his child should be a Roman Catholic, since he looked on
Catholicism as "the best religion, as it is assuredly the
oldest of the various branches of Christianity." It was in
vain that Allegra's mother argued, pleaded, and implored
against Byron's decision. He had promised her at Geneva
that the child, whatever its sex, should never be away from

one of its parents. What are the Italian convent-educated women? asked Claire. Bad wives and most unnatural mothers, licentious and ignorant. How gravely will this treatment of his daughter injure Byron with the world! How fully will it justify Lady Byron in her conduct! "I alone," wrote Claire, "misled by love to believe you good, trusted to you, and now I reap the fruits. . . . I resigned Allegra to you that she might be benefited by advantages which I could not give her. It was natural for me to expect that your daughter would become an object of affection, and would receive an education becoming the child of an English nobleman." Since this was not to be, Claire proposed that she should herself be allowed to place Allegra, at her own charge, in one of the best English boarding-schools, to be chosen by the child's father. "I know not how to address you," continues Claire, "in terms fit to awaken acquiescence to the above requests; yet neither do I know why you should doubt the wisdom and propriety of what I propose, seeing that I have never with regard to Allegra sought anything but her advantage, even at the price of total unhappiness to myself." In addition, Miss Clairmont begged that the opinion of Madame Hoppner might be taken, as that of a person friendly to Byron, free from passion in this matter, and competent to judge fairly of the difference between an Italian and an English education.*

The question as to Allegra's education did not directly concern Shelley, but whatever brought pain to Claire was a matter of deep regret to him. Yet when Byron wrote to him, and when he had consulted with Mary, he did not hesitate in upholding Byron's decision. In no respect could he or Mary discover that Byron had acted unworthily towards Allegra. No doubt Claire, in her letters, had been

* Florence, March 24, 1821.

foolish and provoking ; but her errors were those of unwise love, and therefore she should be forgiven. There was no quarrel with Byron for Shelley to take up ; rather, he hoped that their friendship would renew itself and increase in strength. It would surely be so if Byron could choose as his place of summer residence the Baths of San Giuliano, whither Shelley and Mary were now preparing to remove.

CHAPTER XXII.

SECOND SUMMER AT THE BATHS—RAVENNA.

"THE mountains sweep to the plain like waves that meet in a chasm; the olive woods are as green as a sea, and are waving in the wind; the shadows of the clouds are spotting the bosoms of the hills; a heron comes sailing over me, a butterfly flits near; at intervals the pines give forth the sweet and prolonged response to the wind; the myrtle bushes are in bud, and the soil beneath me is carpeted with odoriferous flowers."

This fragment, written in 1821 in one of Shelley's notebooks, images probably some of the beauty which surrounded him at the Baths of St. Giuliano. From May 8 to October 25, except for a brief absence at Florence, and a somewhat longer visit to Ravenna, he dwelt in quiet under the green hillside, among the shadows of the woods, or sailed hither and thither in his boat upon the waters of the Serchio. Edward Williams and Jane, who was now completely recovered after the birth of her second child—a girl—were four miles distant, occupying the beautiful villa of the Marchese Poschi, under the olive and chestnut woods of Pugnano. There were fears that Williams was suffering from disease of the lungs, but as summer went past these fears diminished, and by the close of the year he was strong and well. During the early months of summer he was

engaged on his play, " The Promise ; or, a Year, a Month,
and a Day," which at the end of July was sent to England
on the chance of its being represented on the boards of
some theatre.   Shelley took a kindly interest in Williams's
dramatic attempt, and had great hopes of its success before
an audience.   For his part, Williams had never met so
interesting, so wonderful a man as his new companion.
" Shelley," he wrote in April, "is certainly a man of most
astonishing genius, in appearance extraordinarily young, of
manners mild and amiable, but withal full of life and fun."
The boat, accordingly, was not idle on the waters which
lay between the Baths and Pugnano.   " It was a pleasant
summer," Mary wrote, "bright in all but Shelley's health
and inconstant spirits ; yet he enjoyed himself greatly, and
became more and more attached to the part of the country
where chance appeared to cast us.   Sometimes he projected
taking a farm situated on the height of one of the near hills,
surrounded by chestnut and pine woods, and overlooking
a wide extent of country ; or settling still further in the
maritime Apennines at Massa."   That poem of radiant
beauty, touched by spiritual sorrow, " The Boat on the
Serchio," has kept fresh and living after half a century the
brightness of a July morning in Italy, with all the prospect
of a long day of freedom and joy upon the stream.

The earlier days at the Baths of Pisa were among the
most memorable days of Shelley's life as a poet.   " Keats
is very ill at Naples," he had informed Claire in a letter
of February 18.   "I have written to ask him to come to
Pisa."   At that time Keats was not at Naples, but in
Rome, enduring the long agony of his last illness.   The
relation of the two young poets before Shelley's departure
from England had been friendly, and on Shelley's side
cordial, yet had not been quite free from difficulties and
misconceptions.   In 1817, Keats had declined Shelley's

invitation to visit him at Marlow, believing that he could best work out the fruits of his genius alone, and fearing that the influences of Shelley's peculiar modes of thinking and feeling might perturb his imagination, or limit its free scope. Keeping thus somewhat isolated, he fancied that Hunt and Shelley were hurt because he had not officiously shown them his "Endymion," and even that they were not indisposed "to dissect or anatomize any trip or slip" he might have made. It is true that Shelley was not quick to discover the full greatness of Keats's powers. When "Endymion" reached him in Italy a year after its publication, he told Ollier that much praise was due to him for having read it, "the author's intention appearing to be that no person should possibly get to the end of it." Yet he found it "full of some of the highest and finest gleams of poetry," and in particular the "Hymn to Pan," in the first book of that poem, was regarded by Shelley as affording "the surest promise of ultimate excellence." On hearing from Mr. Gisborne of Keats's illness in the summer of 1820, Shelley wrote to the invalid (July 27), inviting him to Pisa in words of graceful kindness. He had lately read "Endymion" again, and "even with a new sense of the treasures of poetry it contains, though treasures poured forth with indistinct profusion." "I feel persuaded," he adds, "that you are capable of the greatest things, so you but will." Ollier would send Keats copies of Shelley's books; and as a note of warning against what he regarded as one of the errors of the poetical style of "Endymion," Shelley calls attention to the freedom and variety of style observable in his "Prometheus Unbound" and the "Cenci." "In poetry I have sought to avoid system and mannerism. I wish those who excel me in genius would pursue the same plan."

Keats was gratified by Shelley's kind thought and

friendly words, but he did not accept the invitation to Pisa. Though far from resenting Shelley's counsel in matters of poetical art, he felt that he also was an artist, and was qualified to advise his brother-poet. "An artist," he writes, "must serve Mammon; he must have 'self-concentration' —selfishness, perhaps. You, I am sure, will forgive me for sincerely remarking that you might curb your magnanimity, and be more of an artist, and load every rift of your subject with ore. The thought of such discipline must fall like cold chains upon you, who perhaps never sat with your wings furled for six months together."

It was not until he had received and read the volume containing "Lamia," "The Pot of Basil," and "Hyperion," that Shelley knew Keats aright. "Where is Keats now?" he asked Mrs. Hunt on November 11. "I am anxiously expecting him in Italy, when I shall take care to bestow every possible attention on him. I consider his a most valuable life, and I am deeply interested in his safety. I intend to be the physician both of his body and his soul; to keep the one warm, and to teach the other Greek and Spanish. I am aware, indeed, in part, that I am nourishing a rival who will far surpass me; and this is an additional motive, and will be an added pleasure." About this time Shelley began a letter to the editor of the *Quarterly Review*, a letter never sent, in which he pleads against the cruel judgment pronounced against "Endymion," while admitting the "false taste" with which the poem is "replenished;" appeals to Gifford's humanity by informing him of the sufferings and injury which, as he believed, the *Quarterly* article had inflicted on Keats; and demands a revision of the sentence of condemnation on the ground of the extraordinary strength and beauty of the fragment "Hyperion" in the recently published volume.

The death of Keats, which took place on the night of

February 23, 1821, was announced in the *Examiner* of
March 25, and it was probably from its pages or from a
letter of Horace Smith, written a week later, that Shelley
received the first tidings of the event. Deep personal
affection for Keats he had never felt; but the untimely
death of a young man of genius, the victim, as he believed,
of unmerited literary persecution, moved him to sorrow and
indignation. The "Adonais," which takes its place in
literature beside the laments of Moschus for Bion, and of
Milton for Lycidas, belongs to that class of elegiac poems
which does not aim at perpetuating the memory of the
dead by a monumental portrait, but rather celebrates the
dead through a celebration of grief and an impassioned
meditation upon death. We do not know Keats more truly
when we have read Shelley's poem, but our spirits are
attuned to contemplate aright the untimely and sudden
withdrawal, at whatever time or place, of bright things from
earth—a withdrawal which we must lament, yet which is
only apparent and not real. The chief portrait contained
in the poem is that incidentally introduced of Shelley
himself.

> "He, as I guess,
> Had gazed on Nature's naked loveliness,
> Actæon-like, and now he fled astray
> With feeble steps o'er the world's wilderness,
> And his own thoughts, along that rugged way,
> Pursued, like raging hounds, their father and their prey.

> "A pard-like Spirit beautiful and swift—
> A Love in desolation masked—a Power
> Girt round with weakness."

Yet, though it contain no sculptured portrait of Keats,
"Adonais" is the costliest monument in verse ever erected
to the memory of an English singer. Before its close the
poem rises into an impassioned hymn of immortality—the

immortality of that spirit from which man arises, in which he lives and moves, and to the blessed life of which he returns at last.

An untoward incident came to trouble Shelley at the moment when he was putting the last touches to his "Adonais." "I hear that a bookseller of the name of Clark," he wrote to Ollier on June 11, "has published a poem which I wrote in early youth, called ' Queen Mab.' I have not seen it for some years, but inasmuch as I recollect it is villanous trash ; and I dare say much better fitted to injure than to serve the cause which it advocates. In the name of poetry, and as you are a bookseller (you observe the strength of these conjurations), pray give all manner of publicity to my disapprobation of this publica- tion ; in fact, protest for me in an advertisement in the strongest terms. I ought to say, however, that I am obliged to this piratical fellow in one respect, that he has omitted, with a delicacy for which I thank him heartily, a foolish dedication to my late wife, the publication of which would have annoyed me, and indeed is the only part of the business that could seriously have annoyed me— although it is my duty to protest against the whole. I have written to my attorney to do what he can to sup- press it, although I fear that, after the precedent of Southey, there is little probability of an injunction being granted."

It was not in Shelley's power to restrain the publication of "Queen Mab ;" the work, being calculated to do injury to society, had ceased to be the property of its author But he could publicly disclaim connection with the issue of the volume, and this he did in a letter to the editor of the *Examiner*. Yet he would not have it imagined that he had changed sides in speculation or in politics, or had become an advocate or exponent of the spirit of reaction

"I am a devoted enemy to religious, political, and domestic oppression," he declared in the *Examiner ;* "and I regret this publication, not so much from literary vanity, as because I fear it is better fitted to injure than to serve the sacred cause of freedom." The Society for the Suppression of Vice lost no time in instituting proceedings against the publisher Clark. Such prosecutions seldom attain the end of their promoters ; and the one poem of Shelley's which can truly be said to have had a popular career, is the poem whose circulation both its author and those persons most opposed to him in opinions attempted to restrain

On August 2 arrived a letter from Byron, earnestly requesting that he might see Shelley at Ravenna. The Countess Guiccioli's father and brother had lately been expelled on political grounds from the Romagna, and she herself had fled to Florence. We cannot doubt that Byron's letter informed Shelley of his own approaching departure from Ravenna, and it is natural to suppose that Shelley's thoughts would turn to his former favourite, Allegra, now in the convent at Bagnacavallo. Byron's purpose was to seek a shelter with the Gambas and the countess in Switzerland, and on July 23 he wrote to Hentsch, the Genevan banker, desiring him to engage a house for himself on the Jura side of the Lake of Geneva, and another in the same neighbourhood for the family of the Gambas. At that time Byron intended to remove Allegra from the convent, and take her with him to Switzerland. But before the close of July either his intention was altered, or he had not thought well to inform Shelley of his plans. Although Shelley and Mary approved of Byron's action in placing Allegra in a convent, where her father from a distance of a few miles might visit her at his pleasure, they could not but feel that the position of the child would be different when her father should be away beyond the Alps. With neither parent to watch over her, or be present with her in case of illness, what might not be Allegra's fate?

At ten o'clock, on the night of August 7, Shelley reached Ravenna, and was received by Lord Byron at the Guiccioli Palace. The hours of that night went by in endless converse, and dawn was in the sky before the pair retired to rest. Politics, poetry, personal affairs, were discussed.) Lord Byron seemed to Shelley to be "greatly improved in every respect—in genius, in temper, in moral views, in health, in happiness." His attachment to the Countess Guiccioli had rescued him from the coarse and reckless libertinage of the evil days at Venice, and in the phrase of Shelley, whose respect for the marriage bond as such was slight, he was becoming "a virtuous man." "Poor fellow!" Shelley wrote on the morning after his arrival, "he is now quite well, and immersed in politics and literature. . . . We talked a great deal of poetry and such matters last night, and, as usual, differed, and I think more than ever. He affects to patronize, a system of criticism fit for the production of mediocrity, and although all his fine poems and passages have been produced in defiance of this system, yet I recognize the pernicious effects of it in the 'Doge of Venice;' and it will cramp and limit his future efforts, however great they may be, unless he gets rid of it. I have read only parts of it, or rather he himself read them to me, and gave me the plan of the whole."

With such talk on impersonal topics Shelley's letter endeavoured to set Mary's heart at ease as to her husband's present temper, before it introduced a subject of painful interest, which must shock her moral sense and agitate her feelings. Slander and calumny had long been familiar to Shelley and Mary. Their irregular union, and their rash conduct in the early days, had not alone subjected them to such censure as was natural and just, but had in a peculiar degree exposed them to the aspersions of base and malicious tongues. When in 1814 they fled to the Continent, accompanied by Claire Clairmont, and when, soon after, Godwin was rescued from his distress by Shelley's generosity, it was given out that Shelley had purchased of Godwin his two daughters for sums of eight hundred and seven hundred pounds respectively. When, through the consideration of Shelley and Mary for Claire in her difficult position, she became an inmate of their house at Marlow, the gossips rightly conjectured that Allegra was Miss Clairmont's child. Who, then, could be the child's father except Shelley? These were slanders of old date, and though the *Literary Gazette*, in its article on "Queen Mab," had revived the charges in language of outrageous violence, it did not distinctly specify any new series of horrible crimes which should be laid at Shelley's door. In the spring of 1820, the rascal Paolo Foggi had attempted to extort money from Shelley by threatening to charge him with hideous misdoings; but the affair had been placed in a lawyer's hands, and Paolo, it was believed, had been crushed. Shelley had not spent many hours in the Palazzo Guiccioli before he learnt from Byron that Paolo and Elise had been to work against him with Mr. and Mrs. Hoppner, and not without success.

Shelley to Mary Shelley.

Ravenna, August 7, 1821.

* * * * * * *

Lord Byron has also told me of a circumstance that shocks me exceedingly, because it exhibits a degree of desperate and wicked malice, for which I am at a loss to account. When I hear such things, my patience and my philosophy are put to a severe proof, whilst I refrain from seeking out some obscure hiding-place, where the countenance of man may never meet me more.   It seems that *Elise*, actuated either by some inconceivable malice for our dismissing her, or bribed by my enemies, or making common cause with her infamous husband, has persuaded the Hoppners of a story so monstrous and incredible that they must have been prone to believe any evil to have believed such assertions upon such evidence.   Mr. Hoppner wrote to Lord Byron to state this story as the reason why he declined any further communications with us, and why he advised him to do the same. Elise says that Claire was my mistress; that is very well, and so far there is nothing new; all the world has heard so much, and people may believe or not believe as they think good.   She then proceeds to say that Claire was with child by me; that I gave her the most violent medicine to procure abortion; that this not succeeding she was brought to bed, and that I immediately tore the child from her and sent it to the Foundling Hospital—I quote Mr. Hoppner's words—and this is stated to have taken place in the winter after we left Este.   In addition, she says that both I and Claire treated *you* in the most shameful manner; that I neglected and beat you, and that Claire never let a day pass without offering you insults of the most violent kind, in which she was abetted by me.

As to what Reviews and the world say, I do not care a jot, but when persons who have known me are capable of conceiving of me—not that I have fallen into a great error, as would have been the living with Claire as my mistress—but that I have committed such unutterable crimes as destroying or abandoning a child, and that my own!   Imagine my despair of good!   imagine how it is possible that one of so weak and sensitive a nature as mine can run further the gauntlet through this hellish society of men!   *You* should write to the Hoppners a letter refuting the charge, in case you believe, and know, and can prove that it is false, stating the grounds and proofs of your belief.   I need not dictate what you should say, nor, I hope, inspire you with warmth to rebut a charge which you only can effectually rebut.   If you will send the letter to me here, I will forward it to the Hoppners. Lord Byron is not up.   I do not know the Hoppners' address, and I am anxious not to lose a post.

Shelley to Mary Shelley.

[Ravenna, Thursday, August 9, 1821.]

MY DEAREST MARY,

I wrote to you yesterday, and I begin another letter to-day, without knowing exactly when·I can send it, as I am told the post only goes once a week. I dare say the subject of the latter half of my letter gave you pain, but it was necessary to look the affair in the face, and the only satisfactory answer to the calumny must be given by you, and could be given by you alone. This is evidently the source of the violent denunciations of the *Literary Gazette,* in themselves contemptible enough, and only to be regarded as effects which show us their cause, which, until we put off our mortal nature, we never can despise—that is, the belief of persons who have known and seen you that you are guilty of the most enormous crimes. A certain degree and a certain kind of infamy is to be borne, and, in fact, is the best compliment which an exalted nature can receive from the filthy world, of which it is its hell to be a part; but this sort of thing exceeds the measure; and even if it were only for the sake of our dear Percy, I would take some pains to suppress it. In fact, it shall be suppressed, even if I am driven to the disagreeable necessity of prosecuting Elise before the Tuscan tribunals.

"It was necessary to look the affair in the face"— necessary for Shelley in 1821 ; necessary, since attention has been already directed to the matter, for Shelley's biographer to-day. And, indeed, good is brought out of evil. The happiness is great to witness how all these foul and shameful things are burnt away for ever by the clear flame of a woman's indignant love.

Mary Shelley to Shelley (enclosing a letter to Mrs. Hoppner).

MY DEAR SHELLEY,

Shocked beyond all measure as I was, I instantly wrote the enclosed. If the task be not too dreadful, pray copy it for me. I cannot.

2 K

Send that part of your letter which contains the accusation. I tried, but I could not write it. I think I could as soon have died. I send also Elise's last letter : enclose it or not as you think best

I wrote to you with far different feelings last night, beloved friend. Our barque is indeed " tempest-tost ;" but love me, as you have ever done, and God preserve my child to me, and our enemies shall not be too much for us. Consider well if Florence be a fit residence for us. I love, I own, to face danger ; but I would not be imprudent.

Pray get my letter to Mrs. Hoppner copied for a thousand reasons. Adieu, dearest ! Take care of yourself—all yet is well. The shock for me is over, and I now despise the slander ; but it must not pass uncontradicted. I sincerely thank Lord Byron for his kind unbelief.

Affectionately yours,
M. W. S.

Friday.

Do not think me imprudent in mentioning E's illness at Naples. It is well to meet facts. They are as cunning as wicked. I have read over my letter ; it is written in haste ; but it were as well that the first burst of feeling should be expressed. No letters.

Mary Shelley to Mrs. Hoppner.

Pisa, August 10, 1821.

MY DEAR MRS. HOPPNER,

After a silence of nearly two years I address you again, and most bitterly do I regret the occasion on which I now write. Pardon me that I do not write in French ; you understand English well, and I am too much impressed to shackle myself in a foreign language ; even in my own my thoughts far outrun my pen, so that I can hardly form the letters. I write to defend him to whom I have the happiness to be united, whom I love and esteem beyond all living creatures, from the foulest calumnies ; and to you I write this, who were so kind, and to Mr. Hoppner, to both of whom I indulged the pleasing idea that I have every reason to feel gratitude. This is indeed a painful task. Shelley is at present on a visit to Lord Byron at Ravenna, and I received a letter from him to-day, containing accounts that make my hand tremble so much that I can hardly hold the pen. It tells me that Elise wrote to you, relating the most hideous stories against him, and that you have believed them. Before I speak of these false-hoods, permit me to say a few words concerning this miserable girl. You well know that she formed an attachment with Paolo when we proceeded to Rome, and at Naples their marriage was talked of. We all tried to dissuade her; we knew Paolo to be a rascal, and we thought so well of her that we believed him to be unworthy of her. An accident led me to the knowledge that without marrying they had formed a connection. She was ill; we sent for a doctor, who said there was danger of a miscarriage. I would not throw the girl on the world without in some degree binding her to this man. We had them married at Sir R. A'Court's. She left us, turned Catholic at Rome, married him, and then went to Florence. After the disastrous death of my child we came to Tuscany. We have seen little of them, but we have had knowledge that Paolo has formed a scheme of extorting money from Shelley by false accusations. He has written him threatening letters, saying that he would be the ruin of him, etc. We placed them in the hands of a celebrated lawyer here, who has done what he can to silence him. Elise has never interfered in this, and indeed the other day I received a letter from her, entreating, with great professions of love, that I would send her money. I took no notice of this, but although I know her to be in evil hands, I would not believe that she was wicked enough to join in his plans without proof. And now I come to her accusations, and I must indeed summon all my courage whilst I transcribe them, for tears will force their way, and how can it be otherwise? You knew Shelley, you saw his face, and could you believe them? Believe them only on the testimony of a girl whom you despised? I had hoped that such a thing was impossible, and that although strangers might believe the calumnies that this man propagated, that none who had ever seen my husband could for a moment credit them.

He says Claire was Shelley's mistress, that—— Upon my word, I solemnly assure you that I cannot write the words. I send you a part of Shelley's letter that you may see what I am now about to refute, but I had rather die than copy anything so vilely, so wickedly false, so beyond all imagination fiendish.

But that you should believe it! That my beloved Shelley should stand thus slandered in your minds—he, the gentlest and most humane of creatures—is more painful to me, oh! far more painful than words can express. Need I say that the union between my husband and myself has ever been undisturbed? Love caused our first imprudence—love, which, improved by esteem, a perfect trust one in the other, a confidence and affection which, visited as we have been by severe calamities (have we not lost two children?), has increased daily and knows no bounds. I will add that Claire has been separated from us for about a year. She lives with a respectable German family at Florence. The reasons for this were obvious : her connection with us made her manifest as the Miss Clairmont, the mother of Allegra ; besides, we live much alone, she enters much into society there, and, solely occupied with the idea of the welfare of her child, she wished to appear such that she may not be thought in after-times to be unworthy of fulfilling the maternal duties. You ought to have paused before you tried to convince the father of her child of such unheard-of atrocities on her part. If his generosity and know-ledge of the world had not made him reject the slander with the ridicule it deserved, what irretrievable mischief you would have occasioned her! Those who know me well believe my simple word—it is not long ago that my father said in a letter to me that he had never known me utter a falsehood—but you, easy as you have been to credit evil, who may be more deaf to truth—to you I swear by all that I hold sacred upon heaven and earth, by a vow which I should die to write if I affirmed a falsehood,—I swear by the life of my child, by my blessed beloved child, that I know the accusations to be false. But I have said enough to convince you, and are you not convinced? Are not my words the words of truth? Repair, I conjure you, the evil you have done by retracting your confidence in one so vile as Elise, and by writing to me that you now reject as false every circumstance of her infamous tale. You were kind to us, and I will never forget it ;

now I require justice. You must believe me, and do me, I
solemnly entreat you, the justice to confess that you do so.

MARY W. SHELLEY.

I send this letter to Shelley at Ravenna, that he may see it,
for although I ought, the subject is too odious to me to copy it.
I wish also that Lord Byron should see it; he gave no credit to
the tale, but it is as well that he should see how entirely fabulous
it is.

If Mary, with Shelley's letter before her, asked herself,
"What is Byron's attitude in this affair?" no other answer
was possible than "the attitude of a friend, communicating
to Shelley, whom he had invited to Ravenna and whom
he was 'delighted to see,' a monstrous calumny in order
that it might be met and contradicted." But, in fact, less
than five months before the present time, Byron had used
a portion of Paolo's hideous story as a reason to justify
him to Mr. Hoppner for his disregard of Claire's petition
against entrusting the education of her child to the sisters
of an Italian convent. The Italian convent-educated women,
Claire had pleaded, are ignorant and profligate, bad wives
and most unnatural mothers. When forwarding Claire's
letter to Mr. Hoppner, Byron appended a note: "D^r.
Hoppner,—The moral part of this letter upon the Italians,
etc., comes with an excellent grace from the writer, now
living with a *man* and his *wife*, and having planted a child
in the Foundling, etc." He had promised Mr. Hoppner
that the accusations should be concealed from Shelley. In
the talk of the first night at Ravenna they were disclosed;
and now Mr. Hoppner must learn that his secret had been
betrayed, and that Byron had too readily accepted a cruel
calumny against the woman whom he had wronged, and
against an innocent friend. Such a humiliating position
could not be agreeable to one of Byron's temper.

Shelley to Mary Shelley.

Thursday [August 16], Ravenna.

I have received your letter, with that to Mrs. Hoppner. I do not wonder, my dearest friend, that you should have been moved with the infernal accusation of Elise. I was at first, but speedily regained the indifference which the opinion of anything or anybody, except our own consciousness, amply merits, and day by day shall more receive from me. I have not recopied your letter;* such a measure would destroy its authenticity, but have given it to Lord Byron, who has engaged to send it with his own comments to the Hoppners. People do not hesitate, it seems, to make themselves panders and accomplices to slander, for the Hoppners had exacted from Lord Byron that these accusations should be concealed from *me.* Lord Byron is not a man to keep a secret, good or bad; but in openly confessing that he has not done so, he must observe a certain delicacy, and therefore wishes to send the letter himself, and indeed this adds weight to your representations. Have you seen the article of the *Literary Gazette* on me? They evidently allude to some story of this kind. However cautious the Hoppners have been in preventing the calumniated person from asserting his justification, you know too much of the world not to be certain that this was the utmost limit of their caution. So much for nothing

Mary's letter of vindication, entrusted to Byron under a pledge that he would forward it to the Hoppners, did not pass out of his hands, and was found among papers of his after his death. It remains with us, however, to effect Mary's purpose in a larger sense than she had conceived, and to witness against the baseness of the man who thought

* Mrs. Shelley probably meant that Shelley should keep the copy himself; but as in her agitation, when writing to Mrs. Hoppner, she "could hardly form the letters," and her "hand trembled so much that she could hardly hold the pen," it is not surprising that Shelley should think that she was unwilling to expose such tokens of excitement to comparative strangers.

to spare his own vanity at the cost of the honour of his friend.*

Having as far as possible dismissed from his mind the painful impressions left by Lord Byron's disclosure, Shelley occupied himself in visiting the antiquities of Ravenna. The melancholy waste left by the Adriatic in its retreat cast its spell on his imagination. He looked with a certain interest at the tomb of Theodoric and the mausoleum of Galla Placidia ; but for the beauty of its mosaics and symbolic sculptures he had only a contemptuous glance ; they were rude and tasteless, with scarcely a trace of the antique. But one tomb in Ravenna was sacred to Shelley—Dante's tomb—and there he worshipped. At evening, Byron and he would ride through the sombre pine forest, "Ravenna's immemorial wood," in which the elder poet wrote, at the request of his mistress, to whom it is dedicated, "The Prophecy of Dante." In some quiet spot a pumpkin would be set up as a mark for pistol-shooting ; and Shelley observed with pleasure that, although having had less practice of late than Byron, he fell little short of his rival in exactness of aim.

The way of life at the Palazzo Guiccioli was not to Shelley's liking, but during a short visit he could accommodate himself to the habits of his host. "Lord Byron," he wrote to Peacock, "gets up at two. I get up, quite

* To end this affair, it need only be added that Miss Clairmont met Elise Foggi at Florence in April, 1822, and accused her of having uttered these calumnies to Mrs. Hoppner ; whereupon Elise wrote (April 12), in exceedingly bad French, to Mary Shelley, denying that she had ever said anything to Mrs. Hoppner against either Mary, Claire, or Shelley. She enclosed a letter intended for Mrs. Hoppner, saying that she was extremely astonished to hear that Mrs. Hoppner had spoken or written to Byron "des horreurs contre Mademoiselle Clairmont." "Je puis déclarer avec le plus grand certitude," she adds, " que j'ai jamais rien veuz dans la conduite de Mademoiselle qui pouvait autoriser le moindre remarque [?] pervers."

contrary to my usual custom (but one must sleep or die, like Southey's sea-snake in 'Kehama'), at twelve. After breakfast we sit talking till six. From six till eight we gallop through the pine forests which divide Ravenna from the sea ; we then come home and dine, and sit up gossiping till six in the morning. I don't suppose this will kill me in a week or fortnight, but I shall not try it longer. Lord Byron's establishment consists, besides servants, of ten horses, eight enormous dogs, three monkeys, five cats, an eagle, a crow, and a falcon ; and all these, except the horses, walk about the house, which every now and then resounds with their unarbitrated quarrels as if they were the masters of it." "After I have sealed my letter," Shelley adds in a postscript, "I find that my enumeration of the animals in this Circæan Palace was defective, and that in a material point. I have just met on the grand staircase five peacocks, two guinea-hens, and an Egyptian crane. I wonder who all these animals were, before they were changed into these shapes." Not the least striking of these wild creatures was Tito the Venetian, who acted as Shelley's valet—"a fine fellow with a prodigious black beard, who has stabbed two or three people, and is one of the most good-natured-looking fellows I ever saw."

The third, fourth, and fifth cantos of "Don Juan" were now about to be published, and with the fifth canto, which Byron read aloud, Shelley was astonished and delighted ; every word seemed to him stamped with immortality. "I despair of rivalling Lord Byron, as well I may, and there is no other with whom it is worth contending." The marvellous ease and power of Byron's poetic style were acknowledged by Shelley ; nor did he find in this fifth canto—that which tells of Juan's rejection of the advances of Gulbeyaz—"a word which the most rigid assertor of the dignity of human nature could desire to be cancelled. It fulfils, in a certain degree, what I have long preached of producing—something wholly new and relative to the age, and yet surpassingly beautiful." On the other hand, Shelley could not accept Byron's principles or approve his practice in the writing of dramatic poetry. Byron, for his part, spoke with enthusiasm of "Prometheus Unbound," pronounced an unfavourable judgment on the "Cenci," and said not a word of "Adonais." "Certainly," wrote Shelley, "if 'Marino Faliero' is a drama, the 'Cenci' is not."

The domineering force of Byron's genius produced in Shelley a painful sense of his own powerlessness to play a part in the world of literature. "I write nothing," he tells Peacock, "and probably shall write no more. It offends me to see my name classed among those who have no name. If I cannot be something better, I had rather be nothing. . . . My motive was never the infirm desire of fame ; and if I should continue an author, I feel that I should desire it. The cup is justly given to one only of an age ; indeed, participation would make it worthless ; and unfortunate they who seek it and find it not." "The demon of mistrust and pride lurks between two persons in our situation," he wrote of Byron and himself, to Mary, "poisoning the freedom of our intercourse. This is a tax, and a heavy one, which we must pay for being human. I think the fault is not on my side, nor is it likely, I being the weaker." And to Leigh Hunt he complains of the "canker of aristocracy" which existed in the midst of "many generous and exalted qualities" in Byron's character, and which needed to be cut out. It is evident that a simple, cordial, and abiding friendship was impossible between two such men.

Yet for the time there was more of attraction than repulsion in Byron's presence. The Countess Guiccioli and her brother desired to leave Italy for some time, and settle

in Switzerland. Byron, although he had so far yielded to
their wishes as to order a house in the neighbourhood of
Geneva, now inclined to seek a home in Tuscany or Lucca
and persuaded Shelley to write a letter to the countess in
support of the Italian scheme. "It seems destined," say
Shelley, "that I am always to have an active part in every
body's affairs whom I approach." Shelley's representation
had the desired effect; the countess yielded, and begged
as a favour that Shelley would not leave Ravenna without
"Milord." Florence, where his mistress now resided, was
crowded with gossip-loving English. Byron was therefore
disposed to fix on Pisa as his place of abode, where he
would require a large and magnificent house unfurnished.
The neighbourhood of Claire, and her close relations of
friendship with Mrs. Mason, were perceived by Shelley to
be a difficulty. "Gunpowder and fire," he writes to Mary,
"ought to be kept at a respectable distance;" but in every
case something must be risked. It did not follow because
Byron settled in Pisa that the plans entertained by Shelley
and Mary of wintering in Florence need be changed; the
pros and *cons* should be well considered. "Judge," he
writes to Mary—"*I know you like the job*—which scale is
overbalanced." And then as if a gust were blown back upon
his senses from the loathsome calumny credited by the
Hoppners, "My greatest content would be utterly to desert
all human society. I would retire with you and our child
to a solitary island in the sea and build a boat, and shut
upon my retreat the floodgates of the world. I would read
no reviews and talk with no authors. If I dared trust my
imagination, it would tell me that there are one or two
chosen companions beside yourself whom I should desire.
But to this I would not listen—where two or three are
gathered together, the devil is among them. And good,
far more than evil impulses, love, far more than hatred, has

een to me, except as you have been its object, the source
f all sorts of mischief.

With Lord Byron, the Williamses, and other friends in
'isa, Shelley believed that there would be a security and
'rotection for him and those who were dear to him which
'night not be had in Florence, where English visitors were
umerous.

But one thing seemed to Shelley of more urgent im-
ortance than even the consideration of plans for his own
ousehold. What was to be the fate of the solitary child
1 the convent of Bagnacavallo? "Our first thought," he
'rote to Mary, "ought to be Allegra, our second our own
'lans." On the night of his arrival at Ravenna, Byron had
poken about his daughter. "Allegra, he says, is grown
ery beautiful," Shelley wrote to Mary, "but he complains
hat her temper is violent and imperious. He has no
1tention of leaving her in Italy; indeed, the thing is too
nproper in itself not to carry condemnation along with
:. Contessa Guiccioli, he says, is very fond of her; indeed,
cannot see why she should not take care of it, if she is
ɔ live as his ostensible mistress. All this I shall know
1ore of soon." Before the Swiss scheme had been aban-
oned, Shelley urged upon Byron the duty of taking
Allegra with him, and represented to him the moral
angers of a convent education. "This was all settled,"
e writes to Mary; "and now, in the change of his plans
ɔ Tuscany, I wish to hold him to the same determination
f taking her with him. But how can I do this if I have
othing in Tuscany to propose better than Bagnacavallo?
Iis own house is manifestly unfit, and although no longer
theatre of Venetian excesses, is composed entirely of
issolute men-servants, who will do her nothing but mischief.
ɔ, then, any family, an English or Swiss establishment,
ny refuge, in short, except the Convent of St. Anna, where

Allegra might be placed. Do you think Mrs. Mason coul
be prevailed upon to *propose* to take charge of her? I fea
not. Think of this against I come. If you can now se
or write to Emilia, ask her if she knows any one wh
would be fit for this purpose. But the circumstance tha
most presses is to find a maid to attend her from Ravenn
to Pisa, and to take charge of her until some better plac
than his own house shall be found for her—some perso
less odious and unfit, if possible, than the Italian woma
whom he seems to have fallen upon."

Our latest picture of Allegra is that drawn by Shelle
in the letter (August 15) to Mary which contains his anxiou
inquiries as to where she should be placed when con
ducted to Pisa. "I went the other day to see Allegra a
her convent, and stayed with her about three hours. Sh
is grown tall and slight for her age, and her face is some
what altered. The traits have become more delicate, an
she is much paler, probably from the effect of imprope
food. She yet retains the beauty of her deep blue eye
and of her mouth, but she has a contemplative seriousnes
which, mixed with her excessive vivacity, which has no
yet deserted her, has a very peculiar effect in a child. Sh
is under very strict discipline, as may be observed fror
the immediate obedience she accords to the will of he
attendants. This seems contrary to her nature, but I d
not think it has been obtained at the expense of muc
severity. Her hair, scarcely darker than it was, is beauti
fully profuse, and hangs in large curls on her neck. Sh
was prettily dressed in white muslin, and an apron of blac
silk, with trousers. Her light and airy figure and he
graceful motions were a striking contrast to the othe
children there. She seemed a thing of a finer and a highe
order. At first she was very shy, but after a little caressing
and especially after I had given her a gold chain which

ad bought at Ravenna for her, she grew more familiar,
nd led me all over the garden, and all over the convent,
unning and skipping so fast that I could hardly keep up
ith her."

The Countess Guiccioli's request that Shelley should
ot leave Ravenna without Byron received a courteous
eply, but his chivalry did not oblige him to comply with
er wishes to the letter. It was probably on August 17
hat, resisting the importunity of his host, who desired him
o prolong the visit, he left the Palazzo Guiccioli, and saw
Ravenna sink in the distance amid its forest and marshes.
The visit to Ravenna, although he suffered horrible pains
t first, which he attributed to the water of the place, had
erved his health. "My spirits," he told Mary, "are much
mproved; they had been improving, indeed, before I left
he Baths, after the deep dejection of the spring." In a
ew days he was restored to his home of love under the
live and chestnut woods of the Baths of Pisa.

Byron lingered at Ravenna; but before the end of
August the Countess Guiccioli and her father were in Pisa,
nd had made Mary's acquaintance. "La Guiccioli," Shelley
wrote to Mr. Gisborne, some two months later, while she
till waited impatiently for Byron—"La Guiccioli . . . is a
very pretty, sentimental, innocent Italian, who has sacrificed
n immense fortune for the sake of Lord Byron, and who,
f I know anything of my friend, of her, and of human
nature, will hereafter have plenty of opportunity to repent
her rashness." The Lanfranchi Palace, the stateliest on
he Lung' Arno, said to have been built in parts after the
design of Michael Angelo, had been taken for Byron by
Shelley. It was his hope to add to his little group of
Pisan friends Leigh Hunt, who of late had suffered much
n health and fortune in his English home.

Since the autumn of 1820 Leigh Hunt had been

seriously ill; during many weeks he ceased to write fo
the *Examiner*, and hinted that he must give up even th
Indicator. In January, 1821, Mrs. Hunt, almost in despai
wrote to Mary Shelley, entreating that her husband, hersel
and her children might all be transplanted perforce to Italy
Their circumstances were indeed full of difficulty—the prin
cipal writer for the *Examiner*, which was their chief mean
of support, disabled by illness; his brother, the proprietor, in
prison, undergoing the penalty for rash speaking in hi
journal; some of the children exchanging the discomfor
of measles for the acuter misery of scarlet fever; little
Mary, the gayest of the gay, moaning in the anguish o
rheumatism; the baby given over in convulsions; Mrs. Hunt
hardly allowing herself time to wipe her eyes, and followed
from room to room by her ghost of a husband. During
Shelley's visit to Ravenna he heard from Byron of the gift
of his "Memoirs" to Moore, and of Murray's purchase of
the manuscript for two thousand pounds. Shelley's instant
thought was for his friend in England, poor and ailing, and
of the power which Byron possessed to lighten his burden
of distress. But Byron was not a man of whom he could
ask a pecuniary favour, even on behalf of a common friend.
Something better, as it seemed, than a gift of money was
the outcome of his conferences with Byron. It was proposed by Byron that Leigh Hunt should come to Italy,
and go shares with himself and Shelley in a periodical, in
which each of the contracting parties should publish all
their original compositions. The profits, which must be
considerable, should be shared between them. Shelley did
not choose to shackle himself in the free expression of his
opinions by partnership with others who might suffer on
his account, and his pride or sense of self-respect forbade
him, who as an independent writer had never obtained a
hold upon the public, from seeking to shine with a borrowed

plendour and sharing profits which he had not contributed
o earn.   But it was otherwise with Hunt ; he had already
a large circle of admirers, and had long been prominent as
a Liberal journalist.   Shelley wrote accordingly from Pisa to
his friend, informing him of Byron's proposal, and urging
his immediate departure from England.   Hunt's spirits,
easily set dancing, now leaped with pleasure, and the blood
ran lightly through his veins.   "We will divide the world
between us," he wrote, "like the Triumvirate, and you shall
be the sleeping partner, if you will ; only it shall be with
a Cleopatra, and your dreams shall be worth the giving of
kingdoms."

In the early days of September, just when Leigh Hunt
heard the good news which brought him to Italy, Shelley
with Mary started on a holiday excursion northwards to
the coast, desiring to ascertain whether it would be feasible
to spend a summer at Spezzia.   The relations between
Mary and Claire had been cordial of late, so Claire also was
of the party.   A faint chill touches our spirits when we
see in Mary's journal for the first time the name of the
place of doom.   "*Saturday, September* 8.—Journey to
Spezzia.   Dine on the road under the trees.   Arrive at La
Spezzia."   But the September days were bright, and after
sunset the glory of the moon was on the sea ; the bay on
which they rowed or sailed was lovely to enchantment, with
its hills of vine and olive and chestnut, and villages nestling
under the cliffs.   And as they returned they lingered under
the old castle at Massa, and saw the grey peaks of the
marble-quarried hills of Carrara under the magic of the moonlight.   On the day of their arrival at the Baths the weather
broke, but they pushed on to Pugnano to tell Edward and
Jane Williams the story of their happy wanderings.

"I am full of thoughts and plans," Shelley wrote to
Leigh Hunt in August, "and should do something if the

feeble and irritable frame which encloses it was willing to obey the spirit." Of the larger designs which occupied his imagination, he did not achieve one ; but a sudden inspiration in the late summer or early autumn of 1821 produced a work remarkable as a poet's vision of contemporary events, and a prophecy arising out of that vision. Interested in the cause of Greece, not only on general grounds, but because their friend, Prince Mavrocordato, was a chief actor in the great drama, Shelley and Mary read eagerly the newspaper reports of the progress of the war. In Shelley's lyrical drama the actual occurrences are idealized ; a perspective is created for the imagination ; the words of the snowy-bearded, glittering-eyed Ahasuerus—the immortal wanderer—sound strange indeed, yet hardly miraculous, amid the wonderful chants of the captive Greek women and the soft lullabies of the Indian slave. In the " Persæ " of Æschylus Shelley found a precedent, and to a considerable extent a model, for his poetic treatment of contemporary history ; but the projected prologue to his drama, of which a magnificent fragment was written, recalls rather the opening of the Book of Job, or the prologue to Goethe's " Faust," than the play of Æschylus.

He regarded his poem, not as a work of art like " Adonais," but as "a mere improvise," deriving its interest solely from the intense sympathy which he felt with the cause he would celebrate. To Prince Mavrocordato the " Hellas " is dedicated in words of admiration and ardent sympathy. The last stanza of the final chorus of the drama is a prayer that the brooding wings of the bird of peace— the dove, and not the eagle—may soothe our weary world to rest.

CHAPTER XXIII.

WITH BYRON IN PISA.

THE dedication to "Hellas" is dated November 1. On that day Claire Clairmont was on her way back to Professor Bojti's at Florence ; just before she entered the narrow streets of Empoli, Byron with his travelling train passed her on the road, as he drove forward to take possession of the Lanfranchi Palace. Five days earlier (October 25), Shelley and Mary had left the Baths, and entered the new apartment, which they had furnished for themselves, at the top of the Tre Palazzi di Chiesa on the Lung' Arno, just opposite Byron's prouder dwelling-place. Their rooms had the advantage of looking south over the country towards the sea, thus avoiding the bustle and ill odours of the town. Shelley, whose temperament was that of a salamander, loved the sun alike in winter and summer ; and its vivifying rays expanded the buds and leaves of plants with which Mary made bright her sitting-room, and which still bloom for us in the verses on the Zucca, and the description of the magic plant in that unfinished drama which has the enamoured enchantress for its heroine. Here he hoped to gather his books about him--Calderon, Goethe, Kant, Plato, and the Greek dramatists ; here he desired to "entrench" himself amid his studies "like a spider in his web." Once again he felt the powerful attractions of Spinoza's genius,

2 L

and dictated to Williams (November 11–13) considerable fragments of a translation of the "Tractatus Theologico-Politicus," which Shelley thought might be printed at Pisa, and to which Byron consented to lend his name. In the afternoons Mary drove with the Countess Guiccioli—"a nice pretty girl," so Mary describes her, "without pretensions, good-hearted, and amiable," who with her young brother, Pietro Gamba, was often an evening visitor at the Tre Palazzi. Sometimes, from the lower flat which they occupied in the same house, Edward and Jane Williams came upstairs, and Shelley would read aloud to them and Mary. In reading aloud, the soft vibrating tone of Shelley's voice, "emphatic, pleasant, and persuasive," acquired a "sustained song-like quality," which came out more strongly when he recited verse. On occasions Shelley's presence would be required at one of Byron's weekly dinners at the Palazzo Lanfranchi, "when," he writes, "my nerves are generally shaken to pieces by sitting up contemplating, the rest making themselves vats of claret, etc., till three o'clock in the morning." Byron's love of banter, mystification, and cynicism but half sincere, often made his conversation wearisome ; but with Shelley he would talk seriously and confidentially. Shelley's resolute yet gentle opposition to received opinions, his unshrinking yet amiable warfare with the world, amused Byron, and at the same time excited his admiration. Mephistopheles, in "Faust," calls the serpent who tempted Eve "my aunt, the renowned snake ;" and Byron insisted that Shelley was one of her nephews walking about on the tip of his tail ; "his bright eyes, slim figure, and noiseless movements, strengthened, if they did not suggest, the comparison." But if Byron smiled at the snake, he also recognized with a certain delight his frankness, courage, and hardihood of opinion. Moore had taken upon himself the duty of warning Byron against his intended coalition with Shelley and Hunt. "To-day I had another letter warning me against the Snake," said Byron. "He alone, in this age of humbug, dares stem the current, as he did to-day the flooded Arno in his skiff, although I could not observe he made any progress. The attempt is better than being swept along as all the rest are, with the filthy garbage scoured from its banks." "As to poor Shelley," he writes in a letter to Moore, "who is another bugbear to you and the world, he is, to my knowledge, the *least* selfish and the mildest of men—a man who has made more sacrifices of his fortune and feelings for others than any I ever heard of. With his speculative opinions I have nothing in common, nor desire to have."

Shelley's contention now was not with the Founder of the Christian religion, but with historical Christianity, and on December 12, 1821, it seemed to him that he stood in presence of a signal example of the fatal spirit of fanaticism and cruelty which superstition engenders. While he and Mary were walking on that day with Edward and Jane Williams, a rumour reached them of a high crime and misdemeanour committed in the Infanta's duchy of Lucca, and of its intended punishment. The sacramental cup, or the wafer-box, had been sacrilegiously stolen from a church ; the elements had been scattered about the church or spilt upon the road. Happily the culprit was now in the hands of justice, and it was decreed that on the morrow he should die at the stake. Shelley, Medwin, and Byron instantly held a council as to what measures should be taken to save the offender's life. Might they not ride next morning to Lucca, Shelley asked, rescue the prisoner, and hurry him away to the Tuscan frontier, where he might be safe ? The English residents should sign a memorial to the Grand-Duke, who happened to be in Pisa, begging for his inter-position ; Lord Guilford might be moved to use his influence.

Meanwhile, it would be prudent to make sure of their facts. Taaffe, gallantly forgetful of a broken head testifying to the skill in horsemanship on which he prided himself, was off and away to Lucca, and when he returned with the true story, the excitement was at an end. The criminal, a priest, had fled to Florence, where he had given himself up to the police. It had been decided that he should not be handed over to the authorities at Lucca except on condition that he were dealt with, not by Spanish law, but by the milder code of Tuscany. That Shelley's "fellow-serpent" should be scotched for an act of theft and impiety was not unreasonable.

Companionship with Byron had made Shelley once more a rider, and the exercise on horseback had served his health. Even in winter and wild weather his boat was to be seen at times breasting the current of the Arno. But to a considerable extent during these winter months his horse stood him in stead of the canoe. When Byron first came to Pisa, he arranged with his friends to practise pistol-shooting in the garden of the Lanfranchi Palace ; but all firing within the city walls was forbidden by the governor. After a while, a quiet spot, suitable for his purpose, was discovered in a vineyard to the east of the city, and thither Byron and his pistol club—Shelley, Williams, Medwin, Taaffe, Pietro Gamba—would ride in the afternoon. A half-crown placed in the slit of a cane, which was fixed in the ground, served often for a mark. Although his hand trembled, Byron was an excellent marksman. Shelley, whose hand, says Medwin, was all firmness, almost equalled him in accuracy of aim. It is satisfactory to have evidence that the author of "The Sensitive Plant" showed no lack of steadiness of nerve and eye.

The Mediterranean storms which strewed the coasts with wrecks in the winter of 1821, did not endanger the lives of

Leigh Hunt and his family. On November 15, they had embarked at Blackwall on board a small brig, in which, cooped in a cabin, narrow, chill, and dim, they endured some days of miserable tossing and tumbling about the Channel. The winds seemed as if they had been commissioned by Lord Castlereagh to baffle the hopes of the some-time editor of the *Examiner*. By the end of the year the voyagers had got as far as Dartmouth, where parting from their hapless brig, they decided to proceed to Plymouth and there wait for a more favourable season. If they were lucky in their next vessel, said Hogg, writing in January, 1822, they might hope to spend next Christmas at Falmouth. At the Palazzo Lanfranchi, the ground floor —clean and spacious rooms—had been set apart by Byron for Hunt's accommodation, and Mary Shelley had been busy buying furniture (for which Byron insisted on paying), and arranging it so that all might be neat and comfortable on her friend's arrival.

Before the close of January Shelley had heard that the Hunts were still in England, and it was evident that a large family could not subsist on the air, or on grass of the roadside. "My dearest friend," Shelley wrote (January 25), "I send you by return of post £150, within 30 or 40 of what I had contrived to scrape together. How I am to assemble the constituents of such a sum again I do not at present see; but do not be disheartened—we will all put our shoulders to the wheel. Let me not speak of my own disappointment, which, great as it is at not seeing you here, is all swallowed up in sympathy with your present situation. Our anxiety during the continuance of the succession of tempests which one morning seemed to rain lightnings into Pisa, and amongst others struck the palace adjoining Lord Byron's, and turned the Arno into a raging sea, was, as you may conceive, excessive, and our first relief was your letter from Ramsgate. Between the interval of that and your letter of December 28, we were in daily expectation of your arrival. Yesterday arrived that dated January 6." Shelley could not incur any obligation in the matter of money to Byron, nor place the burden of relieving the Hunts on his shoulders. Would it be possible, he asked Hunt, to find a publisher willing to purchase for £150 or £200 the copyright of the play of "Charles the First" on which he was now engaged? In any case, it was expedient that Hunt should hasten to Italy—"debts, responsibilities, and expenses will enmesh you round about if you delay, and force you back into that circle from which I made a push to draw you." To linger and loiter must prove in every way inexpedient. Already Byron was faltering with respect to his project of the new quarterly—the *Hesperides* or the *Liberal,* whichever it should be named. Yet, while urging Hunt forward, Shelley added a prudent word of warning against leaving England until some means of support other than that to be derived from the projected quarterly had been secured. Hunt's renewed entreaties that he should ask a loan of money from Byron, at length overcame Shelley's resistance. "Hunt had urged me more than once," he wrote to Byron (February 15, 1822), "to ask you to lend him this money. My answer consisted in sending him all I could spare, which I have now literally done." Shelley did not think that Hunt's promise to pay in a given time was worth very much ; but he undertook to be himself responsible for any engagement which Hunt might have proposed to Byron. More important, however, than any loan of money was Byron's disposition with reference to the project of the *Liberal.* Before the close of February, difficulties unconnected with Hunt had arisen, as we shall afterwards see, between Shelley and Byron ; but Shelley's regard for the interests of his friend called forth whatever tact he possessed, and he succeeded in holding Byron to his original design, although manuscripts of the impatient poet were ready for publication and were eager to see the light. "I imagine," Shelley wrote to Hunt, "it will be no very difficult task to execute that which you have assigned me—to keep him in heart with the project until your arrival. . . . Particular circumstances, or rather, I should say, particular dispositions in Lord Byron's character, render the close and exclusive intimacy with him in which I find myself intolerable to me ; thus much, my best friend, I will confess and confide to you. No feelings of my own shall injure or interfere with what is now nearest to them—your interest ; and I will take care to preserve the little influence I may have over this Proteus in whom such strange extremes are reconciled until we meet—which we now must, at all events, soon do."

The opening year had not brought Hunt to Pisa, but it added to the circle of Shelley's acquaintances one remarkable figure. Edward John Trelawny, the younger son of an officer in the army belonging to an old Cornish family, now in his thirtieth year, had led a life of wandering and adventure by sea and land ; he had gathered no great store of book-learning, and was but half-educated from a scholarly point of view, but he had looked on life and the world with the eyes of a man of genius who was also a man of action. He viewed the conventional rules and proprieties of society with impatient scorn ; the received opinions could take no hold upon his mind ; every atom of his nature was alive with vivid life ; he was a modern pagan, with generous instincts and a romantic imagination ; and as picturesque in person as he was original in character. At Geneva he had heard of Shelley from Thomas Medwin—his inspired boyhood, his genius, his virtues, and sufferings. Now it was Trelawny's

intention, in company with Edward Williams and an old
naval friend, Captain Daniel Roberts, to hunt during the
winter months in the wildest parts of the Maremma, and
he had shipped his guns and dogs for Leghorn. From
Genoa he had driven to Pisa to find Williams, and to form
the acquaintance of Shelley and Byron, with whom he hoped
to spend the following summer, boating in the Mediterranean.

"The Williamses," he writes, in a well-known and delightful chapter of his "Recollections," "received me in their
earnest cordial manner; we had a great deal to communicate to each other, and were in loud and animated conversation, when I was rather put out by observing in the
passage near the open door, opposite to where I sat, a pair
of glittering eyes steadily fixed on mine; it was too dark
to make out whom they belonged to. With the acuteness
of a woman, Mrs. Williams's eyes followed the direction of
mine, and going to the doorway she laughingly said—

"'Come in, Shelley; it's only our friend Tre just arrived.'

"Swiftly gliding in, blushing like a girl, a tall thin
stripling held out both his hands; and although I could
hardly believe, as I looked at his flushed, feminine, and
artless face, that it could be the poet, I returned his warm
pressure. After the ordinary greetings and courtesies he
sat down and listened. I was silent with astonishment:
was it possible this mild-looking, beardless boy could be the
veritable monster at war with all the world? . . . I could not
believe it; it must be a hoax. He was habited like a boy,
in a black jacket and trousers, which he seemed to have
outgrown, or his tailor, as is the custom, had most shamefully
stinted him in his 'sizings.' Mrs. Williams saw my embarrass-
ment, and to relieve me asked Shelley what book he had in
his hand. His face brightened, and he answered briskly—

"'Calderon's "Magico Prodigioso." I am translating
some passages of it.'

"'Oh, read it to us!'

"Shoved off from the shore of commonplace incidents that could not interest him, and fairly launched on a theme that did, he instantly became oblivious of everything but the book in his hand. The masterly manner in which he analyzed the genius of the author, his lucid interpretation of the story, and the ease with which he translated into our language the most subtle and imaginative passages of the Spanish poet, were marvellous, as was his command of the two languages. After this touch of his quality I no longer doubted his identity ; a dead silence ensued ; looking up I asked—

"'Where is he?'"

"Mrs. Williams said, 'Who? Shelley? Oh, he comes and goes like a spirit, no one knows where or when.'"

Trelawny, whom Hunt pictures "with his knight-errant aspect, dark, handsome, and mustachioed," interested Shelley and Mary more perhaps than any acquaintance whom they had made since Prince Mavrocordato sailed for Greece. "A kind of half-Arab Englishman," so Mary described him to Mrs. Gisborne, after some three weeks' intimacy, "whose life has been as changeful as that of Anastasius, and who recounts the adventures of his youth as eloquently and well as the imagined Greek. He is clever : for his moral qualities I am yet in the dark. He is a strange web which I am endeavouring to unravel. I would fain learn if generosity is united to impetuousness, nobility of spirit to his assumption of singularity and independence. He is six feet high ; raven black hair, which curls thickly and shortly like a Moor's ; dark-grey expressive eyes ; overhanging brows ; upturned lips, and a smile which expresses good-nature and kind-heartedness. His shoulders are high, like an Oriental's ; his voice is monotonous, yet emphatic ; and his language, as he relates the events of his life, energetic

and simple, whether the tale be one of blood and horror or
of irresistible comedy. His company is delightful, for he
excites me to think ; and if any evil shade the intercourse,
that time will unveil—the sun will rise or night darken all."
That he interested Shelley's imagination is manifest from the
idealized portrait of Trelawny which appears in the "Fragments of an Unfinished Drama" of the year 1822—a drama
undertaken for the amusement of his little circle of Pisan
friends. The pirate of the enchanted isle is Trelawny,
glorified by the poet's imagination—

> "He was as is the sun in his fierce youth,
>   As terrible and lovely as a tempest."

But Shelley's romantic hero does not once appear in person
in the few scenes which were written of this drama of
fantasy.

While Trelawny thus became for Shelley's imagination
a figure exalted by an element of romance, Shelley for his
part engraved on Trelawny's brain and heart an image
deep, clear-cut, and indelible. "There was a marked
individuality," he writes, "in Shelley. In habits, manners,
and all the ordinary occurrences of life, he never changed.
He took no notice of what other people did ; brave, frank,
and outspoken, like a well-conditioned boy, well-bred and
considerate for others, because he was totally devoid of
selfishness and vanity." His bodily vigour seemed to
Trelawny to be considerable, and his health far from fragile.
"I often saw him in a state of nudity, and he always reminded me of a young Indian, strong-limbed and vigorous,
and there were few men who would walk on broken ground
at the pace he kept up ; he beat us all in walking, and,
barring drugs and accidents, he might have lived as long
as his father—to ninety." In his face the most striking
feature were the luminous eyes which had shone upon

Trelawny from the dusk when he first visited the Tre Palazzi. "I caught sight of Shelley's bright eyes in the distance," says Trelawny; "I always recognized Shelley by his eyes." Yet these bright eyes were for ever poring upon books, and seemed rather to drink in light than dimness from the page of Plato, or Spinoza, or Calderon, or Goethe. "He set to work on a book, or a pyramid of books; his eyes glistening with an energy as fierce as that of the most sordid gold-digger who works at a rock of quartz, crushing his way through all impediments, no grain of the pure ore escaping his eager scrutiny."

His mental activity, says Trelawny, was infectious; "he kept your brain in constant action." Though a lover of study and of solitude, he was social and cheerful. If Mary "threatened" him with a musical party, he might indeed pathetically plead to be let off; yet in society, if the fit of abstraction were not on him, he had perfect ease of manner, "omitting no occasion of obliging those whom he came in contact with, readily conversing with all or any who addressed him, irrespective of age or rank, dress or address." But if Shelley could be amiably pliant in matters indifferent, he was resolute and even stubborn when he had fixed his will upon an object. "I always go on until I am stopped," he said, "and I never am stopped." He never wavered, declares Trelawny; he was unalterable.

Before Trelawny arrived at Pisa, he had been informed by Edward Williams of his own hope and Shelley's that the two households might form a party next summer at Spezzia. "Have a boat we must," Williams had written, "and if we can get Roberts to build her, so much the better." When, on the day after his arrival, Trelawny paid his second call at the Tre Palazzi, he brought with him the model of an American schooner, whereupon followed discussion of boats and boating, and before the friends parted it was settled that a boat thirty feet long should be built for Shelley and Williams, and a letter was written by Trelawny to Captain Roberts at Genoa to begin his ship-building at once. In her transcript of Williams's journal, Mrs. Shelley appends a note to the entry for January 15 : "Thus on that night—one of gaiety and thoughtlessness—Jane's * and my miserable destiny was decided. We then said, laughing each to the other, 'Our husbands decide without asking our consent, or having our concurrence ; for, to tell you the truth, I hate this boat, though I say nothing.' Said Jane, 'So do I ; but speaking would be useless, and only spoil their pleasure.' How well I remember that night! How short-sighted we are! And now that its anniversary is come and gone, methinks I cannot be the wretch I too truly am."

Three weeks later, on February 7, Shelley and Williams started for Spezzia to take houses for the summer colony —too large a colony, Mary feared, for unity, since Byron and the Countess Guiccioli, and Pietro Gamba, and Tre-lawny, and Captain Roberts were all to be of the party.

Only one house at all suitable could be found ; "however, a trifle such as not finding a house," writes Mary, "could not stop Shelley ; the one found was to serve for all." But some weeks must pass before a suitable time for seaside residence arrived.

Spring in 1822 woke up early and with extreme beauty. In the first days of March the breeze was sweet and clear, and there was already a glow in the sunshine. "The hedges are budding," Mary wrote to Mrs. Hunt, "and you should see me and my friend Mrs. Williams poking about for violets by the sides of dry ditches ; she being herself

> 'A violet by a mossy stone
> Half hidden from the eye.'

---

* Jane Williams.

. . . Our good cavaliers flock together, and as they do **not**
like *fetching a walk with the absurd womankind,* Jane (*i.e*
Mrs. Williams) and I are off together, and talk morality
and pluck violets by the way. I look forward to many
duets with this lady and Hunt. She has a very pretty voice,
and a taste and ear for music which is almost miraculous.
The harp is her favourite instrument." The indefinable
charm which Mrs. Williams exercised over those whom
she approached was felt even more strongly by Shelley
than by Mary. As a youth his imagination had dwelt
chiefly on the heroic qualities in women—the valour of
pure love, intellectual courage, strength of character, a
passion for reforming the world. The Cythna of his
"Revolt of Islam" embodied his ideal. Now he acknowledged before all else the exquisite charity of woman, the
grace of feminine tenderness—tenderness not of the heroic
kind which can probe a wound to heal it, but that which
lulls our pain as with some delightful anodyne, and trances
the troubled sense, if only for an hour.

"Williams," Shelley wrote to Leigh Hunt, "is one of
the best fellows in the world ; and Jane his wife a most
delightful person, who, we all agree, is the exact antetype
of the lady I described in 'The Sensitive Plant,' though
this must have been a *pure anticipated cognition,* as it was
written a year before I knew her." Her taste for music
and her elegance of form and motions compensated in some
degree, Shelley told Mr. Gisborne, for her lack of literary
refinement. She seemed "a sort of spirit of embodied
peace" in the midst of a circle of tempests. In the happiness of his friends, Edward and Jane, there was for Shelley
something radiant and worshipful, like the brightness of
a spring morning ; Jane, with her grace, and suavity, and
bland motions, and soothing words, was conceived by him
as the dispenser of an exquisite felicity, to which her husband

had a first claim, but the overflow of which might be Shelley's own. How could he adequately express his pleasure in her gentleness, her penetrating charity, her ineffable tenderness? She should be the Queen of Amity and halcyon hours, with Edward Williams for a fortunate Prince Consort, and he should be her humble troubadour; or call the pair Ferdinand and Miranda, with Shelley for their faithful Ariel.

During the winter and spring weeks he did not feel that he possessed courage and ambition enough for great poetical enterprises. He occupied himself from time to time with translations, admirably executed, from the Homeric hymns, from Goethe's "Faust," from Calderon's "Magico Prodigioso."

In the first days of the opening year, he set himself to make a forward movement with his tragedy of "Charles the First," which had lingered long, and of which only some disconnected fragments had been written; but the difficulties of an historical drama entangled him. It was "the devil of a nut to crack." "A slight circumstance," he told Leigh Hunt, "gave a new train to my ideas, and shattered the fragile edifice when half-built." And in April, "I have done some of 'Charles the First;' but although the poetry succeeded very well, I cannot seize on the conception of the subject as a whole, and seldom now touch the canvas." The fragments which we possess contain admirable dramatic writing; but they give no evidence that the tragedy would have had that central pulse which sends life and force through every member of a breathing and moving piece of dramatic art. History but faintly interested Shelley; it is doubtful whether he could ever have found motives in a broad historical theme as inspiring to his genius as those which gave life and being to the "Cenci."

But although Shelley now lacked the courage and energy needful to carry him through a sustained work of imagination, fortunate hours brought into existence a series of lyrical poems as delicate as Ariel had ever sung before, under green boughs or by the yellow sands. These were the songs made for Miranda and her Prince Ferdinand; they have in them a touch of the sadness of renunciation, like that of music that creeps upon the waters,

> "Allaying both their fury and our passion
> With its sweet air."

The songs and poems inspired by Jane Williams were given to her husband or to Jane, to be read by themselves alone. The loveliest of them all is that which accompanied a guitar—Shelley's gift to Jane. Seeking for Shelley in the pine forest near the sea, and guided by an old man who had seen "l'Inglese malinconico who haunts the woods," Trelawny came upon a deep pool of dark glimmering water, by the side of which lay a hat, books, and loose papers. "The strong light streamed through the opening of the trees. One of the pines, undermined by the water, had fallen into it. Under its lee, and nearly hidden, sat the poet, gazing on the dark mirror beneath, so lost in his bardish reverie that he did not hear my approach. . . . He was writing verses on a guitar. I picked up a fragment, but could only make out the first two lines—'

> '*Ariel to Miranda*—Take
> This slave of music.'

It was a frightful scrawl; words smeared out with his finger, and one upon the other, over and over in tiers, and all run together in most 'admired disorder;' it might have been taken for a sketch of a marsh overgrown with bulrushes, and the blots for wild ducks; such a dashed-off daub as self-conceited artists mistake for a manifestation of genius. On my observing this to him, he answered, When my brain gets heated with thought, it soon boils,

and throws off images and words faster than I can skim
them off. In the morning, when cooled down, out of the
rude sketch as you justly call it, I shall attempt a drawing.'"
Shelley's note-books and loose pages of manuscript bear
out Trelawny's description, though this particular poem is
not found among them; page after page often repeating
the same lines or a single stanza, written with pen or pencil,
varied again and again with a text actually visible in the
process of creation.

Towards the close of March occurred an untoward incident
which threatened serious consequences for a time. On
Sunday, the 24th, Byron, Shelley, Trelawny, Captain Hay
(a Maremma hunter), Count Pietro Gamba, and Taaffe were
returning from their evening ride, and had nearly reached
the Porta alle Piagge, just beyond the eastern end of the
Lung' Arno, when a dragoon galloped through the midst
of them, jostling against Taaffe. "This nice little gentleman," writes Mary to Mrs. Gisborne, "exclaimed, 'Shall
we endure this man's insolence?' Lord Byron replied,
'No; we will bring him to an account;' and Shelley
(whose blood always boils at any insolence offered by a
soldier) added, 'As you please!' So they put spurs to
their horses (*i.e.* all but Taaffe, who remained quietly
behind), followed, and stopped the man, and fancying that
he was an officer, demanded his name and address, and
gave their cards." Serjeant-Major Masi, who had drunk
too freely, replied with oaths and bluster, and an announcement that he arrested them all. Dashing forward, Byron
and Gamba passed the gate and its guard, purposing,
says Mary, to fetch arms from the Palazzo Lanfranchi.
Before the others could follow, Masi had drawn his sword,
and calling upon the guards to stop them, began to slash
to right and left. It was Shelley who had first overtaken
him and compelled him to halt, and at Shelley he now

aimed a desperate sabre-stroke. Using his cap as a shield, Shelley warded the blow of the blade; but the hilt struck him on the head and knocked him from his horse. A second time the fellow struck at him while he was down, and might have seriously injured him but for the prompt interposition of Captain Hay's cane. The cane was cut in two, and Shelley's defender received a wound upon the face. Upon this Masi in alarm fled, and on the Lung' Arno encountered Byron returning to the scene of the affray. Hurrying forward in the dusk, he had reached in his flight the Lanfranchi Palace, when a servant of Byron's, imagining that the dragoon had killed his master, rushed forward, struck at him with a pitchfork, and wounded him severely in the side. The man rode on a few paces, then with a cry fell from his horse, and was borne to the hospital to the ringing of the *misericordia* bell. The beginning of the affair had been watched by the Countess Guiccioli and Mrs. Shelley from the carriage in which they followed the riders. Edward and Jane Williams, whether at their own lodgings or the Lanfranchi Palace we know not, first heard of the exciting adventure from Trelawny. "Trelawny," writes Williams in his journal, "had finished his story when Lord Byron came in, the countess fainting on his arm; Shelley sick from the blow; Lord Byron and the young count foaming with anger; Mrs. Shelley looking philosophically upon this interesting scene; and Jane and I wondering what the devil was to come next." By-and-by entered Taaffe, with an announcement that the sergeant's wound was considered mortal. Whereupon the English party sallied forth, that they might be the first to proffer an accusation; and presently all returned, writes Williams, "mutually recriminating and recriminated."

For a time after this event Pisa was no longer dull; rumours chased one another through the town. An

Englishman, named Trelawny, it was reported, had been
left dead at the gate ; Lord Byron was mortally wounded—
it was Byron who told the news, while Trelawny was sipping
brandy-and-water by his side. Taaffe, the assassin—so
Taaffe himself overheard, while walking on the Lung' Arno
—was secreted in Lord Byron's house, "guarded by bull-
dogs." Lord Byron, with all his servants and four English
gentlemen, were captured after a desperate resistance ; forty
brace of pistols were found in the Palazzo. Meanwhile
Sergeant-Major Masi, being honoured with the surgical
attendance of Vaccà, was in truth recovering, and Byron's
servants—Tita, the bearded Venetian, and Vincenzo—both
entirely innocent of the assault, in the interests of justice
were imprisoned. It was Shelley's opinion that Masi, on
recovering, would demand the satisfaction of a gentleman,
which, he added, ought not to be refused. The affair, which
for a while made so much noise, was, as he said, "a trifling
piece of business enough." Yet at a later period it served
the Government as one ground among others for exiling
Count Pietro Gamba and his father, whose share in the
revolutionary intrigues at Ravenna was not forgotten.

The scheme of a summer colony on the Bay of Spezzia,
of which Byron, the Countess Guiccioli, and Pietro Gamba
were to be members, had been abandoned almost as soon
as it had been conceived. Even were houses for so large
a party to be obtained near Spezzia, Shelley could hardly
have endured a whole summer of Lord Byron's close companionship. In February, he wrote to Hunt, expressing a
strong repugnance to the continuance of such intimacy
with Byron as that which had of late subsisted between
them. At no other time did Byron's character present
itself to Shelley in colours so dark. When he quitted
Ravenna in August, 1821, he understood that Byron had
determined that Allegra should not be left behind him,

alone and friendless, in the convent of Bagnacavallo ; he
hoped that an arrangement might be made by which Claire
should have the happiness of seeing her child once more.
During September and October, Claire waited about Leghorn, Pisa, and the Baths of St. Giuliano, expecting that
Allegra some happy day would be in her arms.   But when
Byron, after long lingering, left Ravenna, Allegra was not
with him.   In Claire's journal occur from time to time
little entries which show with what passionate affection her
heart yearned for sight of the child, who was to her the
best and dearest thing on earth.   "*April* 12, 1821.—When
the ' Divina Comedia,' after being lost in the troubles of
the civil war, was found and brought to Dante, he pressed
it to his heart and exclaimed, ' It appears to me as if I
had recovered my lost immortality.'   So would it be to me
if I recovered my lost Allegra as if I had come back to the
warmth of life after the stiffness of the grave, so cordially,
cheerily would my feelings flow in their hitherto choked
channels.   *June* 6, 1821.—Towards Wednesday morning I
had a most distressing dream—that I received a letter which
said that Allegra was ill and not likely to live.   The dreadful grief I felt made awaking appear to me the most
delightful sensation of ease in the world.   Just so, I think,
must the wearied soul feel when it finds itself in Paradise,
released from the trembling anguish of the world.

When Byron arrived at Pisa in November, and Allegra
was not with him, Mr. Tighe, moved by Claire's distress,
set off, she tells us, on a journey of inquiry to Venice and
Ravenna ; he desired to obtain information about the
convent in which Allegra was confined ; and to learn what
was the disposition of the Countess Guiccioli, whose good
offices with Byron on behalf of the child Claire had some
thought of soliciting.   The Shelleys, said Mr. Tighe, were
not to know of his journey, for they would be sure to

divulge the matter to Byron, which would do infinite harm.
His report with respect to the convent was far from reassuring. In the marshes of the Romagna lurked a fever,
which at times came forth and ravaged the district of
Bagnacavallo. The convent was one of Capuchin nuns,
whose poverty and austerity unfitted them for the work of
educating the young; hardly any persons of better rank
than petty tradespeople would send their children to such a
place. The food was said to be meagre, and in winter there
was no fire at which the little ones could warm their
perishing hands and feet. "What pangs of anguish I
suffered in the winter of twenty-one," wrote Claire, "when
I saw a bright fire, and people and children warming themselves by it, and knew my darling never saw or felt a
cheerful blaze." Acting under the advice of Lady Mountcashell, she addressed a letter to Byron, in which she represented to him the dangers of residence in such a convent as
that of Bagnacavallo to a child of tender years, using, she
declares, "not one word of reproach." She entreated him
to place Allegra with some respectable family in Pisa, or
Florence, or Lucca. She, the mother, would not, if such
was his desire, go near the child; nor should Mary or
Shelley without his consent. No answer was returned to
this letter. In a month, Claire wrote again to the same
effect, alleging in explanation that she supposed her former
letter to have been lost. Still no answer. In February,
1822, Miss Clairmont entertained a design of removing to
Vienna, where her brother Charles lived, there to obtain a
situation of some kind, and advance, under conditions more
favourable than Italy afforded, with her study of the German
language. But she longed before her departure to embrace
her child. It seemed a lucky moment for approaching
Byron, for the death of Lady Noel, tidings of which reached
Pisa by February 15, made him possessor of a considerable

property, and for other reasons might naturally have put him in good humour. Accordingly, on the 18th, Claire plucked up courage, and wrote as follows.

Claire Clairmont to Byron.

I am extremely glad to hear that, by your succession to a large fortune, your affairs have become more prosperous than ever. I wish and pray that you may have health to enjoy yourself many long years, with every other accordant circumstance that can combine to make a person happy. You will perhaps not believe that I sincerely wish this for your sake, and therefore I venture to wish it for Allegra's. I do not say that I write now upon her account, but, on the contrary, solely upon my own. I assure you I can no longer resist the internal inexplicable feeling which haunts me that I shall never see her any more. I entreat you to destroy this feeling by allowing me to see her. I waited two months in the autumn, expecting from all you professed to see her every week, and when on the sudden you would no longer allow it to be, a melancholy fearfulness came over me, which has never since passed away. This was owing to the cruel disappointment I felt, and which may perhaps mislead my judgment; but to what besides a determined hatred can I attribute your conduct? I have often entreated Shelley to intercede for me, and he invariably answers that it is utterly useless. I am not wanting in feelings of pride, but everything yields to the extent of my present unhappiness, which grows daily towards despair, and induces me in spite to address you in hopes of an alleviation of my misery. If I could only flatter myself that you would not harden your heart against me, I might indulge the hope that you would grant what I ask.

I shall shortly leave Italy for a new country, to enter upon a disagreeable and precarious course of life; I yield in this not to my own wishes, but to the advice of a friend whose head is wiser than mine. I leave my friends with regret, but indeed I cannot go without having first seen and embraced Allegra. Do not, I entreat you, refuse me this little, but only, consolation. If, instead of the friendly office I request, you resolve to humiliate me by a refusal, success in what I attempt will be impossible, for I know not where I shall gather even the spirit to begin it. I have experienced that I can conquer every feeling but those of nature ; these grave themselves on the breast with thorns, and while life lasts they make the sharpness felt. I am sensible how little this letter is calculated to persuade, but it is one of my unhappinesses that I cannot write to you with the deepness which I feel ; because I know how much you are prejudiced against me, and the constraint which this inspires weakens and confuses all I would express. But if you refuse me, where shall I hope for anything?

The weather is fine, the passage of the Apennines quite free and safe. The when and where of our meeting shall be entirely according to your pleasure, and with every restriction and delicacy that you may think necessary for Allegra's sake. I shall abandon myself to despair if you refuse ; but indeed if your reason, my dear Friend, cannot be persuaded to alter the line of conduct you have hitherto pursued towards me in all that concerns Allegra, it were better that I were dead. So I should escape all the suffering which your harshness causes me. But hope in the present state of my spirits is necessary to me, and I will believe that you will kindly consent to my wish. How inexpressibly dearly will I not cherish your name and recollection as the author of my happiness in the far-off place to which I am obliged to go, and amidst the strangers who will surround me ! My dear Friend, I conjure you do not make the world dark to me, as if my Allegra were dead. In the happiness her sight will cause me I shall gain restoration and strength to enable me to bear the mortifications and displeasures to which a poor and unhappy person is exposed in the world. I wish you every happiness.

CLAÏRE.

Florence, Tuesday, February 18, 1822.

This appeal left Byron unmoved except by anger against the writer. After three miserable days, Claire hastened to Pisa to consult with Mr. Tighe and Lady Mountcashell, Shelley and Mary, and on February 25 was again at her work in Florence. Mr. Tighe and Lady Mountcashell were for decisive measures, and were vigorously supported in their views by Elizabeth Parker. There was talk of an attempt to rescue Allegra by stratagem; nothing, said Elizabeth, but Lord Byron's death would free the child, and were she its mother she would stab or shoot him. Mary and Shelley, while strongly of opinion that Allegra should in some way be taken out of Byron's hands, thought it prudent to temporize and watch for a favourable opportunity. It was probably about this time, though Miss Clairmont, writing late in her life, referred it to a somewhat earlier date, that Shelley, at Claire's entreaty and with much reluctance, made an experiment on Byron's feelings by representing to him the mother's growing anxiety and suffering on her child's account. Byron's "only reply," says Miss Clairmont, "was a shrug of impatience, and the exclamation that women could not live without making scenes. He never had seen the convent; yet he confessed he had not made the smallest inquiry as to whether what I had stated was true or no." Elizabeth Parker, an orphan girl sent by Mrs. Godwin to live with Lady Mountcashell, a firm and affectionate friend of Claire's, wrote to the unhappy woman, relating what Shelley had told on the preceding evening at Casa Silva respecting his interview with Byron. "I never saw him [Shelley] in a passion before," said Elizabeth; "last night, however, he was downright, positively angry. . . . Mr. Shelley declared to Lady Mountcashell that he could with pleasure have knocked Lord Byron down; for when he mentioned that you were half-distracted with alarm about the child's health, and also that you were yourself in very declining health, he saw a gleam of malicious satisfaction pass over Lord Byron's countenance. 'I saw his look,' Mr. Shelley said; 'I understood its meaning; I despised him, and I came away.' These were his own epigrammatic words. Afterwards he said, 'It is foolish of me to be angry with him; he can no more help being what he is than yonder door can help being a door.' Mr. Tighe then said, 'You are quite wrong in your fatalism. If I were to horsewhip that door, it would still remain a door; but if Lord Byron were well horsewhipped, my opinion is he would become as humane as he is now inhumane. It is the feeble character or the subserviency of his friends that make him the insolent tyrant he is.' This observation Mr. Shelley repelled; he said others were free, of course, to use the law of coercion; he disapproved it, and the only law that should ever govern his conduct should be the law of love. The discussion appeared to be getting warm, these two think so differently; therefore Lady Mountcashell carried Mr. Shelley off to read Euripides, and the subject dropped."

An undated fragment of a letter from Mary to Claire, and a short letter from Shelley, also undated, probably belong to a period subsequent to Miss Clairmont's return to Professor Bojti's house at Florence, when it seemed to Claire that another interview and consultation were desirable.

Mary Shelley to Claire Clairmont.

My dear Claire,

Shelley and I have been consulting seriously about your letter received this morning, and I wish in as orderly a manner as possible to give you the result of our reflections. First, as to my coming to Florence; I mentioned it to you first, it is true, but we have so little money, and our calls this quarter for removing, etc., will be so great that we had entirely given up the idea. If it would be of great utility to you, as a single expense we might do it; but if it be necessary that others should follow, the crowns would be minus. But before I proceed further on this part of the subject, let me examine what your plans appear to be. Your anxiety for Allegra's health is to a great degree unfounded. Venice—its stinking canals and dirty streets—is enough to kill any child ; but you ought to know, and any one will tell you so, that the towns of Romagna, situated where Bagnacavallo is, enjoy the best air in Italy. Imola and the neighbouring *paese* are famous ; Bagnacavallo especially, being fifteen miles from the sea and situated on an eminence, is peculiarly salutary. Considering the affair reasonably, Allegra is well taken care of there ; she is in good health, and in all probability will continue so.

No one can more entirely agree with you than I in thinking that as soon as possible Allegra ought to be taken out of the hands of one as remorseless as he is unprincipled. But at the same time it appears to me that the present moment is exactly the one in which this is the most difficult. Time cannot add to these difficulties, for they can never be greater. Allow me to enumerate some of those which are peculiar to the present instant. Allegra is in a convent where it is next to impossible to get her out ; high walls and bolted doors enclose her ; and more than all, the regular habits of a convent, which never permit her to get outside its gates, and would cause her to be missed directly. But you may have a plan for this, and I pass to other objections. At your desire Shelley urged her removal to Lord Byron, and this appears in the highest degree to have exasperated him. He vowed that if you annoyed him he would place Allegra in some secret convent ; he declared that you should have nothing to do with her, and that he would move heaven and earth to prevent your interference. Lord Byron is at present a man of twelve or fifteen thousand a year ; he is on the spot ; a man reckless of the ill he does others, obstinate to desperation in the pursuance of his plans or his revenge. What then would you do, having Allegra on the outside of the convent walls ? Would you go to America ? The money we have not, nor does this seem to be your idea. You probably wish to secrete yourself. But Lord Byron would use any means to find you out ; and the story he might make up—a man stared at by the Grand-Duke, with money at command, and above all on the spot to put energy into every pursuit, would he not find you ? If he did not, he comes upon Shelley. He taxes him ; Shelley must either own it or tell a lie ; in either case he is open to be called upon by Lord Byron to answer for his conduct —and a duel—I need not enter upon that topic, your own imagination may fill up the picture.

On the contrary, a little time, a very little time, may alter much of this. It is more than probable that he will be obliged to go to England within a year ; then at a distance he is no longer so formidable. What is certain is that we shall not be so near him another year. He may be reconciled with his wife, and though he may bluster, he may not be sorry to get Allegra off his hands ; at any rate, if we leave him perfectly quiet, he will not be so exasperated, so much on the *qui vive*, as he is at present. Nothing remains constant, something may happen — things cannot be worse. . . .

Then we are drearily behindhand with money at present Hunt and our furniture has swallowed up more than our savings You say great sacrifices will be required of us. I would make many to extricate all belonging to me from the hands of Lord Byron, whose hypocrisy and cruelty rouse one's soul from its depths. We are, of course, still in great uncertainty as to our summer residence. We have calculated the great expense of removing our furniture for a few months as far as Spezzia, and it appears to us a bad plan. To get a furnished house we must go nearer Genoa, probably nearer Lord Byron, which is contrary to our most earnest wishes. We have thought of Naples. [*Fragment of letter ends.*]

Probably accompanying this letter of Mary, the following letter went to Claire from Shelley.

Shelley to Claire Clairmont.

I have little to add to Mary's letter, my poor dear friend, and all that I shall do is to suspend my journey to take a house until your answer. Of course, if you do not spend the summer near us, I shall come to Florence and see and talk with you. But it seems to me far better on every account that you should resolve on this, and tranquillize yourself among your friends. I shall certainly take our house *far* from Lord Byron, although it may be

impossible suddenly to put an end to his detested intimacy. *My*
coming to Florence would cost ten or twenty crowns; Mary's
much more; and if, therefore, we are to see you soon, this money
in our present situation were better spared.

Mary tells you that Lord Byron is obstinate and *awake* about
Allegra. My great object has been to lull him into security until
circumstances might call him to England. But the idea of contending with him in Italy, and defended by his enormous fortune,
is vain. I was endeavouring to induce him to place Allegra in
the institute at Lucca, but his jealousy of my regard for *your*
interests will, since a conversation I had with him the other day,
render him inaccessible to my suggestions. It seems to me that
you have no other resource but time and chance and change.
Heaven knows, whatever sacrifices *I* could make, how gladly I
should make them if they could promote your desires about her.
It tears my heart to think that all sacrifices are *now* vain. Mary
participates in my feelings, but I cannot write. My spirits completely overcome me.

Your ever faithful and affectionate

S.

Come and stay among us. If you like, come and look for
houses with me in our boat; it might distract your mind.

"It is of vital importance," Shelley wrote to Claire,
"both to me and to yourself, to Allegra even, that I should
put a period to my intimacy with Lord Byron, and that
without *éclat*. No sentiments of honour or justice restrain
him (as I strongly suspect) from the basest insinuations, and
the only mode in which I could effectually silence him, I
am reluctant (even if I had proof) to employ during my
father's life. But for your immediate feelings, I would
suddenly and irrevocably leave the country which he inhabits, nor ever enter it but as an enemy to determine our
differences *without words*. But at all events I shall soon
see you, and then we will weigh both your plans and mine.
Write by next post."

Calmer counsels prevailed when Shelley wrote to Claire

on the morning of that Sunday on which the street-broil
with Sergeant-Major Masi took place, and he could then
condemn her wild projects for effecting Allegra's liberation.

Shelley to Claire Clairmont.

Pisa, Sunday morning [March 24, 1892].

MY DEAR CLAIRE,

I know not what to think of the state of your mind, or
what to fear for you. Your late plan about Allegra seems to me
in its present form pregnant with irremediable infamy to all the
actors in it except yourself; in any form wherein *I* must actively
co-operate with inevitable destruction [word cancelled by Claire].
I could not refuse Lord Byron's challenge ; though that, however
to be deprecated, would be the least in the series of mischiefs consequent upon my [word cancelled by Claire] intervention in such
a plan. I say this because I am shocked at the thoughtless
violence of your designs, and I wish to put my sense of their
madness in the strongest light. I may console myself, however,
with the reflection that the attempt even is impossible, as I have
no money. So far from being able to lend me three or four
hundred pounds, Horace Smith has lately declined to advance six
or seven napoleons for a musical instrument which I wished to
buy for Jane at Paris ; nor have I any other friend to whom I
could apply.

You think of going to Vienna. The change might have a
favourable effect upon your mind, and the occupations and exertions of a new state of life wean you from counsels so desperate
as those to which you have been lately led. I must try to manage
the money for your journey, if so you have decided. You know
how different my own ideas are of life. I also have been struck
by the heaviest inflictions almost which a high spirit and a feeling
heart ever endured. Some of yours and of my evils are in
common, and I am therefore in a certain degree a judge. If you
would take my advice, you would give up this idle pursuit after
shadows, and temper yourself to the season, and seek in the daily
and affectionate intercourse of friends a respite from these perpetual and irritating projects. Live from day to day, attend to

your health, cultivate literature and liberal ideas to a certain extent, and expect that from time and change which no exertions of your own can give you.   Serious and calm reflection has convinced me that you can never obtain Allegra by such means as you have lately devised, or by any mea[ns to be *] devised. Lord Byron is inflexible, and you [are] in his power.   Remember, Claire, when you rejected my earnest advice, and checked me with that contempt which I have never merited from you, at Milan, and how vain is now your regret !   This is the second of my sibylline volumes ; if you wait for the third, it may be sold at a still higher price.   If you think well this summer, go to Vienna ; but wherever you go or stay, let the *past* be past.

I expect soon to write to you on another subject respecting which, however, all is as you already know.   Farewell.

Your affectionate

S.

On April 10, Shelley invited Claire to Pisa, and urged her to become one of their summer party at the seaside.

Shelley to Claire Clairmont.†

[Pisa, April 10, 1822.]

Mary has not shown me her letter to you, and I therefore snatch an instant to write these few lines.

Come, my best girl, if you think fit, and assure yourself that every one—I need not speak for myself—-will be most happy to see you ; but I think you had better wait a post or two, and not make *two* journeys of it, as that would be an expense to no purpose, and we have not an overplus of money.   In fact, you had better resolve to be of our party in the country, where we shall go the moment the weather permits, and arrange all your plans for that purpose.   The Williamses and we shall be quite alone, Lord Byron and his party having chosen Leghorn, where their house is already taken.

---

* The paper is torn.
† The postmark and an entry in Claire's journal fix the date of this letter.

Do not lose yourself in distant and uncertain plans, but systematize and simplify your motions at least for the present.

I am not well. My side torments me; my mind agitates the frame which it inhabits, and things go ill with me—that is within —for all external circumstances are auspicious.

Resolve to stay with us this summer, and remain where you are till we are ready to set off. No one need know of where you are; the Williamses are [* sure?] people, and are alone.

Before you come, look at Molini's, what German books they have. I have got a " Faust" of my own, and just now my drama on the Greeks is come.† I will keep it for you.

> Affectionately and ever yours,
>
> S.

On April 15, Claire arrived at Pisa, and on the same day came news from Spezzia that the houses on which Shelley and Williams had reckoned for their summer quarters were not to be had on any terms. Neither at Genoa, where Captain Roberts had made inquiries, nor at Leghorn or Monte Nero, could a suitable villa be found by Williams. While at Pisa the Florentine advocate, a talkative, good-humoured buffoon, was examining and taking depositions in order to bring to a final issue the affair of the wounded dragoon, Williams, accompanied by Jane and Claire, started for Spezzia, to make one more search for houses on the bay. They cannot have been many hours on their journey, when Shelley and Mary received tidings of sorrowful import, which Mary chronicles in her journal with the words "Evil news." Allegra was dead. The plots and plans to remove the child, so dear to her mother's heart, from the enclosure of her convent were all unneeded now. Typhus fever had raged in the Romagna; but no one wrote to inform her parents of the fact. "She had no friends," Mary told Mrs. Gisborne (June 2), "except the

---

* Word doubtful.   † " Hellas," published by the Olliers.

nuns in the convent, who were kind to her, I believe. But
you know Italians ; if half of the convent had died of the
plague, they would never have written to have had them
removed ; and so the poor child fell a sacrifice. Lord
Byron felt the loss at first bitterly ; he also felt remorse,
for he felt that he had acted against everybody's counsels
and wishes, and death had stamped with truth the many
and often-urged prophecies of Claire, that the air of the
Romagna, joined to the ignorance of the Italians, would
prove fatal to her." On the second day after their departure, Williams, Jane, and Claire were back in Pisa
bringing the report that one house, and only one, could be
found, and that unfurnished—the Villa Magni, situated
between Lerici and San Terenzo. "Return to Pisa," writes
Williams in his journal. "Meet Shelley ; his face bespoke
his feelings." Dreading perhaps some violent outbreak of
passion from Claire—and Byron was still hard by in the
Lanfranchi Palace—Shelley resolved to conceal the mournful
tidings from her as long as possible. It was her wish to
return to Florence ; but Shelley would not have it so. She
must remain with Mary, and both must instantly set forth
for Spezzia, where Mary should use every effort to obtain
possession of the vacant house. Trelawny would act as
their escort. Shelley himself would see to the removal of
the furniture by boats to Lerici. Although no second house
had been discovered, the Williamses must also come, and
bring their furniture. " Like a torrent hurrying in its course,"
so Mary tells Mrs. Gisborne, he carried all before him ;
Claire, Mary, the Williamses, Trelawny, yielded to the
insistence of his will. On April 26, Mary, Claire, and Trelawny were on their way to Spezzia, Claire unconscious of
the burden which oppressed the hearts of her friends. Next
day, Shelley, with Jane and Edward Williams, started to
meet the boats at Lerici. On Sunday morning, April 28,

the aspect of affairs, especially for the Williamses, did not look promising. "Arrive at Lerici at one o'clock," Williams writes in his journal. "The harbour-master called. Not a house to be had. On our telling him we had brought our furniture, his face lengthened considerably, for he informed us that the dogana would amount to £300 English, at least. Dined, and resolved on sending our things back without unloading—in fact, found ourselves in the devil of a mess."

"Dearest Mary," wrote Shelley on that afternoon, "I am this moment arrived at Lerici, where I am necessarily detained, waiting the furniture which left Pisa last night at midnight ; and, as the sea has been calm and the wind fair, I may expect them every moment. It would not do to leave affairs here in an *impiccio*, great as is my anxiety to see you. How are you, my best love, and how have you sustained the trials of your journey ? Answer me this question, and how my little babe and Claire are.

"Now to business. Is the Magni house taken ? if not, pray occupy yourself instantly in finishing this affair, even if you are obliged to go to Sarzana, and send a messenger to tell me of your success. . . . I am anxious to hear from you on every account."

The obliging harbour-master, Mr. Maglian, undertook to allow the furniture to come on shore ; he would consider the villa to which it should be removed as a sort of depôt until further leave came from the Genoese government. All was well with Mary ; she had taken Casa Magni. No house, indeed, could anywhere be found for the Williamses ; but Shelley was not to be baffled—he would contrive to give them rooms. On May 1, the whole party had taken possession of their new abode, and the hastily furnished rooms were getting into a state of disorderly order. "Passed the evening," writes Williams, "in talking over our folly and our troubles."

CHAPTER XXIV.

LAST DAYS.

CASA MAGNI, the house taken by Shelley for his summer residence—a white house with arches which once had been a Jesuit convent—is situated near the fishing village of San Terenzo, in the depth of a cove on the eastern side of the Bay of Spezzia. A steep hill shelters it behind, from which the olive-trees had been removed by the proprietor of 1822 (reputed to be insane), in order to make room for a young plantation of forest-trees. "Some fine walnut and ilex trees," wrote Mrs. Shelley long after, "intermingled their dark massy foliage, and formed groups which still haunt my memory, as then they satiated the eye with a sense of loveliness." Eastwards over the precipitous rocks of fantastic form a rugged, winding footpath led to the little town of Lerici, with its white flat-roofed houses by the water's edge, and its conspicuous castle looking across the bay to Porto Venere. The hoary mountain slopes; the varied rocks of volcanic formation ; the waters, violet and green, of the tideless Mediterranean ; the deep southern sky ; the fishers' black huts, clinging below the little cliffs like swallows' nests ; the lonely house, which stood almost amid the waves,—made up a scene at once beautiful and strange. "Sometimes the sunshine vanished," writes Mrs. Shelley, "when the sirocco raged—the 'ponente' the wind was called on that shore.

2 N

The gales and squalls that hailed our first arrival surrounded the bay with foam ; the howling wind swept round our exposed house, and the sea roared unremittingly, so that we almost fancied ourselves on board ship. . . . The natives were wilder than the place. Our near neighbours of San Terenzo were more like savages than any people I ever before lived among. Many a night they passed on the beach singing, or rather howling ; the women dancing about among the waves that broke at their feet, the men leaning against the rocks and joining in their loud wild chorus. We could get no provisions nearer than Sarzana, at a distance of three miles and a half off, with the torrent of the Magra between ; and even there the supply was very deficient. Had we been wrecked on an island of the South Seas, we could scarcely have felt ourselves further from civilization and comfort ; but, where the sun shines, the latter becomes an unnecessary luxury, and we had enough society among ourselves."

The house in 1822 consisted of a ground-floor and one story. The ground-floor, which was unpaved, was used for storing boat-gear and fishing-tackle, and might almost have been reached by the waves. Two staircases, one public, the other intended for a private staircase, led to the large dining-hall, off which to the rear was Mrs. Williams's bed-room ; while the seaward rooms, occupied by Mary and Shelley, faced each other on opposite sides of the central hall. All these rooms "had once," says Trelawny, "been whitewashed." An outhouse was occupied by the servants The special advantage which Casa Magni owned, beside its noble prospect and lovely surroundings, was a terrace or verandah of considerable width, which ran the whole length of the house, and was precipitous to the sea. The windows of Mary's and Shelley's rooms looked upon this terrace, and an occupant of the dining-hall could step out, and in a moment stand in presence of a landscape and sea-view of unimaginable loveliness.

In spite of a cloudy sky, with dashes of rain, on the morning after they had entered their new abode, Shelley and Williams were off to fish, but with small success. That evening the wind rose, and the waves began to cry and knell against the rocks. Claire, seeing perhaps the scanty accommodation of the house, insisted that she must return to Florence. The others, in order to consult in private, retired to Jane Williams's room. While they were seated, talking over what should be done, Claire entered, perceived the disturbance her entrance had caused, and in an instant with prophetic heart divined the cause of their trouble—her best-beloved Allegra was dead. It was Shelley's part to break the truth to her in its cruel details. "You may judge," Mary wrote to Mrs. Gisborne, "of what was her first burst of grief and despair." Next day (May 3) she was calmer; her chief desire was to look at the coffin before its transit to England, and if possible to possess a likeness of her child and a lock of her golden hair. Through Shelley's endeavour these wishes were in part gratified; a miniature portrait of Allegra remained with her to the day of her death. After a while, in place of her former agitations and plots and passions, a mournful tranquillity possessed her; she seemed to Mary to have reconciled herself to her fate; but in truth her heart protested to the last against the cruelty which had deprived her of a sight of her little one, and had consigned the bright child far from a mother's care to the fever-stricken convent of the Romagna. On May 21, Claire bade farewell to her friends at Casa Magni, and set forth on her road to Florence.

Shelley and Williams waited impatiently for the arrival of the boat which Captain Roberts had undertaken to see built for them, along with Byron's larger craft, at Genoa.

To launch through the surf the flat-bottomed boat which they had brought from Pisa was not easy, now that the full moon seemed to have swayed the currents of the tide less Mediterranean, and swung the heavy swell upon the shore. Shelley's health during these days was excellent, and he was eager to sail abroad; yet the excitement of recent agitation, caused by Allegra's death and Claire's passion of grief, left him at times somewhat shaken in spirit. "After tea, walking with Shelley on the terrace," Williams writes in his journal (May 6), "and observing the effect of moonshine on the waters, he complained of being unusually nervous, and stopping short, he grasped me violently by the arm, and stared steadfastly on the white surf that broke upon the beach under our feet. Observing him sensibly affected, I demanded of him if he were in pain. But he only answered by saying, 'There it is again—there!' He recovered after some time, and declared that he saw, as plainly as he then saw me, a naked child (Allegra) rise from the sea, and clap its hands as in joy, smiling at him. This was a trance that it required some reasoning and philosophy entirely to awaken him from, so forcibly had the vision operated on his mind. Our conversation, which had been at first rather melancholy, led to this; and my confirming his sensations by confessing that I had felt the same, gave greater activity to his wandering and ever-lively fancy."

Such moonlight visions were forgotten when, on the afternoon of Sunday, May 12, the pacers on the terrace descried a strange sail rounding the point of Porto Venere, which in due time proved to be the eagerly expected boat. A Mr. Heslop and two English seamen had brought her from Genoa; they had encountered rough seas, and spoke most highly of her performances. "She does, indeed," writes Williams, "excite my surprise and admiration. Shelley and

ı walked to Lerici, and made a stretch off the land to try
her, and I find she fetches whatever she looks at. In short,
we have now a perfect plaything for the summer." To
Shelley it was the fulfilment of his happiest anticipations
for the golden months of the year. Trelawny tells us how
he and his friends would outline the boat in her actual
dimensions upon the sands of the Arno, and how Shelley
and Williams, having a map of the Mediterranean spread
before them, would squat in their imaginary cabin with faces
as grave as that of Columbus and his companions. Now
Shelley was the possessor of such a winged bark as he had
loved to imagine in his verse, and the Mediterranean sang
its song of invitation. Twenty-eight feet long by eight
feet wide, the boat looked almost twice her size. The
model, obtained from one of the royal dockyards, had been
brought by Williams from England, and he had insisted,
against Trelawny's advice and that of the builder at Genoa,
that his model should be closely followed : had he not been
himself aboard ship as a boy, and ought not he to know
what was right ? The boat was without a deck, strongly
built, schooner-rigged, and for her size carried ample sail.
" It took," says Trelawny, " two tons of iron ballast to bring
her down to her bearings, and then she was very crank in
a breeze, though not deficient in beam." Charles Vivian,
a sailor-lad aged eighteen, quick and handy, who had
helped to bring her round from Genoa, remained to assist
Williams and Shelley in working the boat. The prudent
counsel of Trelawny, to add to the crew a Genoese sailor
accustomed to the coast, was rejected by Williams, who
had confidence in his own knowledge and skill. Nor,
indeed, was he wanting in these, though he did not possess
that promptitude of action which constant practice alone
ıan give. Shelley's seamanship was of a kind better suited
to one of his own imagined boats of rare device, with prow

of magic moonstone, than to a cranky craft on a sea of capricious temper. He could read and steer at the same time, he averred, the one process being mental, the other mechanical. "You will do no good with Shelley," Trelawny exclaimed to his companion, "until you heave his books and papers overboard, shear the wisps of hair that hang over his eyes, and plunge his arms up to the elbows in a tar-bucket." But if Shelley read as he traversed the streets of Pisa, why should he not keep his beloved Plato, or Goethe, or Calderon beside him while he held the tiller and speeded over the rippling waters?

"Fine, after a threatening night," Williams wrote in his journal of May 22. "After breakfast, Shelley and I amused ourselves with trying to make a boat of canvas and reeds as light and as small as possible—she to be eight and a half feet long and four and a half broad." Shelley was delighted, says Trelawny, with this fragile toy; if it capsized in shallow water, his glee was none the less as the crisp waves curled up and over him. He liked to paddle sea-wards, safe in his skiff at least from "land bores;" and then to let it drift "until the sea breeze came and lapped up its side over the gunwale and drove him to the shore." On one occasion he persuaded Jane Williams with her children to enter the frail bark, the gunwale of which was in consequence sunk within a hand's-breadth of the water's edge. From the shadows he pulled round a promontory into deep blue water; then rested on his oars in dreaming mood, musing, pondering. On a sudden he raised his head, and with brightening face exclaimed joyfully, "Now let us together solve the great mystery." Jane, with feminine adroitness, beguiled her uncanny oarsman to thoughts of the shore, and when she saw the sandy bottom snatched up her babes, and clambered out so hurriedly that the punt capsized. "Edward and I," writes Trelawny, who was then a visitor at Casa Magni, "picked them up ; the bard was underneath the boat, and rose with it partly on his back, and was not unlike a turtle, or a hermit crab that houses itself in any empty shell it can find." "Solve the great mystery!" exclaimed Jane. "Why, he is the greatest of all mysteries. Who can predict what he will do?"

In one particular only did their summer plaything displease Shelley and Williams. With words that had in them a touch of extravagance, Shelley still acknowledged the genius of Byron. "I do not write," he told Horace Smith. "I have lived too long near Lord Byron, and the sun has extinguished the glowworm." But he had drawn away from personal relations with Byron, and was resolved that henceforth they should move apart. "I shall see little of Lord Byron," he wrote to Mr. Gisborne (June 18), "nor shall I permit Hunt to form the intermediate link between him and me. I detest all society—almost all, at least— and Lord Byron is the nucleus of all that is hateful and tiresome in it." And to Horace Smith, "I, who could never have been regarded as more than the link of the two thunderbolts, cannot now consent to be even that." That anything belonging to him should be a perpetual reminder of Byron would be hateful and intolerable to Shelley. His boat was originally to have been built for him, in partnership with Trelawny and Williams. Trelawny had chosen the name "Don Juan," and Shelley did not raise an objection. The partnership was dissolved before the boat was launched ; * she became the property of Shelley alone, at the cost of £80, and he and Mary named her the *Ariel*. "Lord Byron," writes Mary to Mrs. Gisborne (June 2), "chose to take fire at this, and determined that she should

---

* The wish to escape Trelawny, Shelley tells Mr. Gisborne (June 18), induced him to become the sole proprietor. Trelawny's close connection with Byron probably alienated Shelley.

be called after the poem ; wrote to Roberts to have the name painted on the mainsail ; and she arrived thus disfigured. For days and nights full twenty-one did Shelley and Edward ponder on her anabaptism, and the washing out the primeval stain. Turpentine, spirits of wine, buccata, all were tried, and it became dappled, and no more. At length the piece has been taken out, and reefs put, so that the sail does not look worse. I do not know what Lord Byron will say, but, lord and poet as he is, he could not be allowed to make a coal-barge of our boat." * Shelley, in writing to Trelawny, did not betray his vexation, and named the boat as Trelawny had proposed that she should be christened.

"Percy is well," wrote Mary of her boy, "and Shelley singularly so ; this incessant boating does him a great deal of good." Through storm and calm the days went by ; it seemed a blissful pause in the impetuous race of life ; a trance of silent wonder and beauty after so much excitement, so much pain, so much eager aspiration, and baffled enterprise and disappointment. Now a gale encircled the bay with whirling foam, and the waves broke upon the beach with a sound like that of booming artillery ; now the waters were covered with purple nautili, " Portuguese men-of-war," as the sailors call them, which told of a lull after wild weather ; now the sun was conquering the sea-mists brought by the south-west wind ; or thunder-clouds gathered on the mountains, and the landscape shimmered in the heat ; or the voyagers drove along the bay in the evening wind under the summer moon, "until," as Shelley writes, " earth appears another world."

---

* Williams writes in his journal of May 17, " Unbent the mainsail and took it to Maglian to see if the letters which Lord Byron, in his contemptible vanity, or for some other purpose, begged of Roberts to inscribe on the boat's mainsail ; all in vain " (*sic*).

It was a pause in the race; a season for renewal of strength, and unconscious growth, before the putting forth of higher powers. "I do not go on with 'Charles the First,'" Shelley wrote (June 18). "I feel too little certainty of the future and too little satisfaction with regard to the past to undertake any subject seriously and deeply. I stand, as it were, upon a precipice, which I have ascended with great, and cannot descend without greater peril, and I am content if the heaven above me is calm for the passing moment." But from the heights to which he had climbed he could look down on life and all its sad, mad, joyous, piteous pageantry. While in the shimmering heat of the summer days Shelley rested in his boat which weltered on the waters, or gazed forth from shore on the mystic splendour of the sea in its breathing calm, or on the endless trooping of the waves; or while he sat on moonlight nights among the rocks, his shallop close at hand, and, the rippling and lapping all around, he wrote the greatest and the wisest verses among all that he has written. "The Triumph of Life," begun at Pisa, is the expression of Shelley's mind in its mood of highest musing and imagining during the days upon the Gulf of Spezzia. It is no simple joyous mood, rather one of high, sad strength, pathetic renunciation, with insight gained from error, and serenity attained through passion. The poem contains the promise for Shelley's poetry, and perhaps for Shelley's life, of a reconcilement between his pursuit of the ideal and his dealings with actual events and living men and women. The triumphal car of life rolls forward in Shelley's vision amid the mad troop of those who hasten they know not whither; while, bound to the conqueror's chariot, are the world-renowned captives, who, for any lure that life can offer, had yielded up their freedom, or, having fought a vain fight, had been defeated. But all are not there, either in that fierce and obscene crowd or among those melancholy captives. Socrates is not there; nor is Jesus. To know one's self, and to know the Highest, this and this alone makes it impossible that life should ever defeat us or deceive. For, knowing these, we shall know the world, and temper our heart to its object, loving well, yet wisely, not with the self-abandoning passion of Rousseau, not even with the purer and loftier error of Plato. "Good far more than evil impulses," Shelley had written to Mary from Ravenna, "love far more than hatred, has been to me, except as you have been the object of it, the source of all sorts of mischief." Henceforth he would be on his guard against the errors of love—against identifying any mortal object with that for which alone man's being is made; he would love what he had found best and truest in life; but even this with a knowledge that it is not the absolute, and with a touch of renouncement in his adhesion Such is part of the ethical or spiritual import of Shelley's noble fragment. In the general outline of its imaginative treatment and in its metre the poem follows Petrarch's "Triumph of Love," and this fact may encourage us to believe that Shelley did not design to extend the poem to great length, and that our loss in its incompleteness is less serious than some have supposed. In the details of its imagery there is a Dantesque manner rarely found in Shelley's writings. If we may venture to hope that in the existing fragment we possess a considerable portion of the entire poem, we yet must read it with a sense, at once proud and mournful, that the "Triumph of Life" may have been but the starting-point for a new and higher development of the writer's genius.

Shelley's mood this summer was one of unusual joy. Yet, while taking a vigorous part in life, he would henceforth hold loosely by it, and never become its captive slave. At times he dreamed that a day might arrive when, if the anguish of an irrevocable malady possessed his senses, he might himself lightly sever the link which bound him to this world. Meanwhile he would play his part in the world earnestly and with activity. Two extracts from letters written within a few days of each other, and both within a few days of Shelley's death, exhibit these different aspects of his mind. " Should you meet with any scientific person," he wrote to Trelawny on June 18, "capable of preparing the *Prussic Acid, or essential oil of bitter almonds*, I should regard it as a great kindness if you could procure me a small quantity. It requires the greatest caution in preparation, and ought to be highly concentrated ; I would give any price for this medicine. You remember we talked of it the other night, and we both expressed a wish to possess it ; my wish was serious, and sprung from the desire of avoiding needless suffering. I need not tell you I have no intention of suicide at present, but I confess it would be a comfort to me to hold in my possession that golden key to the chamber of perpetual rest." But for a denizen of our earth, activity, not rest, is the law of existence. " It seems to me," Shelley wrote to Horace Smith, with reference to Moore's warnings against the dangerous influence exercised by him over Byron—"it seems to me that things have now arrived at such a crisis as requires every man plainly to utter his sentiments on the inefficacy of the existing religious, no less than political systems, for restraining and guiding mankind. Let us see the truth, whatever that may be. The destiny of man can scarcely be so degraded that he was born only to die ; and if such should be the case, delusions, especially the gross and preposterous ones of the existing religion, can scarce' supposed to exalt it. If every man said what he it could not subsist a day. But all, more or themselves to the element that surrou' contribute to the evils they lament by the hypocrisy that springs from them." Shelley, the armed soldier of ideas, was still alert and vigilant. But if ever his zeal was destructive, it was not so now. He abhorred superstition chiefly because it lies like a shadow between man and God, and the eclipse hanging over heaven is worshipped in place of the true sun.*

"I still inhabit this divine bay," Shelley wrote on June 29, "reading Spanish dramas, and sailing, and listening to the most enchanting music." The music was that of Jane's guitar, played at evening on the terrace, or on board the *Ariel* while she sailed slow beneath the moon. The simple melodies affected Shelley more deeply than could music more complex and abstruse. "If the past and the future could be obliterated," he says, "the present would content me so well that I could say with Faust to the passing moment, 'Remain thou, thou art so beautiful.'" And again, "My only regret is that the summer must ever pass, or that Mary has not the same predilection for this place that I have, which would induce me never to shift my quarters." Mary, indeed, could not find the same pleasure in life at San Terenzo that Shelley had, whose days were spent drinking in the joy of the sun, the breeze, the waves. Again there was promise that a babe would be theirs before the winter came, and Mary, weak and nervous, had little capacity to enjoy the compensations afforded by her surroundings for the roughness and discomforts of life at Casa Magni. The toils of housekeeping for two families taxed her strength. The very excess of

---

* " And Gregory, and John, and men divine,
    Who rose like shadows between man and God,
    Till that eclipse, still hanging over heaven,
    Was worshipped by the world o'er which they strode
    For the true sun it quenched."
                                    " Triumph of Life."

beauty oppressed and persecuted her overwrought nerves —beauty in whose midst she lay powerless, which encircled her as with some woven spell, or which held her passive under a very nightmare of loveliness.

During these days Mary was aware that things went ill with her father, and that Shelley, through his regard for her, was concealing the truth. "The die, so far as I am concerned, seems to be cast," Godwin had written to her on April 19, "and all that remains is that I should entreat you to forget that you have a father in existence. Why should your prime of youthful vigour be tarnished and made wretched by what relates to me? I have lived to the full age of man in as much comfort as can reasonably be expected to fall to the lot of a human being. What signifies what becomes of the few wretched years that remain?" "This day," he wrote a fortnight later, "we are compelled by summary process to leave the house we live in, and hide our heads in whatever alley will receive us. If we can compound with our creditor, and he seems not unwilling to accept £400 (I have talked with him on the subject), we may emerge again." "The Godwins," Shelley had written to Mr. Gisborne in April, "are for ever plotting and devising pretexts for money; none of which, however, they get; first, because I *can't;* and secondly, because I *won't.*" In May, Shelley was convinced that Godwin was indeed in dire distress. He wrote to Horace Smith begging that he would advance the sum of £400; but Godwin had already applied in that quarter and in vain. It was not in Smith's power to lend such a sum, nor did he believe that the loan would benefit Godwin, whose proper course would have been to take the benefit of the Insolvent Act. Why should he call upon his friends to give him their money to pay away to strangers, commissioners, and assignees? Such letters as those of Godwin could not be placed in Mary's hands while she was weak and ailing ; yet something must be told her in reply to her inquiries about her father. Shelley's difficult duty was to protect her from sudden shock or prolonged suffering, and at the same time to keep open, if possible, such communications as might be safely permitted between her and her father. " It is not my intention or my wish," he wrote to Mrs. Godwin (May 29), " that the circumstances in which your family is involved should be concealed from her, but that the details should be suspended until they assume a more prosperous character, or at least the letters addressed to her, or intended for her perusal on that subject, should not convey a supposition that she could do more than she does, thus exasperating the sympathy which she already feels too intensely for her father's distress, which she would sacrifice all she possesses to remedy, but the remedy of which is beyond her power."

" I described to you the place we were living in," wrote Mary to Mrs. Gisborne, in a letter which recalls the incidents of the great sorrow that closed her youth ; " our desolate house, the beauty yet strangeness of the scenery, and the delight Shelley took in all this ; he never was in better health or spirits than during this time. I was not well in body or mind. My nerves were wound up to the utmost irritation, and the sense of misfortune hung over my spirits. No words can tell you how I hated our house and the country about it. Shelley reproached me for this. His health was good, and the place was quite after his own heart. What could I answer ? That the people were wild and hateful ; that though the country was beautiful, yet I liked a more *countryfied* place, and that there was great difficulty in living ; that all our Tuscans would leave us, and that the very jargon of these *Genovese* was disgusting. This was all I had to say, but no words could describe my feelings ; the beauty of the woods made me weep and shudder ; so vehement was my feeling of dislike, that I used to rejoice when the winds and waves permitted me to go out in the boat so that I was not obliged to take my usual walk among tree-shaded paths, alleys of vine-festooned trees—all that before I doted on, and that now weighed on me. My only moments of peace were on board that unhappy boat—when, lying down with my head on his knee, I shut my eyes and felt the wind and our swift motion alone."

At five o'clock on the morning of June 6, Shelley and Williams started in the *Ariel* for Via Reggio to meet Claire on her way from Florence to Casa Magni. Baffling morning breezes fell at noon into a calm ; the heat was excessive ; and the boat lay for hours like a log on the water. When evening came they were no further than Massa, and had lost the chance of bringing Claire round by sea. "At seven," Williams writes in his journal, "rowed in to Massa beach ; but on attempting to land we were opposed by the guard, who told us that the head person of the fort (of two rusty guns) being at Festa, that as he was not able to read (*sic*), we must wait till the former arrived. Not willing to put up with such treatment, Shelley told him at his peril to detain us, when the fellow brought down two old muskets, and we prepared our pistols, which he no sooner saw we were determined to use than he called our servant to the beach, and desiring him to hold the paper about a yard from him, he suffered two gentlemen who were bathing near the place to explain who and what we were. Upon this, the fellow's tone changed from presumption to the most cowardly fawning, and we proceeded to Massa unmolested. Slept at Massa about three miles inland." Next day, after beating slowly round Magra Point, Shelley and Williams reached home in the afternoon a few hours before the arrival of Claire, who had travelled from Via Reggio by land.

In good time Claire arrived ; on the next day or the next but one Mary Shelley was seriously unwell, and for a week she remained in a condition which caused grave anxiety to her friends. On the morning of Sunday, June 16, came the threatened calamity—a dangerous miscarriage. Her life, probably through Shelley's promptitude and decision, was saved. " I was so ill," Mary afterwards wrote to Mrs. Gisborne, "that for seven hours I lay nearly lifeless—kept from fainting by brandy, vinegar, eau-de-Cologne, etc. At length, ice was brought to our solitude ; it came before the doctor, so Claire and Jane were afraid of using it ; but Shelley overruled them, and by an unsparing application of it I was restored. They all thought, and so did I at one time, that I was about to die." Claire's presence at Casa Magni at such a crisis had its uses ; yet to the invalid she did not bring comfort or repose of mind. " Claire is with us," Shelley wrote to Mr. Gisborne (June 18) ; " and the death of her child seems to have restored her to tran-quillity. Her character is somewhat altered. She is viva-cious and talkative, and, though she teases me sometimes, I like her. Mary is not, for the present, much discontented with her visit, which is merely temporary, and which the circumstances of the case rendered indispensable."

Over-fatigue and the alarm caused by Mary's illness strained Shelley's nerves, and afflicted him in sleep with frightful visions. " I think it was on the Saturday after my illness [June 22]," wrote Mary, " while yet unable to walk, I was confined to my bed, in the middle of the night I was awoke by hearing him scream and come rushing into my room ; I was sure that he was asleep, and tried to waken him by calling on him, but he continued to scream, which inspired me with such a panic that I jumped out of

bed and ran across the hall to Mrs. Williams's room, where
I fell through weakness, though I was so frightened that
I got up again immediately ; she let me in, and Williams
went to Shelley, who had been wakened by my getting
out of bed. He said that he had not been asleep, and
that it was a vision that he saw that had frightened him.
But as he declared that he had not screamed, it was certainly
a dream and no waking vision. What had frightened him
was this. He dreamt that, lying as he did in bed, Edward
and Jane came in to him ; they were in the most horrible
condition—their bodies lacerated, their bones starting
through their skin, the faces pale yet stained with blood ;
they could hardly walk, but Edward was the weakest and
Jane was supporting him. Edward said, ' Get up, Shelley ;
the sea is flooding the house, and it is all coming down.'
Shelley got up, he thought, and went to his window that
looked on the terrace and the sea, and thought he saw the
sea rushing in. Suddenly his vision changed, and he saw
the figure of himself strangling me, that had made him
rush into my room ; yet, fearful of frightening me, he dared
not approach the bed, when my jumping out awoke him,
or, as he phrased it, caused his vision to vanish. All this
was frightful enough, and talking it over the next morning,
he told me that he had had many visions lately. He had
seen the figure of himself, which met him as he walked on
the terrace, and said to him, ' How long do you mean to
be content ? '—no very terrific words, and certainly not prophetic of what has occurred. But Shelley had often seen
these figures when ill ; but the strangest thing is that Mrs.
Williams saw him. Now Jane, though a woman of sensibility, has not much imagination, and is not in the slightest
degree nervous, neither in dreams or otherwise. She was
standing one day—the day before I was taken ill—at a
window that looked on the terrace with Trelawny ; it was

day ; she saw, as she thought, Shelley pass by the window, as he often was then, without a coat or jacket ; he passed again. Now, as he passed both times the same way, and as from the side towards which he went each time there was no way to get back except past the window again (except over a wall twenty feet from the ground), she was struck at seeing him pass twice thus, and looked out and seeing him no more she cried, 'Good God ! can Shelley have leapt from the wall ? Where can he be gone ?' 'Shelley ?' said Trelawny ; 'no Shelley has past. What do you mean ?' Trelawny says that she trembled exceedingly when she heard this ; and it proved, indeed, that Shelley had never been on the terrace, and was far off at the time she saw him."

News to rejoice Shelley reached the Villa Magni on June 19. The Hunts, who had left Plymouth more than a month since, were at last in the harbour of Genoa ; the children in the best of health and spirits, the elders not the worse for their voyage ; in a few days they would pass Lerici on their way by sea to Leghorn, and Hunt's eyes might perhaps distinguish from the vessel's side the white house on the water's edge inhabited by his friends. Shelley would have hastened at once to Genoa, but that Hunt's letter had been delayed in its transmission from Pisa, and he feared that the travellers might have started for Leghorn before he could reach Genoa. It was glorious midsummer weather ; too dry and sultry for the crops, but hardly too hot for Shelley's enjoyment. At Parma the labourers were forbidden to work in the fields between ten o'clock and five ; prayers for rain were offered up in the churches, and relics were borne in procession. The *Ariel,* which for a while had been beached, was run from shore, in order that, on hearing of Hunt's departure from Genoa, Shelley might immediately put to sea and chase the *David Walter* to

Leghorn. While waiting thus in the long monotony of
glowing summer days, a happy incident took place. A
parcel of Shelley's books which had arrived from England
in May, and had been sent unopened to Genoa to be inspected by the ecclesiastical authorities, lest it should contain any immoral or seditious publication, at length was
delivered into the hands of the owner. Here was abundant
pasturage for the coming July days after Shelley's return
from Leghorn. Among other works which enjoyed the
permission of the Church was "Queen Mab" in Clark's
pirated imprint, to which Williams turned with eager
curiosity, finding it an astonishing work, containing admirable passages of verse, and notes as subtle and elegant as
their author could write to-day.

By July 1 news had reached Casa Magni of Hunt's departure from Genoa ; on that day at noon a fine breeze
sprang up from the west ; it was a chance not to be missed
of a prosperous sail to Leghorn. Mary, whose illness had
been followed by nervousness and low spirits, could hardly
bear that her husband should leave her. Undefined fears
for little Percy's health and life possessed her. "I called
Shelley back two or three times," she afterwards wrote to
Mrs. Gisborne, "and told him that if I did not see him
soon, I would go to Pisa with the child ; I cried bitterly
when he went away." At Lerici, Captain Roberts came
on board the *Ariel;* and by nine o'clock that evening they
had cast anchor, astern of Byron's yacht the *Bolivar,* in
the port of Leghorn. At that hour the Health Office was
closed, and it was not possible for the seafarers to land ;
accordingly they procured cushions from the larger vessel,
and lay down to sleep under the open heaven and the
stars of the July night.

With morning came ill tidings. A brawl at Byron's villa
at Monte Nero had given the government the excuse they

desired for banishing Count Gamba and his family from
Tuscany. Byron in consequence would instantly quit the
country ; he would sail for America, or journey, as he had
intended some months since, to Switzerland. Trelawny
must at once start for Genoa in the *Bolivar*, and there make
arrangements for the carriage of Byron's yacht to the Lake
of Geneva. Such reports heard from the deck of the
Bolivar received confirmation when Shelley landed. If
Byron should quit Italy, what was to become of Hunt ?
what of the project of the journal ? The damp cast on
Shelley's hopes for his friend, however, must not dull his
welcome to Italy. Already, indeed, he had given Hunt
most cordial greeting by letter. "A thousand welcomes,
my best friend, to this divine country," he had written on
June 19; "high mountains and seas no longer divide
those whose affections are united. We have much to think
of and talk of when we meet at Leghorn ; but the final
result of our plans will be peace to you, and to me a greater
degree of consolation than has been permitted me since we
met." Now, in the hotel at Leghorn, the long-parted friends
were once more face to face. Thornton Hunt remembered
after many years the cry with which Shelley rushed into his
father's arms : "I am inexpressibly delighted ; you cannot
think how inexpressibly happy it makes me." During four
years of absence each of the two had somewhat altered in
appearance. "I have become since you saw me," Leigh
Hunt had written, with a touch of playful exaggeration,
"an elderly gentleman, with sunken cheeks, and temples
that throb at the least touch of emotion—joy especially."
Shelley, on the contrary, had grown in manly vigour. His
brown hair, indeed, was sprinkled with grey ; but his chest
seemed of larger girth ; "his voice was stronger, his manner
more confident and downright, and although not less emphatic, yet less impulsively changeful." With characteristic

kindliness and energy, he undertook to see the Hunts comfortably settled in the rooms prepared for them at Pisa
in the Lanfranchi Palace, and insisted on bringing Vaccà
to visit Mrs. Hunt, who still suffered from the illness
consequent on her cares, anxieties, and exhaustion of the
preceding year. Vaccà's opinion was unfavourable, and
Hunt's spirits, already shaken by the coldness and caprice
of Byron, sank low when he heard how slight was the hope
that his wife could outlive the year. Vaccà was mistaken.
Mrs. Hunt lived until 1857. It was Shelley's task on the
one hand to sustain Hunt's drooping courage, and on the
other to screw, if possible, Byron's mind to the sticking-
place about the journal. "Between ourselves," he had
written a few days since to Horace Smith (June 29), " I
greatly fear that this alliance will not succeed ; for I, who
could never have been regarded as more than the link of
the two thunderbolts, cannot now consent to be even that ;
and how long the alliance between the wren and the eagle
may continue I will not prophesy." For Hunt's sake it
was now necessary that Shelley should endeavour to fix the
vacillating will of Byron, and bind him to the fulfilment
of his engagement. And, as in many other instances, he
bore down all opposition and effected his purpose. Byron
would settle in Lucca ; . Hunt should have the copyright
of " The Vision of Judgment " for his first number. " This
offer," Shelley wrote to Mary, " if sincere, is *more* than enough
to set up the journal ; and, if sincere, will set everything
right." With the success of his effort on his friend's be ·
half, Shelley's spirits rose. On July 4, while the affairs of
Hunt were still entangled, he had written in a melancholy
strain to Jane Williams, with no other motive than to give
relief to a vague sadness, which he dared not express in
his letter to Mary, whose dejection was already too profound. " How soon those hours past," he wrote to Mrs.

Williams, "and how slowly they return, to pass so soon again, and perhaps for ever, in which we have lived together so intimately and happily! Adieu, my dearest friend. I only write these lines for the pleasure of tracing what will meet your eyes. Mary will tell you all the news." And to Mary on the same day, "How are you, my best Mary? Write especially how is your health, and how your spirits are, and whether you are not more reconciled to staying at Lerici, at least during the summer. You have no idea how I am hurried and occupied. I have not a moment's leisure, but will write by the next post." By Sunday, July 7, his work had all been done, and the day was given to happy idleness. Acting as guide to the sights of Pisa, he visited the Leaning Tower with Hunt, and together they listened to the pealing organ in the Duomo. "He was looking better," writes Hunt, "than I had ever seen him; we talked of a thousand things—we anticipated a thousand pleasures." When on that day he called to take leave of Lady Mountcashell, he seemed to her in better health and spirits than she had ever known him, his face burnt by the sun, and his heart light because he had succeeded in rendering his poor friends tolerably comfortable. Yet the ground-tone of his disposition, Hunt thought, was less sanguine than it had been in former times. "If I die to-morrow," Shelley said to Mrs. Hunt, "I have lived to be older than my father; I am ninety years of age."

When darkness fell, adieus were said. Hunt entreated his friend, if the weather were violent on the morrow, not to give way to his daring spirits and venture to sea. For reading on the voyage, Shelley took with him Hunt's copy of the last volume of Keats—that containing the noble fragment of "Hyperion." "Keep it," said Hunt, "till you give it to me with your own hands." And so the friends parted, and Shelley's post-chaise drove through the dark along the road to Leghorn.

The weather had held on in unabated heat and glare and oppressive July splendour. "Processions of priests and religiosi," wrote Williams in his journal (July 4), "have for several days been active in their prayers for rain ; but the gods are either angry, or nature is too powerful." The aspect of the sky on Monday morning, July 8, seemed to portend a change ; there was a thunderstorm, but it rolled away, and all again was fair. The forenoon was spent by Shelley in necessary business in the town ; he visited his bankers' with Trelawny, obtained a supply of dollars, and made purchases of articles needed for the housekeeping at Casa Magni. A light breeze, blowing in the direction of Lerici, sprang up. Captain Roberts was not without apprehension that the elements were brewing a tempest. "Stay," he said, "until to-morrow, to see if the weather is settled." But Edward Williams for days had been eager to return ; in seven hours, he declared, they would be at home. Shelley's fit of extravagant good spirits that morning did not predispose him to a surly prudence, and he would not say nay to the desire of his friend. By midday, or a little later, they were on board the *Ariel*, having with them the sailor-lad Charles Vivian, who had been in charge of the boat. Trelawny, in the *Bolivar*, proposed to accompany them into the offing, but not having obtained a port-clearance from the Health Office, he was not permitted to carry out his intention. Between one and two o'clock, the *Ariel* sailed out of the harbour, almost at the same moment with two feluccas. Sullenly and reluctantly Trelawny re-anchored, furled his sails, and with a ship's glass watched the progress of his friends' boat. They should have started at early morning, said his Genoese mate, and added, "They are standing too much in shore; the current will set them there." "They will soon have the land-breeze," replied Trelawny. "Maybe," continued the mate, "she will soon have too much breeze; that gaff topsail is foolish in a boat with no deck and no sailor on board." Then, pointing to the south-west, "Look at those black lines and dirty rags hanging on them out of the sky; look at the smoke on the water; the devil is brewing mischief."

Captain Roberts had also kept the boat in view. Standing on the end of the mole, he saw her going at about the rate of seven knots. Anxious to know how she would weather the storm which was visibly coming from the Gulf, he got leave to ascend the lighthouse tower, whence he could still discern her about ten miles out at sea, off Via Reggio, and he could perceive that they were taking in the topsail; then the haze of the storm hid them, and he saw them no more. "Although the sun was obscured by mists," Trelawny writes, "it was oppressively sultry. There was not a breath of air in the harbour. The heaviness of the atmosphere and an unwonted stillness benumbed my senses. I went down into the cabin and sank into a slumber. I was roused up by a noise overhead, and went on deck. The men were getting up a chain-cable to let go another anchor. There was a general stir amongst the shipping; shifting berths, getting down yards and masts, veering out cables, hauling in of hawsers, letting go anchors, hailing from the ships and quays, boats sculling rapidly to and fro. It was almost dusk, although only half-past six o'clock. The sea was of the colour, and looked as solid and smooth as a sheet of lead, and covered with an oily scum. Gusts of wind swept over without ruffling it, and big drops of rain fell on its surface, rebounding, as if they could not penetrate it. There was a commotion in the air, made up of many threatening sounds, coming upon us from the sea.

Fishing-craft and coasting-vessels, under bare poles, rushed by us in shoals, running foul of the ships in the harbour. As yet the din and hubbub was that made by men, but their shrill pipings were suddenly silenced by the crashing voice of a thunder-squall that burst right over our heads. For some time no other sounds were to be heard than the thunder, wind, and rain. When the fury of the storm, which did not last for more than twenty minutes, had abated, and the horizon was in some degree cleared, I looked to seaward anxiously, in the hope of descrying Shelley's boat amongst the many small craft scattered about. I watched every speck that loomed on the horizon, thinking that they would have borne up on their return to the port, as all the other boats that had gone out in the same direction had done."

At eight o'clock Trelawny went on shore. It was then calm ; but during the night the wind blew hard at intervals, with rain and lightning that flashed along the coast, and pealing thunder. At daylight he returned on board ; none of the crews that had fled into harbour from the storm brought tidings of Shelley's boat. "They either knew nothing," writes Trelawny, "or would say nothing. My Genoese, with the quick eye of a sailor, pointed out, on board a fishing-boat, an English-made oar that he thought he had seen in Shelley's boat, but the entire crew swore by all the saints in the calendar that this was not so." A period of anxious suspense followed. On the morning of the third day, Trelawny rode to Pisa, called at the Lanfranchi Palace, inquired whether a letter had been received from the Casa Magni, and was informed that there was none. "I told my fears to Hunt," he writes, "and then went upstairs to Byron. When I told him, his lip quivered, and his voice faltered as he questioned me. I sent a courier to Leghorn to despatch the *Bolivar* to cruise along the coast, whilst I mounted my horse and rode in the same direction. I also despatched a courier along the coast to go as far as Nice."

Meanwhile at Casa Magni anxiety was growing to alarm. During the days of Shelley's visit to Leghorn and Pisa, Mary was slowly regaining strength; but she could not recover her cheerfulness or serenity. When Jane Williams and Claire took their evening walk, she would patrol the terrace, "oppressed with wretchedness, yet gazing on the most beautiful scene in the world." It was in the summer that William died; again a summer had come, and one of excessive heats; was little Percy's life more secure than William's had been? She reminded her trembling heart of the love, peace, competence, which she enjoyed; but tears filled her eyes. "Yet I thought when he, when my Shelley returns, I shall be happy—he will comfort me; if my boy be ill, he will restore him and encourage me. . . . Thus a week past. On Monday, 8th, Jane had a letter from Edward dated Saturday; he said that he waited at Leghorn for Shelley, who was at Pisa; that Shelley's return was certain; 'but,' he continued, 'if he should not come by Monday, I will come in a felucca, and you may expect me on Thursday evening at furthest.'

"This was Monday, the fatal Monday, but with us it was stormy all day, and we did not at all suppose that they could put to sea. At twelve at night we had a thunderstorm. Tuesday it rained all day and was calm—the sky wept on their graves. On Wednesday, the wind was fair from Leghorn, and in the evening several feluccas arrived thence. One brought word they had sailed Monday, but we did not believe them. Thursday was another day of fair wind, and when twelve at night came, and we did not see the tall sails of the little boat double the promontory before us, we began to fear, not the truth, but some illness, some disagreeable news for their detention.

"Jane got so uneasy that she determined to proceed the next day to Leghorn in a boat to see what was the matter. Friday came, and with it a heavy sea and bad wind. Jane, however, resolved to be rowed to Leghorn, since no boat could sail, and busied herself in preparations. I wished her to wait for letters, since Friday was letter-day. She would not, but the sea detained her; the swell rose so that no boat would venture out. At twelve at noon our letters came; there was one from Hunt to Shelley; it said, 'Pray write to tell us how you got home, for they say that you had bad weather after you sailed on Monday, and we are anxious.' The paper fell from me. I trembled all over. Jane read it. 'Then it is all over!' she said. 'No, my dear Jane,' I cried, 'it is not all over, but this suspense is dreadful. Come with me—we will go to Leghorn; we will post, to be swift and learn our fate.'

"We crossed to Lerici, despair in our hearts; they raised our spirits there by telling us that no accident had been heard of, and that it must have been known, etc. But still our fear was great, and without resting we posted to Pisa. It must have been fearful to see us—two poor, wild, aghast creatures, driving towards the sea to learn if we were to be for ever doomed to misery. I knew that Hunt was at Pisa, at Lord Byron's house, but I thought that Lord Byron was at Leghorn. I settled that we should drive to Casa Lanfranchi, that I should get out and ask the fearfu question of Hunt, 'Do you know anything of Shelley?' On entering Pisa, the idea of seeing Hunt for the first time for four years under such circumstances, and asking him such a question, was so terrific to me that it was with difficulty that I prevented myself from going into convulsions. My struggles were dreadful. They knocked at the door, and some one called out, 'Chi è?' It was the Guiccioli's maid. Lord Byron was in Pisa. Hunt was in bed, so I was to see Lord Byron instead of him. This was a great relief to me. I staggered upstairs; the Guiccioli came to meet me smiling, while I could hardly say, 'Where is he—Sapete alcuna cosa di Shelley?' They knew nothing; he had left Pisa on Sunday; on Monday, he had sailed; there had been bad weather Monday afternoon; more they knew not.

"Both Lord Byron and the lady have told me since that on that terrific evening I looked more like a ghost than a woman; light seemed to emanate from my features, my face was very white, I looked like marble. Alas, I had risen almost from a bed of sickness for this journey. I had travelled all day; it was now twelve at night, and we, refusing to rest, proceeded to Leghorn—not in despair —no, for then we must have died, but with sufficient hope to keep up the agitation of the spirits which was all my life. It was past two in the morning when we arrived. They took us to the wrong inn; neither Trelawny or Captain Roberts were there, nor did we exactly know where they were, so we were obliged to wait until daylight. We threw ourselves drest on our beds, and slept a little, but at six o'clock we went to one or two inns to ask for one or the other of these gentlemen. We found Roberts at the Globe. He came down to us with a face which seemed to tell us that the worst was true, and here we learned all that had occurred during the week they had been absent from us, and under what circumstances they had departed on their return."

Yet all hope was not extinct. The boat might have been blown to Corsica or Elba, and, not knowing the coast, they might have sailed still further. It was said that they had been seen in the Gulf. "We resolved to return,"

Mary Shelley continues, "with all possible speed; we sent a courier to go from tower to tower along the coast to know if anything had been seen or found; and at nine a.m. we quitted Leghorn, stopped but one moment at Pisa, and proceeded towards Lerici. When at two miles from Via Reggio we rode down to that town to know if they knew anything. Here our calamity first began to break on us. A little boat and a water-cask had been found five miles off. They had manufactured a *piccolissima lancia* of thin planks stitched by a shoemaker, just to let them run on shore without wetting themselves, as our boat drew four feet of water. The description of that found tallied with this; but then this boat was very cumbersome, and in bad weather they might have been easily led to throw it overboard. The cask frightened me most; but the same reason might in some sort be given for that. I must tell you that Jane and I were not now alone. Trelawny accompanied us back to our home. We journeyed on, and reached the Magra about half-past ten p.m. I cannot describe to you what I felt in the first moment when, fording this river, I felt the water splash about our wheels. I was suffocated. I gasped for breath. I thought I should have gone into convulsions, and I struggled violently that Jane might not perceive it. Looking down the river I saw two great lights burning at the *foce;* a voice from within me seemed to cry aloud, 'That is his grave.'

"After passing the river I gradually recovered. Arriving at Lerici we were obliged to cross our little bay in a boat. San Terenzo was illuminated for a festa. What a scene The waving sea, the scirocco wind, the lights of the town towards which we rowed, and our own desolate hearts, that coloured all with a shroud. We landed; nothing had been heard of them. This was Saturday, July 13, and thus we waited until Thursday, July 25 [an error for

July 18], thrown about by hope and fear. We sent messengers along the coast towards Genoa and to Via Reggio—nothing had been found more than the *lancetta.* Reports were brought us; we hoped; and yet to tell you all the agony we endured during those twelve days [an error for *six*] would be to make you conceive a universe of pain, each moment intolerable and giving place to one still worse. The people of the country, too, added to one's discomfort; they are like wild savages. On festas, the men and women and children in different bands—the sexes always separate—pass the whole night in dancing on the sands close to our door, running into the sea, then back again, and screaming all the time one detestable air—the most detestable in the world. Then the scirocco perpetually blew, and the sea for ever moaned their dirge. On Thursday, 25th [an error for 18th], Trelawny left us to go to Leghorn to see what was doing or what could be done. On Friday [the 19th], I was very ill, but as evening came on I said to Jane, 'If anything had been found on the coast, Trelawny would have returned to let us know. He has not returned, so I hope.' About seven o'clock p.m. he did return. All was over; all was quiet now; they had been found washed on shore."

Two bodies, some three or four miles apart, had been found upon the beach; one near Via Reggio, in the Duchy of Lucca, the other in Tuscan territory. The latter, found on July 16 or 17, had been buried in the sand thirty hours before Trelawny's arrival at the spot. The former, cast ashore on the 18th, was seen by him on the following day. The parts of the body not protected by clothing were fleshless. "The tall slight figure," writes Trelawny, "the jacket, the volume of Sophocles * in one pocket, and Keats's poems

* The " Sophocles " of Trelawny's " Recollections " (1858) is changed to "Æschylus" in his "Records" (1878). Mr. Garnett, in his article on

in the other, doubled back as if the reader, in the act of reading, had hastily thrust it away, were all too familiar to me to leave a doubt on my mind that this mutilated corpse was any other than Shelley's." The body of Williams was much more mutilated ; "it had no other covering than the shreds of a shirt, and that partly drawn over the head, as if the wearer had been in the act of taking it off, a black silk handkerchief tied. sailor-fashion round the neck, socks, and one boot, indicating also that he had attempted to strip. . . . It was not until three weeks after the wreck of the boat that a third body was found—four miles from the other two. This I concluded to be that of the sailor-boy Charles Vivian, although it was a mere skeleton, and impossible to be identified. It was buried in the sand, above the reach of the waves." *

"Is there no hope ? " Mary Shelley inquired of Trelawny, after a dreadful interval of silence, when on Friday, July 19, he reappeared unexpectedly at Casa Magni. He could not answer, but left the room and sent the servant with the children to the two widowed women. Next day (July 20) he conducted them from the hearing of the waves to Pisa, where they might have the comfort of Hunt's companionship. The body of Shelley's beloved boy lay in the cemetery at Rome ; and Mary recalled to mind the stanzas of "Adonais" which tell of its living beauty in the midst of sorrow. There all that was earthly of her dearest one should rest. Unhappily, a difficulty arose from the strict quarantine laws of the Italian coast, which forbade that

"Shelley's Last Days," also says "Æschylus." In August, 1886, I had in my hands the volume preserved at Boscombe Manor as that found in Shelley's pocket, and I made certain that that volume is Sophocles. It has been stated that the volume of Keats's poems was doubled back at "The Eve of St. Agnes."

* In a letter to Leigh Hunt, Miss Clairmont informs him of a report of July 14 that the bodies had been found three miles from Via Reggio.

bodies cast upon the shore, and buried in quicklime amid the sands, should be disinterred. By the exertions of Trelawny and the kindly aid of Mr. Dawkins, English _chargé d'affaires_ at Florence, the permission of the authorities for the removal of the bodies was obtained. It had occurred to the friends of Shelley and Williams that if the bodies were consumed by fire upon the sands, and only the ashes preserved, all objection arising from the quarantine laws would cease, and that the subsequent difficulties as to reburial would be diminished. The form of permission, however, obtained by Trelawny and presented to the Governor of the Tower of Migliarino, at the Bocca Lericcio, made no mention of the intended burning of the bodies, and it needed some little persuasion to obtain his consent.

An iron furnace of the dimensions of a human body had been made at Leghorn under Trelawny's direction. He had also ordered two small boxes of oak, about the size of writing-desks, lined with black velvet, having a brass plate affixed to each, setting forth in Latin the name, age, country, and fate of the deceased. On August 14, Trelawny, with an English friend, Captain Shenley, sailed from Leghorn in the _Bolivar_, and after a tedious passage of ten or eleven hours, anchored off Via Reggio. Having landed, and arranged with the officer in command of the Tower of Migliarino, he despatched a letter to Byron at Pisa, informing him and Hunt that all was ready for noon on the following day. By that hour, on August 15, he stood upon the beach where lay the body of Edward Williams, some eighteen paces from the breaking surf. A squad of soldiers in working dresses, armed with mattocks and spades, under the superintendence of a quarantine officer, was at hand. Byron and Shenley, accompanied by an officer with foot soldiers and some dismounted dragoons, soon joined him. A considerable group of spectators from the neighbourhood stood at a little distance. The gnarled root of a pine tree marked the spot where the body lay. Fuel had been brought, but needlessly, for driftwood on the beach and timber fallen from a stunted pine-forest close at hand would have afforded an abundant supply. "The heat was intense, the sand being so scorched as to render standing on it painful. Mr. Shenley and myself were occupied with the soldiers in clearing away the sand, and we anxiously watched the first appearance of the body. I first pulled out a black silk handkerchief, then a collar of a shirt, which from its peculiarity I knew to be my friend's, and a boot, which we compared with one brought for the occasion, and which removed every doubt. . . . Lord Byron had often declared he could recognize Williams by the form and peculiarities of his teeth ; he examined the jaw, and said that, had nothing else remained, he would have sworn to his identification. Having now made a funeral pile with faggots all around and green branches on the top, I set fire to it. Lord Byron, Mr. Leigh Hunt, Mr. Shenley, and myself gathered round, throwing on it frankincense, salt, and wine.

"Lord Byron, looking at the shapeless, limbless mass, as it was taken from its sandy grave, said, 'What is a human body ? Why, it might be the rotten carcase of a sheep for all I can distinguish ;' and further continued, pointing to the black handkerchief, 'Look, an old rag retains its form longer than he who wore it ! What a humble and degrading thought, that we shall one day resemble this !' He then pointed out the peculiar appearance of the flames at this moment. The body and skull, which burned fiercely, gave them a silvery and wavy look of indescribable brightness and purity." "Let us try the strength of these waters that drowned our friends," said Byron. "How far do you think they were when their boat sank ?" He stripped and swam

2 P

from shore, with Shenley and Trelawny as his companions in the waters. "Before we got a mile out, Byron was sick and persuaded to return to the shore. My companion, too, was seized with cramp, and reached the land by my aid." At half-past three, nothing was left of the funeral pile, except a quantity of blackish-looking ashes, mingled with white and broken fragments of bones. These were placed in the oaken box, and consigned to the care of Byron and Hunt.

Next day (August 16), the ceremony was repeated for the body of Shelley at a spot three or four miles nearer to the Gulf of Spezzia. Again Hunt and Byron were present, having driven hither in a carriage ; again the Health Officer and the soldiers, among them on this second occasion some mounted dragoons. The people from the surrounding district flocked in crowds to witness so strange a spectacle. "The sea, with the islands of Gorgona, Capraja, and Elba, was before us ; old battlemented watch-towers stretched along the coast, backed by the marble-crested Apennines glistening in the sun, picturesque from their diversified outlines ; and not a human dwelling was in sight." Three white wands stuck in the yellow sand from low-water to high-water mark indicated, but not with precision, the place of burial. An hour of silent toil went past before they had discovered the lime in which the body lay concealed ; suddenly a mattock with a dull hollow sound struck the skull, causing a general shudder, while the men drew back. The furnace being placed and surrounded by wood, the remains were removed from their shallow resting-place. It was Byron's wish that the skull, which was of unusual beauty, should be preserved ; but it almost instantly fell to pieces. Of the volume of Keats's poems which had been buried with Shelley's body, only the binding remained and this was cast upon the pyre. Although the fire was

greater than that of the preceding day, the body was but
slowly consumed. Three hours elapsed before it separated ;
it then fell open across the breast ; the heart, which was
unusually large, seemed impregnable to the fire. Trelawny
plunged his hand into the flames and snatched this relic
from the burning. The day was one of wide autumnal calm
and beauty. "The Mediterranean," says Leigh Hunt,
"now soft and lucid, kissed the shore as if to make peace
with it. The yellow sand and blue sky were intensely
contrasted with one another ; marble mountains touched the
air with coolness ; and the flame of the fire bore away
towards heaven in vigorous amplitude, wavering and
quivering with a brightness of inconceivable beauty."
During the whole funeral ceremony a solitary sea-bird
crossing and recrossing the pile was the only intruder that
baffled the vigilance of the guard.

Byron, who could not face the scene, had swum off to
his yacht. Leigh Hunt looked on from the carriage.
Having cooled the furnace in the sea, Trelawny collected
the fragments of bones and the ashes, and deposited them
in the oaken box. All was over. Byron and Hunt
returned to Pisa in their carriage. Shenley and Trelawny
bearing the oaken coffer, went on board the *Bolivar*. The
relics of Shelley's heart, given soon after by Trelawny to
Hunt, were, at Mary Shelley's urgent request, supported by
the entreaty of Mrs. Williams, confided to Mary's hands.
After her death, in a copy of the Pisa edition of "Adonais,"
at the page which tells how death is swallowed up in
immortality, was found under a silken covering the em-
browned ashes, now shrunk and withered, which she had
secretly treasured.

When the *Bolivar* arrived off Via Reggio on August 14,
she fell in with two small vessels hired by Trelawny at
Leghorn for the purpose of ascertaining, by the means used

to recover sunken vessels, the spot at which Shelley's boat
had foundered. They had on board the captain of a
felucca, in which Roberts had observed several spars
belonging to the *Ariel.* The captain declared that he
had seen the *Ariel* at the moment of her disappearance;
it was four in the afternoon, the boy was at masthead,
when thwart winds struck the sails ; they had looked away
for an instant, and looking again the boat was gone. They
could not, said the captain, get near her, and passing three
quarters of an hour later over the spot where they had seen
her, no wreck was visible. For six days Trelawny's sailors
dragged the bottom, and at length succeeded in ascertaining
the position of the foundered boat, about two miles off the
coast of Via Reggio, but were unable to bring her up.
When, in September, Captain Roberts raised her from ten
or fifteen fathoms of water, his first impression was that
she had been swamped by a heavy sea ; it was evident,
from the position in which things were found in her, that
she had not capsized. The two masts were carried away
just above the board, the bowsprit broken off close to the
bows, the gunwale stove in, and the hull half full of blue
clay. A closer examination showed that many of the
timbers on the starboard quarter were broken, which led
Roberts to infer that she had been run down by a felucca
in the squall. At Leghorn this was the received opinion ;
but it has been suggested by Peacock that during the
dredging operations so light a craft may have been seriously
injured. "Among the various conjectures respecting thi
lamentable event," writes Leigh Hunt, "a suspicion was
not wanting that the boat had been run down by a larger
one with a view to plunder it. Mr. Shelley was known
to have taken money on board. Crimes of that nature had
occurred often enough to warrant such a suspicion." In
1875, it was stated by Sir Vincent Eyre, writing in the

Times, that an old fisherman who had died twelve years
before at Sarzana confessed to a priest that he was one
of five who, seeing the English boat in great danger, ran
her down, thinking that Byron was on board, and that they
should find gold. Sir Vincent Eyre's informant, a lady living
in a villa overlooking the Bay of Spezzia, had heard the
story from an Italian nobleman to whom it had been
communicated by the priest. This account was accepted
by Trelawny as solving that which for half a century had
been to him a mystery. We know too well how such a
story as that of the fisherman and the priest may come
into existence without the slightest foundation in fact.
"The Italian sailors," it has been well observed, "could
not have attacked Shelley's boat in broad day, amongst the
many small craft scattered about; and the subsequent
darkness and tempest . . . would, one have thought, have
given them enough to do to take care of themselves. On
the whole, it seems most probable that the collision, if
collision there was, was accidental." * We are not over-
curious to penetrate that tempestuous mist which veiled
Shelley's boat. He had often contemplated death, and its
terror had been subdued to a solemn awe. "Are you
going to join your friend Plato?" were almost the last
words written to Shelley by Jane Williams. It was thus
that he thought of death, hoping that death itself, like this
life of ours, might be but part of the inwoven design, glad
and sad, on that veil which hides from us some high reality.
Williams, who could swim, though not well, had made a
struggle for his life. Shelley probably accepted the inevitable with an instant comprehension that the end had come
—the end, or the beginning. He had often declared,
says Trelawny, that "in case of wreck he would vanish
instantly, and not imperil valuable lives by permitting

* Mr. R. Garnett, in his article "Shelley's Last Days."

others to aid in saving his, which he looked upon as valueless."

The casket or coffer containing Shelley's ashes was entrusted by Trelawny to a Mr. Grant, of Leghorn, who consigned it to Mr. Freeborn, a merchant correspondent of his at Rome, who also seems to have held the position of English Consul in that city.* By December 7, 1822, Mr. Freeborn had received the casket. The old Protestant burial-ground, where lay the body of Shelley's boy, having been closed, the casket, incased in a coffin, was placed in the new cemetery hard by. To quiet the authorities the usual ceremonies were observed. They sought for the body of the child to place it near his father's ashes, but it could not be found. All was done, says Severn, "as by the hands of friends." Among the few persons who were present at the burial were General Cockburn, Sir C. Sykes, Severn, Kirkup, Westmacott, Scoles, Freeborn, and the Revs. W. Cook and Burgess.

Visiting Rome in the spring of 1823, Trelawny found Shelley's grave amid a cluster of others. "The old Roman wall," he writes, "partly enclosed the place, and there was a niche in the wall formed by two buttresses—immediately under an ancient pyramid, said to be the tomb of Caius Cestius. There were no graves near it at that time. This suited my taste, so I purchased the recess, and sufficient space for planting a row of the Italian upright cypresses. . . . There was no 'faculty' to apply for, nor bishop's licence to exhume the body. The *custode*, or guardian, who dwelt within the enclosure, and had the key of the gate, seemed to have uncontrolled power within his domain, and scudi, impressed with the image of Saint Peter with the two keys, ruled him. Without more ado masons were

---

* Leigh Hunt, in a letter to Severn, dated "Genoa, December 16, 1822," mentions these facts, but does not call Freeborn the English Consul at Rome.

hired, and two tombs built in the recess. In one of these when completed I deposited the box with Shelley's ashes, and covered it with solid stone, inscribed with a Latin epitaph, written by Leigh Hunt." The words inscribed upon the stone are the following :—

PERCY BYSSHE SHELLEY

COR CORDIUM

NATUS IV AUG. MDCCXCII

OBIIT VIII JUL. MDCCCXXII

" Nothing of him that doth fade
But doth suffer a sea-change
Into something rich and strange."

The vacant grave was reserved by Trelawny for his own resting-place. The lines from Shakespeare's "Tempest" were added by him to the words of Leigh Hunt's choice, "Cor Cordium."

Mary Shelley returned to England in the autumn of 1823. On February 21, 1851, she died. Shelley's son, Percy Florence, succeeded to the baronetcy on the death of his grandfather in April, 1844.* In the monument, by Weekes, which Sir Percy and Lady Shelley erected in the parish church of Christchurch, Hants, the feeling of Mary's heart, confided to the pages of her journal after her husband's death, is expressed in marble. In Boscombe Manor, Bournemouth, in an alcove devoted to that purpose, the portraits, relics, journals, note-books, and letters of Shelley and Mary, duly ordered by Lady Shelley's hands, were preserved with love and reverence. The murmur of pine woods, and the resonance and silvery flash of the waves of our English sea, were near to solemnize and to gladden the heart.

* Shelley's first son—the child of Harriet Shelley—had died in boyhood.

INDEX.

Reprinted from Stereotype Plates by W. & J. MACKAY & Co., LTD.,
Fair Row, Chatham.